Conceptualizing Security for India in the 21st Century

Editor
Gautam Sen

ATLANTIC
PUBLISHERS & DISTRIBUTORS (P) LTD

Published by

ATLANTIC

PUBLISHERS & DISTRIBUTORS (P) LTD

B-2, Vishal Enclave, Opp. Rajouri Garden,
New Delhi-110027
Phones : 25413460, 25429987, 25466842

Sales Office
7/22, Ansari Road, Darya Ganj,
New Delhi-110002
Phones : 23273880, 23275880, 23280451
Fax : 91-11-23285873
web : www.atlanticbooks.com
e-mail : info@atlanticbooks.com

ISBN 81-269-0788-6

Printed in India
at Nice Printing Press, Delhi

Acknowledgments

This book is an anthology of papers presented at NISDA Security Conference 2005. I therefore wish to record my sincere thanks and gratitude to the eminent contributors who have participated in this Inaugural Annual Conference of NISDA and presented their thoughts on the theme of "Conceptualizing Security in the 21st Century".

I take this opportunity to record our thanks to all those who have supported our endeavours in building NISDA as an institution. The vision and foresight of the University Grants Commission has been pathbreaking and has allowed us to set up an institution, which is one of its kind within the university system.

While the list of our well-wishers is long and many have been a tremendous source of encouragement for all of us at NISDA, I would like to specially thank Dr. Ashok S. Kolaskar, Vice Chancellor, University of Pune, whose support has meant that we have had the cooperation of the various departments of the University in our endeavours. Also, thanks are due for the support of Shri. Ratnakar Gaikwad (IAS), Director General, YASHADA, that enabled us to hold this inaugural annual conference in YASHADA premises and avail of the excellent conferences facilities there in a manner befitting the stature of the institute and the distinguished participants.

Special thanks are due to all the team members of NISDA. Arpita Anant painstakingly pursued the contributors to procure the final version of papers and did the copyediting, Aravind Yelery brought to bear his considerable computer skills to produce the proof copy and Rajashree Nighojkar helped in organizing the Conference to run it smoothly. Ravindra Nalawade, the Office

Superintendent, did a yeoman work to ensure all logistics were in place, including the financial details. Without such a dedicated team the work would not have been complete. In the end we are grateful to Dr. K.R. Gupta, Chairman, Atlantic Publishers & Distributors (P) Ltd., New Delhi, to bring out the manuscript in the form of a book.

Gautam Sen

Preface

In the 21st century, conceptualizing "security" and the academic approach to Security Studies has undergone a major transformation. One can observe a paradigm shift in this vital area of investigation. Thus conceptualizing security, achieving passive/active human centric security and involving university-based institutions to undertake security studies due to the impact of a change in the world system, has become major challenge facing us. The end of Cold War has brought about the loss of a quantified bipolarity and has ushered the polarization of intent, capability and power (military and non-military). With the breaking up of the former Soviet Union and the evolution of information technology, multipolar nodes of power have emerged having nuclear capabilities with potential to deploy and threaten the use of Weapons of Mass Destruction (WMD) even when the history of the post-1945 period till date has not precipitated an all out nuclear war. It has therefore been necessary to examine the very nature of "Security" and "Security Studies" in a holistic fashion.

Considering the above, it was imperative that the concepts of security and the process of conceptualizing the same had to be congruent to security studies and security analysis/policy making at normative levels. In a sense, conceptualizing security has three definite aspects—the abstraction, theorization and the implementation. Since nation-states despite being asymmetrical to each other on more than one count, will continue to remain as prime actors in the foreseeable future as a unit of analysis in international relations and international system, the role of military will continue to remain an important factor. However, it will be superimposed by the non-strategic dimensions of security to ensure a human-centric rationale of security needed by every nation-state to acquire and protect, to bring about stability and peace in an interdependent atmospherics influenced by transnationalism.

Therefore, conceptualizing security and giving a sense of direction for implementation of security policies will require bridging the gap between the realm of ideas and the domain of public policy making, the latter being an offshoot of the organizations at the government and non-government levels are empowered to examine holistically the totality of security considerations. As a market driven new world order is emerging because of globalization, the changing self-perceptions of nation-states will impinge on the manner in which they articulate their security concerns and coping strategies. We have to therefore consider that both financial and technological aspects will operate and play a significant role based on resources and opportunities. It is in this emerging scenario that the institutions of higher education like the universities will bridge the gap between the realm of ideas and the domain of public policy and provide the nation-states with the capacity to evolve policy relevant options for national security policy making.

Hence conceptualizing security and the role of security in the 21st century will have to be examined from the perspectives of social sciences, military, bureaucratic, political and human security through the implementation of non-strategic dimensions. NISDA's Security Conference aimed to approach the basic theme of "Conceptualizing Security in the 21st Century" through an in-depth discussion on security perspectives so as to provide a conceptual and an operational model for our understanding of security in the 21st century.

Gautam Sen

Contents

List of Contributors

U.P. Thakur, Scientist 'G', DRDO, Defence Machinery Design Establishment, Secunderabad.

C. Narasimha Rao, Director, Centre for Scientific Socialism and Head, Department of Rural Development, Acharya Nagarjuna University, Nagarjuna Nagar

Gopalji Malviya, Head, Department of Defence and Strategic Studies, University of Madras.

Shrikant Paranjpe, Department of Defence and Strategic Studies, University of Pune.

Prashant Agarwal, Reader, Department of Defence and Strategic Studies, University of Allahabad.

Sanjay Jain, Lecturer, Department of Law, University of Pune.

Abdul Khadeer Taj, Reader, Department of Defence and Strategic Studies, University of Pune.

Sohan P. Modak, G.R. Ramachandran Fellow, Institute of Genomics and Integrated Biology, CSIR, New Delhi.

Santishree Pandit, Executive Director, International Centre, University of Pune.

Harsh Kumar Sinha, Lecturer, Department of Defence and Strategic Studies, D.D.U Gorakhpur University, Gorakhpur.

V.N. Bhoraskar, Prof. of Physics, Department of Physics, University of Pune, Formerly Director, Microtron Radiation Lab, Indore (an Autonomous Institution of the UGC).

Hari Saran, Reader, Department of Defence and Strategic Studies, D.D.U Gorakhpur University, Gorakhpur.

Air Marshal A.K. Trikha, PVSM, AVSM, VSM (Retd.), Chair Professor, Air Power & National Security Studies, NISDA,

University of Pune, Former Commandant of National Defence Academy, Khadakwasla, Pune.

Vijay S. Khare, Lecturer, Department of Defence and Strategic Studies, University of Pune.

Prasad Rane, Associate Fellow, Institute for Defence Studies and Analyses (IDSA).

Gen. Shankar Roychowdhury, PVSM, AVSM (Retd.), Former Chief of the Army Staff and Former Member of Parliament.

Gen. V.P. Malik, PVSM, AVSM (Retd.), Former Chief of the Army Staff.

Lt. Gen. H.M. Khanna, SYSM, PVSM, AVSM (Retd.), Former Southern and Northern Army Commander.

M.R. Joshi, Former Director, R & D Engineers, Dighy, Pune.

Vishal Katariya, Chair, Intellectual Property Rights Studies, University of Pune.

Aniruddha G. Joshi, Chief Investigator, Centre for Information and Network Security, University of Pune.

Ankush R. Kulkarni, Research Associate, Centre for Information and Network Security, University of Pune

Lt. Gen. D.B. Shekatkar, PVSM, AVSM, VSM (Retd.), Chhatrapati Shivaji Chair Professor in Policy Studies, Department of Defence and Strategic Studies, University of Pune.

Pramod Kale, Director, VLSI Design and Research Centre, University of Pune and Former Director of Vikram Sarabhai Space Launch Station, Sriharikota.

K.B. Powar, Former Vice Chancellor, Shivaji University, Kolhapur, Former Director General, Association of Indian Universities and presently Advisor to V.C., D.Y. Patil Vidyapeeth.

Leena Parmar, Head, Department of Sociology, Rajasthan University.

P.A. Ghosh, Lecturer, Bhosala Military College, Nashik.

Rajendra Prasad, Head, Department of Defence and Strategic Studies, DDU Gorakhpur University, Gorakhpur.

1

Conceptualizing Security for India in the 21st Century

U.P. Thakur & C. Narasimha Rao

Why We should Conceptualize Security for the 21st Century?

Security has been defined and understood variously by various experts on various occasions ranging from "the ability of a nation to protect its internal values from external threats" to "the preservation of its core values critical to the nation-state from external and internal threats." You are deemed to be secure "when you don't have to sacrifice your interests to avoid war and are able to maintain them by war, if challenged." The notion of security has spanned from "territorial integrity" through "national interest" and "the political, economic and social well-being to the government policy" aimed at the creation of favourable national and international conditions for the protection or extension of national interests against existing or potential enemy threats." National security thus "comprises every action by which a society seeks to assure its survival or realizes its aspiration internationally." Why then we talk about "Conceptualizing security in the 21st century?" What changes have prompted us to rethink about the security paradigm of yesteryears? Does it mean the basic parameters in the context of which we defined security earlier no longer exist? Yes, the 21st century has presented an entirely new canvas for security, it has different kinds of interests at play, with different actors and interest groups which are making the security concept of 20th century irrelevant to a great extent.

We must therefore conceptualize security for the 21st century because the context has changed, the forces we have to fight with have changed, the tools and techniques with which we can fight effectively are new, the players are new, their attitudes are new. And all these are in permanent changeable state and unpredictable. Things change in nanoseconds, not in days and months. The very scale of measure has changed. The measure by which you define victory or defeat has changed. It is no longer Himalayan border we are fighting for, we are fighting forces external and within that are dynamic and unpredictable. If it is 21st century, we can't conceptualize war doctrine for the 20th century.

The dissolution of Soviet Russia, the end of the Cold War, the reality of unipolar world, the equalizing force of information technology, the emerging technologies of bio and nano—all these have brought in newer forces at work and in war. It is a different world, and different time. We have to conceptualize security differently. It is more so for India—the India that does not change, the India that always thought itself to be safe and secure, but was always proved wrong, must see reason to change—to secure itself and its people in the new age of knowledge economy.

Which of the sources of security is the most fundamental? The one which if provided can also provide all the others? We must examine this question in relation to various elements of security so that the basic element is brought out. Conceptualisation of security also involves the question of what and whose interest you protect, how you protect, who all are involved in protecting. Is it only army that is supposed to protect while others keep watching. Also, the issue of where the protection begins—is it at border alone or in every home and field? Is security a geographically and temporally static concept? One cannot overlook the way information technology and globalisation have made security everybody's problem.

The concept of protection must be replaced by the concept of progress and development, the concept of defence must yield to the concept of proactive force capability. We must shift security philosophy to a positive action agenda for the overall growth and progress of the nation, where every citizen, every activity, every sector and every entity becomes the generator of strength and power, and contributes to the strength and might of the nation.

How We Conceptualize It?

One way is to scan history, culture, and the wars that have been fought and the lessons they carry for us. Interpolate them on the present and future scenario and project security for future. This may be the best logical way for conceptualizing the security for 21st century. However, to assume that the whole of the 21st century would remain what it is today with dynamically evolving information technology, biotechnology and nano-technology will be too simplistic. The concept whatever we arrive at must take note of the dynamics of factors. It can be local but must be compatible with universal phenomena. Today to think of a military and its policy to remain confined to the boundary of a country is naïve. One must have sub-continental and continental strategy to remain unimpregnable. This demands technological upgradation of military systems, and our thinking process. We can't predict future but we can certainly base our projection on historical, sociological, psychological, economic, political, and technological moorings.

Historical Perspective

To think of a futuristic planning for security of India requires us to reflect back on how in the past Indians handled security threats, whether they perceived any security threat at all. Where they went wrong in perception of security threat and what was the quality of response when a threat came. Indian history is replete with instances to show that India had been in deep slumber, seemed to perceive no sense of security threat over the entire historical spectrum. She seemed to be in "a world of her own," assured of a false sense of safety between the confines of northern Himalayas and the southern seas as natural protection barrier, similar to the mood prior to 1962 in contemporary India. A strong central regime between 321 and 233 BC, was no doubt provided by the Mauryans which eclipsed after Ashoka the Great. Gupta empire between 320 AD and 467 AD was just a tributary empire of allegiances by regional kings to a *Maharajadhiraj*, without the direct central governance of Ashoka, Akbar or Curzon and without the direct governance and integration. There was no attempt to knit this land mass into a Nation State. And this didn't stand the onslaught of the Huns and their sovereignty vanished after 500 AD. Harsha Vardhan remained confined to the north before the Muslim invasion from Sindh in the 8th century and from Kabul in the 11th and 12th centuries. The 332 years of the Sultanates of Delhi saw five dynasties Ghor, Slave, Khalji, Saiyyids and Lodis, rising and falling, each lasting ephemerally for few years, conquering India for plunders and revenue, not for state building. We have truly followed them to this day. The Afghan-Turkish rule not only regionalized India but impoverished it also economically and culturally. Then came Sher Shah Suri, Akbar and the great Mughals when Aurangzeb gave India its first really strong, central governance since Ashoka. This period extended over a century and half, with a rise in economic development with 22 per cent share of the world trade, which came down to 2 per cent in 1950 and 0.6 per cent in 2000.

No Pan-Indian Perception

The British empire extended over Burma and Sri Lanka with strategic buffer state in Afghanistan and in Tibet. However, independent India didn't learn from the British who inherited Albuquerque's Indian Ocean Maritime Strategy Concept and secured unchallenged naval power in the three critical points of the Cape of Good Hope, the Malacca Straits and the Oman Straits. This vast strategic concept to which was added the Suez Canal after 1870, didn't open the eyes of independent India's leaders who failed to inherit this comprehensive strategic concept.

India's contemporary history too depicts a historical lack of an organized geopolitical and military or even good tactics in battlefield. What we find is, between Alexander in the 4th century BC, Ghazni and Ghori in the 11th and 12th century AD, Babar in the 16th century and the British in the 18th century and 19th century, India and Indians remained unconcerned and disinterested in how their country was being plundered, destroyed and abused. No awakening, there seemed to be no pan-Indian perception of external threat, and no organized strategic response. And this lack of perception of a common culture and a common threat by the Marathas and the Sikhs was visible before the third battle of Panipat in 1761 against the Abdalis leading to an absence of a joint response. This divisiveness in Panipat in 1761 indirectly created a power vacuum for conquest by the British in the next century with the defeat of the Marathas. Indians continued to overlook the loot and mayhem committed on their motherland. While foreign invaders captured India again and again through commerce, brutality and technology, India kept accepting whoever came with no word of protest and no sense of shame. Indian kings fought against themselves over a loaf of their ego, helped foreign invaders to see the defeat of the other Indian kings and in the process got themselves liquidated. This internal bickering, back stabbing, and lack of cohesiveness has continued to this day. This knowledge economy has given you an opportunity to wrest the lost political space, provided you are able to convert this knowledge into technology for development, for management, weapons and war.

The Egoistic Cage

Prithvi Raj lost to Ghori in the two battles of Tarain in the 12th century, partly because of the old egoistic idea of a retreat by Ghori being mistaken for the defeat without any follow up. The symbols of status mattered, not the power of battlecraft. We find the same pattern repeated by Babar's smaller army at Panipat in 1526 and at Khanua in 1527 against Rana Sanga. It was just the absence of a sense of strategy and battlecraft for decisive victory, which could also be seen centuries later in Kashmir in 1947 and in NEFA in 1962—the same lack of "a killer instinct" and the lack of a purpose. Not very different happened at Tashkent and at Shimla, the shear defeat in diplomacy what you won in wars.

Though the last three Indian powers—the Marathas, Tipu Sultan and Ranjit Singh confronted the British between 1790 and 1842, the Marathas were a sadly divided house between the nominal heads, the Peshwas, the Holkars, the Scindias, the Gaikwads and the Bhonsles. This was an abject lesson in disunity even within the same dynastic, linguistic and cultural groups. Tipu and Ranjit Singh could not stand against the superior economic and maritime power of the British which triumphed on account of a subcontinental and oceanic strategy and battlecraft. It is a pitiable lesson for India where her monarchs remained isolated and insulated from developments around in technology, craft and doctrines.

Independent India with the Same Mindset

Independent India too remained preoccupied with the hangover of its past. It paid no attention to realistic geopolitical and the future planning of state security strategy, which resulted in the Chinese debacle of 1962. The then PM when asked about his perception of security threat, asserted that his government saw no security threat, that he believed in peace and that there was no need for an army—the same detachment to the reality of geopolitics. However, the same army saved two-third of Kashmir when the Pak-Afghan raiders came two months later. But the folly of that unmilitary mindset prevented the complete repulse of the raiders that led to the loss of PoK when India had the power to do it, the mindset that Prithvi Raj exhibited. India again displayed a lack of political prudence in accepting a UN ceasefire and the conditional plebiscite proposal, when it was in a position to enforce its victory. Our leaders in the past and in the contemporary times remained in an ivory tower of their own.

Sardar Patel's warning in as early as 1950, twelve years before the Chinese war, about China's future hostile intentions went unheaded. Patel died without his threat perception being given due weightage leading to India's humiliating defeat in 1962. And we have shamefully forgotten the humiliation without ever learning a lesson. The 1962 debacle was the result of the lack of an organized diplomatic and military strategy and a replay of the traditional "*Maharajadhiraj* concept." It was not the professional decision of a modern government with a state apparatus for strategic security—something for which India is still groping even after 59 years of independence.

The Bangladesh war in 1971 was the only decisively, planned strategic effort involving intelligence and the paramilitary. But the model victory in the field was lost at the political level through Shimla agreement without solving the PoK issue. India keeps bleeding to this day! It was so similar to Prithvi Raj's indecisive failure to pursue a wounded Ghori when the advantage was his.

While failure to clinch initial military advantage gave Ghori a chance to retreat to Kabul, recoup and return to victory in 1192; the failure of India to solve PoK issue when India was in a position to do so in 1971 has made independent India suffer from terrorism. So similar, same response and mindset we live with!

Realistic Conceptualization

While conceptualizing security for India in the 21st century these traits, these mindsets and the casualness, and attitudes so typical of us in dealing with matters of life and death, and things of national security, must not be lost sight of. It looks like it is our national identity and culture we can't rid off. The inadequacy, indecisiveness, lack of strategy and vision, absence of planning and management must be adequately and comprehensively factored into any process of conceptualization. And the roadmap for India's security needs to incorporate the compensating and supplementary agenda. It is important that Indians at all levels be educated, tutored and indoctrinated to shun these complexes and mental frame as a part of security vision. The total population needs to be sensitized on security so that they are completely involved in security thinking, planning and management. Let us discuss the different aspects of security to spell out a road map for India's defence and development.

Defence and Development

The national consensus on security, defence and foreign policy is missing today. All are not one on what is nationalism, what are national priorities, what are the issues of national security and what should be done to strengthen India. There are people who question, poor don't have a stake in India's security, first feed them, defence comes later. The question of defence and developmental requirements must figure in any security conceptualization for economic growth only can sustain defence expenditure. There is no question of a choice between the two, given the kind of threats that exist within and without.

Economic reforms have left small-scale, rural industrialization untouched giving room to uneven development and social unrest. Reforms are also silent on human development, education, health, child nutrition, drinking water, women's welfare and empowerment. Rural areas remain ignored. Opportunities for personnel and social advancement for people in rural areas are limited. Food security is one of the most important issues in India's security management. But the state schemes ostensibly designed for public welfare, such as the public distribution system have not benefited the poor. A minimum of social security net has not yet been constructed.

Reforms when not implemented in letter and spirit may create havoc to social and economic fabric of the nation. It is difficult to expect reform to be carried out by an administrative set up that for decades has functioned as an inert, arbitrary, corrupt and uncoordinated monolith. Government machinery that does not itself allow reform in its own backyard would derail the complete programmes and is a security risk. The nation's health depends on how we perceive this risk and factor into our security calculation.

Internal Security

India's present has inherited so much of the past that it is just its reflection. Its social and economic scenario always in turmoil has become more tumultuous with the waves of globalisation and the information revolution. The latter has brought in the environment of high expectation for better living and a desire for equality. Security concept should be conceived for the society that has a large gap between poor and rich for centuries, where information flow is now causing aspiration to catch up with the rest but lack of opportunities find frustration leading to social tension, agitation and violent expression. Conflicts have also been emanating from social and economic injustice and from the tide of cultural nationalism and ethnic consciousness. Diverse conflicts—political, social, economic, and cultural and psychological, borne out of self-consciousness, aspirations and self-identity in the backdrop of globalisation of values, freedom and democracy are dotting India. National security is at stake if this freedom is not channelised constructively.

There are also non-conventional and non-military threats arising out of terrorism, ethnic conflicts, fundamentalism, natural disaster that impinge upon security of the country. The breakup of the Soviet Union and Yugoslavia seem to have eroded the very sanctity and legitimacy of pluralistic societies as well as the multiethnic, multilingual and multi-religious states. And India has enough of these fissiparous tendencies. Caste-based, religion-based and ethnic and linguistic parties are weakening the consolidation of the Indian Republic as a strong nation. Centre-State relations are uneasy because of the demand for restructuring relation between the central and the state government. Rapid economic reforms have also widened the chasm between urban and rural population and accentuated the regional imbalance in development, employment, income and industrialization with poor becoming poorer and rich becoming richer. Criminalisation of electoral politics and increasing level of corruption are leading to disenchantment and skepticism about politicians and political institution. While easy availability of information and globalisation in a democratic set up are leading to higher aspirations and social tension, newer technologies also play the role to bridge the gap between poor and rich. Security of India in the 21st century must be seen in this background.

Political Perception and Globalisation

Security has political perception too which is driven by globalisation. Globalisation theorists focus upon the world as a system and attend to the global processes transcending and operating almost autonomously from individual society or nation. Globalisation is considered a replacement of the cold war system because it has led to the emergence of a global market place and the rise of "homogenous" global culture that is understood essentially to be the spread of "Americanisation on a global scale," the security connotation of which must be qualified for incorporation into our security philosophy and management socially, economically, politically and technologically.

The 1999 Human Development Report, defines globalisation as "global markets, global technology, global ideas and global solidarity, enriching the lives of people everywhere, and involves new markets, new actors, new rules and norms and new tools of communication," each of which has implications for Indian security, impacting every aspect of national life and societies. Indian markets for "American goods," but American markets not for Indian goods; global technology with "technological restrictions and sanctions;" global ideas synonymous with American philosophy and views; and, global solidarity connoting the alignment with the only superpower make Indians suspicious of globalisation whether it is in the interest of India and if it is intended to serve the purpose of American interest alone. However, if the country strengthens itself technologically to the extent that it can lead the market, the direction of market gets reversed and globalisation benefits you. It means only "fittest would survive," the rest gets finished. Technology has the edge over others in deciding the direction of flow in the market and helps conceptualize security on a common platform. If globalisation is the "intensification of economic, political, social and cultural relations across borders" it is important globalisation enters our security design and calculation in its entirety. This requires that the fear of cultural invasion, market capitalization, technological onslaught, Americanisation, civilizational clash, loss of national, ethnic, linguistic and religious identity which are stalking the nation states and fear of danger to their security must be calculatively addressed into any security analysis of India.

While envisioning India's future security we cannot overlook Huntington's hypothesis which says that "fundamental source of conflict in the new world will not be primarily ideological or primarily economic, but cultural" and which has been condemned by peace theorists who advance the philosophy of "dialogue of civilization" instead of "clash of civilization." Huntington talks in another article titled, "A lonely Super Power?" the need of the American Global Leadership to save the world community from the total anarchism, with a view to maintaining "Western predominance" and "protect" Western interests and promote Western political and economic values. These pronouncements indicate the intentions behind the veil of globalization. While globalisation will be promoted in some pretext or another, every country would protect its national interest to the hilt, protect its geographical boundaries, its ideologies and values. How you do it forms the process of conceptualizing security.

It is evident that after the establishment of the WTO in 1995, a kind of new war is perceptible—a trade war, and very

very cold trade war between and among the developed and developing nations; the developed nations protecting their serfs at any cost, and the persisting controversy over social chapter that includes the environment, human rights, and labour standards only indicate that "globalisation" has not changed the mindset of the "Cold War period," and India has to fight its own battle for its own commercial and other interests—through diplomacy and bargains at various levels. It is a multi-front war fought in multiple ways through multiple means. Any conceptualization of security must recognize the reality of commercial, social and human interests of India.

The way naked power was exhibited by the strategic coalition of the United States and Britain in this liberalized and globalised world against the so-called rogue states—Iran, Iraq, Libya and North Korea and remember, India was clubbed with them and also the way Pakistan was declared a major non-NATO ally in the fight against terror is a grave message for the security thinkers and planners of India—how narrow the globalised world is! Is globalisation a ruse to smoothen the ugly and rough faces of petty interests? Things have only changed for the worse. The globalised world is much more dangerous than the world of the cold war era. Only self-interest matters. India must discover where her interests lie and find ways and means to fulfil those interests. Principles and ideologies do not count, nor should they handicap our policy-makers in charting out a security vision. At least now India should wake up to the geopolitical reality.

The international relations theorists' argument that nature of power politics has changed and it is through the "collective security" approach that big powers take punitive action to maintain peace and security in the world is contested by the realistic school of thought that does not see the basic difference in the power value, individual or collective. This arrogance is mainly because of the technological leadership they have. The mastery of technology for development, economy and weapons has bestowed upon them uncanny political perception and unparalleled maneuverability and flexibility in decision-making. Technology today is the single propeller of political decisions taken in the world's capitals. A proper security response to the unilateralism must be ingrained into our visualization of security planning and organization for the twenty-first century.

Emerging World Order

Any conceptualization of Indian security has to take note of the developments and attitudinal changes occurring the world over after the end of the cold war. What is observed is a sort of democratization of international relations that has resulted in not only the nation-states but even the non-state actors influencing the international opinions and politics, because of the increased interaction caused by information technology. An incremental erosion of state sovereignty is perceptible mainly due to technological empowerment. The US has emerged as the overwhelming centre of power. And India is not happily placed in this changed scenario because of its past baggage of ideological postures and the present strategic requirements placing its security under great stress. Can we think of widening India's security agenda despite the issues of human rights, good governance and management of environment being linked to security issues? What will be our response to security issues when countering terrorism, though focus of concern has been applied with a selective, nation-specific interest dominated by the superpower? One thing is clear, India must find its security paradigm and solution itself. How do we secure India in this complex situation, is the question to be answered by Indian security mind alone.

India's current security concern is to cope with this complex, competitive and one-sided international pressure compounded by the reality of unipolar force. The pressure on conformance to economic and technological regimes being considered necessary by the great powers for ensuring stable new world order require strategic response. It is essential that in the evolving international dynamics, India go overboard to forge new relationships, strategic ties and defence equations keeping its interests in view across the globe with various alliances and associations. Diversified economic and technological links with a number of countries to share the resources would be the foundation for future security of India.

State security, that involves territorial integrity, internal unity and cohesion, sovereignty in fashioning policies, and the ability to choose options related to foreign relations, defence and socio-economic development need new conceptualization for all these criteria territorial, political and economic, internal unity and cohesion, and sovereignty—affecting the autonomy of nation-state are under question in the new emerging world order. The question is how we picturise the security for India so as to secure her despite the dynamics of the world order. How we fashion our security concept so that it is tuned to the evolving philosophy of new world order, taking into cognizance the Western concept based on peace, justice, cooperation, collective security system, rule of law, human rights, democracy and good governance as also the developing countries' concept based on equality, equity and sovereignty. Conceptualizing security with these contesting ideological platforms is a major challenge. The view that the concept of sovereignty in the globalisation process has lost much of its relevance given the inevitable global interdependence need to be countered adequately because the meaning and concept of globalisation cannot be extended to where it becomes a real security threat to the state. State sovereignty is also being subjected to what is being referred to as neo-multilateralism which is being promoted by the United States. It is a new framework for international security to conduct security consultations and informal defence cooperation under Article 51 of the chapter of the United Nations that allows countries of different regions to put in place regional defence and security arrangements on their own initiative but outside the framework of the UNO and its security council.

India has limited options in these irreversible globalisation processes but can certainly make serious attempt to expand and diversify them, that must find expression in the rationalization of security framework. No single model or paradigm in international relations can explain the complex nature of the emerging world order. Nor is there any uncontested security model that can fit in the interconnected and interdependent but unipolar world. India has to evolve its own security concept and content that can successfully lead her to achieve aspirations in the emerging world.

Technology in the Driver Seat

If the world has entered into the age of information-intensive warfare, if all the elements of security, food, energy, environment, economy, social and political thinking, defence and development and everything else are shaped and guided by technologies, what is India's response to this technological onslaught? Are we prepared to meet the nation's technological requirements today and in future? This means, have we worked over insights gained from our historical and recent failures and fallacies, technological and operational experiences in development and war in the past and since independence? We must make an honest technological review of what is happening today, what we are doing and what we are capable and incapable of and draw up the gaps not only to be filled up but match with the best in the world to avoid the blunders we are so used to repeat.

If technology is driving the defence and development thinking, if our internal security is guided and controlled by technological strength, when the political perception and globalisation processes are being shaped by the input of technologies and also of the force behind emerging world is the technology of today, technology must become not only one of the major element in the conceptualization of security for this century but the very strategic road map for security can be drawn up only with the technological formulation. All technologies—biotechnology, nanotechnology, information technology and communications, satellites and GPS, artificial intelligence and robotics, electronics and embedded systems have given tools not only to fight wars and win them with pin-pointed accuracy but also the techniques and wherewithal to produce more food, industrial products, medical facilities and other ways to develop economy faster and dynamically attuned to the need of the country. Where we stand while the G-8 and other countries are entering into the arena of war controlled and executed by IT, BT and NT. You are secure only when you prepare to face the worst. It is important we assess ourselves in the light of technological developments sweeping the militaries of the advanced world. Why can't we work on the concepts covering the technological challenges in the area of robotics, ground combat vehicles without men inside them, performing command, control and communications on the move in a network centric mode, ability to engage and kill targets beyond the line of sight using netted weapon system, ability to produce all-weather platforms that can carry sensors and communication systems to ensure that a network-centric force can see and communicate over its entire battlespace, and the design and development of netted sensors that have the ability to identify and locate targets anywhere on the battlefield. Why can't we work on nano and bio weapons? Why can't our universities and institutions shift to R&D that have direct application in fields, factories and battlefields?

Advanced technologies for unprecedented intelligence, surveillance and reconnaissance capabilities coupled with ground, air and space sensors networked into a common integrated operational picture need to be pursued. Today's technologies have placed the soldiers and actors in economy in a new tactical framework with poorly defined frontlines while smart weapon system concept and the precision munition technologies along with the unmanned vehicles including the combat ones, their development and technologies for tactical, endurance and maritime and air launched applications are the scenarios the nation must be prepared for technologies that generate wealth and opportunities must be pursued zealously.

High tech weapons in the hands of misguided individuals and with states can wreak havoc. These technologies with little cost can provide extraordinary power to smaller and weaker nations to equalize otherwise unequal nations. Nations can now resort to asymmetry through chemical or biological or nuclear weapons attack to get over the weakness because of size. We must have strategy to meet this new threat. Technology is again the solution.

It is not the warfare alone but the whole social and economic discourse has changed because of technology. Technology is the most important single factor to boost economy of a nation and their people and has acted as great equalizer. Technological advances in IT and communication have increased the awareness of people, made them politically conscious and changed the way politics is conducted and also the way nation-states are governed. It is technology that has set the political thinking moving for interaction and cooperation across the globe. Globalisation and all its offsprings are the direct offshoots of technological revolution.

Technology today as in the past is in the driver seat for social, economic, and political well-being and military prowess. Development of technology has been accelerated in the knowledge economy and so is the case with military technology. It is the technology that can increase industrial productivity, it is the technology that will bring another green revolution and it is this technology again that will boost all your endeavour. Technology is the common denominator for comprehensive overall security of a nation, for technological weakness is the weakest link in the nation's development and defence. India must find its anchor in technology paradigm for conceptualizing its security in 21st century.

India must Prepare for the Eventuality

How we plan for security into the future, when we see our neighbours have biological weapons, space and cyberspace become the battleground and terrorists wield even more asymmetric and destructive threats? "We have to expect the unexpected and plan to be shocked." We shouldn't be surprised if by 2015, biological weapons could be in the hands of our adversaries. Should we not expect that non-state actors—terrorist groups in and around the country and the like will have some sort of weapons of mass destruction? The scenario of a major act of cyber terror by a government or terror group causing the collapse of our vital communication infrastructure such as air traffic control is not imaginary. The increasing ease of developing biological weapons and the difficulty of determining whether an outbreak is the result of a natural occurrence or deliberate attack may make biological warfare against humans, crops or animals relatively more attractive, particularly to those engaged in low level, long-term conflicts. It is expected that after 2015, biological weapons will become more sophisticated and tuneable with respect to duration, survivability, transmission, lethality and resistance to countermeasure. This is where the thrust of our security strategy should dictate our planning for future security.

Biotechnology is also likely to influence the battlefield in many other ways. It is predicted that by 2030, behaviour controlling chemicals, bionics and germ line engineering could be used to enhance the fighting power of military forces. Weapons of mass effect would expand to include the threats from delayed lethality—and non-lethal weapons; e.g. electromagnetic pulses, radiological and carcinogenic chemical weapons. India would also need to prepare for asymmetric strategies such as attacking civilian population, denying entry to forces, striking deploying and deployed forces, disabling satellites and other force multipliers, and hacking military and civilian computer networks would be normal. There is every possibility for research into space platforms shifting from sensors and communication to weapons. Our security in this scenario depends on how India plans to face these eventualities.

Security Enablers for India

What all would cnable India to secure itself from the emerging complex environment? The only way India can ensure its security is by having a regional and global view in the context of its national interest, which would also determine its security strategy including maritime security strategy. While people, especially the political, bureaucratic, technocrat and working class must be sensitised to have national security perspective while taking decisions, a strong sense of history for strategic awareness must also be inculcated. A strong centre with stable central authority is required with political will and power to maintain internal and external security, and with a clear strategic vision in political, diplomatic, economic and military affairs. India not only should have a strong economic foundation, internal and external, for both development and defence security, but also an effective police and military power backed by skilled professional diplomacy and alert intelligence services. Properly trained human resources in political, economic, military and technological matters, with low social corruption and social divisiveness only can translate conceptual security into a reality.

Today being the knowledge economy, it is technology that determines the strength and agility of the economy and the might of the army. Whether it is agricultural technology, biotechnology, engineering technology, or military technology, it is technology that decides the flexibility of the nation. Investment in technology, that gives overall development which in turn sustains investment in military technology is the only option for India for security. And how and where the investment should be made first. Education, that promotes the traits of development of appliances and implements, weapons and munitions, not the education that only enhances research paper meant only for self-advancement. Application-oriented research and development—whether in science or technology, political science or psychology, it is the usability that should be the criterion for judging the work.

Technology Choices for India

India has been struggling for strategic technologies that have been hardly coming. We must change our approach to develop technology, to engineer and reengineer technology and to create technologies to get an upper edge in defence and development. We have not learnt the art of innovation and novelty that make things different and brings high value. Our emphasis all along has been on fundamental research that has been of no use to our day-to-day requirement. We must direct ourselves towards making things which can alter the status-quo of our economy and military. Remember, today's developments are mainly in the combination technology for value addition and application enhancement. National energies must be diverted toward this end. For example, much of the cleverness, and the inherent operational capability of air system now lie in the software. Airframe and engine development is certainly not rampant in the same way as progress in computers, sensors and communication equipment. Thus it is possible to keep an ageing airframe operationally viable by updating its mission system. We see this trend the world over.

One of the principal ways to compensate for modest size and sometimes lack of technological edge is through attention to selection, training and ethos. Despite the manifest differences between the past, present and likely future challenges, technologists must proceed in the direction of acquiring the ability of airpower to shape the environment and to pave the way for low-cost victory in the subsequent land battle. There is a need to exploit fully the ability of air forces to switch roles rapidly and adapt tactics to changing situations. We must acquire expertise in electronics, for accurate, timely, and tactical intelligence and be able to dominate the electronic spectrum. And then we must make pragmatic and carefully considered investment decisions.

Technology may be taking us places but, the overwhelming influence of the human spirit is achieving success in the battle and for that development of human resource is a prerequisite. What we are witnessing now is the "tenth military revolution," where vision incorporates technology in new concepts and organizations. Our conceptualization can be technology-intensive. In general, the trends have always been clear: "getting beyond the human limitations, achieving better speed, range, precision and effect, to surprise and to preserve command and control." We must activate toward this end. In the past, it was tried to exploit the most out of every technology separately in order to give precision capability, future systems will rely upon the integration of at least two different technologies as a basis for achieving robust solutions. Technology could be the harbinger of strength for India provided our vision incorporates technology at conceptual stage.

What India should Do?

India must go for quantitative and qualitative strategies both and develop "offset strategy" with emphasis on qualitative advantages from innovative technologies to offset the quantitative advantages enjoyed by enemies. Three different approaches to technological innovation may be adopted. One, make incremental improvements to the system as new technology could be applied to existing concepts. New models of aircraft or weapons that go higher, faster, further and demonstrate ever increasing advances in roll, pitch and turn rate. It must design strategy beyond the available possibilities. Two, apply innovative technology in ways which produce revolutionary impacts and lead to new operational concepts to deny an enemy the sanctuaries of whatever worth. Synthetic Aperture Radar, LANTIRN and LONGBOW targeting systems may be cited as examples for this kind of technology. Space-based sensor systems provide a global awareness and will enable you dominate your enemy. Three, implement programmes that would allow us to leap frog enemy systems and their associated operational and doctrinal thinking. Application of stealth for air-breathing platforms, and the deployment of geo-stationary sensors in space to provide a permanent presence for missile launch warning are the futuristic scenarios one can work upon.

It is not just a game of superiority today, but a case of whether your enemy has this, or whether you need this edge and working out to get that edge. The fusion of air and space power will give you new options with greater promise of success. Space-based knowledge cannot only reduce the logistic problem of transportation but also the risk to human lives. The combat effectiveness of ground forces can just be increased by providing more, better and rapid information. A presence in space will also allow you to see the other side of the hills.

There have been great strides in the areas of increased computational power, avionics, miniaturization and informational technology, the impact of which when combined with the traditional characteristics of airpower have strategic role in shaping India's technological power in the 21st century. The core competencies of rapid global mobility, precision engagement, information superiority, and agile combat support are greatly contributed by aerospace forces. Aerospace superiority tops the list of competencies because it is the enabler for all other competencies and capability of air force as well as for surface forces.

India must create and integrate space forces into the mainstream of the air force because the future would see a larger percentage of the mainstream space related. We should stop asking, in what technologies we should invest to improve our precision strike capability. Instead we should ask which technology we should choose, because there exists a wide variety and growing number of technologies. Decision-makers need to find the optimal mix among these technologies that could provide maximum operational punch at minimum cost.

Conclusion

Threat to India's security from the concept of the "danger of dual technologies falling into the hands of irresponsible states" is basically a techno-security threat that need to be countered by strategic innovation of technologies. The continuing handicap in updating and sustaining India's technological capabilities is the greatest stumbling block in ensuring India's security. Can India be secure without securing emerging military and non-military technology for defence and development? Liberalisation under globalisation philosophy has more restriction, selective controls and denial of important resources like oil, energy, technology and technical equipment beyond a certain degree of sophistication. If technology determines our security status, it is a serious issue and needs action plan to develop and employ leading edge technologies. Shall we keep complaining and bemoaning on what is given to our adversary while we ourselves do nothing to develop and compete? Is it the way to seek security for India? Do we still hope to get technology from somewhere to meet the challenge posed by the same powers who preach us about "dual" technologies and we keep sitting idle? The post-Cold War scenario has left India alone and made it urgent and essential to look into technological aspects of Indian security.

Today it is technological prowess that decides economic, military and political muscle of a state. The present is witnessing a relentless march of technology driving not only war fighting doctrines and defence strategies but also the economy and the entire spectrum of national and global processes, entities and above all social thinking and political and diplomatic postures. Technology is the enabler of globalisation process as well as of security. IT, cybertechnologies, nanotechnology, biotechnology, cognitive science and many other technologies have revolutionalised military thinking, political dialogues, and social and economic activities. Since both technologies and strategies naturally transform each other, it is essential to include technology as the significant element of security thinking. Things become simpler if you recognize technology as a liberator as well as a defender, as an equalizer as well as an edge-provider.

In the liberalized environment, the role of private sector in defence preparedness need to be examined along with the question if government controlled defence R&D is capable of meeting the diverse and fast changing needs of the country. If economy can be liberalized, why military technology remain shackled to government control and regulation.

Yes, technology is the solution. But how will we get it? Not through isolating ourselves in ivory tower. But, through cooperation and co-creation, through sharing and mutuality. In this century, sharing will bring more experience to the table and will more rapidly convert information to knowledge and to technology. As more and more of sharing about engineering aspirations, co-creation, and vision take place throughout society, the conversion of information to knowledge will yield the pursuit of engineering wisdom. This co-creation would lead to technologies of unprecedented complexity and unparallel novelty shortening the gap between the dream and reality, between development and defence and between threat and security.

2

Dialectics of Governance and Comprehensive Security in India

Gopalji Malviya

Introduction

The concept of security is dynamic and multi-dimensional. Post-Cold War debate on national security has significantly brought new definitional changes. And post-9/11 has further accelerated the security discourse to new angles. The paradigm shift brought new focus like human security and human development. The genesis of comprehensive security was found in this realisation. Post-Cold War discourse on security also realised that threats to national security could emulate from many directions. These not necessary from military centric threats. These may come from lack of economic growth and opportunities, external commercial factors, internal instability, natural disaster, health-hygiene, ecological and environmental degradation, poor governance and intra-state conflicts. Thus, to deal with such complexity nation-state need to develop comprehensive capabilities rather than mere military build-up.

The existing state centric approach to national security confined to the defence of the country against territorial aggression has been widened to the idea of security that is inclusive of larger sets of threats to the people of the state. In this context arrival of the nuclear weapons on the Indian sub-continent, have added urgency to the need for a fresh look at national security beyond its military dimension.[1] Hence, a wider range of issues that includes economic, environmental, societal, education and governance in addition to the political and military factors deserve a comprehensive attention to the national security.

'Comprehensive Security' is all an all embracing phrase that need to be anchored in the security of states as well as in condition of human security, because national security is dependent on and inseparable from the loyalty and well-being of all citizens who, in turn are connected with and vulnerable to regional and international trends including the globalisation process.[2]

India's security policy has been basically a policy to defend our territory, sovereignty and freedom. This seems to be inadequate for a variety of reasons, prominently, because it fails to make a distinction between external and internal threats to its national security and its magnitude and linkages between both. Threat from within has not been given appropriate attention from the ruling elites and security managers, since '50s. Minor threats, events from various quarters have gained momentum over a period and transformed into a major source of security threat. These internal dimensions to India's security threats gained intensity in the last two decades.

The politico-administrative lethargy has led to decline of vital institutions. Vitiation of electoral process rampant corruption at every levels of authority, ever-growing violence in the society, criminalisation of politics and politicisation of criminals, creation of vote banks and lack of accountability raises the important question whether governance is the core issue for ensuring India's national security. If one peeps through the corridors of post-independent history of India, it would be seen that following issues have gradually emerged and transformed into major source of internal security. Over a period these crises also raised a question of governance and security and also put a question mark on federal structure of India.

- Militancy in Kashmir.
- Khalistan Movement in Punjab.
- Ethno-political movements in North-East.
- Naxalite activities; Left wing extremism.
- Tamils sub-nationalism blend with LTTE sponsored violence.

- Regional aspiration for Bodoland, Jharkhand further fuelled, similar cry for Uttaranchal, Vidarbha, Poorvanchal, Ladakh, Jammu, Haritpradesh, Telangana and Gorkhaland.
- Caste-based violence seeking to change societal hierarchies.
- Communal violence in certain parts of the country.
- Intra-State conflicts.
- Proliferation of small arms.

Genesis of these could be seen through 1950s but now it has gained political overturns. Some of these were political aspirations and dissatisfactions later converted as the mass movements. External actors fuelled some of these insecurities, thereby, in accordance to suit their agenda to destabilise India. Thus clearly identified as externally fostered internal threats.

The architect of modern India and the Prime Minister of independent India, Nehru took stubborn view that security came from peace rather than peace from security. Nehruvian model of security looked upto macro-dimension of grand strategy by building roads, dams, and industrialisation, etc. but failed to identify or foresee the micro-level of security threats.[3] Lack of institutionalised thinking and coherent security policy failed to address the security priorities. Also gradual assault on security governance was due to *ad hoc* choices, interim and incremental approach of decision-making. Absence of credible public document laying down its defence doctrine or well-defined security policy has been the subject of continued debate amongst the academia and intellectuals in the country for many years. Even Parliamentary Estimate Committee has made critical mention for absence of clearly articulated security policy.[4]

Security Governance in India

The act of ruling or controlling with authority is called governance. It is also a value-loaded concept. The challenge for civil-society is to ensure that the discourse on governance remains in the public space occupied by the citizens and is not hijacked into the headquarter of global institutions or classrooms. The biggest obstacle in developing society is the lack of both policy-making and institutional capabilities, a condition, conducive to large-scale lawlessness and corruption. Fruits of governance cannot be achieved without law enforcement and adherence to rule of law. Globally people seek good governance for political and economical reasons. Politically good governance is an issue of democracy, public accountability, transparency and fairness.

Like many concepts, governance is a term with many interpretations. Some equate it with Government and some equate it with democracy. Governance implies structure and processes for determining use of available resources for the public good. Therefore, the meaning of governance is complex. It is more than multi-party elections, a judiciary or democracy and a parliament. Good governance does not mean 'to rule', but to govern. Good governance implies:

- Universal protection of human rights.
- Laws that are implemented in a non-discriminatory manner and Rule of Law.
- An efficient, impartial and quick judicial system.
- Transparent public agencies and official decision-making.
- Accountability for decisions made about public issues and resources by public officials.
- Devolution of resources and decision-making power to local levels and bodies in rural and urban areas.
- Participation and inclusion of all citizens in debating public policies and choices.
- Corruption free Government.
- Utilisation of full potential for productivity.
- Societal peace and secured life for citizens.

The institutions of governance in India have largely failed to provide socio-economic and political opportunities to millions of its people. Progress towards better governance will be impossible without the protection of the basic rights of the people and their participations in developmental activities. Democratic governance is measured by the levels of people's participation. Free and fair elections, accountable elected representatives, and availability of information, people's role in decision-making, women's participation and fulfilling the expectations of common human being. Legitimate government is not necessarily considered as good governance. Poor living conditions, and voiceless masses remain at the margin. Widespread feudalism, income disparity, absence of internal democracy within political parties has eroded the faith in real democratic values. In Indian political systems a hard-core criminal or history-sheeter can get elected in Parliament and State Assemblies. Poor attendance in the temple of democracy is a clear indication of the mood and preferences of the elected representatives.[5] The growth of regional and smaller parties and unstable coalition has led to instability and insecurity. Fragmented Assemblies and Parliament are unable even to enact the laws that are essential for good governance.

In India we have evolved a political environment of 'collective violence,' in which each break down in law order prepared the ground and justification for the next round. Various efforts of innovative reconciliation have not seen the desired results. The other precedence is the Indian states highly developed capacity to accommodate those practitioners of violence and crime who commit this against the innocent people and security forces. From Kashmir to North-East, from Punjab to Andhra Pradesh, the Indian state is engaged with the extremist groups who have been indulging in large-scale violence and the state and its machinery trying to make peace with these recognised offenders and their ideologues.

Ruling elite in New Delhi persists in continuing the dialogue of sorts with the Hurriyat Conference, Naga Separatists Groups, representatives of People's War Group and leaders of Left wing extremism.[6] This periodic ritual continues to reach out for an accord or peace. Despite their commitment to use violence against security forces. Whether this is weakness of the security governance or compulsions of democratic politics of civilised society or the ultimate political will to rediscover the possibility of reconciliation and cooperation with 'branded criminals.' The Indian state has to decide how long to engage in such unproductive orchestration. Now time has come to think "This far and no further."

As 'Law and Order' is a state subject, whenever, political violence in a massive scale breaks out in a state, the police become the first responder. Police in India are trained, equipped and mentally conditioned to deal with civil disorders only. When confronted with serious threats to internal security like terrorism, insurgency and other proxy war situations, they find it difficult to respond effectively. In such a situation, States seek the expert assistance of paramilitary forces. As paramilitary forces, other than Central Reserve Police Force (CRPF) are raised, trained and equipped to meet a specific need of national security, when deputed to deal with large scale disorders and proxy war situations, they are required to quickly modify and reorient their operational doctrines to meet the situation at hand. Though the paramilitary forces in India have acquitted themselves well in handling internal security problems, much valuable time has been lost before successes are recorded.

Often the authorities call in the Army to aid civil authorities to meet Internal Security situations more as a numerical supplement to PMFs and Police than for its expertise. As Army's ethos is 'Victory at all Costs,' their internal security operations have created more problems than they were meant to solve. Human Rights violations, excessive use of force, lack of coordination with civil authorities etc. are among the recurring complaints against the army, when deployed on internal security duties.

The all enveloping crisis of governance in India is apparent from inability of the State to govern, in contra-distinction to rule which has strengthened the phenomena of human governance, transcending other contentions. Manifestation of poor governance is eminently apparent; they are exemplified by the wasteful use of scarce resources, unresponsive administration at its cutting edge, pervasive at all levels; little policy coherence to address the issues and concerns impinges upon citizen.[7] These manifestations of poor governance include lack of decentralisation and devolution, and unimaginative dealings with minority, decay of established institutions and self-centred ruling elite. There is also a paucity of documentation of what constitutes the ruling elites' understanding of the threat to national security, issues and concerns as a part of comprehensive security.[8]

The main problem of governance in democratic and plural societies is meeting their populations' raising expectations molded by their exposure to electronic media. Multi-cultural and multi-ethnic characteristics of these societies require adequate space being provided for diverse community to live in harmony.

Also civil society does not exist in India because of prevailing socio-economic and political environment does not permit this. Our country lacks any political culture suitably needed for a civil society. Deliberate attempts have been made to weaken the civil structure by the forces of status quo and power hungry ruling elite. The fragile societal forces also provide the ruling class to exploit them. These are primarily variety of hurdles for a viable civil society in India.[9] They are lack of political culture, lack of accountability, religious fundamentalism, element of militancy/terrorism, state sponsored terrorism, controlled media, class difference, economic fragility, poor governance, rampant corruption.

Regrettably, the compulsions of electoral policies dictate the use of communal, caste, and class divisions by the political masters to consolidate their respective vote banks. This is bound to generate social conflicts and violence in society. This electoral politics lies at the roots of governance and security. Money and muscle power obviously become the important ingredients for this phenomena. The problem is also perceived to be with the politics and politicians who have reduced the agenda of governance in pursuit of power. The dilemma before the State is that it can reform itself while remaining party to its sustained misgovernance.

The role of judiciary too has come under scanner. Despite various judicial review, remarks and public interest litigation, there is an erosion of public confidence in judiciary. Lack of effective access to justice, huge backlog of cases, long delay, persistent corruption and decimal convictions has only weakened the fabric of judicial systems in the country at all levels. Administration of criminal judicial system need immediate and an urgent attention for speedy justice, fair trial and appropriate corrective measures.

Dissent, violence, militancy and terrorism on one hand, and politicians-criminal nexus on the other hand, blend with lawlessness and rampant corruption has caused the enfeeblement of government, especially its police and criminal justice system in India. If a concerted campaign is to be launched against drugs and arms smuggling, child and women trafficking or other such crimes serious efforts are bound to fail. This is precisely because of profiting mafias have higher reaches with ruling establishments. Hence, these issues cannot be addressed as long as it is linked with the crisis of governance. The very machinery of governance, thus, insidiously becomes a source of insecurity.

Sense of security is an inseparable element of human existence. The notion of human security is a prime conceptual leap forward in the quest of security. Its linkage between individual national and international securities could be explained. Well-being of a citizen or secured lifestyle of an individual must form the basis of national security considerations, for simple reason that it is these individuals who form this nation. Human security, therefore, pertains above all to the safety and well-being of "all the people everywhere...in their homes, in their jobs, in their streets, in their communities, in their environment".[10]

The new security discourse has enveloped the idea of that the security of people's need to be placed ahead of other security concerns. The Commission on Human Security embraced this movement beyond the traditional state-centric view of security. It defines "protecting the vital core of all human lives in ways that enhances human freedom and human fulfilment."

Hence, the respect of human security, their dignity, rights and freedom are paramount before the state. Therefore, the objective of human security flows from state to individuals. The focus changes from military-centric security to human development; from territorial security to food, water, shelter, education, health, employment and environmental guarantees. These profound transitions are essential formulation from classical sense of security to the human security.

The concept of human security deserves a comprehensive look covering various dimensions of human existence as mentioned in UNDP report "...a state in which the human being is without threat and ill-treatment...."[11] The concept of human security seeks to define the basis of security as a comprehensive and integrated matrix of needs and rights, from which all individual and social values flourishes and be optimized. While security the State is an essential element for survival but the essence cannot be restricted to merely well-being of the State itself. Classical formulations of security are the protection and welfare of the nation, whereas what is central or should be central is the protection and welfare of the individual/citizen/ human being. A conception of security that centred above all on the sanctity of the individual may be called as human security.[12]

The constituents of human security, of every individual, not just the region needs to be looked into. Here security through development comes into focus; security of all people, everywhere, in every environment. The prevalence of high-risk diseases like AIDS/HIV and diabetes, in various parts of India, indicate the need for stronger, workable and more efficient public health infrastructure. Politically Indian states throw a challenge to governance and federalism. The states at times act in a manner that questions the authority of the Centre and poses concern to the integrity of the nation. The mushrooming of several ideological groups like the PWG, TNLA that possess sub-nationalist agenda like separatism and seek to achieve ideological aims is another ominous trend.

Communalism has emerged as one of the greatest threats to internal security and creating widespread disorder in the country and promoting disunity and disharmony amongst the population by affecting economic growth and thus weakening the nation. Exploiting the 'injured psyche' of the minorities in India hostile neighbour is busy fomenting communal conflicts in India. The rabid hate rhetoric of Hindu fundamentalists, further worsened the communal situation.

Demands for sharing economic and political power, increase in literacy, growing unemployment amongst the educated youth and the urge towards upward mobility etc. have galvanized the erstwhile downtrodden to raise their voice against social inequalities and injustice resulting in caste and class conflicts in many parts of India.[13] Uneven regional developments are likely to be a major concern to India's federal structure. Though it may not be imminent but not improbable in near future. If the corruption in government transcends certain limits, that may lead to popular discontent and pose not only law-order problem but also threats to internal security.

While this implies that India is endowed with vast wealth and potential of human capital, it also entails new problems and threats. The huge coastline requires constant surveillance, especially as waters are considered "porous borders" that could easily serve for arms, ammunitions and illegal trafficking of other contraband goods. Attacks on Indian fishermen and even naval personnel by neighbouring countries are another problem. Water is the elixir of all life. In today's world of global warming and scant resources, water may be in the forefront of human conflict. This is seen as a growing problem in various parts of India, especially when it brings into force the conflict between federal units of the nation and as well as a tussle between the centre and states.

Link between governance and internal source of conflict is important on any reckoning and particular relevance to India. It is generally believed that under a democratic government country provides a 'safety valve' that could dampen or minimize internal source of conflicts. But here the reality is different. There is also a link between democracy and human development, because a good government must guarantee citizens certain basic liberties for promotion of their progress and their expansion of the social opportunities. Democratic process could facilitate the framing and enactment of laws that reflects popular aspirations, but effective implementation and enforcement of the same remains with the mighty-ruling elite. It is here that good governance could do the best. The basic question thus arises:

- Is the government accountable to the people it governs?
- Is Indian State providing good governance addressing the security aspirations of the common man?
- Is their social justice and dignified life for common people governed?
- Is there transparency and respect for human rights?

Governance and security has assumed greater importance in recent years. While the crime rate is ever growing in the country, the **abductions** and **extortions** has almost become an industry for criminal mafia and ***rangdari*** and ***supari*** culture is fast emerging as new brand of threats to our society. Cyber and hi-tech crimes and various other forms of illegal activities like money laundering, hawala transactions and human trafficking is on the rise. Basic question before us whether law-order machinery has collapsed? Or the pillars of governance have weakened? Or the states with all its agencies have failed to perform its designated role. Whether the statecraft will be able to bring rule of law and strict enforcement what is guaranteed to its citizens.

Conclusion

National strategy covers the complete gamut of activities of government and is not limited to military centric security alone. It has to govern various functions of the state. Hence assessment of all micro-macro threats, its magnitude and its sources is necessary to build up a threat matrix. National Security Strategy flows from overall national strategy and is a sub-set of the former cannot be conceived in a vacuum.[14] Hence articulation of national security is paramount for emerging power status of India.

Complex security threats need effective security management. It is urgently required to review and refurbish each and every element of the entire security apparatus across various wings of the central and state governments. While varied steps are required to improve governance on all fronts certain administrative reforms, enactment of new laws and legal modalities are essential to ensure effective functioning of the security management apparatus.[15] India is endowed with able and competent security managers who are capable of changing the landscape of comprehensive security in India. But whether there is a collective wisdom and political will to assert? Well, competency alone cannot provide results without ability to act. Hence competency and ability both is needed to address comprehensive security issues in India.

NOTES AND REFERENCES

1. Raghavan, V.R. ed. *Comprehensive Security for South Asia.* New Delhi: Delhi Policy Group, [2000], p. 1.
2. Mansingh, Surjit. India. *In*: V.R. Raghavan, ed. *Comprehensive Security for South Asia.* New Delhi: Delhi Policy Group, [2000], pp. 140-41.

3. *See Also*: Karnad, Bharat. *India's Place in the World: Democratic Peace, Raison d'état and Co-operative Security. In*: M. L. Sondhi, ed. Democratic Peace: the Foreign Policy Implications (ICSSR). New Delhi: Har-Anand, 2000, pp. 14-15.
4. India, Defence (Ministry of -), Standing Committee on Defence on Demand of Grants. Imprudent Defence Planning: Needs An Enhanced Approach. Report 19. *Vayu,* V.III, 2003, pp. 17-18. ***See Also:*** Jasjit Singh. *Defence A Profile of Five Decades. In:* Hiranmay Karlekar, ed. Independent India: The first fifty years. New Delhi, Oxford University Press, 1998, pp. 94-95.
5. ***See for details***: Chari, P.R. ed. *Security and Governance in South Asia*. New Delhi: Manohar Publications, 2001.
6. Khare, Harish. Ritual of Retribution, Obligations of Reconciliation. *The Hindu,* dt. 18th August, 2005.
7. Chari, P.R. Governance and Security. *The Hindu,* dt. 3rd November 2001.
8. Chari, P.R. Governance and Security. *The Hindu,* dt. 3rd November 2001.
9. Malviya, Gopalji. *Counter Terrorism: An Agenda for Co-operative Security in South Asia. In*: Lakshmi Krishnamoorthy et al. Responding to Terrorism: Challenges to Democratic Societies. Madras: Book Venture, 2003, p. 227.
10. Maqbub ul Haq. *New Importants of Human Security*. RGICS Paper No. 17, New Delhi: Rajiv Gandhi Institute for Contemporary Studies, 1994, p. 1.
11. *Widely known details on the Concept of Human Security are found in:* UNDP. Redefining Security: The Human Dimension. *Current History,* May 1995, pp. 229-36.
12. Bajpai, Kanti, The Idea of Human Security. *International Strategic Journal.* V. 40, (3), 2003, pp. 198-203. *See Also:* Kanti Bajpai. Beyond Comprehensive Security: Human Security. *In*: V.R. Raghavan, ed. *Comprehensive Security from India's Region.* New Delhi; Delhi Policy Group, 2001, pp. 1-25.
13. Rammohan Rao, P.S. Key Note Address. *In:* Gopalji Malviya, ed. *Security Dimensions of Peninsular India*. Chennai: CSA, 2005, p. 15.
14. Sundarji, K. Media and National Security. *Trishul*, V.IV (1), 1991, pp. 29-33.
15. Vohra, N.N., Managing Security Through Fixed Tenures? *The Hindu*, Chennai, dt. 20th October 2005. ***See Also***: Vinod Saighal. *Restructuring South Asian Security*. New Delhi: Manas Publications, 2000, pp. 236-44.

3

Process of Making India's Security Policy: Role of the Legislature

Shrikant Paranjpe

A policy is defined as a purposive course of action taken by those in power in pursuit of certain goals or objectives. Public policies are policies adopted and implemented by government bodies and officials.[1] David Easton argues that public policies are formulated by the 'authorities' in any political system. These include the elders, paramount chiefs, executives, legislators, judges, administrators, councillors, monarchs, etc.[2] Policies need to be differentiated from goals or objectives. Goals or objectives are indicative of the final end to be achieved. These goals are usually a product of certain values that are cherished and are considered desirable. These values may sometimes be defined as beliefs and are held by those who define the goals. They by themselves need not provide any direction or a path to be taken for the achievement of the objective, for that is a matter of policy. Thus in the context of a nation state one can talk of certain national values or belief systems that are the 'core values' held by that state. The goals that the state seeks to achieve would be in consonance with the values held by the state and that the policies formulated would provide the direction to be taken by the state in achieving those set of values/goals. Policy making involves decision-making, but every decision is not a policy decision. A policy decision involves an action to reject, alter or accept a preferred policy alternative.

Policy formulation comprises of four main aspects:[3] (a) predicting and defining areas where policy formulation is required; (b) the process of formulating policy; (c) planning programmes and projects to achieve the purposes of policy; and (d) reviewing the policy for a more effective feedback. In the first stage long range plans are formulated. It is here that a linkage is sought to be developed between identifiable goals and demarcating areas that require formulation of a policy. In the second and third areas, policy options are proposed keeping in mind their effectiveness, costs, availability of support systems, etc. In the final stage a policy review is conducted for a feedback on the policy that is implemented.

Security policy, in a wider sense, encompasses the economic, industrial, and technological base; the cohesiveness of the socio-cultural structure; the resilience and stability of the political system; and the efficacy of diplomacy. This also opens up the question of compatibility between national and international security.[4] There is a need to temper the military capability approach to security policy with factors like diplomacy and science and technology. There is also the need to realize the linkage between domestic policy and national security policy. An important aspect of this linkage is the factor of costs. A national security policy ultimately rests on political decisions about the role that the nation is to play in international politics.[5] Defence planning and preparation, in particular, are conditioned by social and political objectives.[6]

India's security policy is to be understood within a much wider framework than the one that has been conventionally used for the study of 'defence' policy. There has been a tendency to look at the security policy through the conceptual lenses of the armed forces of a nation—hence its identification with the term defence policy. Even though this approach to security is fundamental, it is not exclusive to the understanding of the broad range of security issues that a nation faces. Therefore, Indian security doctrine needs to be anchored in a framework that considers rapid and well-managed socio-economic development for the people a primary strategic priority.[7]

Drawing of Boundaries

The term policy has come to acquire a meaning that goes beyond being a mere statement of intent and purpose; it accepts the growing need for greater internal consistency and rationality. Consequently, the efforts to analyze a policy would have two categories: one that attempts to understand the context and the dynamics of policy making process and two, the substance of the policy. The former would require the analyst to be familiar with different aspects of the policy making process including the identity of the participants, legal requirements, ability to assess the situation, anticipate and deal with problems, etc. The latter requires a fair knowledge of the subject at hand.

This paper uses the institutional approach to policy analysis[8] to understand the making of India's security policy. The state is a web of governmental structures and institutions through which it performs various functions. An ideal state is a guardian of interests of all the sections of the community, accommodating and reconciling diverse interests and ensuring that public policy is compatible with the preferences of the majority. In pluralist democratic societies the various agencies that constitute the channels of communication for the making of public policy include the legislature, political parties, interest groups, judiciary, media, etc. Public policy is formulated and implemented by governmental institutions. The government has the legal authority to make policies, the application is universal and the state has the coercive authority to implement the policies.

Public policy is thus concerned with power since policy making is essentially a manifestation of power. The sources of power which effect change and influence the making of policy are diverse. At one level they are the non-official groups who seek to influence those who are vested with official power. These include the individual citizen, the media, interest and pressure groups and political parties. These non-official sources influence the policy process by initiating, vetoing, planning, adjudicating, controlling, moralizing, theorizing, cooperating and agitating.[9] The official policy-makers occupy formal offices of the political community. They include the legislature, executive and the bureaucracy.

Policy making in India is shaped by the following features that constitute the basis of the Indian constitutional system:

(i) India is a sovereign democratic republic. It accepts

the concept of popular sovereignty with the people expressing their opinion through duly elected representatives. The democratic system of governance requires that the public opinion be articulated by the representatives with accuracy and that in case they fail to do so they be replaced (through the due process of elections).

(ii) In the Indian context, this representation is achieved through the Parliamentary system of governance. The Parliamentary system requires the ministers (executives) to be members of the Parliament and be accountable to their decisions to the Parliament. The term 'government' includes the civil service (bureaucracy) which is the agency used by the executive to implement policy. They are required to be politically neutral and accountable for their actions.

(iii) India is a federal state. While there are overriding powers that the Central government may exercise in case of an emergency, the constitution specifies a division of powers between the Centre and the States.

(iv) Public policy in India conforms to India's socio-economic philosophy. This philosophy governs the key area of internal security policy.

In a complex system of governance a vast number of social, political, economic, cultural, administrative etc. forces may seek to influence India's security policy-making. In a Parliamentary system the Executive, as the Government, holds the power to take initiative in the formulation and implementation of policy. The study of the input into policy making by the Executive relates to the identification of players whose interest and behaviour have an important effect of the governmental actions. In the present Indian context this would include the bureaucratic network around the Prime Minister and the Council of Ministers. It would also include the Higher Defence Organisation apparatus, the staff agencies of the Defence Ministry and the input provided by the Armed Forces. The question about the role that the Legislature plays as an input into policy making is determinant on the contextual situation of the issue under consideration and the (political) environment in which the policy is being made. This input into the policy making at this stage is likely to be both, contextual and substantive in its content. This network of input givers would also constitute the agencies that provide a feedback to the Executive on policy. This paper looks at the role of the Parliament as one of the important agencies in the process of making India's security policy.

Conceptual Framework

The activities of Legislatures can be grouped into three broad categories: those pertaining to policy making, representation and system maintenance.[10] In the Indian case the executive and the legislature are closely interlinked because of the parliamentary system of government. It may perhaps be difficult to distinguish who was responsible for making of policy, the executive or the legislature. But given provision of accountability of government, the legislature is bound to have some role in the process. The representational activities of the legislature are those where it seeks to articulate the societal interests. This is where the role perception of the parliamentarian becomes important. System maintenance activities include support for the government, conflict management and conflict resolution within the political system.

The Parliamentary system works on two integrated principles that appear contradictory: the concept of the supremacy of the Parliament and the power of the Executive, as the Government, to take initiative in the formulation and implementation of policy. The former is a constitutional position while the latter has a political base. The concept of control of the Parliament on the Executive's sphere of activity flows from the idea of responsible government. Executive privilege and the role played by the Parliament in influencing the Executive in its actions forms the crux of the debate on Parliament's role in the making of India's security policy. In India this role is played through general debates on various issues, appointment of committees, parliamentary questions, and various motions moved on the floor of the House, etc. Executive control, on the other hand, is exercised through the system of party discipline—in case of the Parliamentary procedures through the Whip and though the threat of dissolution of the Parliament. In reality, however, the balance depends upon the nature of majority held by the government in power and the leadership of the Prime Minister.

This paper starts with the following broad hypothesis:

- Given the nature of security policy decision-making its inherent secrecy and specialization, decisions tend to be made public only after they are taken or implemented.
- Given the *post facto* publication, public scrutiny is performed as a feedback on the government's decision-making process.
- It is likely, in some circumstances, that public "feedback" is sought even before the actual announcement of policy, at the stage of policy formulation. This could be done to understand the 'mood' of the nation or to stall issues.

Parliament and Security Policy

The formulation of Indian security policy in the early years of independence had almost been the exclusive domain of Pandit Nehru. The basic principles of security policy grew out of the domestic and international compulsions of that period. The debacle of 1962 and Nehru's death in 1964 brought in changes in the situation. The exclusivity of decision-making dissipated and there emerged some degree of debate within the government circles. The openness of debates notwithstanding, one observes a historical tendency to keep security issues outside the scope of public scrutiny. This arises from two main reasons: the need for urgency and secrecy in decision-making and the specialized nature of the subject.

Three factors have dominated India's security policy: The first is the regional threat perception that focuses primarily on the neighbours Pakistan and China, and subsequently the other regional powers. The threat from Pakistan and China is predominantly a threat of conventional border conflicts. Over the years other dimensions such as insurgency, support to militancy, and concerns about nuclear weapons have further complicated this relationship. In case of the other regional powers, the threat is an indirect one; it may manifest itself through intervention in favour of or covert and overt support to anti-India forces. The second factor is the urge for self-reliance. This could mainly be seen in the context of India's relations with the West and the former Soviet Union. The threat perception in this case rested on a wide spectrum of relations including those dealing with trade and commerce (especially in armaments). Of some significance has been the effort to secure a transfer of technology in the purchase of foreign equipment. It also rested on the approaches these countries took in the context of Cold War conflicts and consequent repercussions of India's national interests. A military connection with the former Soviet Union appeared to satisfy some of these interests. The third dimension of India's security policy is the debate over the validity of the concept of self-determination is the basis of this legitimacy. However, this concept works in two mutually opposite directions—as a unifying force and as a divisive one as well. Indian security policy has had to confront itself with these questions, whether in the context of demands for separatism or autonomy.

During the early years of Independence, India's security policy followed two main trends: one represented India's urge to retain newly won independence in the practice of security policy even while upholding its peace policy; the second reflected in the application of these principles in the context of building regional solidarity and the spread of regionalism. But regionalism never became a fundamental concern of Asian states. Inter-state conflicts caused by unsettled boundaries, existence of large minorities, clash of elites, etc. were some of the serious obstacles. The onset of the Korean war and the resultant Korean system of alliances ended attempts at regional solidarity. From Bandung onwards there was a slow shift towards the development of a "neutralist" policy that addressed itself to the global concerns of the Cold War conflict. The fundamental tenets of peace and independence were to become the foundations of the new non-aligned policy. The security dimensions of the non-aligned approach were to draw on these basic tenets. They ensured that the strategic doctrine of a country focused on the fundamentals of national interest, as defined by the approaches of peace and independence, and thereby enabled one to structure a security policy to ensure the goals. Such a perspective on non-alignment[11] considered the Cold War a contextual perspective within which the definitions of interest had to be articulated. This ensured its continuing validity as a security policy in the days of the Cold War and the period of détente. The post-Soviet scenario has raised new questions about this approach that would be discussed further.

Until 1962, there was very little debate on defence policy in India. This was mainly because of the lack of expertise and the apparent success of Nehru's nonaligned policy. Unlike the Nehru phase, the post-Nehru debates appeared to use the power approaches to security policy. These debates were[12] to remain within the broad parameters of international relations, except when they discussed defence matters in a technical sense or reflected on the experiences of the 1962 and 1965 wars. It must be noted, however, that the foci of most of the debates remained issue based or sectoral in nature and rarely covered overall security policy. A.P. Rana describes the discussion on security policy in India mainly as "debating literature."[13]

The debates on security policy in the Indian Parliament have been viewed in a diverse perspective.[14] At one level, there is an appreciation that the members are well informed and the quality of the debates is good. None of those interviewed expected a large number of members to participate in debates on security policy. Increasing complexity of the international situation and the variety and the abundance, often contradictory, of material available has only complicated the issue. There is a broad agreement that the library-based information has not been used by the average parliamentarian, while there is a great deal of dependence on the press. There is little effort made by the Ministry to brief the members on subjects that may prove to be controversial. Informal dialogue by the Ministers with the members has been restricted to very few members, nowadays of only the ruling party.

While security policy formulation has remained almost exclusively in the hands of the Executive, this includes the political executive and the bureaucracy, the Parliament has emerged as a participant mainly in the feedback process. Cases like the resignation of Krishna Menon, debates on NPT, debates on

Morarji Desai's stand on the Tarapur Atomic Power Plant, discussion on the Kargil conflict, India's nuclear tests of 1974 and 1998, Indian policies towards the United States, etc. have seen active debates on the floor of the House.

Role of the Parliament

The Constitution of India contains provisions that are broad and generalized. The Parliament has exclusive powers to make laws with regard to the following subjects:[15]

(i) Foreign affairs, all matters which bring the Union into relation with any foreign country;
(ii) Diplomatic, consular and trade representation;
(iii) United Nations;
(iv) Participation in international conferences;
(v) Entering into treaties and agreements with foreign countries; war and peace;
(vi) Foreign jurisdiction;
(vii) Extradition;
(viii) Piracy and crimes committed on the high seas or in the air, etc.

However there are three important issues on which certain conventions have developed on the basis of constitutional provisions:[16]

(i) *Declaration of war*: The legislative power of the Parliament extends to making laws in regard to war and peace, but the Parliament has no power to declare war, whether a state of war exists, to terminate the state of war, enter into armistice or conclude peace, etc. This power is exercised by the President on the advice of the Council of Ministers. The parliamentary control over this aspect is only indirect, in form of debates, resolutions and motions in the Parliament.
(ii) *Treaty Making*: The task of conducting treaty negotiations with foreign powers is essentially a part of the functions of the Executive. It is not obligatory to seek approval of the Parliament to such treaties unless the treaty itself has such provisions.

(iii) *Diplomatic representation and recognition of governments*: Matters relating to diplomatic representation and recognition of governments are decided by the Cabinet without Parliamentary approval.

A key question that is raised on the issue of the role of the Parliament is did the Parliament go beyond pure discussion? There could be two answers to this question. One would focus on the government's willingness to involve the Parliament as a participant in the formulation of policy and the other on the ability of the Parliament to take independent decisions. The former operates on an *ad hoc* basis, in the case of the latter there are structural hurdles.

At the structural level, the Parliament comes into the picture through various committees and the discussions on the floor of the House. In 1992 the system of departmentally related Standing Committees was introduced. These committees look into the Demands for Grants pertaining to the various ministries papers on policy matters referred to them by the Speaker. One notable case of a committee was that of the Estimates Committee of the Indian Parliament that in its Nineteenth Report on the Ministry of Defence raised some crucial questions about India's Defence policy. The Ministry of Defence, in its statement to the Estimates Committee, stated that India's Defence policy has basically been a policy to defend the territory, sovereignty and freedom of the country. The Estimates Committee considered this a needless oversimplification of the concerned policy. It felt that India should have a national security doctrine which not only takes a long-term view of the country's security requirements but also looks into problems of internal security.[17]

The Indian Parliament has used several procedures and opportunities to influence the formulation and conduct of security policy. There is a fairly large degree of coordination between the Government and the party in power. The parliamentary party is often consulted where an issue requires knowledge of the public opinion, the Congress Party, for example, had a system of standing committee on foreign affairs. There is very little literature available on the nature of informal contacts between the parliamentarians and the government. Informal discussion with members[18] who participated in the debates on security issues presents a varied perspective. On the one hand, there has always been a complaint that the government has shied away from revealing information on various subjects on the pretence of national security. On the other there appears to be an acceptable level of informal cross-party dialogue on various security-related issues. This dialogue was most visible during the governments of Rajiv Gandhi, various non-Congress coalition governments headed by V.P. Singh, Chandrashekhar, Deve Gowda and Gujral, the Narsimha Rao government and the first real non-Congress government of Vajpayee. This informal dialogue appears to have died out since then.

An important method that appears to have been used to involve the Parliament in policy formulation can be described as a system of "inspired questions." The government can deliberately introduce a question in the Question Hour through a Member so as to get an opportunity to explain its stand in form of an answer. Such a question may be introduced while the line of action is still being debated by the government as it seeks a feed-back on the possible line of action prior to actual announcement of policy. The answers may also provide a third party observer an indication of the line of thinking of the government.[19] There is, however, a disagreement on the veracity of the concept of the 'inspired question.' While some legislators agreed to the use of the method, others denied its existence.[20]

One of the early expressions about the ability of the Parliament to deal with world politics is found in John Locke's writings. However, unlike Locke, who had not granted the Parliament any significant role in this area, the British and American systems have sought to balance the executive privilege with a need of a popular control of the Parliament. In the parliamentary system like India the issue of control is far more complicated as there is a need to balance the concept of supremacy of the Parliament and the prerogative of the executive. Executive privilege on the one hand, and the ability of the Parliament to influence policy on the other, is the crux of the role of the Parliament in formulation of security policy.

NOTES AND REFERENCES

1. R.K. Sapru, *Public Policy: Formulation, Implementation and Evaluation*, (Delhi: Sterling), p. 3.
2. David Easton, 'An Approach to the Analysis of Political Systems', *World Politics*, Vol. 9 (1), April 1957, p. 384.
3. Ishwar Dayal, 'Organisation for Policy Formulation,' K.D. Madan, et al., *Policy Making in Government* (New Delhi: Publications Division, 1982), p. 142.
4. Approaches to security were dominated by militarized perspectives of "national" security. These have been criticized as being "ethnocentric." Barry Buzan's approach, on the other hand, includes political, economic, societal, environmental as well as military considerations. See : Barry Buzan, *People, States and Fear* (London, 1983), pp. 214-42. Also of related interest is P.M. Kamath's argument in "Trends in the Study of National Security-Making and Implementation", *Strategic Analysis* (New Delhi), Vol. XIV, No. 4, July 1991, pp. 429-40.
5. K. Subrahmanyam, *Our National Security* (New Delhi, 1972), pp. 8-9.
6. Government of India, Ministry of Defence, *Annual Report, 1964-65* (New Delhi), p. 1.
7. Jasjit Singh, "Affordable Credible Defence of India," *Strategic Analysis* (New Delhi), Vol. XVI, No. 11, Feb. 1994, p. 1381.
8. Other approaches include David Easton's Systems approach and the Rational Policy Making model.
9. Charles Lindblom, *The Policy Making Process* (New York: Prentice Hall, 1968), pp. 30-31.
10. Michael Mezey, *Comparative Legislatures* (Duke University Press, 1979), p. 29.
11. K. Subrahmanyam, "Defence Policy and Analysis," in *ICSSR Survey, A Survey of Research in Political Science, Vol. 5 : International Relations* (New Delhi, 1988), p. 250. For a realist approach to Nonalignment, see also A.P. Rana, *Imperative on Nonalignment: A Conceptual Study of India's Foreign Policy Strategy in the Nehru Period* (Meerut, 1978).
12. The ICSSR Survey on Research in International Relations and Defence Policy and Analysis by A.P. Rana and K. Subrahmanyam has been an excellent basic source on defence/security policy. See, *A Survey of Research in Political Science, vol. 5: International Relations* (New Delhi, 1988). There is general agreement about the relative lack of interest in Indian defence policies in the Nehru era. Chris Smith argues otherwise. Rohit Handa also tends to substantiate this view. Some of the other works include: Lorne J. Kavic, *India's Quest for Security: Defence Policies, 1947-65* (New Delhi, 1960); S.S. Khera, *India's Defence Problem* (New Delhi, 1968); Raju G.C. Thomas, *The Defence of India: A Budgetary Perspective of Strategy and Politics* (Meerut, 1978); P.V.R. Rao, *Defence Without Drift* (Bombay, 1970); Chris

Smith, India's Ad hoc Arsenal : Direction or Drift in Defence Policy?, SIPRI Study (Oxford, 1994); Rohit Handa, *Policy for India's Defence* (New Delhi, 1976).

13. A.P. Rana, "International Relations," in Rana and Subrahmanyam, n. 12, p. 31.
14. Interviews with Parliamentarians.
15. *Foreign Policy of India* (New Delhi: Lok Sabha Secretariat, 1987), p. 11. Also see Art. 253 of the Indian Constitution.
16. *Ibid.*, pp. 13-14.
17. Estimates Committee, 1992-93, 10th Lok Sabha, 19th *Report, Ministry of Defence: Defence Force Levels, Manpower Management and Policy* (New Delhi, 1992).
18. Interviews with Parliamentarians.
19. Two instances of such questions refer to the questions raised about Indian nuclear testing in 1974. Mrs Gandhi in her replies to the Parliament in 1972 and again in 1973 made it clear that the Atomic Energy Commission was reviewing the progress in the technology of underground testing of nuclear devices from both, the theoretical and experimental angle. See: Lok Sabha *Debates*, Vol. XX93, No. 4, 15 November 1972, Col. 49 and Rajya Sabha *Debates*, Vol. LXXXVI, No. 4, 15 November 1973, Col. 138-39.
20. Interviews with Parliamentarians.

4

India's Nuclear Strategy: A Challenge to Decision-Making Process

Prashant Agarwal

Decision-making and Higher Defence Management has been the most critical area in any country's national security management. For a common man the essence of decision-making is the formulation of various options or alternatives and choosing one of them, subsequently. The basic purpose is being to make judgment on 'more desirable' option. The science of 'operational research' and 'qualitative analysis' has developed certain procedures for such decision-making. These methods incorporate certain mathematical techniques to identify an 'optimum course of action under a given situation.' This method is known as analytical approach to decision-making and is most successful in the areas where problems are well defined. But there are number of decision-making problems including that of military which are not amenable to such treatment. It is because these problems are complex involving human lives and are ill-defined because of non-availability of information and limited options.[1] This is an area where the entire process of decision-making will be on litmus test. Any delay or a wrong decision may be catastrophic.

In view of the highly militarized environment, infusion of nuclear and advanced technologies, and multifarious threats ranging from terrorism and insurgency to drug trafficking have not only altered the security environment but also make the national security management and decision-making process exceptionally complex and too serious a business to be tackled carefully. In the 21st century, national leaderships, particularly of nuclearized countries, will have to consider an extraordinarily large number of factors and complex issues in managing national security. In the democratic set-up it is difficult for the political leadership to take the right security decisions without considering professional advice from agencies involved directly or indirectly in security management. Similarly, it is equally impossible for bureaucracy to be proficient on all issues of national security. Hence, it is essential for every nation to have a well-established and functioning Higher Defence Management system which can consider various issues and concerns while formulating the national security strategy. At the apex level, therefore, there is a need for creation of various channels that are able to provide comprehensive analysis of security issues, recommend the right operational strategy and carry out comprehensive planning for long-term security management both during peace time and war.

In the domain of Higher Defence Management, close interaction between civilians and the military constitutes a critical as well as controversial relationship in any country, whether democracy or dictatorship. Ideally, civilians and the military are from two distinct domains, each with a specific set of functions. While the decision to go to war is made by the political establishment, the military is responsible for the actual conduct of war on the battlefield.[2] Yet this relationship is not as simple as it appears at a first glance. There often emerge situations in which the traditional division of labour between civilians and the military becomes blurred. For example, in the case of nuclear doctrine of any country it is a challenging job for the policy-makers to assign responsibilities to the various military and non-military organizations.[3] Close coordination between the various organizations which involved in the decision-making process and its implementation is the key for the success of any doctrine. From this perspective, if we analyze the Indian Nuclear Doctrine one can find several positive and negative points in it. It is also necessary for us to closely analyze this doctrine because, since the nuclear tests in 1998, several analysts have pointed out towards the lack of strategic doctrine and command and control capabilities to accompany India's nuclear programme.

Broadly speaking there are two ways through which one can structuralized its nuclear command: the first is centralized and the second is decentralized command.[4] Most of the newly nuclearized countries generally adopted the centralized command structure for their nuclear forces. In this type of structure, complete centralization of the nuclear forces is represented by the linkage of all nuclear weapons to the central command post headed by the political head of the country (either the President or the Prime Minister depends on the form of government). Control in this set-up was as centralized as physically possible. India has also adopted the centralized command structure to implement its nuclear doctrine. In a broader perspective, India's nuclear doctrine can be summarized as follows:

1. Building and maintaining a credible minimum deterrent;
2. A posture of 'No-first-use'—nuclear weapons will only be used in retaliation against a nuclear attack on Indian territory or on Indian forces anywhere;
3. Nuclear retaliation to a first strike will be massive and designed to inflict unacceptable damage;
4. Nuclear retaliatory attacks can only be authorized by the civilian political leadership through the Nuclear Command Authority;
5. Non-use of nuclear weapons against non-nuclear weapon states;
6. However, in the event of a major attack against India, or Indian forces anywhere, by biological or chemical weapons, India will retain the option of retaliating with nuclear weapons.

In order to implement this strategy a Nuclear Command Authority (NCA) has also been established. In the chain of Command: there would be a political council headed by the Prime Minister, the composition of this would probably the same as the Cabinet Committee on Security. To execute the decisions of the political council there would be an Executive Council under the National Security Advisor. The Commander-in-Chief of the Strategic Forces Command (SFC) will control, manage and administer the nuclear forces. Nuclear assemblies are with DRDO, the weapon cores are with the Atomic Energy Commission and delivery systems are with the services.

The current nuclear strategy of India requires that India should at least maintain:

1. Sufficient, survivable and operationally prepared nuclear forces,
2. a credible command and control system,
3. effective intelligence and early warning capabilities,
4. comprehensive planning and training for operations in line with the strategy, and
5. the will to employ nuclear forces and weapons.

The deficiencies of such a centralized command system are quite obvious. The entire control system can be disabled by enemy's first strike fired at the Central Command structure. Thus, this form of command system is too just vulnerable to attack to ever be a credible deterrent.[5]

Another problem with this type of structure is that it places too much control of civilian authorities over military leadership. The political leadership of any country generally lacks both information processing abilities and the management and technical background needed to perform this function. As the size of the nuclear forces grows, as measured by the number of launchers or the number of warheads, the span of control of the central command grows exponentially large, which might create complex and critical situations before the decision-makers to take right decision at right time.

Several other gray areas in both strategy and command structures are:

- A pivotal role has been accorded to the NSA, who heads the Executive Council and would function as a vital link between the political and military wings of the NCA and also function as the Principal Secretary to the Prime Minister. He remains busy tackling both domestic and international crisis.
- Nuclear weapons assemblies are with the DRDO, the weapons are with AEC and delivery systems are with the services. How these dispersed assets would be brought together and the system worked in a wartime situation

when communications could get affected and quick decision-making is needed, has not been clarified.

- In Indian set up, the civil-bureaucratic structure has diffused accountability, and does not reveal who is accountable to whom, or what would be the line of succession if a decapitating strike succeeds.
- What would be the structure of the second strike capability—a key factor for the credibility of the minimum nuclear deterrence policy. Thus, how many nuclear warheads are essential for the credibility of the policy is a big question mark as it is dependent on various factors and likely targets.
- Who will determine what should constitute minimum deterrence remains unresolved between the scientific and strategic community, while no requirements seems to have been forwarded by the armed forces.
- How India would respond if it will be attacked with CBWs by a non-state actor, given the volatile situation in South Asia.
- How much funds are committed towards Nuclear Command and Control.

The only way out of this problem is to organize the command organization away from fully centralized control, and the only real way to do this in a world where military organizations are responsible for security is to structure the nuclear command in such a way that it meshes with the organizational structure of the military. Without such command organization, the absence of well defined hierarchy would lead to an information overload that would derailed the entire decision-making process.

In order to create a credible nuclear command and control system for India it is necessary for us to scrutinize the command and control systems of the other nuclear powered countries. In the British nuclear command and control system, the Royal Air Force plays a key role in the delivery and safety of UK's nuclear arsenal. The PM of UK is authorized to take decision for deployment and use of nuclear arsenals. Under the American law the command of nuclear weapon employment is vested with the President of the United States. The US President exercises control over nuclear weapons through The National Command Authority. It comprises the President, the Secretary Defence, and the Joint Chiefs of Staff. The US nuclear command and control system caters for the worst nuclear scenario, by earmarking a line of succession for continuous nuclear weapon command and control. In the event of death and incapacitation of the President a 16-member line of succession has been designated. After the President, the Vice President, Speaker of the House of Representatives, the Chairman of the Senate, the Secretary of State and so on will exercise command of the vast US nuclear arsenal.[6] In France, the President exercises close control over the deployment and employment of nuclear weapons. In fact, the National Command Post for ordering release of nuclear weapons and directing their use has been built, complete with operational communications in the basement of Elysee Palace in the heart of Paris. Russia's vast nuclear arsenal is controlled by the President. Under Command Russian Air Force, Strategic Forces Command and Rocket Forces Command, are tasked to carry out nuclear operations when required. India can also think about the creation of a Nuclear Command Authority on the US pattern.

In India, the entire nuclear command should be placed under the three-member National Command Authority (NCA) comprising the Prime Minister, the Defence Minister, the Chairman Chief of Staff Committee for the command and control of nuclear weapons at the highest level. India's nuclear weapons and nuclear forces must be under the command and control of the highest political authority, i.e. the Prime Minister of India. The authority to launch nuclear weapons must rest with the Prime Minister. The Defence Minister and the Chairman COSC need to be chartered to authenticate weapon release orders. The order will then go through the various formations of the Primary Strategic Command Centres and from these to Secondary Command Centres or actual nuclear weapon units scattered in all over the country. Besides this structure, a well defined line of succession will also be prepared so that in the event of emergency national security can be taken care off.

NOTES AND REFERENCES

1. K.J. Radford, *Complex Decision Problems: an Integrated Strategy for Resolution*, Printice Hall Company, Virginia, 1977.
2. Karl Von Clausewitz, *On War*, Princeton University Press, 1976.
3. Maxwell D. Taylor, *Precarious Security*, W.W. Norton & Company, New York, 1976.
4. Paul Bracken, *The Command and Control of Nuclear Forces*, Yale University Press, New Haven, 1983.
5. *Ibid.*
6. Maxwell D. Taylor, *Precarious Security*, *op. cit.*, f.n. 3.

5

Aviation Security: Evaluating the New Anti-Hijacking Policy of India*

Sanjay Jain

In this brief paper, an attempt is being made to critically analyze the most recent Anti-hijacking policy of Government of India, which it unfolded on the eve of Independence Day. As is clear, terrorists often resort to hijacking of aircrafts to compel the states to fulfil their demands. However, apart from this, they are also trying to convert these aircrafts into missiles so as to inflict enormous amount of damage in terms of life and property. Till recently, the response of Government to take on the terrorist in cases of hijacking or kidnappings was very soft as is evident from the episode of Kandhar. We are also aware of the story in which how the former home minister's daughter was used by the Kashmiri terrorists to get the release of some of the most notorious terrorists. For the same our Government has also faced constant criticism from various quarters.

However, with the uncovering of the new policy to take on with terrorists in cases of their being involved in hijacking of planes, government is trying to send a clear signal to them that no longer, it adopts a softy attitude towards them.

In foregoing pages I would briefly critique this policy. In the first section, I would briefly deal with changing dimensions of

---

* This paper has been prepared for presentation in the conference "Conceptualizing Security in the 21st Century" 18th-20th Nov. 2005 organized by National Centre of International Security & Defence Analysis (NISDA), University of Pune, Pune.

the concept of security with special reference to human security. I would argue that all policies dealing with any type of security, including national security or public security must be in conformity with the paradigm of human security.

Section two then goes on to briefly review and highlight important organizations and key International legal norms having a bearing upon aviation security and aviation terrorism. It is argued there that the law is still in its infancy in this area, and lack of rigor and uniformity.

In section three, having taken a bird's eye view of International scenario, I would provide the framework of the newly modified anti-hijacking policy instituted by Cabinet Committee on Security.

In the next section, I would briefly examine as tc whether this new policy withstands the test of constitutionality? I would also try and answer the question whether it was appropriate for government to first uncover this policy outside the Parliament without taking it in confidence, particularly at a time when Parliament was in session?

Finally, I would argue that the policy is perfunctory in nature and has a number of drawbacks and it does not touch several important issues like, whether or not Government of India is liable to pay compensation to the victims of a brought down plane, if the same is not owned by it?

I would like to conclude by arguing that national security is not only a political issue and it needs to be tackled with by adopting a cohesive and strategic perspective, may be by providing a more vocal and effective role to the National Security Advisory Council.

SECTION 1—CHANGING DIMENSIONS OF SECURITY

Obviously, the newly instituted anti-hijacking policy's prominent focus is security of strategic locations in particular and national security in general. Therefore, it would be interesting to have a bird's eye view of jurisprudence of security and critically examine the policy in the light of its modern perspective.

Undoubtedly, there is a paradigmatic shift in the understanding and appreciation of conception of security. Unlike present connotation of security, which is much more broader and holistic and therefore it is perceived as human security; the nineteenth century version of security was considerably narrower and was influenced predominantly by doctrine of police power under which the State is liable to secure life, liberty and property of the citizens against invasion of any kind. Of course, the modern notion of human security is not free from its critics and it is argued by many observers that concept of human security is too broad and universal in nature and under it; it is not easy to appreciate regional and local considerations, peculiar to a particular nation. In my humble opinion, although security indeed involves local and regional considerations, there is no gain saying the fact that we have to balance[1] these considerations in the light of the global standards. However, this gives rise to a number of tricky and complex questions, viz. whether human security should be a universal concern beyond national boundaries and whether the principles of human rights and individual freedom should be integral to human security? A detailed discussion of these questions lies beyond the scope of this paper; nevertheless suffice it to say that in the name of security, human rights and fundamental freedoms cannot be given a go by.

As a matter of fact, if one looks at the definition[2] of the term human security from a benevolent perspective, most of the misgivings would evaporate because "by making no distinction between civil, political, economic, social and cultural rights, human security addresses violations and security threats in an integrated, multi-dimensional and comprehensive way and provides a practical framework for identifying the specific rights and obligations that are at stake in a particular situation of insecurity."[3] Thus, "by focusing on individuals and communities and by looking at policies and institutions that not only protect but also empower individuals and communities, human security creates genuine possibilities for people to live in safety and dignity, thereby strengthening the partnership between states and citizens and complementing state security."[4] Furthermore, "human security promotes policies that not only empower individuals to benefit from economic growth and development but also protects them in times of insecurity and crisis. And, in this regard, human security recognizes and enhances the inter-linkages between security and development."[5]

Thus, it becomes evident from the above discussion that human security provides us an important perspective to problematize critique and if required, question the traditional discourse on security from the standpoints of violation of human rights, for being lacking in proper focus on human development and for being narrow in its approach.

If I were to link the aforesaid discussion to the topic at hand then I would have to make an attempt to critique the newly modified Anti-Hijacking Policy in a manner I have just observed, i.e. to say, whether this policy is in conformity with the broad parameters of human security. To answer this question, first I will have to examine the actual contents of the policy, which I propose to do in the third section. However, prior to discussing its contents, I would make a brief review of aviation terrorism with special reference to hijacking.

Background and History of Aviation Terrorism

Since its early beginnings, the aviation industry has been a target for acts of violence and terrorism. Today, modern terrorism and international civil aviation are closely linked. It is unfortunate to note that most major advances in aviation security have occurred as a direct result of terrorist activities.

Three distinct phases[6] in aviation terrorism have emerged during the last 50 years:

- Phase 1: 1948 to 1968—flight from persecution or prosecution.
- Phase 2: 1968 to 1994—the political phase.
- Phase 3: 1994 to date—the aircraft as a weapon of destruction.

- These phases are marked by major terrorist incidents including Lockerbie, Scotland in December 1988 and the events of September 11, 2001. Hijacking and sabotage have been a consistent approach used by terrorists, what has changed is the philosophy behind the attacks.[7]

Phase 1: 1948 to 1968—Flight from Persecution or Prosecution

Spanning 1948 to early 1968, this era was characterized by air piracy or 'hijacking' of aircraft where individuals fleeing a State to avoid persecution or prosecution viewed hijacking aircraft as a fast and convenient means of achieving this aim. An early example occurred on 6th April 1948 when three crew members (including the pilot) and twenty-one of the twenty-six passengers hijacked a Ceskoslovenske Aerolinie (CSA) internal flight from Prague to Bratislava landing in the US Occupation Zone in Munich. Whilst as a primary means of escape, hijacking has reduced; recent events in China demonstrate that it is not totally obsolete. During the early part of 2003, a number of hijackings were reported where individuals were attempting to reach Taiwan from China.

Phase 2: 1968 to 1994—The Political Phase

The apolitical nature of aviation terrorism experienced in Phase 1 changed during this phase. 1968 is seen as the beginning of 'modern terrorism' and the link between politics and terrorism against civil aviation. Although hijacking was still the civil aviation terrorists' most popular tactic (between 1967 and 1996, of the 1,033 incidents against airlines 914 (88%) were hijackings)[8], the terrorist organizations began to use hijackings and bombings as a way of calling attention to their cause. The aircraft was seen as a proxy for the State with the terrorists attempting to utilize the vast media potential of a hijacking or bombing to exert pressure on the State to change its policy or policies. The objectives of these attacks were invariably to:

- Embarrass their opponents (governments and other terrorist organizations).
- Damage the economy of the target State.
- Use it as a tool for extortion, either for the release of imprisoned colleagues and/or for money.

This phase is marked by three significant acts of aviation terrorism:

- In June 1985, Lebanese terrorists diverted TWA flight 847 en route from Athens to Beirut. One passenger was killed during the two-week ordeal; the remaining

155 passengers were released. This hijacking, together with an upsurge in Middle East terrorism, resulted in a number of US actions, among them the International Security and Development Cooperation Act of 1985 that made Federal Air Marshals a permanent part of the FAA workforce.

- 1985 also saw the bombing of an Air India flight when ground staff allowed a bag with no confirmed seat holder to be checked through to its final destination. This incident led to the inauguration of the International Civil Aviation Organization's (ICAO) Aviation Security Panel and the rewriting of Annex 17. [Annex 17 (Security) is a security manual containing operating guidelines and training programmes—it is considered the 'rulebook' on aviation security and outlined later in this section.]
- On December 21, 1988, en route from London to New York, a bomb brought down Pan Am flight 103 over Lockerbie, Scotland. All 259 people onboard were killed, as well as 11 people on the ground.

Phase 3: 1994 to date—The Aircraft as a Weapon of Destruction

This phase is considered to have begun on December 24, 1994, when Algerian terrorists hijacked Air France flight 8969, en route to Paris from Algiers. The French government refused the aircraft landing rights at Paris as they had received intelligence that the hijackers intended to blow up the aircraft over the city.[9] On diverting to Marseilles, French police commandos stormed the aircraft and successfully rescued the passengers and crew.

This incident marked a change in tactics for terrorists. Their use of terrorism directed against civil aircraft was not new; using the aircraft to target an entire city was. International civil aviation had become a battleground for terrorists and aircraft a weapon.

More recently on 11th September 2001, four passenger aircraft were hijacked with two of the aircraft deliberately flown into the New York World Trade Centre. Both 110-storey buildings were demolished within an hour of impact, killing more than 2,800 people. A third aircraft was deliberately flown into the Pentagon in Washington DC. The events of 11th September 2001 signaled a major change in terrorist activity.

With the advent of suicide attacks, the intention is to inflict maximum collateral damage and loss of life. Phase 3 is considered the most dangerous era and certainly the most difficult to defend against. This unprecedented attack resulted in an immediate and drastic heightening of air transportation security across the world.

In the next section, I propose to deal briefly with the international legal framework to combat aviation terrorism.

SECTION 2—INTERNATIONAL LEGAL FRAMEWORK TO COMBAT AVIATION TERRORISM

In this section a brief review is made of important international organizations and legal norms to combat aviation terrorism.

(A) ORGANIZATIONS

From the early part of the 20th century, two aviation bodies have been at the forefront of international civil aviation:

- International Civil Aviation Organization (ICAO—the aviation wing of the United Nations).
- International Air Transport Association (IATA—the trade association of the world's scheduled airlines).

When aviation terrorism first threatened commercial air services, both organizations took a leading role and many of today's standards, procedures and legislation owe their origins to this early reaction. More recently, two other international organizations have been working with ICAO and IATA to enhance aviation security:

- The European Civil Aviation Conference (ECAC).
- Airports Council International (ACI).

There are also two organizations at the centre of aviation security policy in the USA—

- Federal Aviation Administration (FAA).
- Transportation Security Administration (TSA).

(1) International Civil Aviation Organization (ICAO)

The International Civil Aviation Organization (ICAO), a non-governmental organization body within the United Nations, came into being on 4th April 1947. ICAO was formed as a result of the ratification of the treaty developed at the Convention on International Civil Aviation (also known as the *Chicago Convention*) on 7th December 1944. ICAO comprised 188 contracting States in November 2003.[10]

ICAO's aims and objectives are to "develop the principles and techniques of international air navigation and to foster the planning and development of international air transport."[11] ICAO's role in enhancing civil aviation security has concentrated on the development of standards and recommended practices (SARPs).

These standards and practices comprise 18 technical annexes to the Chicago Convention and, where implemented, provide a consistent and appropriate level of security worldwide. ICAO's SARPs are developed and published through a tiered committee structure. Member states are urged to implement these SARPs. It is important to note that ICAO has no powers of enforcement over its members and governments are able to 'opt out' of regulations which, for one reason or another, they find unacceptable. A combination of three ICAO initiatives: Annex 17 (Security); a Security manual containing operating guidelines and training programmes—should enable any State to develop its own efficient response to terrorism aimed against civil aviation.[12]

(2) International Air Transport Association (IATA)[13]

IATA, originally founded in 1919, is the trade association for the world's scheduled airlines. Flights by these airlines comprise more than 95 per cent of all international scheduled air traffic.

IATA's principal goal, included in its articles of association, is to "promote safe, regular and economical air transport for the benefit of the peoples of the world, to foster air commerce and to study the problems connected therewith."

IATA's membership comprises more than 280 airlines worldwide, ranging from major scheduled carriers to small inter-island operators.

IATA's secretariat has, from the beginning of terrorist activity against civil aviation operations, adopted a role of developing new initiatives to counter terrorism.

(3) European Civil Aviation Conference (ECAC)

ECAC was founded in December 1955 by 19 States as an intergovernmental organization. In close liaison with ICAO and the Council of Europe, ECAC's aim is to "promote the continued development of a safe, efficient and sustainable European air transport system that has regard to environmental requirements."[14]

In so doing, ECAC seeks to harmonize civil aviation policies and practices amongst its Member States and promote understanding on policy matters between its Member States and other parts of the world.

ECAC's activities are consultative in nature; however, decisions are not binding on its Member States. Thus, any action taken by the Conference has to be transformed into national law and policies in order to become mandatory.

ECAC is a subordinate body to ICAO and regional in its responsibility. Four Member States (UK, France, Germany and Italy) are G7 powers and permanent members of the ICAO Council. The USA and Canada, both members of the G7, have permanent observer status at ECAC meetings.

(4) Airports Council International (ACI)

While ICAO, IATA and ECAC remain at the forefront of international aviation rule making, ACI has also played a role in enhancing aviation security across the world. ACI is the representative industry body of the world's airports with a membership comprising 554 airports and airport authorities operating over 1,500 airports across 169 States and territories.[15] With similar goals to IATA, ACI sees its role as fostering co-operation among airport administrations and with other partners in world aviation. In this capacity, ACI provides a forum for airport administrations to meet and discuss a wide range of mutually beneficial subjects.

(B) INTERNATIONAL LEGAL NORMS

The past 30 years have seen some key pieces of legislation introduced as a consequence of aviation terrorism. It lies beyond the scope of this paper to discuss all the International legal norms dealing with aviation security, I would only focus on some of the most important measures.[16]

(1) ICAO Tokyo Convention

In the early 1960s, the international aviation community recognized the growing seriousness of air piracy. In 1963, the Convention on Offences and certain other Acts committed on Board Aircraft (known as the Tokyo Convention) was drafted, requiring the prompt return of hijacked aircraft and passengers.[17]

(2) ICAO-Annex 17

The ICAO annex that governs aviation security is Annex 17[18] (Security: Safeguarding International Civil Aviation Against Acts of Unlawful Interference). Annex 17 is considered to be the rulebook of aviation security and details what is required to produce a valid national aviation security programme. Annex 17 is seen as a compromise document designed to balance the needs of civil aviation seen through the eyes of security specialists with political and economic considerations demanded by the wide-ranging membership of ICAO. The 1985 bombing of the Air India flight led to the inauguration of ICAO's Aviation Security Panel and the rewriting of Annex 17. Amendment 10 to Annex 17, which came into force on 1st July 2002, is believed to represent the most substantial revision that the Annex has undergone.

(3) The Hague[19] and Montreal Conventions

On 16th December 1970, 50 nations signed the Convention for the Suppression of Unlawful Seizure of Aircraft (the Hague Convention). This convention categorized hijacking as a criminal rather than as a political act. The 1971 Montreal Convention,[20] which came into force in 1973, strengthened the earlier agreement. Following the loss of Pan Am flight 103, ICAO proposed a revision to the Warsaw Convention of 1929, the legislation that addresses compensation in cases of international air accidents. This revision, to the Montreal Convention, came into force on 4th November 2003,[21] almost 15 years after the Lockerbie disaster, and replaces the Warsaw Convention.

(4) ECAC Document 30

ECAC's Document 30 (Doc 30) is the European aviation security 'manual,' developed over the past 30 years by ECAC's

Member States and containing the European aviation security policy. First authorized in 1985, Doc 30 was largely based on ICAO's international security procedures (Annex 17). More recently, this has turned full circle with policies adopted by ECAC in Doc 30 subsequently being included in ICAO Annex 17. The events of 11th September 2001 resulted in a revision to Doc 30, which was completed early in 2002.[22]

(5) New EU Rules on Aviation Security following the 11th September 2001 Attacks

On 10th October 2001, the European Commission proposed the adoption and enforcement of common security rules for civil aviation across the Member States. Based on ECAC Document 30, these rules aimed to increase aviation security for both international and domestic flights.

The main objectives of the Regulation were to:

- Establish and implement appropriate community measures, in order to prevent acts of unlawful interference against civil aviation.
- Provide a basis for a common interpretation of the related provisions of the Chicago Convention, in particular its Annex 17.

These objectives were achieved by the setting up of common basic standards for aviation security measures and appropriate compliance monitoring mechanisms.

The rules were predominantly concerned with:

- Control of access to sensitive areas of airports and aircraft.
- Control of passengers and their hand luggage.
- Control and monitoring of aircraft hold luggage.
- Control of cargo and mail.
- Training of ground staff.
- Definition of specifications for the equipment for the above controls.
- Classification of weapons and other items which it is prohibited to bring on to aircraft or into the sensitive areas of airports.

In view of the degree of technical detail of the standards to be implemented in the draft Regulation, the Commission proposed adopting the implementing measures needed with the support of a committee of representatives of the Member States. The measures would be implemented gradually in a realistic manner to take account of the time needed to train personnel and alter infrastructure. In the event of a more specific threat, Member States would be able to adopt special measures.[23]

(6) Regulation (EC) No. 2320/2002 and Associated Implementing Legislation[24]

In December 2002, through Regulation (EC) No. 2320/2002, the Commission established common rules in the field of civil aviation security across all Member States. Based on the current recommendations of ECAC Document 30, the main objectives of the Regulation were to:

- Establish and implement appropriate Community measures, in order to prevent acts of unlawful interference against civil aviation.
- Provide a basis for a common interpretation of the related provisions of the Chicago Convention, in particular its Annex 17.

The level and quality of aviation security in Europe is widely considered to have improved significantly since the introduction of Regulation (EC) No. 2320/2002. For the first time minimum standards have been mandated on the Member States. This has followed years of inertia in the implementation of common security standards caused by the voluntary nature of the ECAC Doc 30 requirements.

These objectives were achieved by the setting up of common basic standards for aviation security measures and appropriate compliance monitoring mechanisms.

The regulation put forward a number of requirements:

- Within 3 months following the enforcement of this Regulation, each Member State "shall adopt a national civil aviation security programme in order to ensure the application of the common standards referred to."

- Each Member State shall designate an appropriate authority responsible for the coordination and the monitoring of the implementation of its National Aviation Security Programme (NASP).
- Within 6 months following the enforcement of the Regulation, each Member State shall require its appropriate authority to ensure the development and implementation of a national civil aviation security quality control programme so as to ensure the effectiveness of its national civil aviation security programme.
- Each Member State shall ensure that their airports and air carriers providing services from that State establish, implement and maintain airport and air carrier security programmes appropriate to meet the requirements of its national civil aviation security programme. These programmes shall be submitted for approval and monitored by the appropriate authority.
- Each Member State shall require the appropriate authority to ensure the development and implementation of a national civil aviation security training programme.
- Commission Regulation (EC) No. 622/2003 laying down measures for the implementation of the common basic standards on aviation security.
- Commission Regulation (EC) No. 1217/2003 of 4th July 2003 laying down common specifications for national civil aviation security quality control programmes.
- Commission Regulation (EC) No. 1486/2003 laying down procedures for conducting Commission inspections in the field of civil aviation security.
- Commission Regulation (EC) No. 1138/2004 establishing a common definition of critic parts of security restricted areas at airports.

US Initiatives

While taking a review of various international organizations legal norms pertaining to aviation security, a brief reference is also essential to the development in USA in this area, particularly in the aftermath of 9/11.

(1) Federal Aviation Administration (FAA)

The Federal Aviation Agency was established in 1958 as the branch of the US government responsible for the safety of civil aviation. The agency changed its name to the Federal Aviation Administration (FAA) in 1967, and became part of the Department of Transportation (DoT). Since then the FAA has been the leading authority for the civil aviation industry in the US. The FAA's mission is to provide a safe, secure and efficient global aerospace system that contributes to national security and the promotion of US aerospace safety. The FAA issues regulations, rules and guidelines to all aviation equipment operators in the US and the rest of the world through Airworthiness Directives, Federal Aviation Regulations (FARs) and Special Federal Aviation Regulations (SFARs).

(2) The Transportation Security Administration (TSA)

Enactment of the Aviation and Transportation Security Act (ATSA) on 19th November 2001 resulted in the establishment of the TSA, a department within the US Department of Homeland Security. The TSA has overall responsibility for the security of all modes of transportation within the US. The TSA's objective is to protect all of the US' transportation systems (including aviation) "to ensure freedom of movement for people and commerce."[25] ATSA and the TSA have resulted in fundamental changes being made to the way in which aviation security operates and is managed in the US. For the first time in US history, aviation security is the responsibility of a single branch of government.[26]

Thus to conclude, the Tokyo, Hague and Montreal Conventions provide the basis for international law in respect of unlawful interference with aircraft. Despite ICAO's efforts, the voluntary nature of enforcement of its rules and guidelines means that effective aviation security exists in only a minority of States around the world.

Having taken stalk of global developments in brief let me now turn to India.

SECTION 3—NEW ANTI-HIJACKING POLICY OF INDIA

Hijacking has happened 12 times in India. The last one was on December 24, 1999, when IC-814 from Kathmandu to Delhi was hijacked to Kandhar via Amritsar and Lahore. It has taken almost five years for the government to make up its mind as to how it will deal with hijacking. It is more than a coincidence that all these hijackings of Indian planes had their source, support or landing in Pakistan, which quite convincingly demonstrate, how Pakistan (at least till recently) had adopted a very organized and strategic terrorism policy against India.

On this background, let me provide first a brief outline of the policy followed by its critique.

Brief Outline of the Policy

The government, in its landmark anti-hijack policy cleared by Cabinet Committee on Security (CCS), has said that any foreign-registered aircraft hijacked in Indian skies will not be allowed to land in the country. According to the policy, all efforts will be made to ensure that the plane makes a safe and quick exit from Indian airspace. Indian fighters will escort the plane and ensure that 25 nautical miles airspace is cleared around the hijacked aircraft. However, the policy does take note of India's international obligations and allows for permission to land in unavoidable circumstances—for instance, when a plane has run out of fuel. In such a case, further action will be taken in consultation with the country concerned.

On the other hand, if an Indian registered aircraft has been hijacked, the policy will be to get it to land at one of the Indian airports. The CCS decision is clear that once the hijacked plane has landed in an Indian airport, all efforts should be made not to allow it from taking off again.

In such a situation, the policy is that without any prior orders, airport personnel will make all attempts to immobilize the aircraft and prevent it from taking off. This can be done by bringing fire tenders or turning off the runway lights.

The policy processes may be summarized as under:

On noticing any suspicious activity or in case an aircraft issues a hijack alert, the ATC Watch Supervisory Officer (WSO) will inform the Joint Control and Analysis Centre (JCAC) manned by IAF officials.

- The JCAC will observe and analyze the situation with the help of inputs from the ATC. Based on this, it will alert the IAF's operational wing, which is responsible for giving orders to fighter aircraft.

- Once an aircraft has been declared "rogue"—after it has ignored ATC and Air Defense warnings—the WSO will be asked to activate the Central Committee headed by the Director General of Civil Aviation (DGCA). This will automatically set into motion all other procedures, with the Committee of Secretaries on Aircraft Hijack (COSAH)[27] acting as the Crisis Management Group and CCS as the apex decision-making body. COSAH and CCS will also communicate with the executive authority which will be the Central Committee with officers from relevant ministries and agencies to carry out orders.[28] This committee will maintain a panel of negotiators, psychiatrists and linguists to deal with the situation.

If the aircraft aligns itself to a strategic target like Rashtrapati Bhavan, Parliament House and other important government installations, it will be declared a 'threat' and the CCS can take a decision to shoot it down.

According to detailed procedures that have been adopted for shooting down a commercial plane, it has to be first ascertained without doubt that the hijacked aircraft will hit a strategic target. For this assessment a three-stage classification process has been put in place:

- *Doubtful Aircraft*: A plane deviating from allotted course, not complying with ATC instructions and its transponder is not responding will fall in this category.
- *Rogue Aircraft*: A doubtful aircraft, which ignores advice of the Air Traffic Control (ATC), and continues to deviate. It switches off its transponder and does not respond to radio telephony.
- *Threat Aircraft*: A rogue aircraft that takes no cognizance of ATC warnings or that of air defense fighter aircraft and whose flight path is aligned to a strategic target like Rashtrapati Bhavan, government installations, Parliament House etc.[29]

It is only when a plane falls in the third category that a decision to shoot it down will come into play. Such a decision will be taken by the CCS, the apex body for handling hijack situations. However, in case of shortage of time, the Prime Minister, Defence Minister or Home Minister—whoever can be reached first—will take a call.

Still, there are situations where a plane could turn a threat while landing or taking off. This offers very little reaction time and so in such a case, the authority will vest with the Air Force.[30] However, the decision would have to be taken by an official senior to the Assistant Chief of Air Staff (Operations). However, the decision to declare a "rogue" aircraft as a threat lies with the Air Headquarters—the executive authority in such a situation.

The policy also makes it clear that the pilot of the fighter aircraft will not take an independent decision, regardless of what the hijacked aircraft may do. In fact, fighters will have to maintain a distance of over 500 feet from the hijacked aircraft while carrying out any interception exercise.

To ensure the best contact options between the aircraft and the ATC, the policy requires all airlines in India to provide for alternate communication equipment on board their planes. This includes cellular or satellite-based phones.

Besides, the policy makes it mandatory for all airports to put in place a contingency plan that has to be approved by the Bureau of Civil Aviation Security. This plan will cater to an Aerodrome Committee which has to be headed by the concerned Home Secretary in state capitals, District Magistrates in districts and by Airport Director in aerodromes outside the airport. The policy caters for armed intervention to end a hijack. While the decision to storm an aircraft will be taken by the CCS, the NSG team will have to be airborne within two hours of the hijack accompanied by the central negotiating team.

In case, the Cabinet Secretariat is unable to provide an aircraft for this, the NSG can take a commercial plane but it has to be airborne at the earliest. The punishment to a hijacker will be death penalty.

Thus, it becomes clear from the aforesaid discussion that these new guidelines are dictated by a policy doctrine which states that any attempt to hijack an aircraft will be considered as an act of aggression against the country and will, thus, prompt a response fit for an aggressor.

To sum up, events of 9/11 not only exposed fundamental human errors in aviation security but they also brought to the surface the audacity with which aeroplanes can be transformed into lethal missiles. The challenges posed by the terrorists to the superpower brought upside down the whole thinking about security and all over the world strategists and planners began to emphasize upon "homeland security and public security." World around strategists and policy-makers began to visit afresh the domain of aviation security with renewed vigor and determination. However, unfortunately legislative activity all around the world appears to have influenced very faintly the scenario in India and therefore they have ended up with a perfunctory and overwhelmingly bureaucratic policy.

SECTION 4—CRITICAL APPRISAL

A close look at this policy which we have just seen makes it clear that it has a number of problems.

However, before highlighting them, let me raise few vital questions, Whether the Anti-hijacking policy as such is in consonance with Human Rights and Human Security? Whether the approach of the government as reflected in the policy at hand is incongruous with its overall policy to combat terrorism in our country? Whether or not state should adopt a clearly defined and articulated policy to secure all forms of transportation against terrorist's strike?

While answering the first question it is quite plausible to argue that in order to secure one of the vital human rights i.e. freedom of movement, state has to ensure a secured and risk free aviation environment and therefore formulation of a cohesive, clearly articulated and strategically sound policy is an imperative. However, what may be contested is its contents, because if at one hand risk free aviation environment is to be ensured to safeguard the interests of the passengers, equally state has to also clearly balance its interest of securing strategic locations from the wrath of a threat aircraft. Indeed, it is far too easy to talk about this balancing in theory; however, it may become practically difficult to exactly identify the factors to undertake this delicate task of balancing.

The answer to the second question is far from being simplistic. Clearly, the Government of India does not have any general and static policy to combat terrorism in different parts of country. For example, while tackling the terrorism in Kashmir government is ready to negotiate with the militants unconditionally; on the other hand so far as terrorism of North-Eastern states like Manipur is concerned, the government has taken a very tough stand, whereas so far as Naxalism of Bihar and Andhra Pradesh is concerned the policy is appeared to be extremely wishy washy. Thus, looked at from the lens of a strategist, we are combating the problem of terrorism by adopting differing mechanisms how far it is viable is a matter of debate.

So far as third question is concern, government must adopt a broad and general policy statement; instead government has merely focused upon aviation environment and by almost completely ignoring other forms of transportation, has exposed itself to criticism. We are very much aware as to how railway tracks are being sabotaged, buses are being bombed and bogies of the trains are being burned. It would have been in the fitness of the things, if India would have followed the US approach by enacting legislation along the lines of "Aviation and Transportation Security Act 2001."

On this background, let me now discussed some of the inherent problems with which the policy at hand suffers.

(1) Legal Difficulties
(2) Ethical Problems
(3) Logistical Difficulties

Legal Difficulties

Since fundamental law of our country is our Constitution, the question which I abruptly must ask is, whether this policy withstands the test of constitutionality? In other words, whether this policy is in accordance with the letter and spirit of the Constitution of India. The answer to this question has two strands.

The first strand has a focus on Parliamentary Democracy and accordingly, it is argued that any major issue must be brought to the notice of Parliament and any decision on the same should be taken only after it is fully and squarely discussed by the Parliament. Clearly, issues like negotiating with the hijackers of a plane or bringing down the plane if it becomes a threat to the strategic locations of our country like Nuclear Installations, Parliament House, Rashtrapati Bhawan, etc. are certainly major issues and any decision to have a particular position about them, backing of Parliament is essential. If the modified policy is viewed in the light of the aforesaid then it becomes clear that in fact, the policy was inaugurated by the Central Government in a press conference with the media and the same led to the criticism that it provided a backseat to the Parliament in the whole issue. In my humble opinion, the criticism is justified because the action of the government is clearly in violation of basic structure of the constitution, parliamentary democracy being one of its vital features[31] and the discussion on the second strand would add further force to this contention.

The second strand focuses upon Article 21 of our Constitution. It lays down "no person shall be deprived of his life and personal liberty save as procedure established by law." Now, in a given situation, if it becomes expedient due to security reasons to bring down a plane and if the plane is brought down it would bound to result in deprivation of lives of not only those who are on board the plane but it might also result in loss of lives and property of people of a particular area in which its debris fall. Whether the deprivation of right to life of certain persons in this scenario is backed by support of Article 21? Obviously, under Article 21, for any deviation of rights guaranteed by it should be enacted in a law passed by the Parliament. It has been made clear by a long line of precedents[32] that to take away right to life or personal liberty, Parliament has to pass a law and it must also provide a just, fair and reasonable procedure there. Clearly, in this case there is no intervention of Parliament and therefore, any order of the government asking for bringing down the plane is *ultra vires* Article 21.

Finally, the policy clearly adopts an escapist approach by discriminating between hijacks of the planes owned by India and of foreign origin. Does it not amount to arbitrariness, thereby violating Article 14? Moreover, when the hijacked plane is in the Indian skies, than it is an issue not only of terrorism but there is also concern about the safety of the passengers on board the plane. Obviously, even foreigners have protection of Article 21,[33] as soon as the plane is in the Indian skies. Therefore, in stead of driving the plane away out of Indian space, as envisaged by the policy, it would have been most appropriate if, government would have shown the willingness to take constructive measures. From the standpoint of terrorism too, it is clearly unjustified to simply drive the terrorists away from our country and close the matter. At a time when clarion call of the world is to fight terrorism across the boundaries, the same cannot be watered-down by invoking doctrine of sovereignty.

Here, reference is also essential to three important legislations,[34] which have been enacted by Parliament in this area, viz. Tokyo Convention Act, 1975, Anti-hijacking Act, 1982 and the suppression of unlawful acts against safety of civil aviation acts 1982. Curiously enough, the new policy statement of the government does not make any reference to these laws. As a matter of fact, earnestness of government would have been clearly reflected, if it would have resorted to amend these laws in the light of the recent developments around the world. Thereby providing an occasion to open a nationwide debate on the same. Alternatively it would have been also possible for government to promulgate an ordinance and provide legal sanctity to its aspirations. However, by not following either of these two recourses, government has quite justifiably exposed itself to criticism for being not serious and not concern about this matter.

Another legal difficulty may arise in the context of restitution. The policy is utterly silent on the aspect of payment of compensation to the victims of the tragedy.[35] We have to also think about a scenario in which a foreign company owned aircraft being brought down resulting in deaths and destruction of the property. Who will pay the compensation in such a case? There is also hardly any consideration given to the issue of funding of private airliners.[36]

Ethical Problems

From the standpoint of ethics also the policy is problematic. A terrorist can hijack a plane only if there is a human failure on the ground letting him to fly. Thus, after fallibility of the staff of a concerned airport, innocent passengers of the ill-fated aircraft are being lectured to make sacrifices for their nation. But, is it ethically and morally justified to expect sacrifices for somebody's ghastly mistakes while performing his or her duties? Are we not coercing the passengers to die for the mistakes of certain careless individuals? It is not easy to provide answers to these questions. Moreover, policy is totally silent on the issue of negotiating with the hijackers in case on board the plane are high profile VIPs or their relatives. Whether in such a scenario also we will have no negotiations and as a last resort can the plane be brought down?

Last but not the least, should the State prefer to show its strength and toughening attitude towards certain paranoid elements of the society or terrorists on the dead bodies of innocent civilians? The questions require serious debate.[37]

Logistical Difficulties

From the standpoint of logistics also, policy has several wink links. Thus, there is an elaborate procedure as to how:

(a) The NSG team would be organized

(b) CCS has to meet and discuss the case

(c) Prime Minister must take decision in absence of CCS

(d) In absence of Prime Minister, Home Minister or Defence Minister has to act

(e) And only in most urgent situations, higher officials of the Air Force must take the decisions.

When one closely looks at all this, one can immediately realize logistical difficulties. Whether aforesaid is possible in such a short span of time when action rather than an interaction is the need of the hour? What happens, e.g. if there is no consensus in the meeting of CCS?

Thus, the above discussion makes it clear that though superficially policy may appear to be high sounding, it has a number of loopholes. Secondly, it is also arguable that government has completely ignored role of National Security

Advisory Board in the scenario and on the other hand it has overburdened the policy with bureaucratic details.

CONCLUSION

To reiterate the above discussion, looked at from the paradigm of human security, the policy has number of loopholes. Government in a bid to secure strategic locations has failed in not properly balancing the concerns of public security and the interest of the passengers. When, one looks at the security scene of our airports than one cannot but help to comment that the present policy is like constructing the castle in the air without solid foundation on the ground. There are still others who quite convincingly argue that the policy is nothing but a pious declaration and may be altered conveniently according to the political situations.

However, being an optimist and being a student of law it would be inappropriate on my part to be altogether dismissive, and hence I would like to pause by hoping that very soon government would legally cloth its intentions by doing the needful.

NOTES AND REFERENCES

1. See generally M.C. Abad, Jr., "The Challenge of Balancing State Security with Human Security." Paper presented at the 9th Harvard Project for Asian and International Affairs Conference, Beijing, August 2000.
2. The Commission on Human Security (CHS) defines human security as the protection of "the vital core of all human lives in ways that enhance human freedoms and human fulfilment. Human security means protecting fundamental freedoms—freedoms that are the essence of life. It means protecting people from critical (severe) and pervasive (widespread) threats and situations. It means using processes that build on people's strengths and aspirations. It means creating political, social, environmental, economic, military and cultural systems that together give people the building blocks of survival, livelihood and dignity" [*Human Security Now*, p. 4]. Human security is far more than the absence of violent conflict. It encompasses human rights, good governance and access to economic opportunity, education and health care. It is a concept that comprehensively addresses both "freedom from fear" and "freedom from want." Available at www.ochaonline.un.org/law
3. *ibid.,* supra note 2.
4. *ibid.,* supra note 2.
5. *ibid.*

6. The phases are provided for the sake of systematic discussion and as will be seen, events overlap from one phase to the other.
7. Civil Aviation Security Financing Study, 2004. Available at europa.eu.int/comm/transport/air/safety/doc/studies/2004.
8. Ariel Merari, "Attacks on Civil Aviation: Trends and Lessons," in Aviation Terrorism and Security, Paul Wilkinson and Brian Jenkins, 1999.
9. Peter Harclerode, *Secret Soldiers*, 2001.
10. ICAO website, *Contracting States* www.icao.int
11. ICAO website, *Objectives of ICAO*. www.icao.int
12. *Aviation Terrorism and Security*, Paul Wilkinson and Brian Jenkins, 1999.
13. For further information see www.iata.org
14. ECAC website.
15. ACI website, November 2003.
16. The International Air Services Transit Agreement, 1944, The International Air Transport Agreement, 1944, The Protocol on the Authentic Quadrilingual Text of the Convention on International Civil Aviation, 1944, The Hague Protocol, 1955, The Guatemala City Protocol, 1971, The Additional Protocol No. 1, 1975, The Additional Protocol No. 2, 1975, The Additional Protocol No. 3, 1975, The Guadalajara Convention, 1961, The Geneva Convention, 1948, The Rome Convention, 1952, The Hague Convention, 1970, The Montreal Protocol, 1988, The Montreal Convention, 1991, The Montreal Convention, 1999, The Cape Town Convention, 2001, The Cape Town Protocol, 2001, The Consolidated Text of the Cape Town Convention and Protocol.
17. Govt. of India has ratified this convention. See The Tokyo Convention Act, 1975.
18. Airport Security—The objective of airport security will be to safeguard the passengers, crew, ground personnel, the general public and the airport infrastructure against unlawful acts as per ICAO Standards and Recommended Practices laid down in Annexure-17 to the Chicago Convention. Excerpted from the "Policy of Aircraft Infrastructure" Ministry of Civil Aviation, Govt. of India, available at http://civilaviation.nic.in/
19. India has also ratified Hague Convention 1970 by enacting Anti-hijacking Act 1982, see *infra* section 4.
20. Govt. of India has ratified this convention. See The Suppression of Unlawful Acts against Safety of Civil Aviation Acts, 1982.
21. ICAO website—www.icao.int/icao/en/nr/2003/pio200314.htm
22. Thena Position Paper Security Issues, 4 October 2002.
23. *ibid.*, at supra note 5.
24. *ibid.*, supra note 5.
25. available at website www.tsa.gov/

26. Other aviation security initiatives of US includes Passenger Profiling and Magnetometers (Metal Detectors), Baggage Screening, Introduction of the Explosives Detection Canine Team, 100% Hold Baggage Screening (HBS), Passenger & Baggage Reconciliation, Federal Marshal Programme, The Commission on Aviation Security and Terrorism, The Gore Commission, id at supra note 5.
27. A Committee of Secretaries on Aircraft Hijack (COSAH), consisting of Foreign, Home, Defence and Civil Aviation secretaries apart from heads of intelligence agencies and the Principal Information Officer will form the Crisis Management Group and co-ordinate with the CCS.
28. Pranab Dhal Samanta, "Hijacked foreign planes can't land in India," *Indian Express,* August 14, 2005. See also http://www.eians.com/stories/2005/08/14/14sint.shtml.
29. Pranab Dhal Samanta, "Hijacked foreign planes can't land in India," *Indian Express*, August 18, 2005.
30. In the US too, the decision to shoot an aircraft vests with the President, Vice-President or the Secretary of Defense. In case the time is short, the Commander of the North American Air Space Defense Command can take a call. In France, under such circumstances, an identified officer at the airport takes orders directly from the Prime Minister. *Ibid.* supra note 28.
31. Keshvanand Bharti *v.* State of Kerala 1973, supp. SCR.
32. See Maneka Gandhi *v.* Union of India 1978, 1 SCC, 248 and other subsequent verdicts of Supreme Court and High Courts of India.
33. See AIR 2000 SUPREME COURT 1988 "Chairman, Railway Board *v.* Mrs. Chandrima Das".
34. All these legislations are confined to proscribing certain acts as offences and do not empower the government to go as far as it has gone. In other words all the laws are the pieces of punitive and criminal legislations and have been enacted mainly with a view to conform to the relevant international conventions. Even, Article 73 of the Indian constitution empowering the central government to exercise its executive powers would not be of any avail because exercise of executive power is subject to Article 21 of our constitution.
35. India has not yet ratified Convention for the Unification of Certain Rules for International Carriage by Air signed at Montreal on 28 May 1999* (The Montreal Convention, 1999) which has fundamentally transformed the rules of civil aviation including compensation.
36. "Charges Fly, US asks India for security details on funding sources of Jet Airways, under the suspicion of its Nexus with Al Qaeda." *Indian Express*, 4-7-2005.
37. From stand point of basic principles of Jurisprudence the policy clearly militates against the fundamental notions of natural law theory and human rights paradigm.

6

Conflict Resolution and Human Security

Abdul Khadeer Taj

This paper entitled "Conflict Resolution and Human Security" is based on the following hypotheses:

1. Social/Human conflict is an omnipresent reality. It cannot be eradicated completely, at best it can be managed, de-escalated, controlled and resolved...paving way for the evolution of a stable Social/Human system.
2. International conflicts (bilateral, regional and global) exists due to instable international system since conflict generate instability and instability is the root cause for security threat: only a stable international system guarantees international, regional and bilateral security by creating a favorable (peaceful) environment, conducive to conflict resolution (local, regional and global) and provide sustainability to the nation-state.
3. By resolving the challenges to the non-strategic dimensions of security threat at National, Transnational and International level, through sharing of national and international resources among developed and developing nation-states, human security is best guaranteed.

Conflict

Human/International conflict is a social phenomenon of immense complexity and variety. It is characterize by multiple causation both with respect to its origin and development. It can emerge due to a single or numerous primary issues. Primary issues through the processes of proliferation and escalation[1] may become intertwined with a diversity of secondary issues. Thus conflict is a mixture of objective and subjective or sociological and psychological variations.[2]

There is an analogy between social and international conflict. As conflict has its existence at individual and societal levels, similarly it has its existence at international level.[3] Nation-states in their quest for stability, welfare, prestige, defense, security, self-identity, self-reliance and sustainability usually pursue incompatible policies. Incompatible policies generate clash or conflict of interests with each other. The existence of this phenomenon of incompatible interests and policies among nation-states cannot completely be eradicated. Since incompatible interests and policies are directly co-related with conflict, therefore, conflict is the omnipresent reality of human existence and human security.

It cannot be assumed that international conflicts are simply the product of misunderstanding and misperception among international actors. In fact, most of the conflicts involves real clash of interests and ideologies centering on incompatible goals and structural realities.[4] Therefore, it cannot be eradicated completely from human and international society. However, adjustment of incompatible policies can be attained through mutual understanding, accommodation, reconciliation, bargaining and various other confidence-building measures.[5] Thus management and resolution of conflict can be attained.

International conflict appears inherently open to certain self-aggravating mechanisms, which foster escalation on to a variety of dimensions. There are strong and powerful tendencies for conflict escalation moves to be reciprocated often in the interest of precaution, economic benefits, pride, security and defense.[6] On the contrary conflict de-escalation and conciliatory acts are not reciprocated so easily and readily. Most of the aspects of conflict behavior of social entities are predominantly understandable and modifiable reactions to a complex and difficult environment, rather than due to inherent and unchangeable properties of the entities themselves or of their relationship. This is not to deny the significance and vitality of the socio-structural determinants of conflict, but to pinpoint that these and many other aspects can be dealt with and modified if the parties to the conflict are genuinely interested.[7]

Human/social conflict within a group sometimes helps to revitalize the existing norms, material base and social dynamics or contributes to the emergence of new norms and social dynamics. In this sense conflict is a mechanism for adjustment of norms, material base and social dynamics adequate to new environment and conditions. Hence conflict is an inevitable component of transition and transformation dialectics.[8] Further, conflict is characteristically reflected in a mixture of functional and dysfunctional actions and counteractions. And it would be oversimplification to characterize conflict exclusively as either negative or positive.[9]

As pointed out earlier that conflict has both the characteristics, i.e. functional and dysfunctional. Conflict is desirable only in its functional aspect for the stimulation of human progress.[10] Indeed it is in the conflict situation that the finest co-operative and creative spirit manifests and asserts. An individual or a nation-state at perfect peace may not be fully capable of constructive actions. It is a historical reality that great works of art, significant inventions and important movements are initiated by those who are confronted with challenges and crisis. Hence conflict is desirable as long as it is evocative and creative, the movement it turns out to be destructive and catastrophic, it has to be controlled, managed and de-escalated and resolved.

Conflict *per se* does not seem to be necessarily destructive and evil. It may have and often does have constructive values. And conflict de-escalation and resolution endeavors possess both integrative and creative values. According to Arthur Larson,

> One of the challenges of warless world is to enable the individuals and nation-states to learn to engage in conflict without recourse of war.[11]

As stated earlier conflict *per se* has both the functional and dysfunctional dimensions. It is necessary to control dysfunctional aspects of conflicts, through various conflict building measures (CBM), techniques and methods such as, adjustment, accommodation, reconciliation, bargaining, negotiation, dialogue, meditation, moot, arbitration and regulation on the issues which generate conflict, depending on the suitability of one of these techniques. It appears in the contemporary international scenario that the traditional peaceful institutional means, such as, international organization and international law have with minor exceptions failed in resolving international conflict.

It has been observed that the quest for conflict resolution and national security has been the core objective of nation-state's policies from time immemorial. But the concern for national security and conflict resolution acquired greater significance in the contemporary international system due to advancement in nuclear science and technology and the catastrophic nature of nuclear weapons and nuclear warfare. It is the recognition and realization of this potential threat to human existence and survival that has recognized the need for conducting international conferences of the present type from time to time to provide with an opportunity to the conflict resolution and security studies experts to meet, interact and exchange views with a view to evolve viable conflict resolution techniques to avoid annihilation, destruction and catastrophe.

In the contemporary era conflict resolution through the application of physical force appears to be increasingly inapplicable.[12] Present era is known for negotiation, dialogue, reconciliation, compromise and diplomatic activities among nation-states on various conflicting issues.[13] These negotiations and dialogues are of various nature, but among them, in my opinion 'bilateral approach' seems to be most suitable, because parties in conflict, themselves know best 'where the shoes pinches' and about the extend to which mutual accommodation and bargaining is possible. In addition bilateral approach assists to keep the Super Power and Great Powers away from the local and regional conflicts and check their meddling in the local and regional affairs. Thus keeping the local and regional affairs at a regional and local level to deal by the local and regional powers and a guarantee for greater interaction among the local and regional powers.

I would like to draw the attention of this august participants on a question raised by John Galtung about the applicability of 'interdisciplinary approach' to the study of contemporary questions of international relations. Galtung observed the problem of exploring the range of possibilities for international stability and security as follows:

> Development: Which gives an opportunity to present basic values, basic trends, the state of affairs, in the world.
>
> Conflict: Which gives an opportunity to discuss what happens when values, goals and interests are in conflict, to discuss conflict dynamics and conflict resolution.
>
> Peace: Which gives an opportunity to discuss how development and creative approach to conflict can come together, in the fight against direct as well as structural violence.
>
> Future: Which gives an opportunity to project all this on the screen of the future analyzing trends, making proposals for actions.[14]

During the process of conflict resolution, the first step appeared to be followed is to analyze the nature of conflict, holistic conceptualization of disputants views on the issues of conflict. And provide with an opportunity to the conflicting parties to participate for negotiation, without any outside concern or constraint to reach their own mutually agreed upon agreements and decisions. To effect this parties in conflict must be brought into active and prolong consultations, so that they can breakdown their 'mirror images' of each other's position and reach an acceptable agreement. Though a 'genuine compromise' may not be possible to attain but may at least lead to working relationship of new behavioral pattern. This would further assist the conflicting parties to initiate the process of greater interaction and to prepare ground to evolve a stable system.

Security

To my mind, holistically speaking in the context of contemporary international scenario, it seems that conceptualization of security has dual dimensions, i.e. strategic and non-strategic. Strategic dimension of security is nation-state centric, while non-strategic dimension of security is human centric, initially within the territorial limits of nation-state and subsequently at transnational and international level. Therefore, the unit of analysis in the first case is nation-state and in the second case individual human being. However, most of the time territorial limits become irrelevant due to interdependence among nation-states, trans-nationalism and globalization. Thus non-strategic dimension of security really becomes truly international in its nature. Challenges to non-strategic dimension of security in any one of the nation-states in the community of nation-states, have its impact on the entire community of nation-states and that's how the concept of 'soft borders' become relevant in the present times.[15]

Further, in the present international system, physical conflicts/ wars (with minor exception) is almost avoidable, due to catastrophic nature of weaponization, advancement in science and technology, nuclear weapons and advancement in the means of diplomacy. Therefore threat to strategic dimension of security is minimized. But on the other hand due to internal instability at political, economic and social levels, in fighting among various political units/competitors, underdevelopment and poverty, at the nation-state level, challenges to non-strategic dimension of security seems to be maximized. Hence efforts have to be maximized to minimize conflict within the territorial limits of the nation-state, by being more accommodative to the just demands of its citizens and being resolving them.

Further, at a nation-state level, governance has to be more alert and conscious to eradicate poverty, provide basic amenities of healthy life, like better living facilities, safe drinking water, better nutrition, better housing facilities, better educational facilities, better health facilities (particularly due to pandemics like HIV/AIDS), better job facilities, better working conditions, better environmental surrounding and should make all possible efforts to satisfy the common men. Thus laying the foundation of a healthy and progressive nation-state and ensuring human centric rationale of security based on interdependence and trans-nationalism, which is the great need of our times. It is this emerging scenario that will dictate the concept of national security and make the nation-states more conscious to be reciprocative to the urgent demands of its public. However, to meet these challenges in a better way, sharing of international resources between developed and developing nation-states become imperative. It is this holistic concept of security that is going to dominate the international system during the 21st century and will hopefully enhance the human security environment.

However, for the time being I will be discussing strategic dimension of security, since I wish to talk in the next few pages about Arab-Israel conflict, Jammu and Kashmir conflict, Afghanistan, Iraq, Iran and North Korean conflicts, where the challenges to human security is predominant and human suffering at its peak.

It could be reasoned that perpetuation of conflictual relations among nation-states generates instability, instability generates security threat, and security threat creates sense of penalty if a particular nation-state fails to face the threat properly. Therefore, security perceptions recognize the concept of national power,[16] to safeguard national interest and to preserve territorial integrity. Since national power appears to be the guarantee for self-reliance, autonomy and self-confidence, self-confidence in turn provides opportunities for development, prosperity and advancement. Hence it is the concept of power, self-reliance, autonomy, self-confidence, development and prosperity of a nation-state, which enhances the national security perspectives.[17]

Further, national security both in its strategic and non-strategic dimensions comprises of all measures that have a bearing to demonstrate strength and viability of a particular nation. Security is a relative concept, no matter whatever the level of progress and prosperity of a particular nation-state, it cannot absolutely feel secured. Hence the concept of security and insecurity are inter-connected, i.e. security *per se* leads to insecurity and insecurity brings consciousness for security. To elaborate it further it is the concept of insecurity, which keeps nations vigilant, and dynamic vis-à-vis, security threat from adversaries and engage them in nation-building processes.

Further an analysis in a historical perspective of international strategic security highlights that nations engaged in creating a power equilibrium-disequilibrium scenario vis-à-vis each other, since it was believed that such a scenario is the best guarantee for national security. And it helps the nations to engage themselves in developmental projects, keeps dynamic, competitive and creative. In this sense conflict and security are inter-related with each other.

Thus it could be concluded that conflict and security are the primary characteristics of human and international society. It is inconceivable to think of human society free of their presence and interaction. Therefore, the basic question with which the conflict resolution experts are confronted is not the elimination or eradication of human conflict but with its management, control, de-escalation and resolution, thus guaranteeing the human security. Conflict being resolved is meaningful only when it is resolved to create harmony, mutual confidence-building, co-operative understanding, peaceful co-existence with a view to evolve stable local, regional and international system as a guarantee to national and human security.

It is the historical fact that Great Powers being the core of international system exercised major influence in international relation's management and functioning. It is as true and valid today as it was in the past. During the post world-war II phase Great Powers due to their political maturity and stability, strategic-military superiority, economic, scientific-technological and industrial advancement influenced and dominated international scenario and they are dominating the present international system too.

Case Studies

In the light of the above presentation, following specific case studies of strategic conflicts and their impact on human security will be discussed.

1. Arab-Israel Conflict

It is one of the oldest conflicts, which is still unresolved. It was active during the entire Cold War phase and few wars have been fought between the Arabs and the Israelis. After each war, efforts were made through diplomatic channels to establish peace and leaders of both the sides were even awarded the Nobel Peace Prize, but it is unfortunate that in spite of this, peace has not been achieved in this region. There is a threshold nuclear power in this region and there is high possibility of making use of nuclear weapons against the non-nuclear states. The Palestinians are the main sufferers and targets over the last

60 years. The rate of casualties per day is between 4-5 persons in the last couple of years. In this region most of the developmental infrastructure like schools, colleges, industrial units, housing, etc. are destroyed daily, thus affecting the human security badly. Israel is a small country surrounded by the entire Arab world and faces insecurity vis-à-vis the entire Arab world and had acquired the nuclear capability to keep the balance. Thus making this region more dangerous in the international system and a possible nuclear flashpoint. Therefore, it requires the urgent attention of the Super Power and the Great Powers to play an active role of peace-makers so that the conflict should be resolved permanently to the satisfaction of the Palestinians and the Israelis, and the precious resources and the human energy which is wasted in the destructive activities should be diverted towards the constructive activities and development can be achieved. Thus, guaranteeing the human security through progress in the fields of education, industrialization, health sector, global interaction in trade and commerce, science and technology and human understanding.

2. *Jammu and Kashmir Conflict*

Like the earlier discussed conflict, Jammu and Kashmir conflict is also very old and affects the security of the entire Indian subcontinent since the last seven decades. This also has the potential to convert peace into international/world war with the nuclear capability. Since most of the participants of this august gathering are well aware of its destructive nature, I will not discuss much about it, however, there is a hope that the recent diplomatic efforts initiated by India, Pakistan and Kashmiris to resolve this conflict will pay the fruits hopefully at an earlier stage. Thus establishing permanent peace in the Indian subcontinent and satisfying all the parties to this conflict and hence guaranteeing human security in this geo-strategically important region.

3. *Afghanistan Conflict*

This conflict is entirely different from above discussed two of them because in this case the two Super Powers were involved, but with the disintegration of the Soviet Union, the Americans are involved presently. It is escalated and exploded to such an extent that the incident of 9/11 was the result of it and this had created a new challenge to the entire world in the form of terrorism and extremism. Americans are feeling difficult to face both these challenges and the entire world is suffering from it in its worst form. For the first time Americans are facing the security challenge from the non-state actors, this puts the US into an awkward position and further fallout of this conflict was the result of Iraq war. We all are well aware of it. This has made a history of its own nature in the present world scenario, where a Super Power is directly fighting a war with the underdog and feeling difficult to come out of it successfully. Further, the repercussions of this conflict has observed in the form of Korean and Iranian conflicts too and gave birth to a new international security scenario where the Americans are at loggerhead with the smaller powers, thus making it difficult for the smaller powers to face the Super Power and on the other hand Super Power's prestige, patience and accountability vis-à-vis the underdeveloped world is at stake.

Conclusion

To avoid such scenario as discussed above the Super Power and Great Powers have to act responsibly towards the security scenario in the international system and should establish goodwill towards the small nation-states through magnanimity, thus winning the confidence of the small countries and laying foundation of new behavioral pattern (democratic) between the less privilege countries and the Super Power and Great Powers.

I will be concluding my presentation with a quotation from our Prime Minister, Dr. Manmohan Singh during his address to the 60th session of the UN Security Council on 15th September 2005 stated that,

> In a democracy, it is the rule of law and transparency which ensure that the interests of the ordinary citizen are upheld. At the global level too, we need to ensure that multilateral rules governing the flow of goods, services and capital take adequate account of the needs of developing countries. The world awaits a "New Deal" that can spur development and create jobs on a global scale. It must

> address the challenge of eradicating mass poverty and pandemics like HIV/AIDS and other communicable diseases.

Further he said that,

> Democratic governance both within nations and in our global institutions would also constitute a powerful weapon in meeting the global scourge of terrorism. We must not yield any space to terrorism. We must firmly reject any notion that there is any cause that justifies it.

The above message is the best guarantee for the human security in the world at this critical moment of international turmoil.

NOTES AND REFERENCES

1. Quincy Wright, 'The Escalation of International Conflict,' *Journal of Conflict Resolution* (Michigan), Vol. 9, 1965, pp. 434-49.
2. Anthony De Reuck and Julie Knight (eds.), *Conflict in Society* (London, 1965) and Elton B. Mc Neil, (ed.), *The Nature of Human Conflict* (Englewood Cliffs, N.J., 1965).
3. Even Luard, *Conflict and Peace in the Modern International System* (London, 1972), pp. 200-03. The word 'conflict' is made used of here in the sense of strained relations *inter se* nation-states.
4. John Galtung, 'Conflict as a way of life,' *Survival* (London), Vol. 12, No. l, January 1970, pp. 13-16 and Michael Haas, *International Conflict* (Indianapolis, 1974).
5. Arthur Larson, *When Nations Disagree* (Baton Rouge, 1961).
6. Kenneth E. Boulding, *Conflict and Defence: A General Theory* (New York, 1962).
7. Jonathan Wilkenfield, *Conflict Behavior and Linkage Politics* (New York, 1973).
8. Lewis A. Coser, *Continuities in the Study of Social Conflict.* (New York, 1967), p. 20.
9. Thomas C. Schelling, *The Strategy of Conflict* (Cambridge, 1960), and C.R. Mitchell, 'Evaluating Conflict,' *Journal of Peace Research* (OSLO), Vol. 17, No. 1, 1980.
10. Nazir A. Kamal, 'Strategy in contemporary world,' *Strategic Studies* (Islamabad), Vol. 1, No. 2, July-September 1977, pp. 15-16.
11. Arthur Larson (ed.), *A Warless World* (New York, 1962), and Anatol Rapoport, *Conflict in Man-made Environment* (Harmondsworth, 1974).
12. F.S. Northedge (ed.), *The Use of Force in International Relations* (New York, 1974), and Osmo Apunan, 'Non-use of Force: A strategy for peace in

Nuclear Age.' *Co-operation and Conflict* (Universitetsforlaget), No. 3, 1977, pp. 171-85.

13. Anatol Rapoport, *Fights, Games and Debates* (Harmondsworth, 1960).
14. John Galtung, 'On Peace Education', in Christoph Wulf (ed.), *Hand Book of Peace Education* (Frankfurt/main, 1974).
15. Barry Buzan, *People, State and Fear.* (New Delhi : Transasia Pub : 1987).
16. Security in its conventional and traditional sense identified with overwhelming power.
17. In the contemporary scientifically-technologically advanced and compact international society the concept of national security becomes more complex and identifies with holistic development, i.e., it includes politico-economic, socio-cultural, civilizational, ethnic, psychological, ideological, geo-strategic, techno-industrial, trade-commerce, transport-communication and military potential as the viable and vital aspects. Experts on national security, such as, Walter Lippmann, Henry A. Kissinger, Robert O. Neil, Peter-Neiller, Donald Hugn, Me Millen Geardward, Christoph-Bertram, Zbigniew Brezezinski, Stephen P. Cohen, Jonathan Alfred and many others reached consensus on the parameters of national security and agreed in being a holistic concept. Further, consensus found among security experts over the means and ends of national security. According to all of them means being the available opportunity for proper implementation of national policies and ends being economic viability, progress, prosperity, and preservation of cultural values and above all protection of territorial integrity from the external threat.

7

Environment and Security: Two Sides of the Same Coin

Sohan P. Modak

There is only one Earth, a body with a hot core of molten lava, a mantle of hard and brittle crust decorated by mountains, valleys, lakes, rivers, seas, oceans and flatlands, deserts and wetlands, marshes and forests, savannahs, ice shelves and ice caps. Over four and half billion years, the earth chemistry has changed in leaps and bounds, forming, through collision of basic elements, complex hydrocarbons, nitrogenous compounds, building blocks of biologically active molecules, catalysts and their assembly evolving from bacteria to plants, animals and the man. Our atmosphere is common to all lands and oceans without regard for nationalities and politics. With the earliest records indicating its origin about 2.5 million years ago, the man has continually strived to understand and harness other living and non-living materials on the earth for the furtherance of human civilization. In doing so, the human activity has continually transgressed the frontiers of the unknown, learned to exploit and exploited the environment to facilitate its biological existence through creation and procurement of replenishable sources of food and nutrients, albeit at the cost of other competing organisms. Such unhindered human activity going hand in hand through uncontrolled reproductive activity has led to the resource crunch setting a firm ground for the establishment of "haves" and "haves not." Human history is defined by conflicts for resource acquisition and possession through cataclysmic cycles of war often complemented by famines due to environmental distortion by changed weather patterns, the march of deserts, storms, hurricanes, volcanoes, earthquakes, Tsunamis and even induction of artificial methods for weather modification to control the troposphere for the benefit of a few or even something more drastic as surreptitious release to the environment of pathogens and engineered organisms acting as time bombs. This has led to the obsession that he, who controls the environment, controls the chemical, physical and biological resources. Environment, therefore, has now become the major security issue transcending any other single issue dealing with the culture, health, spirituality, wealth and leading to a dramatic paradigm shift from the security of the land mass and its resources as an exclusive possession to the mastery and security of the environment as an ultimate assurance of sovereignty. Today, Environment and Security are being used by the clever ones as the two sides of the same coin.

The Atmosphere

The earth is surrounded by the atmosphere composed of 78% N and 21% O, 0.9% Argon and the remaining gases. As one moves away from the earth, the atmosphere becomes increasingly rarified of these gases. With time, some of the Oxygen has changed over to Ozone layer which filters out the harmful ultraviolet radiation from the sun. With industrialization, the atmospheric gaseous balance has changed due to dangerous increase in the levels of CO_2 which trap heat being radiated from the Earth creating the Greenhouse effect. We live in the troposphere where most of weather occurs. Above is stratosphere where originates the global warming. The ozone layer is maintained when ultraviolet rays strike O_2 and free O^- atoms combine with O_2 to form O_3. While ozone is hazardous to health, we benefit from its acts as a filter against the ultraviolet (UV) radiation in sun rays, which cause skin cancer and damage vegetation. UV interacts with ozone and splits into O^- and O_2 which can again recombine to form ozone. In the 20th century, chlorofluorocarbons (CFCs) and similar halogen derivatives were used in refrigeration, aerosols, solvents, etc. These, in addition to the naturally occurring greenhouse gases such as water vapor, carbon dioxide, methane and nitrous oxide, absorb heat and cause the greenhouse effect. Compared to carbon dioxide, methane and nitrous oxide absorb 20-270 times more heat per molecule, while CFCs and derivatives are far more efficient (Figure 1).

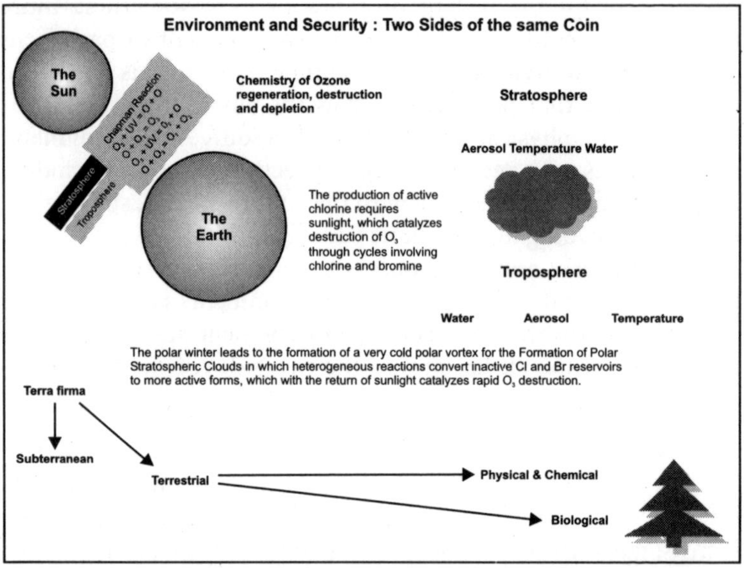

Figure 1

In 1985, it was discovered that, due to ozone depletion, a hole had appeared in the ozone layer over the Antarctic pole through which solar UV could pass unfiltered and create serious hazard to human health. How does that happen? (Figure 2). At earth's poles strong circumpolar wind develops causing the polar vortex. During the polar winter, the South Pole has no sunshine and the polar vortex gets very cold and form polar stratospheric clouds composed of nitric acid and water. CFCs are lighter than air and when released, reach the stratosphere where these are broken down to form free chlorine reservoirs. With return of sunlight, the molecular chlorine in the polar vortex is dissociated into atomic Cl^- by UV which quickly breaks down O_3. This reaction is fast and the Ozone hole is formed. The existence and rapid increase in the Ozone hole was confirmed by European experiments SESAME and THESEO which have also found Ozone appearing at the North Pole. It is now estimated that even after fully banning CFCs, it will take about 30 years for

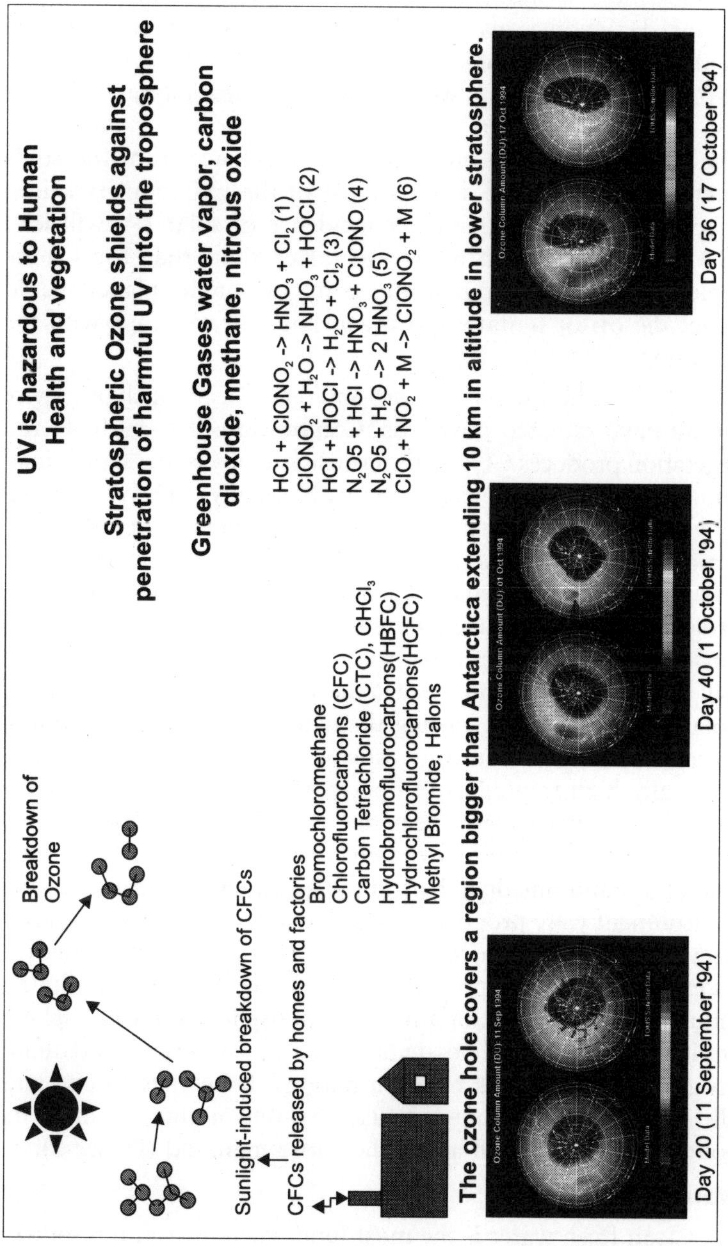
UV is hazardous to Human Health and vegetation
Stratospheric Ozone shields against penetration of harmful UV into the troposphere
Greenhouse Gases water vapor, carbon dioxide, methane, nitrous oxide
Breakdown of Ozone
Sunlight-induced breakdown of CFCs
CFCs released by homes and factories
Bromochloromethane
Chlorofluorocarbons (CFC)
Carbon Tetrachloride (CTC), $CHCl_3$
Hydrobromofluorocarbons(HBFC)
Hydrochlorofluorocarbons(HCFC)
Methyl Bromide, Halons
$HCl + ClONO_2 \rightarrow HNO_3 + Cl_2$ (1)
$ClONO_2 + H_2O \rightarrow NHO_3 + HOCl$ (2)
$HCl + HOCl \rightarrow H_2O + Cl_2$ (3)
$N_2O5 + HCl \rightarrow HNO_3 + ClONO$ (4)
$N_2O5 + H_2O \rightarrow 2\ HNO_3$ (5)
$ClO + NO_2 + M \rightarrow ClONO_2 + M$ (6)
The ozone hole covers a region bigger than Antarctica extending 10 km in altitude in lower stratosphere.
Ozone Column Amount (DU): 11 Sep 1994
Day 20 (11 September '94)
Ozone Column Amount (DU): 01 Oct 1994
Day 40 (1 October '94)
Ozone Column Amount (DU): 17 Oct 1994
Day 56 (17 October '94)

Figure 2

Ozone shield to reform. While the chemistry and physics of Ozone depletion is well established, the role of the magnetic field cannot be overlooked. It is known for some time that the Earth's magnetic field is weakening at an alarming rate over the last few hundred years and that it may eventually disappear. The magnetic field is our first line of defence from the sun's intense radiation as it deflects most of the radiation back into space; without it a far greater incidence of solar UV will lead to Ozone destruction at a rate faster than that for Ozone replenishment. The animal and plant life of the planet would either die off or mutate into organisms that can cope with the radiation.

The greenhouse gases absorb and retain heat which otherwise would have radiated outwards. Combustion of fossil fuels and vegetation produces CO_2 while fermentation by bacteria of animal and plant wastes produces methane. Normally, CO_2 is recovered by vegetation and forest cover, but with rapid deforestation the atmospheric CO_2 levels continue to rise. Increased human activity and decreased plant and dependent animal biodiversity have progressively led the average temperature to rise by about 1°C during the last century. The accumulation of greenhouse gases will lead to an exponential rise in the average temperature causing polar ice caps to melt, raising the temperature of water bodies, increasing evaporation and causing huge hurricanes, storms, unusually high rainfalls and floods and may indirectly provoke earthquakes, particularly near the natural faults in the tectonic plates which constitute dynamic cracks in the earth's crust. Therefore, an immediate halt in the activities detrimental to the environment were proposed in the Rio and Kyoto protocols. But USA, the major producer of greenhouse gases, has refused to cooperate under the pretext of protecting its highly polluting industrial assets and economy. The troposphere and stratosphere environment cannot be demarcated to superpose artificial geographic boundaries between nations. It belongs to one and all. Therefore, continued refusal by one nation to limit its polluting activities will affect the entire mankind (Figure 3).

Water Resources

Clean fresh water is the most fundamental natural resource. Civilizations flourished near river banks like Egyptians on the

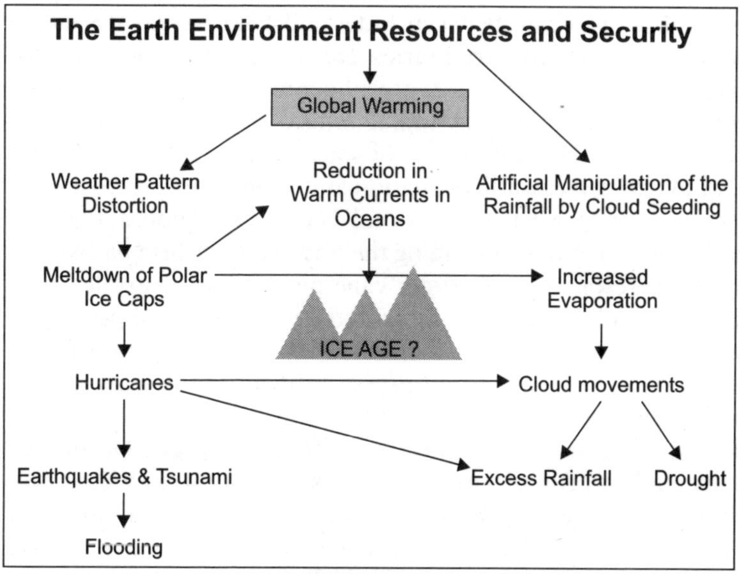

Figure 3

waters of Nile, Sumerians, Babylonians and Persians around Tigris-Euphrates, Indo-Europeans near the Ganges, and water resource was at the origin of ownership of the multitudes of conflicts. The man has exploited wasted and polluted water and caused a continuum of water-stress downstream. The Colorado river no more flows into the sea but peters out in Mexican heartland. The Nile delivers highest amount of agricultural, municipal and industrial wastes to the Mediterranean Sea. China's Yellow river is polluted and often goes dry. Amu Darya and Syr Darya rivers in Central Asia have practically died and rarely reach the Aral sea. All nation states, particularly heavily industrialized ones have polluted their water bodies and created huge health hazards. As rivers flow from one nation to another, it is those downstream that receive the polluted waters. Nations upstream and uplands, controlling water resource through construction of barrages, dams, and cause water scarcity to the populace downstream. This has become a bone of contention among a number of countries and number of states within a nation-state. The Israeli-Jordanian stand-off on the waters of Jordan river, Egypt-Sudan heat on the use of Nile waters, reopening of debate between India and Pakistan on the use of waters of Sindhu and tributaries, etc. are obvious hot points for impending conflicts as water becomes a scarce national commodity. Even within India, refusal of upstream states to acknowledge the water rights of states located downstream has lead to explosive conflict situation and water wars are an annual feature among Karnataka, Tamil Nadu and Andhra Pradesh, with Maharashtra soon joining the fray. Maharashtra has wasted its water resources over sugar cane plantations controlled by a few neo-feudal lords, heavily polluted its agricultural pesticides, fertilizers leading to its salination. Maharashtra has practically exhausted 75% of its aquifers. Libyans have now begun harvesting the huge underground fossil water reservoirs at a rate which will ensure its exhaustion in about 50 years. During the Vietnam War, Americans dumped toxic chemicals in Vietnamese rivers and water reservoirs. The total lack of sensitivity, or a benign neglect, of this problem is of great concern. For example, the Irrigation section of the World Bank, controlled by vested interests, is proposing privatization of water resource. Stupidity has no ends and Andhra was the first state in India to actually help privatize some of its fresh water resource to water bottling industry. Furthermore, the World Bank suggests access to privatized water through conditions such as use of agricultural practices like water sprinklers or drip irrigation which, while good for water saving, will cost heavily and directly benefit private industry, thereby evicting hundreds of thousands of small agricultural households from their basic livelihood. As it is, privatized water is drawn and cleaned at a rate of 20 paise (0.45 cents) per litre and sold at Rs. 12 (35 cents) a litre. Conflicts based on water scarcity, cleanliness and ownerships promise to threaten peace during next 25-50 years leading to radical changes in geopolitical equations. Cleaning up polluted waters worldwide is estimated to cost around 800 billion US dollars while the resource available is less than 10% of that. Every year, about 10 million people die due to diseases caused by polluted water. Stagnated water bodies are harbingers of parasitic diseases. The water wars are a definite worry for the present and the near future.

Atmospheric Engineering

There are serious and sustained attempts by nation states to develop artificial means to control and modify weather patterns. The most innocuous among these is rain cloud seeding by spraying and injecting clouds with silver iodide crystals. But then clouds do not respect the geopolitical frontiers and could be weaponised to cause incessant rains, flash floods or even draughts.

The modern warfare is increasingly using stratosphere and the outer space for weaponization and weapon positioning. With satellites as weapon-platforms, there is increasing attempt to create anti-missile defense through laser weapons like China's Anti Satellite Simulation lasers (ASATS), India's electron accelerating machine Kali 5000, a Microwave Beam Weapon. It is claimed that Kali 5000 would generate bursts of microwaves of gigawatt of power directed to disable incoming enemy missiles. Once miniaturized, such gadgets can be positioned in satellites and used to provoke earthquakes and Tsunamis.

Oil Wars

With the discovery that fossil materials can be used as fuels and developing appropriate technologies to harness these have led to the need to control and own these resources. The 20th century history of the Middle East has been molded by the incessant desire of the Western Industrialized Nations to monopolise fuel resources. After all the Military Industrial State, predicted by Eisenhower, is now a reality in many parts of the world and the major forces of world economy are navigated and controlled by few states which also control major food and water resources. But, the oil resource will disappear along with a number of nation states. The oil industry, which also owns the photovoltaic technology for harnessing solar power, is artificially keeping the price of this technology uneconomical (Figure 4).

Biological Warfare

Panoply of infectious organisms has been used to create biological weapons that can disable or kill human and animal populations. The most popular among these is Anthrax. Others include Tularemia, Staphylococcal Enterotoxin B, Q fever, Botulism, Malaria and even the impending onslaught of genetically engineered microbes and viruses. The weaponization

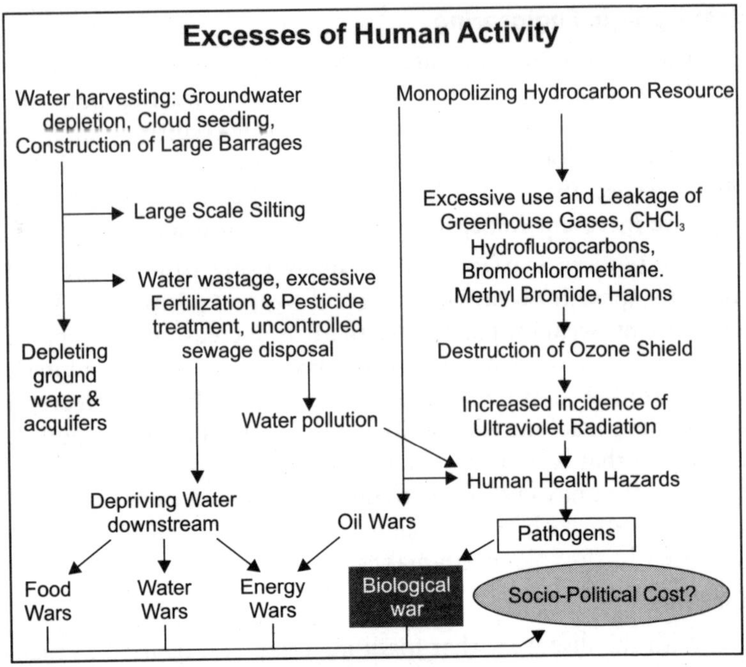

Figure 4

process is cheap and will cost one-thousandth of what it takes to kill using conventional weapons like artillery, bombs and bullets. The delivery systems depend on the nature of the bio-warfare agent ranging from single bullets, missiles or just plain aerosols spread using directed cloud movements. Can one spread lethal infectious agents like viruses using migratory birds? The idea is not new and was actually tested. And, one shudders to think of something like the epidemic of bird flu! It is also well known that the present day HIV is genetically related to the African Ebola virus causing hemorrhagic fever.

'The Earth is the only known habitable place for mankind and maintaining biodiversity on which it depends.'

A traditional disregard of the earth's environment, a multifactorial system, has led to its degradation and caused progressively increased threat to security. Environment knows no geopolitical frontiers. It is owned by all but its manipulation by privileged Nation-States or communities is sowing the seeds of impending disasters like water wars, climate wars, food wars and lead to a state of turmoil never imagined before except in the Science fiction scenarios. Only implementation of rational and alternate energy generating projects and carefully implementing water conservation, good agricultural practices and stopping the fouling of the air will ensure sustainable development and refurbishing our environment back to sanity and promotion of equilibrium among humans and the biosphere. There are no available weapons against the transgression of the environment. Environmental hazards can be created by either slow or fast methods but the restitution is very slow and no armies of the world can contemplate a rapid recovery weapon against pollution. Environment and security are the two sides of the same coin.

8

Beyond Bananas, Beaches and Bases: Feminist Interpretation of Security and a Paradigm Shift in South Asia

Santishree Pandit

The discourse on Security, International Relations and Human Rights has been gendered. They have basically dealt with studying the causes of war and conflict, the development of diplomacy and international law and the global expansion of trade and commerce with no particular reference to people called "men" and "women" *per se*. Indeed the representation of international relations as "high politics" is implicitly gendered, as women are associated with the private sphere of domesticity, morality, subjectivity, passion and femininity. As high politics is thought to be of crucial importance to public power and women are excluded from its work. These political exclusions have been challenged. It is this "malestream" security and international relations that is being challenged, for "what gets left out is often as important as to what is put in and assumed."[1]

The actions of states or more accurately of men acting for states have come to dominate the substance of the theoretical discourses. This paper hopes to grapple with the three different categories and attempt to link them in the concept of Human Security. The issues that will be analyzed are—where does the study of people called women or the social construction of gender and subjectivity fit into the new international order? To what extent do understandings of the co-constitution of sovereign man and gendered states help us to understand and ultimately transform the reproductive practices of international relations, security studies and human rights? The spatialities and geographies of human rights violations have been gendered. Some of the most brutal and cruel cases of human rights violations and abuse are connected to the lack of freedom to move in space by imprisonment at home, whether it is enforced physically, psychologically or philosophically through fear or terrorism or imposed by rules and the cultural meanings of space.

Women's inhibited use of public space is seen as a spatial expression of patriarchy and a violation of human rights. The situation shows that space is never neutral; instead, it affects and is affected by social and power relations in society. The legal exclusivity in human rights discourse have argued that male dominance such as this makes freedom of movement impossible and encroaches upon socio-economic rights. In multicultural societies it has become ever more complex and politically charged in many parts of the world. Spatial planning is never a neutral process. It reflects social and power relations within a society as well as affecting them and, to a large extent, spatial relations actually represent and sometimes also reproduce social relations.[2]

The global perspectives of International Relations of the different discourses, from the feminist and post-modern perspectives, have greatly enriched the entire corpus of knowledge available today. There is no one feminism, no single approach to the construction of feminist theory, but multiple varieties of feminism which often embrace very contradictory and overlapping positions, discourses and practices. The recognition that, there are multiple feminisms has arisen out of the feminist movement itself as different groups of women have challenged a singular, representational feminism and homogenous category of "woman" that do not take into account of differences among women.

Within the feminist theory and gender studies there is an increasing realization that one can no longer understand or explain the varying yet remarkably persistent inequality of women compared with men without the global view of diverse geo-political and economic conditions that have a gender-differentiated causes and consequences. Hence this school performs a dual meta-disciplinary task. They make these discourses gender sensitive and at the same time they bring global perspectives to the study of women which involves elucidating heterogeneity among women, differentiated by hierarchies of race, class, ethnicity, nationality and sexuality, and embedded in global structures and processes.[3] The latter task is essential if one has to deconstruct the multiple oppressions, including gender, sustaining the structural and direct violence of the global political-economic system; and to reconstruct practices of feminist solidarity and resistance in the face of increased fragmentation of labour and identities and the increased mobility of capital and people.

Human Security

Security today has come to be a more umbrella term and all compassing. It is no longer as it denoted during the Cold War years to mean just military security but today it encompasses economic prosperity, social peace and political stability. It is this broadening of definition that is extremely relevant to problems that nullify national borders and state boundaries. The social, economic and environmental trends that are key to human security are increasingly being shaped not only by the fragmentation implied in the rise "tribalism" but also by globalization. It is these contradictory forces that are at work in the global system today. Market, media and monetary exchanges have brought into a reality the idea of Marshall Mc Luhan of the "global village" into a reality.

Although the nation-state is far from being eclipsed, countries and national governments have less and less ability to shape their own destinies. The meaning of borders, community and sovereignty is in flux, and that in turn makes national security a more tenuous concept. As James Rosenau observes, "In the political realm, ...authority is simultaneously relocated upward toward supranational identities, sideward toward transnational organizations and social movements, and downwards toward sub-national groups and communities. In the economic realm, production and distribution facilities are being reorganized in both larger economic units and localized regions. In the social and cultural realms, loyalties and values are being reoriented toward global norms and neighbourhood concerns."[4]

Boundaries of Gender

Knowledge establishes the meaning of bodily sexual difference as binary confers meanings on power relationships and social orderings in general. Gender structures institutions and identities through the asymmetrical social constructs of masculinity and femininity, as opposed to ostensibly biological male-female sex differences. Hegemonic masculinity is associated with autonomy, sovereignty, objectivity, universalism, the capacity for reason/abstraction, and hegemonic femininity with the absence or absolute lack of these qualities. In this construction, to be masculine is not to be feminine; men are therefore 'emasculated' when shown to embody effeminate/feminine characteristics that are associated with women, the second sex. In more abstract terms, masculine identity is achieved by demonstrating its difference from and superiority to a feminine other. Hence, "the binary opposition and the social process of gender relationships both become part of the meaning of power itself: to question or alter any aspect threatens the entire system."[5]

Military training is socialization into masculinity carried to the extremes. Typically soldiers are taught not only to deride the presence of women [and gays/homosexuals whose bodies are labeled feminine/effeminate] but to achieve manhood by virtue of their autonomy from women, their suppression of emotions associated with [feminized] craving for pain, and their protection of women and children. This has been clear from the US cultural constructions of masculinity on killing and expressions of domination over other men, women and children. Rather it requires extreme personal courage to resist such "taken for granted" masculinist constructions of what it means to be a citizen and even a human.[6] At the same time, feminine characteristics signify inferiority and are used to discredit women in power. Questions actually asked by women qua [embodied as] woman as subjects is silenced within this framework of equality or e-man-cipation. In India women in politics are to be seen and not to be heard. One sees the battalion of film stars in Parliament. The exceptions have been Jayalalitha, Mamta, Phoolan and a few others. But one can count these on one's fingers.

Unlike the feminists who valorize femaleness and invert the gender hierarchy of male-masculine over female-feminine, this perspective tries to look at the issue from a human security perspective. For, by, associating women's nature with different, more peaceful, ethical and cooperative ways of being than men's, these positions tend to reinforce oppressive binary gender identities and structures as opposed to explaining how gender hierarchies and other forms of superordination are reproduced and how they can be transformed. These perspectives argue that knowledge which emerges from women's experiences 'on the margins' of world politics is actually more neutral and critical because it is not as complicit with, or blinded by, existing institutions and power relations.[7] Women's political struggles against marginalization and exclusion from status-quo public power impart a strong objectivity to knowing because women often have the most to gain from developing critical understandings of exactly how the world which oppresses them is constructed, and how it might be reconstructed in more egalitarian ways. It makes sense "of men's gendered reactions if we take women's experiences seriously."[8]

Gender as a Variable

The sexist exclusion of women has been challenged here. Women are already in international relations, security and human rights 'if we choose to see them there.'[9] Taking gender seriously involves recognizing over fifty per cent of the world's population, correcting the denial or misrepresentation of women in international politics due to the false assumption that certain male experiences can count for men and women universally and/or that women are simply absent from political activities and not relevant to political-economic processes, especially those at an international level. Globally, women are a disadvantaged group: they own one per cent of the world's property and resources, perform sixty per cent of the labour, are the majority of refugees, illiterate and poor persons, and yet women are central to the social and material survival of families and communities and also at the forefront of environmental, peace, indigenous, nationalist and other critical social movements. International processes and interactions have gender-differentiated causes and consequences, but more importantly the worldwide failure to resolve dilemmas of poverty, pollution, population and nuclear proliferation is inseparable from our failure to understand the contributions and situation of women globally as well as the prevalence and stability of global gender hierarchies.[10]

Men's work gets organized into paid labour while women's work is kept invisible and unpaid. Globalization has come to the developed world by default rather than design. We are all in it before we know that we are in it. Macroeconomic research documents the expanding gender gap in work hours, income, resources and power intensified by Third World debt crises, structural adjustment policies [SAPs], the fiscal squeezing and privatization of welfare states and the globalization of production, finance, labour and economic management.[11] As state economic policies are increasingly governed by the global imperatives of export earnings, international financial markets and comparative labour costs, states fail to deliver social welfare services and to maintain their commitment to full employment and the general well-being of national populations. As the cheapest source of flexible paid labour, the reserve army of labour, women, especially poor women oppressed by race, ethnicity, nationality and class, are also disproportionately vulnerable to the deregulation of labour markets and the privatization of state public sectors in particular. Empirical studies reveal the increasing feminization of poverty worldwide and the gendered nature of the new international division of labour-heavily reliant on women's labour in the export processing zones of developing countries, the growth sex-tourism, migrant domestic labour and male-order brides in attracting foreign exchange in subordinate states, as well as the growing number of female headed households and never-married mothers, and triply burdened by childcare, domestic and wage labour.[12] This means there is a turn to low cost, insecure, often part time or contract based temporary female employment with few social benefits. These changes in the international and gendered divisions of labour have acutely exploited women workers in developing and industrialized countries. They have been constructed, supported and encouraged by multinational corporations and governments everywhere.

Gender as a variable in foreign policy making by exposing the dominant male gender of conventional practitioners and their exhibition of masculine characteristics as strategically rational actors who make life and death decisions in the name of an abstract conception of 'national interest.' Women are rarely insiders of the actual institutions that make and implement foreign policy and conduct war.[13] Women are providers of a whole range of military support services [domestic, psychological, medical and sexual] they are reserve armies in home industries, transnational peace activists, soldiers and mothers of soldiers, and revolutionary actors in national liberation struggles and civil wars. Women are being increasingly recruited into armies worldwide, although they are usually excluded from combat and decision-making roles. Men sacrifice their lives in war to protect the motherland and the home as a mothering space.

Women have been significant activists in foreign policy as well as in critical social movements, organizing for peace, environmental justice and women's liberation transnationally.

Gender as Transformative-Human Security

Cross-cultural understanding and feminist strategies in the context of these multiple standpoints and differences among women, however, demand empathetic cooperation. Cultures operate within both social and spatial contexts within the time dimension that is, different positioning, both socially and geographically, affects the ways cultures are articulated and used, both inside and outside collectivities. This situation poses a dilemma: in a world of so many cultural differences is it possible to discuss human rights issues internationally? An overly simple notion of the relationship between culture and human rights in the world of differences could result in a dichotomous formulation, with universalists falling on one side and the relativists on the other.[14] While Universalists argue that human rights are universal, relativists argue that efforts to "universalize" human rights can be reviewed as an act of imperialism or colonialism. As Radhika Coomaraswamy[15] put it, the discourse between the two approaches is a battle between those who are struggling for democracy, pluralism and ethnic tolerance and those who are strongly nationalistic or believe in return to religious fundamentalism where the community of interests is laid down at birth and by tribe and not on the basis of what is fair, just and equal.

In reality, the universality of human rights is usually undermined by governments who argue that human rights must be subject to the interests of national security, economic strategies and local traditions. When it comes to women's human rights, many governments take a particularly restrictive view with regard to women's equality and freedom to move, or their rights to have free access to resources, because women represent the reproduction of the family, the code of honour and modesty of a society and a nation. Thus, women's human rights abuses are often justified in the name of cultural and moral codes. The main concern should therefore be how to legitimize international human rights within particular cultures and traditions. For planners, this cultural relativity of human rights presents challenges. Should traditional norms and cultural habits causing women's subordination be regarded as "human rights" in order to be taken into consideration in planning schemes and, if so, to what extent should planning schemes play a role, either in changing these norms or perpetuating them? One way of tackling this discourse is to distinguish between human rights, which are universal and determined by international law and human needs which are local in nature and vary from one culture to another. Coomaraswamy acknowledges the diversity, but only within the context of a firm foundation of universally acknowledged human rights and women's rights. Perhaps a more just way to decide whether the cultural and political priorities of a particular patriarchal community should take precedence over the collective will of the international community is to ask what women want and think.

Women in Armed Conflict: The Manipur Experience

Manipur has been a theater of low-intensity armed conflicts for the past few decades. At the root of the conflict, *inter alia*, is the issue of its political status after 1949. Manipur's independence was restored in August 1947 with the departure of British. A constitutional monarchy was established under the Manipur State Constitution Act, 1947 and elections on the basis of universal adult franchise and the secret ballot were held in 1948. However Manipur became a part of the Indian union. There has been insurgency since then. Of late there has been an agitation against the Indian army and several accusations of human rights violations.

The Indian state has been a garrison state and women's rights have been violated. All men are deeply affected by the expectations as well as their desires. In this state there is dominance of national security as against human security, which has led to the supremacy of the soldier. In the name of curbing insurgency, there are gross violations of human rights.

NOTES AND REFERENCES

1. J.B. Elshtain, *Women and War* (New York, 1987), p. 41.
2. R. Cook, *Human Rights of Women* (Philadelphia: University of Pennsylvania Press, 1995).
3. L. Alexandre, "Genderizing International Studies: Revisioning Concepts and Curriculum", *International Studies* Notes 14, 1 (1989), pp. 5-8.
4. James Rosenau (1994).
5. J. Scott and J. Butler (eds.), *Feminints Theorize the Political* (New York, 1992), p. 49.
6. C. Enloe, *The Morning After: Sexual Politics at the end of the Cold war* (Berkeley, 1995), p. 55.
7. Sylvester and R.O. Keohane, "International Relations Theory Contributions of a Feminist Standpoint," *Millennium*, 18, 2 (1989), p. 245.
8. J. Kerr (ed.), *Women's Rights as Human Rights* (London, 1993).
9. G.A. Steurnagel, 'Men do not do Housework! The Image of Women in Political Science' in M. Paudi and G.A. Steurnagel (eds), *Foundations for a Femininist Restructuring of the Academic Disciplines* (New York, 1999).
10. H. Afshar and C. Dennis, *Women and Adjustment in the Third World* (London, 1992).
11. I. Bakker (ed.), *The Strategic Silence: Gender and Economic Policy* (London, 1994).
12. J. Pettman, *Worlding Women: A Feminist International Politics* (Sydney, 1996).
13. N.E. McGlen and M.R. Sarkees (eds.), *Women in Foreign Policy: The Insiders* (New York, 1999).
14. A. Rao, "The politics of gender and culture in international human rights discourse," in J. Peters and A. Wolper (eds.), *Women's Rights as Human Rights* (New York: Routledge, 1995).
15. Radhika Coomaraswamy, "The principle of universality and cultural diversity" in M.A. Schuler (ed.), *Claiming our Place: Working the Human Rights System to Women's Advantage* (Washington D.C.: Institute for Women, Law and Development, 1993).

9

Strategic Culture, Civil Society and War Against Terrorism

Harsh K. Sinha

It was Clemenceau who once said that 'war is much too serious a matter to be left to the Generals.' If he was correct it will also not be incorrect if we say that 'it is also much too serious a matter to be left to the politicians, opinion makers and civil society' because there is a definite lack of strategic culture and awareness evident among these.

In India the public awareness is not in a good shape as far as the security related issues are concerned. It can and has been observed in the popular debate of onions vs N-bomb a few years back or in the people's indifference over the defence deal seams or in a zero-reaction on the Mitrokhin's disclosures. It is rather impossible to find out any example in this domain which could be labeled as public driven change or something alike.

Though in the recent years, there is a growing concern about National Security in India. This concern is the result of many separate but inter-related events like Kargil clash, hijacking of the Indian Airlines flight IC 814 and intensification of the proxy war in Kashmir. Above all, the war against terrorism after 9/11 has awakened India from her dogmatic slumber and there is a new National security awakening becoming evident but still the overall situation is not satisfactory. It is often said that in India the strategic culture is completely absent in the civil society.

This paper is an attempt to assess the level and quality of the security related knowledge of the civil society. For this, the results of different opinion polls related to the war on terrorism have been used as a testing tool. For observing in a comparative manner the results of a Gallup poll conducted among American citizens on the same issues are also referred.

The Pretext

Strategic culture means an environment in which there is an awareness of the National Security goals and problems and a sense of strategic understanding to preserve and promote the National Security. It is rather univocally accepted that in India such a culture is completely absent. Interestingly, Indians and Western thinkers both are agree on this point. Laurus (1976), George Tanham (1995) and Rosen (1997) have offered convincing reasons to support this contention and Ashok Mehta, Subhash Kapila and the Former Indian Minister Jaswant Singh also echo the same sentiments. Thinkers like Sumit Ganguly form a very miserable thin group who disagree with the above contention. This group forgets that strategic culture must be evidenced in observable terms and assuming its ideational existence is nothing but a misplaced idealistic and faulty reality perception.

There are a number of patent reasons for this absence of strategic culture in the country. Reasons are rooted in the history, religion, philosophy, social culture, nationalism and political leadership of the country. Historically, historiography in India was never a systematic intellectual exercise. There is a definite lack of the sense of history. Some attempts have been made to explain this casual and unsystematic approach to history. Jaswant Singh in 'Defending India' says:

> As a constituent of strategic culture, a sense of history, or a recording of it, evaluating and assessing it, and then utilizing it as an input in decision-making has not been there. This absence of a written historical account of India can be variously explained—an account of a lack of unity, there being no one India, that the Indian tradition is more oral, that religious texts, in any event, have always had greater merit. No matter, what the causes, the consequences of this absence (of a sense of history) has significantly affected the development of India's strategic thought.

But some experts like Bharat Karnad who have a little different view point say that it would not be correct to say that the strategic culture was completely absent since ancient times rather it was hampered continuously. As he points out:

> The absence of broad-based preparedness for defence had made India prone to invasions. The body politic, which developed a fatalistic outlook, started to culturally absorb the invaders instead of confronting them. Inured to invasion, strategic thinking in the country was negatively affected and was unable to envisage an 'expansive outlook' or plan 'proactive doctrines.' Indians had developed a race-memory of an inflated sense of achievement and military excellence when in reality defeat and weakness had typified India's experience.

It is really surprising that strategic culture is not fairly evident in a country which has fought four big wars in the five decades since its independence and participated in more than two dozen large or small scale military operations. But the situation is changing drastically. This transformation is happening more by default than intent. After jumbling on the periphery of the National security circuit, at least the country seems to be on the threshold by a National Security awakening. The breakthrough has occurred due to India becoming a nuclear power and continuing with its missile programmes. The liberalization and progressive decontrol of the Indian economy, and its integration with the global economy makes it even more imperative that the political class understands the vast variety of pressures on National Security.

The Setting

There may be several tools to examine the status of strategic culture in the country. We can examine it among ruling elites or intellectuals who usually design the policies but both of them do not represent the common mindset of the civil society so it is better to focus on common man and their general responses on security related issues.

For this study a unique testing tool was applied. To understand the strategic understanding, knowledge of security affairs, general reasoning and the common proclivity of the civil society, results of various opinion polls were used. These opinion polls, conducted by three leading Newspapers were focused largely on the events related to the terrorist attack of 9/11 and the war against terrorism. These three Newspapers were the *Times of India (TOI)*—the largest circulated English daily having a readership of 7.98 crore with its circulation of 1.88 crore copies everyday according to the ABC (Audit Bureau of Circulation) report of the year 2004. The other two dailies were the Hindi dailies *Rashtriya Sahara* and *Dainik Jagran* respectively. It is worth mentioning that according to the above mentioned ABC report *Dainik Jagran* is the largest circulated daily of the country having a readership of 16.40 crore with its circulation of 1.9 crore copies everyday. The results of the opinion polls used for the study were published in these dailies between September 11, 2001 and October 11, 2001.

These Newspapers carry daily opinion polls as their regular column which attracts a very large amount of readership and thus reflect the general psyche and propensity of the civil society. For this content analysis percentage comparisons are made and no attempt is made to test the significance of the difference between various percentages statistically. The opinion statements on which the polls were conducted reflect a high degree of similarity. The similarity shows that the problems of National Security and terrorism have been giving rise to a rich storage of information. Today the opinions are shared in a similar fashion by persons across the globe. In this study responses are classified and presented into 3 categories, i.e. Yes (Y) showing approval, No (N) showing disapproval and cannot say (CS) shows no opinion or indecision.

Besides these three set of the opinion poll results, one other set was studied to examine the strategic culture status of the people of United States. The Gallup Poll Analysis (hitherto be referred as GPA) on 9/11: key trends and indicators of October 12, 2001 available on the website of the Gallup organisation, i.e. www.gallup.org. shows the American public opinion following the terrorist attack on 9/11. The results show the opinion on 25 statements and focused largely on President Bush's reaction to the attack and military action taken by the

United States. Only those statements are considered which were also used in the opinion polls conducted by Indian dailies, so that a comparative study could be done. In this study to examine the status of the strategic culture in the civil society, the basic focus was concentrated on following four points:

1. The quality of the responses, i.e. whether these results reflect the well thought opinion or the superficial kind of knowledge.
2. Consistency and pattern in the responses.
3. Difference between the responses of Hindi and English readers.
4. Comparison between the responses of Indian and US citizens to understand the difference of strategic culture level of both the countries.

Results and Discussions

Problem - 1

It was clearly evident in the responses that most of them were a poor blend of speculations, superficial knowledge and the instant proclivity and because of it they were proved as wrong later. For example:

In an opinion poll conducted by *Rashtriya Sahara* (henceforth referred as *RS*) on September 19 asking whether the Pakistani government would revert to its decision to support United States in the war against terrorism because of the agitations all over in the country—69 per cent responded affirmative which later proved wrong.

Similarly in an opinion poll of *RS* on September 25, 75 per cent respondents were of the view that any campaign against terrorism would not be successful if it associates with Pakistan. 83 per cent respondents 'were observing US hesitation' in attacking Afghanistan in an opinion poll conducted by *Dainik Jagran* (henceforth referred as *DJ*) on 20 September while this percentage decreased by 13 per cent on the same question asked in *DJ* poll on September 29. In an opinion poll conducted by *The Times of India (TOI)* on September 27, 69 per cent respondents were telling that the attack on Afghanistan would run over the years and 83 per cent were of the view (*TOI*,

September 29) that US is heading towards 'another Vietnam' in Afghanistan. All of these examples reflect the poor level of understanding of the civilians regarding security-related issues.

Problem - 2

It is surprising that the readers gave different opinion in response to the similar questions asked in the same newspaper during three consecutive weeks.

On 17 September's poll of *RS* 76 per cent opined that Pakistan will be trapped in a civil war by supporting USA, on 22 September's poll 83 per cent were of the view that there will be a coup in Pakistan.

Similarly till 19th September's poll 69 per cent were of the opinion that Pakistan will do a somersault due to public resistance but by 10th October 67 per cent have changed their mind and only 32 per cent were standing by the previous statement.

This again is surprising to see that when US was finalising its war designs, the civil society in general was in a dilemma with its plan of action. In a *DJ* poll on 20th September 83 per cent of the respondents were of the view that US is hesitant of its attack plan but on 29th of the month, the percentage has reduced by 13. In an opinion poll conducted by *TOI* on 14th September 88 per cent of the respondents were thinking that Osama-bin-Laden was behind the 9/11 attacks. It is interesting to observe that by that time there was no sufficient proof to establish his involvement but when the conspiracy was almost exposed the number of the respondents thinking on the same line was reduced by 15 per cent (*TOI*, 6th Oct.).

Problem - 3

Though the general responses of Hindi and English readers were somewhat similar on the similar questions but the responses of Hindi readers were a bit exaggerated and jingoised. For example in a poll (*DJ*, 15th Sept.) 76 per cent respondents were apprehensive of the possibility of third world war after the 9/11 terrorist attacks whereas only 60 per cent *TOI* readers were thinking so on 17th September's poll.

"Shall India support US attack on Afghanistan?" was a common issue of opinion poll in *RS* and *TOI* (Sept. 16) but the number of the respondents were not the same. The Hindi respondents' percentage was 83 whereas English respondents' percentage was 73 only. Similarly in response to one more common question (shall there be actions against the countries harbouring terrorism/*TOI*, 15th Sept.) the 95 per cent of English readers were in favour of such actions while 76 per cent of the Hindi respondents were answering the same question affirmatively (*RS*, Oct. 1).

Problem - 4

US respondents were more pragmatic and rational whereas Indian respondents were irrational and emotional on the question of US attack on Afghanistan. For example the world famous opinion poll agency Gallup Organization, in its report released on October 12, 2001, detailed the results of opinion polls conducted in the United States just after 9/11 on some 25 questions related to the war on terrorism. One question among these 25 was, How long do you think an attack on Afghanistan would last? The same question was asked by *TOI* in its opinion poll of September 27. Surprisingly the results were very much different from each other. Sixty-nine per cent Indian respondents were of the view that it would last to many years but the number of US respondents thinking on the same pattern was only 22 per cent. While only 4 per cent Indian respondents were thinking that it would last maximum a year only but the number of US respondents thinking so was 26 per cent. Fourteen per cent Indians opined that this operation would last up to few months and 34 per cent US respondents were supporting them. It can be said, that the responses of US citizens were more closer to the fact and their perception was comparatively more logical based on ground realities and good information whereas Indian responses were the outcome of stereotype images and poor knowledge of the ground reality.

So if we summarise the observations, we can find that:

1. Most of the Indian responses were the outcome of the superficial knowledge and understanding of the security affairs largely based on the exaggerated news items carried by newspapers during that period. The answers were stereotype with the hangover of past experiences and information.

2. The answers of the question without open endings (question with subjective assessment) of Yes or No shows the limited knowledge and understanding of the security related issues.
3. There was a lack of consistency in the response of Indian citizens. The same questions were answered at different times showing different results. It again proves that in fact the 'Media' was driving their thoughts and thus responses too.
4. The general responses of Hindi and English readers were similar in tones but different in textures. The responses of Hindi readers were little exaggerated may be because of the jingoistic items published in vernacular press.
5. The difference between the responses of Indian and American citizens can be observed as the classical example of understanding and evaluating the status of the strategic culture of any civil society. The American responses were more pragmatic and rational because they were exposed to good information and better understanding of strategic affairs.

Reasons Responsible

The above discussed study shows clearly that there is a definite lack of strategic culture and awareness in the civil society. Now, what are the reasons responsible for this situation. As it has already argued that there are several reasons rooted in the history, religion, philosophy, social structure, nationalism and political leadership of the country some of these can be observed at length.

1. Referring once again Jaswant Singh in his book *Defending India* we can trace its roots in the history. As he says: whereas ancient Indian texts on every conceivable subject abound—on art and dance and drama, most abundantly on philosophy there are none other than Kautilya, that have detailed the military science of India. There is another factor; of geography, of a sense of territory. Indian nationhood being largely cultural and civilizational and Indian being supremely contented with what

was as unconquerable as is the Spirit. Thus both are absent, a territorial consciousness and a strategic sense about the protection of the territory of residence.

2. Ancient Indian social stratification system placed National Security concerns to be the sole responsibility of a caste. In the four-fold *Vernashram* system (which gave birth to the caste system later), *Kshatriyas* are placed next to the *Brahmins*. The word *Kshatriya* means one who gives protection and security. It was a warrior class and a concern for the security of the kingdom is his prime duty and *Dharma*.

Such exclusiveness made others indifferent to the objectives and goals of the kingdom's security. Bharat Karnad rightly says:

> The Hindu religion imposed a Brahminical order of Indian Society, wherein the responsibility for the defence of the realm lay with a single caste. As a consequence the rest of the society did not relate to political authority except in a ritualistic sense.

Had there been security awareness among the masses in the times of foreign invasions they would not have been a helpless spectator, incapable of offering any resistance.

3. The Brahminical society in ancient India got religious sanctions for the division of labour among these four castes. In *Varnashram* theory the *Varna* was acquired by deeds not by birth. Vishwamitra, a *Kshatriya* could become a *Brahmin* sage and Parashuram, *Brahmin* could become a *Kshatriya* warrior. When caste replaced *Varna* and heredity principle dominated Indian society, being born in a higher caste was considered to be a blessing of fate. Fatalism in Indians made them accept their defeats in a philosophical-designed manner. At times they lived in a mythological world in which they could recall the past glory of their ancestors in the battlefield. As if, the belief in ancestral supremacy in military excellence was not enough they took recourse to philosophy and religion and declared that non-violence is the supreme religion (*Ahimsa paramo dharma*). The theme of non-violence is cultural in Indian thought. It is glorified in theist and atheist philosophies both. Buddhism and Jainism made non-violence a cordial virtue. Yoga considers it as one of the five *Yamas* (*Satya, Ahimsa, Asteya, Brahmacharya,*

Aparigraha), i.e. Truth, non-violence, non-stealing, celibacy and non-holding). It will not be out of place here to mention that Gandhi, the modern day apostle of the non-violence understood the place of non-violence in the life of Indians and could use this non-military non-aggressive tool against the British to free India.

4. Cultural plurality coupled with ethnic diversity has made India always a congregation of many 'nations.' It is not surprising that the concept of Indian Nationhood is of very recent origins. India has witnessed a *fractured nationhood*. Bharat Karnad is aware of this when he says:

> The territory of (ancient) India had consisted of a fractured set of warring kingdoms and principalities of varied ethnic, linguist and socio-religious compositions, which counteracted the development of fixed loyalties.

On a very few occasions, there were attempts to unite these fractured segments into an organizational hold. Before the dawn of Indian Independence with hundreds of princely states, concept of nationhood was an illusion and a National strategic culture could not exist.

5. In 1947, India emerged as a new nation and under the leadership of Jawaharlal Nehru gave armed forces a role that could prevent a military coup. Perhaps Nehru witnessed the number of military coup in newly independent nations. Nehru completely sidelined the Indian Armed Forces from any effective participation in National security decision-making. Here the civil bureaucracy too, had a convergence of interest with the political leadership in that they did not want the emergence of a rival elite with direct access to the political leadership, accuses Subhash Kapila, Nehru may explain this sidelining of the army by saying that he was committed to peace and progress, scientific, industrial and agricultural growth rather than military progress. It may be assumed that Nehru, though a deviant follower of Gandhi, adhered to the principle of peace and non-violence. The need for a strategic culture was not felt till 1962 when the China invaded.

6. There is a definite lack of strategic culture education in leaders and opinion-makers in India. May be because neither the country was a collectivity of war loving caste group nor there was the provision like compulsory military training. The

security goals and problems remained exclusively the concerns of a limited group. Democracy was accepted as a system of governance but National Security matters were put in a veil. In such an environment the politicians and intellectual elites who could cultivate a strategic culture were either ignorant of the importance of strategic culture or they preferred other local issues to it. Even today, few leaders and intellectuals have any understanding of what the term strategic affairs really means. To the majority of them strategic culture implies something to do with defence and military matters.

7. In India the most effective and perhaps the sole source of opinion building is the media. Media, having a penetrating reach and powerful impact always play an important role in public opinion building. In India there are approximately 38,000 titles registered with the registrar of newspapers. Out of these about 3000 publications are brought out regularly. The Indian newspaper society at present has around 720 member publications. It is the worthwhile to note that the Hindi press in India has a wolf's share of the total readership and circulation jiggers.

8. The largest publications in the country, according to the findings of the National Readership Survey, are regional language publications, and not their more high profile English counterparts. According to the Indian Readership Survey (IRS) report of round 2, *Dainik Jagran* (a Hindi Daily) was top on the chart with more than 16.4 crore readership, much ahead with the largest circulated English daily *The Times of India*, which has the readership of 7.09 crore in same period. It is interesting to note here that between these two newspapers, another three dailies were ranked which are *Dainik Bhaskar, Malayala Manorama* and *Anand Bazar Patrika* respectively and all these again were regional language newspapers.

It is observed that in most of the vernacular press, the coverage of defence and security related issues affairs is very low in comparison of English dailies. Since the large chunk of the civil society, thus, is not getting proper dose of the content on security affairs, readers become clueless when asked to react or respond on it. This cluelessness or the unawareness keeps them far from the discussions about the strategic affairs.

And lastly the role of language. Intellectuals used to discuss, read and write in a language which still is not the language of the country. Any discourse, does not matter how much useful it is, if being conducted in English, it automatically goes out of the periphery of a vast chunk of the population.

ANNEXURE-1

Opinion Polls conducted by *Rashtriya Sahara*:

Sept. 13. After terrorist attacks will America attack the terrorist camps all over the world?

Y – 20, N – 60, CS – 20.

Sept. 14. (the same question was repeated.)

Y – 80, N – 20.

Sept. 15. In its fight against terrorism, would America like stronghold on Pakistan?

Y – 60, N – 30, CS – 10.

Sept. 16. If US attacks on Afghanistan should India support it?

Y – 83, N – 16, CS – 1.

Sept. 17. Does supporting US can cause civil war in Pakistan?

Y – 76, N – 24.

Sept. 18. Would US accept Pakistan's demand to keep India aside from this war?

Y – 48, N – 51, CS – 1.

Sept. 19. Will Pakistan somersault to its decision and withdraw its support due to the domestic pressure and turmoil?

Y – 69, N – 28, CS – 3.

Sept. 20. American fight against terrorism is confined to the Laden only.

Y – 81, N – 16, CS – 3.

Sept. 21. Is China's demand justified that any action against Afghanistan must be taken under the supervision of the security council?

Y – 76, N – 24.

Sept. 22. Can there be a coup in Pakistan on the issue of supporting US against Afghanistan?

Y – 83, N – 12, CS – 5.

Sept. 23. America wants Laden dead or alive. Is it possible to catch Laden without a war on grounds?

Y – 16, N – 75, CS – 9.

Sept. 24. Is the demand of Taliban justified that before taking any action against Laden, US must furnish proof of his involvement?

Y – 61, N – 14, CS – 03

Sept. 25. It is possible to fight terrorism keeping Pakistan as ally in it?

Y – 20, N – 75, CS – 5.

Sept. 26. Can Laden take refuge in any other country after leaving Afghanistan?

Y – 48, N – 51, CS – 1.

Oct. 02. Should India play a role in forming of coalition government in Afghanistan?

Y – 74, N – 26.

Oct. 03. After the attack on high security zones like J & K assembly, should it be believed that terrorists are capable of attacking any place?

Y – 74, N – 26.

Oct. 04. Coming Khaleda Zia in power in Bangladesh with her Anti-India image, will the bilateral relations be hampered?

Y – 52, N – 35, CS – 11.

Oct. 05. Is it right to look forward to the US in abolishing terrorism from J & K?

Y – 30, N – 50, CS – 20.

Oct. 06. The rumors of plane hijack are an intelligence failure of the government.

Y – 50, N – 40, CS – 10.

Oct. 07. Not imposing ban on Lashkar-e-Toiba and Jaish-e-Mohammed by US is a diplomatic failure for India.

Y – 70, N – 30.

Oct. 10. The agitations taking place in Pakistan against US attack on Afghanistan will impose new challenges for President Pervaiz Musharaf.

Y – 32, N – 67, CS – 1.

ANNEXURE-2

Opinion Polls conducted by *Dainik Jagaran*

Sept. 14. America has been to such a major attack because it ignored Islamic Terrorism.

Y – 85, N – 14, CS – 01

Sept. 15. Is there a scene of 3rd WW after attack on America?

Y – 76, N – 21, CS – 03

Sept. 16. Is coercing the Kashmiri women to wear Burka a part of terrorism?

Y – 76, N – 23, CS –01

Sept. 18. Will the Musharaf's moves make the America-Pakistan relation friendly again?

Y – 59, N – 37, CS – 04

Sept. 20. Is America showing hesitation in attacking Afghanistan?

Y – 83, N – 16, CS – 01

Sept. 21. Will Muslim Terrorists become more aggressive after attack on Afghanistan?

Y – 65, N – 34, CS – 01

Sept. 22. American war against terrorism only centralize against Taliban and Laden.

Y – 65, N – 34, CS – 01

Sept. 23. Would America be attacked on Afghanistan till now?

Y – 77, N – 21, CS – 02

Sept. 24. American Administration is showing more liberal attitude than required against Pakistan.

Y – 87, N – 09, CS – 04

Sept. 25. Is Pakistan heading towards disintegration?

Y – 89, N – 09, CS – 02

Sept. 27. Should America publish all evidences against Laden before all the countries?

Y – 52, N – 47, CS – 01

Sept. 29. Will America reserve from his intention of attacking Afghanistan?

Y – 70, N – 27, CS – 03

Sept. 30. Will elements associated with SIMI be discouraged after imposing Ban on it?

Y – 67, N – 28, CS – 05

Oct. 01. Is Demand of Ban Organization like VHP & BD correct?

Y – 65, N – 34, CS – 01.

Oct. 02. Will George Bush image fall down if US does not attack on Afghanistan?

Y – 76, N – 23, CS – 01

Oct. 03. Is attack on Kashmir Legislative Assembly, result of Indians weak initiative against terrorism?

Y – 80, N – 18, CS – 02

Oct. 04. Is Government's reaction on the attack on Kashmir legislative Assembly shows it is a fight against terrorism?

Y – 63, N – 36 , CS – 1

Oct. 06. The hijack issue is a case of lapses in security arrangements.

Y – 33, N – 66, CS – 1

Oct. 07. India's image is of a 'Soft State' on the issue of curbing down the terrorism.

Y– 90, N – 9, CS – 1

Oct. 10. Those who support Taliban and Laden, are damaging the Islamic values.

Y – 70, N – 28, CS – 2

Opinion Polls conducted by *The Times of India* (also on www.Indiatimes.com):

Sept. 11. To counter Pak, should India too plan a media blitz at the UN Meet.

Yes – 78 No – 20 Can't say – 2

Sept. 14. Do you think Laden is behind US attack?

Yes – 88 No – 7 Can't say – 5

Sept. 15. Should action be taken against countries that harbor terrorists?

Yes – 95 No – 4 Can't say – 1

Sept. 16. Should India take part in a US strike against Bin Laden?

Yes – 73 No – 24 Can't say – 3

Sept. 17. Are we heading towards World War III?

Yes – 60 No – 34 Can't say – 6

Sept. 19. Should the US rebuild the twin towers of the WTC?

Yes – 79 No – 19 Can't say – 2

Sept. 20. Do you think India can absorb the economic fallout of a conflict in Asia?

Yes – 82 No – 17 Can't say – 1

Sept. 21. Who is India's most wanted?

Dawood – 34 Osama – 37

Chota Shakeel – 28.8

Sept. 22. In the past 7 days, whose performance has been the most impressive.

Vajpayee – 15, Bush – 34, Musharaf – 32,

Mullah Omar – 19

Sept. 23. Which News Channel coverage of the attack on the US cities has been the most impressive?

CNN – 56, BBC – 23,

Fox News – 16, MSNBC – 5

Sept. 24. Where do you think O.B. Laden is hiding?

Pak – 13, Afg. – 34,
China –13, Indonesia – 27,
Chechnya – 13

Sept. 27. How long do you think an attack on Afghanistan would last?

1 yr. – 4%, Yrs. – 69%, Months – 14%,
Weeks – 8%, Days – 5%

Sept. 28. What is the real objective behind the US Plan to strike Afghanistan?

Combating terrorism – 47%

Installing a Pro US govt. – 36%

Revenge – 17%

Sept. 29. Is the US rushing into another Vietnam in Afghanistan?

Yes - 83%, No – 17%

Sept. 30. Why do people watch news about the war on TV?

- To escape the reality around them - 7%,
- To face reality - 20%
- For time pass - 73%

Oct. 01. What is your commitment to the war against terrorism?

- Willing to suffer eco. hardship - 43%
- Just be happy to watch it on TV - 28%
- Would encourage my loved ones to fight - 29%

Oct. 02. As India's PM, what would be your primary concern?

- Nation's finances - 57%
- Terrorism - 41%
- UP Polls - 2%

Oct. 04. What's the first thing that comes to your mind when you think of Afghanistan ?

- Poverty-stricken children - 11%

- Orthodox Muslim clerics - 8%
- Gun-wielding terrorists - 81%

Oct. 06. What do you think of the US evidence against Osama?

- Conclusive - 73%
- Speculative - 18%
- Fabricated - 9%

Oct. 07. What is the thing the government should do in the next 7 days?

- Go for UTI privatisation - 12%
- Deploy sky marshals - 16%
- Expose Pakistan - 63%
- Give Aid to Afghans - 9%

Oct. 08. Is Tony Blair acting as America's foreign minister?

- Yes - 69
- No - 31

Oct. 09. What makes Osama bin Laden?

- Spy network - 26%
- Money power - 29%
- Cunning - 11%
- Links with Pak - 34%

Oct. 10. What worries you most about the US attack on Afghanistan?

- Civilian casualties - 27
- Terrorist reprisals - 28
- Prolonged War - 12
- Unrest in Asia - 33

Oct. 11. What do you find missing in the TV coverage on Afghanistan?

- Taliban's view - 21
- Anti war views - 16
- Afghan's plight - 30
- Bin Laden footage - 33

10

Detection of Landmines: Issues Related to Human Security

V.N. Bhoraskar

Introduction

About 150 years ago fused munitions in different forms were invented in a few countries. Within a short period small size and cheap munition, now called landmines, was used as safety hazard at battlefields and military training camps in several parts of the world. As a result of the two World Wars, in several countries, the military had left pieces of land, each of large areas and containing hazardous planted landmines. In a large number of countries accidents involving forgotten landmines are common and posing a threat to humanity as well as to a section of the animals living in the respective hazardous regions.

According to the reports published by the United Nations, IAEA and other agencies, about 120 million landmines were buried in about seventy countries world over. Even today, with all the advanced technology, more than 110 million anti-personal and tank mines are estimated to be in the ground in different parts of the world. As per the report published in 1997, these landmines are spread over in the world but with high concentration in 12 countries of central South America, 23 countries of Africa, 10 countries of Middle East, 13 countries of Asia and 24 countries of Europe. In Asia, though the concentrations of the landmines grounded during the World War II and subsequent period is significant, however, the number of the landmines in India, Pakistan, Bangladesh, and Nepal in the civilian areas are negligible. It is surprising that around India, there are about 10 million mines in Afghanistan, 9 million in Cambodia and 10 millions in China. The number of landmines in Korea, Sri Lanka, Thailand, Vietnam, Philippines is still unknown. In general the existence of these landmines poses a global threat and therefore efforts are made to destroy all the landmines.

A rough estimate indicates that about 2,000 innocent persons are killed per month all over the world from the accidents occurring due to the hidden landmines. These landmines, though of relatively low cost, have high destructive powers. Due to the cross-border terrorism, war and for such other reasons, landmines are still being planted in the region of the boundaries of the adjacent countries. At the same time a large number of countries are engaged in neutralizing the planted landmine. During the last few years, in some parts of India landmines are being used for the terrorist activities. As a result number of innocent civilians and military persons are killed or severally maimed every year. Under such circumstances, if the present situation is allowed to be continued, then the ratio of the planted mines to those being neutralized will continue to grow in the world for many years in the near future.

Types of Landmines

The explosives which are commonly used in the landmines are TNT, RDX, composition B, Tetryl and C-4. In general two categories of landmines namely the antitank and the antipersonnel are in operation all over the world. The antitank mines (AT) contain explosive in the range of 2 to 10 kg. These mines are buried at a depth of more than 20 cm from the surface. These mines are buried in the ground, roads or other places for destroying vehicles, tanks, etc. Depending upon the types of landmines the pressure required to trigger it may vary from 10 kg to 300 kg. These antitank landmines cause huge explosion followed by destruction of the objects existing around that area.

The antipersonnel landmines are small in size, with diameter varying in range 60 to 120 mm and height varying in the range 40 to 70 mm. The amount of the explosive in this type of mines may vary from 10 to 250 gm. These landmines are buried for killing persons and animals, while passing over that region. The pressure required to trigger the antipersonnel landmine varies in the range 0.5 kg to 50 kg. The antipersonnel mines are of great variety, in terms of weight, size and amount and type of explosive. A rough estimate indicates that there are 700 varieties of the antipersonnel landmines. The antipersonnel mines being small in size, can be planted under the ground at a depth of few centimetres or thrown mechanically or manually on the target. In some cases it can also be dropped on the ground from air.

In all these mines, the main objective is to release energy, which should be as high as possible by the explosive materials and destroy the target. The lethal action of the induced blast is primarily from the shock waves produced in addition to the energy released in terms of heat. In the case of grounded landmine, injuries and destruction are also caused by the impact of the small pieces of the surrounding gravel, metal parts, dirt, etc. evolved as a result of the blast. These mines are made in different shapes using plastic or metal.

Some mines are made with curved shape for easy mounting on a round surface such as trees, poles, etc. In this way the metal pieces can shoot out with high velocities on the target immediately after the blast. These mines can have lethal effect up to a distance of about 50 metres. These mines are normally blasted with a remote control mechanism. Another type of mine is having a large number of metallic pieces with a relative large amount of explosive. This mine has a pin arrangement for initiating explosion. This mine is first thrown up by a detonator coupled to a mechanical system. The other end of the wire which is anchored in the pin is fixed to the ground. During the upward motion of the mine the pin is pulled apart and the fuse is put into action. As a result the mine is blasted and a large number of metal pieces scatter over a large area and induce lethal effects.

The other types of mines are pressure-sensitive and can be exploded by the person carrying it. These types of mines having butterfly-like shape or in other shapes which resembles toys. These types of mines are often used in the public places.

As of today for each landmine cleared, about 20 landmines are planted. These destructive weapons are relatively cheap as compared to their destructive power in both human and economic terms. As a result the ratio of the number of the buried mines to that of the neutralized mines is growing all over the world unless appropriate actions are taken by all the concerned countries, this will lead to a chaotic situation.

Detection of Mines

All over the world, efforts are being made to detect the buried mines and evolve a process for neutralizing the landmines at a fast rate. For this purpose, the process of determining has been divided into two groups: (a) military countermine and (b) humanitarian demining.

One of the effective approaches of the military for demining is to open lanes in the suspected areas by utilizing explosive. In some cases the techniques such as plows and racks are also used to bring the buried mines in the surface area without their explosion. Humanitarian demining refers to the process in which landmines lying in the civilian area are detected and removed without inflicting casualties.

In principle there are several methods for the detection of the landmines but in practice there are a few methods which can be used that too with a low success rate. The main reason behind this is that over the years technology has advanced, and the landmines with small size but with high powers of destruction are being developed. Moreover, these landmines do not have or have very little metallic components and therefore cannot be detected with the conventional metal detectors.

(a) Manual Clearance

In remote places, the convenient method to detect a landmine is through prodding the ground manually. This work has to be carried out by the trained men. In the location of the buried mine, the resistance experienced in digging the ground is relatively low as compared to the normal ground. This is mainly because that portion of the land becomes relatively soft and therefore the experienced person can make out the location of the buried mine easily.

(b) Metal Detector

The landmines which were buried before and immediately after World War II have metallic components. A mine containing iron or other metal parts can be identified with a metal detector. A metal detector consists of a coil in which magnetic field is generated by passing current. The magnetic field is sensed continuously by a sensor. The magnetic field of this coil gets disturbed whenever the coil is brought near any magnetic material. The information acquired by the sensor about the change in the magnetic field is converted into an audio signal. This type of detector can be used to locate landmines containing iron based components.

For the non-ferrous elements, the detector is based on the measurement of conductivity of the soil. The conductivity of the soil surrounding the buried mine is different than that of the normal soil of the ground. This change in the conductivity is caused by the eddy currents produced in the mines and due to the soft soil covering the landmine. This technique is, however, not applicable to the landmines made using plastic, wood, etc. Moreover, presence of metallic pieces in the ground will produce false signals. Recently developed Magnetometers are very effective in detecting ferrous metals. The basic principle is that the earth magnetic field gets disturbed in the surrounding of the ferrous metal buried in the ground. These magnetometers can be used in detecting ferrous metals up to a depth of two to three metres. The drawback of these magnetometers is that it cannot distinguish between a ferrous metal piece and a landmine containing ferrous metal. However, such magnetometers are useful in detecting landmines containing ferrous metal parts.

(c) The Ground Penetrating Radar (GPR)

In this method electromagnetic radiation covering different frequencies around 1 GHz are passed into the ground and the reflected radiations are monitored. The reflections of these radiations vary with the dielectric constants of the soil and the elements of the landmine. By the analysis of the reflected radiation at different frequencies it is possible to detect a landmine buried in the ground up to a depth of a few metres. Recently GPR have been developed which can detect and identify landmine buried up to a depth of 30 metres.

(d) Chemical Method

The vapors emanating from the explosives can be collected and analyzed by chemical methods. Similarly, there are other techniques based on odor sensing and are effective in detecting a landmine from the gases or vapors evolved from the explosive materials. Dogs are known to have ability of sense presence of an explosive through sniffing. Dogs after sniffing the explosive vapors emanating from buried explosives or mines can indicate the location of the explosive materials. This method has its own advantages and disadvantages, however, trained dogs are used for detecting the hidden explosive and landmines.

(e) Nuclear Quadrupole Resonance

In a few countries, a method based on the nuclear quadrupole resonance principle has been developed for the detection of landmines. In this system two types of antenna, one for transmitting the signal and the other for receiving the signal are used. The transmitted R.F. signal into the ground interacts with the landmine and the induced nuclear quadrupole resonance signal is detected. The element nitrogen–14 possess an electric quadrupole moment and therefore electric field generated by the particular molecular arrangements around the nitrogen–14 nuclei provide different sets of excited levels with known energies. The R.F. power is absorbed when such transitions occur among different energy states. This technique is very sophisticated but can be used for the identification of explosives and hidden landmines.

(f) Nuclear Techniques

Neutrons are highly penetrating particles in the ground and therefore their energy and intensity do not vary much while penetrating in the soil over a distance of few tens of centimetres. Similarly, gamma-rays of energies about 1 MeV can also penetrate soil without much loss in the intensity over a distance of about 20 to 30 centimetres. The fast and thermal neutron-induced-reaction analysis technique offers several advantages in the detection of explosives and hence landmines. Elements such as nitrogen, oxygen, carbon, and hydrogen are present in almost all kinds of explosives and propellants. Neutrons on interaction with these elements can induce nuclear reactions. The prompt gamma-rays, characteristic of the elements, are emitted from the respective elements on interaction with neutrons. The energies of the prompt gamma-rays emitted by carbon, hydrogen, nitrogen and oxygen on interaction with neutrons are given in Table 1.

Table 1: Energies of the prompt gamma-rays emitted by the elements on interaction with fast and thermal neutrons

Element	*Gamma-rays energy*	*Neutrons*
Lead	2.6 MeV	Fast
Carbon	4.43 MeV	Fast
Oxygen	6.1 MeV	Fast
Nitrogen	4.9, 5.1 MeV	Fast
Nitrogen	10.8 MeV	Thermal
Hydrogen	2.2 MeV	Thermal

In this method the explosive sample, such as landmine, is exposed to 14 MeV neutrons and during irradiation the energies and intensities of the prompt gamma-rays emitted by the sample are measured by a NaI (Tl) or BGO gamma-ray detector. The recorded gamma-ray spectrum is analyzed and the ratio of the nitrogen to oxygen is estimated. The same approach is also used for estimating the ratio of carbon to hydrogen. It is observed that in the explosive the ratios of nitrogen to oxygen and carbon to hydrogen have typical values which do not exist for other materials. In this way from the measured ratios of the nitrogen to oxygen and carbon to hydrogen, it is possible to identify whether the sample under interrogation is an explosive class material or not.

In the Department of Physics, University of Pune, Pune a 14 MeV Neutron Generator has been built and is in operation for the last 20 years. This machine is being used for studies related to the neutron-induced reactions. Recently experiments on the detection of explosive have been carried out. The concentrations of carbon, hydrogen, oxygen and nitrogen were estimated in a few mock explosive samples. The estimated values of the concentrations of oxygen, nitrogen and carbon are close to that obtained from the chemical composition.

For the detection of landmines it is proposed to design and assemble a small and portable unit of 14 MeV neutron generator such that it can be mounted on a vehicle. The vehicle can take the neutron generator in the field or on the road. The neutrons emitted from the source will enter the ground and interact with the elements of the soil and of the objects. A pair of gamma-ray detectors can be to measure the energy and intensity of the prompt gamma-rays emitted by the elements after interactions with the neutrons.

A facility to measure intensities and energies of the prompt gamma-rays emitted by elements of an explosive has been developed in the Department of Physics, University of Pune, and a schematic diagram of this facility is shown in Figure 1.

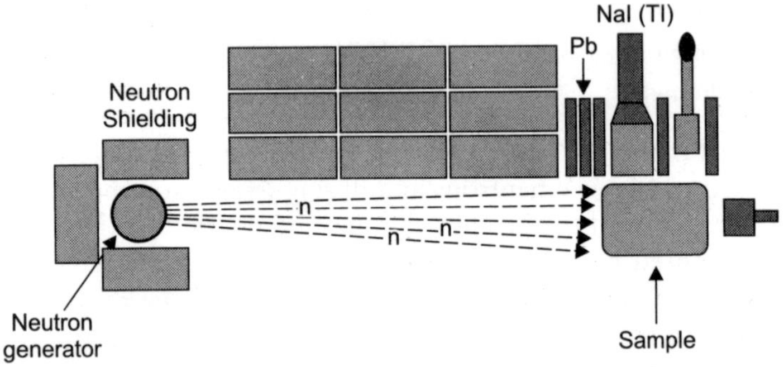

Figure 1: A schematic diagram of the system used for detection of prompt gamma-rays.

From the measured ratio of nitrogen to oxygen and similarly, carbon to hydrogen, it is possible to identify an explosive and hence landmines.

In this laboratory efforts are being made to develop a portable neutron generator system to detect landmines. A schematic diagram of the proposed system is shown in Figure 2.

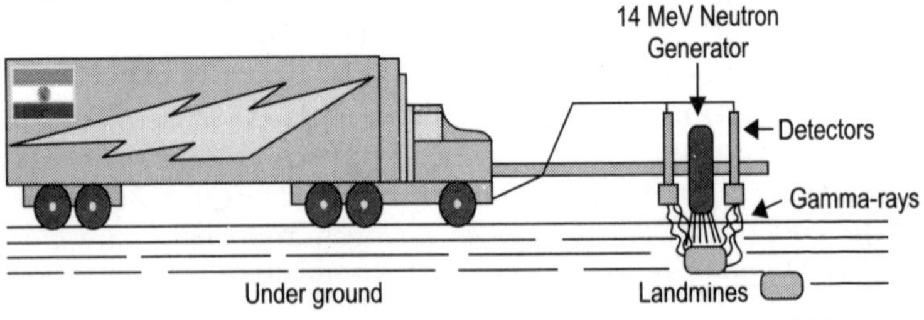

Figure 2: A schematic diagram of the proposed portable 14 MeV Neutron generator system for detection of landmines.

In addition to these methods there are a few other methods such as, Infrared imaging; Acoustics, X-ray scattering, thin film resonator, etc. which have been developed by different countries. However, use of these methods is limited due to several practical difficulties.

Conclusion

Even though, in principle, a large number of methods are available for the detection of explosives, however, so far no method has been found useful in saving lives of the innocent civilians being killed on roads or in public places due to landmines. In the interest of public security it is necessary to develop techniques by which explosives or a landmine carried in a public place or at any place of importance can be detected with a high level of confidence.

REFERENCES

Detection of buried landmines and hidden explosives using neutron, X-ray and gamma-ray probes by Ginacarlo Nebbia and Juergen Gerl, Euro Physics News, p. 119, July-Aug. 2005.

Forensic and Environmental Detection of Explosives by Jehuda Yinon, John Wiley & Sons Ltd. (1999).

Papers contribution from participants of the Advisor Group Meeting, IAEA, Vienna, 9-12 Dec. 1997. Draft for NISDA Security Conference 2005 proceedings.

11

Aerospace Remote Sensing: India's Capability

Hari Saran

In this paper an attempt has been made to explain the concept and types of modern aerospace remote sensing platforms. Use of these information-sweeping platforms by the US in the post-Cold War period operations has changed the very scenario of the battlefield. As a result of technological advancement the range and lethality of weapon systems have increased manifold over the years. The time to hit the target has reduced dramatically. Distances in the battlefield are no longer constrained by communication and targeting barriers. In a modern battlefield timely access to intelligence can be easily and accurately obtained through aerospace remote sensing platforms to match the operational mobility with great effect. Wars have now become high-tech and network centric by nature. In view of the regional threat perceptions, India has shown its concern for acquiring modern high-tech aerospace remote sensing platforms after the Kargil War, 1999. The progress made is reviewed and this paper offers some suggestions for the continuous growth of aerospace remote sensing capability of India.

Aerospace remote sensing means using aerial and space based platforms, whether manned or unmanned to collect secret, precise and timely intelligence of relevance to national security and defence to undertake covert actions. It is a dual use technology. Its information and data mainly geographical and meteorological are being used in various civilian and developmental arenas also.

The twentieth century was the century of scientific revolution. It was the era in which 90 per cent of the science has really occurred. The invention of airplane by Wright Brothers in 1902 provided a great impetus to the emergence of modern aerial photography (Remote Sensing). Since then, the science of photogrammetry and art of photo-interpretation has developed exponentially with the development in instrumentation, camera and films. Space remote sensing activities started in the decade of fifties. The usefulness of images for mapping and other application increased in 1960, with the launching of the first US meteorological satellite TIROS-1. Orbiting satellites images are capable of providing quantitative as well as qualitative information about objects. Today, aerospace remote sensing affords a practical means for frequent and accurate monitoring of the Earth's resources, encompasses all information on or below the Earth.

Remote sensing data (aerial and satellite images) provide a permanent record of topographical features of the area. One can identify mail boxes and lamp posts with the help of their shadows in aerial photographs taken from a height of 3000 m. Development in space technology has greatly enhanced the capabilities of remote sensing, mainly because of its synoptic and repetitive coverage, to gather real-time information.

The art and science of aerospace remote sensing has undergone significant changes since second world war, transforming the very nature of combat. Military forces have benefited hugely by aerospace remote sensing activities in the past decades to meet their longstanding reconnaissance, surveillance and target acquisition requirements. The use of electromagnetic spectrum has added a new dimension to warfare, which infuses the entire battlefield. Though aerospace remote sensing by itself is no longer a secret, its fast expanding frontiers continue to be one of the best kept secrets even today. Various countries have established a separate national surveillance center for managing various activities under their aerospace remote-sensing programme.

In 2004 Russia launched 23 satellites, which was more than any other country. Eleven of these satellites are for military use.[1] Russia currently has about one hundred of these satellites orbiting the Earth. Nowadays satellites are essential to the national security. Military considerations have always been one of the main reasons for the exploration and use of space.

Due to the development in field of long range precision guided weapons the depth of the battlefield is increasing day by day. C_4ISR (Command, Control, Communication, Computer—Intelligence, Surveillance and Reconnaissance) capability has now become the main weapon of warfare.[2] The increasing depth of the battlefield will need for corresponding increase in C_4ISR capabilities to be in a position to manage the battle in future. The linear characteristics of the battlefield have now became useless and outdated due to advancement in the field of aerospace remote sensing and long range precision weapons. Now aerospace remote sensing has become the first line of defence because of its real time information gathering characteristics.

All secret intelligence collection whether it is HUMINT, ELEINT or SININT is the result of penetration. Penetration through technical means (aerial or space) for the collection of various information (photo or images) is an important component of all intelligence collection operation. After space, aerospace is the only medium through which one can penetrate into the area of enemy or neighboring countries to collect various types of information spatial or non-spatial. These informations are necessary for strategic level planning and for tactical advancement. These aerospace remote sensing techniques have amply proved their usefulness in the post-Cold War period operations such as—Gulf War 1991, Kosovo War 1995, Afghanistan War 2002 and Gulf War 2003.[3]

India's security interests in this region call for equipping the armed forces with such aerospace state-of-the-art technological remote sensing platforms to keep an eye on the hostile activities on its periphery. The two traditional rival neighbours, Pakistan and China, are allies and both are boosting their military intelligence, surveillance and reconnaissance capability while fielding increasing number of missiles and modern fighters.

Modern Aerospace Remote Sensing Platforms

Platforms play an important role in remote sensing data acquisition. It may be air-borne, space-borne and ground based, depending upon the objects under surveillance or monitoring on earth surface. Air-borne platforms are normally an aircraft—manned or unmanned and the data products are black and white and colored aerial photographs.[4] Space-borne platforms are generally satellites and data products are black and white images, false color composites (FCCs), computer compatible tapes, compact discs, etc. Various types of satellites are orbiting in the space for different missions.

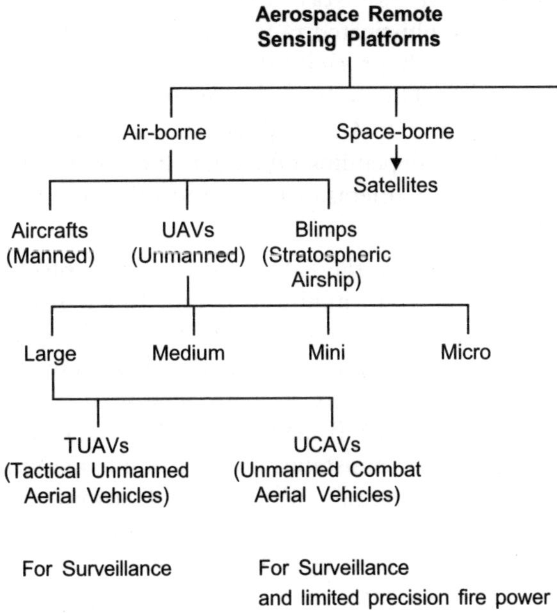

Modern air-borne platforms are unmanned aerial vehicles (UAVs). A large number of various types of UAVs were used in post cold war conflicts by the western countries. The British army used Phoenix-UAVs during operation of Iraq 2003. Whereas Global Hawk, Pioneer, Shadow, Hunter and Predator UAVs were used by US forces in this campaign.[5] During Gulf War in 2003 UAVs were put to work in the hunt for Iraqi leaders and missile launchers.

In Afghanistan operation, barely a dozen UAVs launched 115 Hellfire missiles and laser-designated 525 targets for manned aircrafts to destroy. But in Iraq, where the US deployed a whopping 56 larger UAVs and more than 60 portable ones, UAVs launched 62 Hellfires and designated 146 targets.[6] Until now, the only UAV that the Pentagon has openly stated to be armed with any type of projectile in combat is the Predator UAV, built by General Atomics, San Diego, which has launched Hellfire and Stringer missiles in Afghanistan and Iraq.[7] Clearly UAVs are a permanent part of the US military forces.

The US-based company, Startcom International LLC has developed blimps, that can stay airborne indefinitely at 70,000 feet, carrying sophisticated radar and cameras. It was a 'Stratospheric Airship' (a huge sack filled with helium, an inert gas lighter than air). The helium keeps it afloat, and a combination of solar and fuel cells power it. The blimp can carry 907 kg to 5440 kg, depending on its size. It can carry high-resolution multi-spectral cameras, sensors and other electronic remote sensing devices.[8]

On the basis of their size the UAVs are classified into four categories, i.e. large, medium, mini and micro. Israeli Aircraft Industries (IAI) has developed a supersize, highest flying and long endurance UAV called 'Eitan' (strength). This new UAV has a take-off weight of 4 tons. Its 26 metre wingspan is nearly three times the size of searcher II medium size UAV and it will take off and land without assistance from ground operators, according to an official Israeli military publication.[9] Two lightweight mini naval systems—the US Marine corps 'Dragon Eye' and 'Silver Fox' made their operational debuts in the skies above Iraq. Although researchers are even now striving for much smaller UAVs, the 5 pound "Dragon Lady" is among the smallest in current use.[10]

UAVs payloads are camera, sensor, radar and low level video-camera allowing live transmission of imagery. Smaller micro UAVs (low budget and low tech) are also very useful for battlefield surveillance task. Besides their obvious military uses, UAVs have found application in a variety of civilian uses such as mapping, detection of forest fires, spraying fertilizer, and monitoring roads, nuclear plants and high speed trains. It is hardly surprising that there are currently more than 300 UAVs programmes underway in around 40 countries. Israel has reached a high degree of expertise and marketing sophistication in UAVs.[11]

Airborne-AWACs and JSTAR has become an essential force multiplier, is rightly considered an integral part of any modern powerful airforce. These modern early warning platforms can detect an airspace intrusion at 300 kilometres distance covering of 360 degrees deep within the enemy's territory giving enough time to the air defence commanders to initiate necessary counter measures. These platforms are capable enough to undertake a whole spectrum of tasks including airspace surveillance, airspace management, search and rescue, coastal surveillance, electronic intelligence gathering and the most important of all multi aircraft strike coordination. Only a handful of countries have these airborne platforms.

India's Capability

India has developed both aerial and satellite remote sensing capabilities for national security. Here, aerial photography have been in use since 1920 for aerial survey and for producing topographic maps. The authorized official agency for carrying out fresh aerial photography and providing reprints for India is the Surveyor General of India and Director Survey (Air). Three flying agencies—Indian Air Force, Air Survey Company—Dum-Dum, Kolkata and NRSA, Hyderabad are there in India for aerial photography. They are using four old type of aircraft—Dakota, Avro, Cessna and Canberra. India has not even a single high altitude manned sky planes and modern AWACs plane.

To improve its field surveillance capability, India has purchased more than 100 UAVs, mostly from Israel since 1995. The buying programmes began after the 1999 Kargil War, when the military was not able to track Pakistan-backed fighters in the high altitude combat zone.[12] According to military sources India will need 200 additional UAVs in the next three to five years for surveillance activities. According to them, these pilotless vehicles are the best way to track the enemy activities and forces from sky, in the absence of airborne-warning planes. The Indian MOD is pursuing various options under a strategic decision to increase the use of UAVs in many areas of the armed forces.

Israel Aircraft Industries has supplied the Indian armed forces the Heron and Searcher II systems under contracts worth $ 300 million.[13] The searcher II UAV has been operational with the Israeli Air Force since 1992. It has a wingspan of 28 feet and is designed to carry a 220 pound payload for upto 15 hours at altitude of 20,000 feet. It is equipped with autonomous return mode activation on data link loss.[14] The Heron long range UAV has a wingspan of 55 feet and can carry a payload of upto 500 pounds for upto 40 hours at a maximum altitude of 30,000 feet. India wants to co-produce this UAVs by technology transfer.[15] Israel is currently India's sole source for UAVs.

India's own indigenously UAV (Nishant) development programme is being carried out successfully by DRDO and Aeronautical Development Establishment, Bangalore. Its trial schedule has been completed and limited production is going to start in December 5. It can fly at an altitude of 12,000 feet, has an endurance of 4-5 hours and a range of 100 kilometres. It can carry a 45 kilogram payload.[16] It can detect humans at 2-5 km, trucks at 5 km and building at 12 km, flying at speeds of 150 km per hour.[17] The DRDO is working on increasing its endurance and on multi-spectral stealth materials. The armed forces would use it for target acquisition. India is poised to increase its UAVs fleet in near future. India and Israel have entered into a new phase of partnership to develop three new UAVs—Rustam, Pawan and Gagan.[18] Israel's Aeronautics Defence Systems displayed its advanced UAV system—Dominator, Aerolight, Aerostar and Orbiter UAVs at Aero India Air Show 05.[19]

India's own airborne early warning and surveillance system, which was being developed by DRDO but left apart in January 1999, when the aircraft it was mounted was crashed. India's hard quest for an indigenously developed AWACs turned out to be an utter failure.[20] India is looking to revive its own $ 400 million AWACs project again. According to DRDO Chief V.K. Atre, India has begun talks with Israel about joint production of the Mini-AWACs.[21] After five years, government (CCS) has finally approved the DRDO's AWACs project and sanctioned 1800 crores for the project. The time allotted for this project is seven years. DRDO and Indian Air Force will jointly work for this project.[22]

A trilateral deal had been signed on October 10, 2003, for the US $ 1 billion for three Phalcon system among India, Israel and Russia, with Moscow supplying the IL-76 (Ilyushin) aircraft on which it is to be mounted. Deliveries are scheduled to begin in 2007. Phalcon system will be used for tactical surveillance of airborne targets and collection of ELINT data.[23]

The Phalcon system comprises four sensors, radars, IFF, ESM and communication intelligence, all controlled by a central computer that performs all system level functions, including sensor data integration, tracking data processing, threat identification and assessment, data link processing and display functions for a consistent and accurate picture of the tactical situation.[24] By this system India will be capable of carrying out surveillance sweeps for hundreds of kilometres by day or night in any weather condition. It is India's long awaited dream. In Asia only four countries—China, Singapore, Japan and Taiwan have this Phalcon system.

The US is also pushing India for the sale of the P-3C Orion maritime surveillance aircraft. It can play an important role in long range surveillance and network centric warfare missions. It will be one of the key force multipliers in the modern war scenario. India is also interested in US Hawkeye 2000 airborne early warning and battle management command and control system. With a powerful and highly automated target detection and tracking capability the Hawkeye 2000 has the ability to manage peacetime crisis and wartime operations.[25]

In the field of space remote sensing, India is the sixth country in the world to have the best remote sensing satellites. The Indian space remote sensing programme was initiated in 1970. Since then, the country has crossed many a major milestones. Under remote sensing programme eleven IRS satellites have been launched since 1989. The most significant features of IRS is that it makes possible repeated survey of vast areas in a very short time even when the area is otherwise inaccessible. The repeated coverage of IRS-P_4 is 2 days. IRS-IC, P_3, 1D and P_4 are still working and providing valuable data and imageries. Data from the IRS-IC and ID has become available to the whole world through EOSAT (Earth Observation Satellite Company) of the US. German company 'Euromap' has taken acquisition, archiving and distribution rights for Europe through EOSAT.[26] The

National Remote Sensing Agency (NRSA), Hyderabad under the Department of Space, which is working under the Ministry of Defence is mainly responsible for acquisition, processing and dissemination of satellite/aerial data and training the personnel in various application techniques. Indian armed forces are also using these data, aerial photo and imageries in various fields.

Lessons from the Kargil war made India review its aerospace remote sensing capability. ISRO started a programme to develop and acquire high resolution imaging satellite with one metre resolution sensor and synthetic aperture radars to see through clouds and infrared sights for night vision. Following the December 1999 lifting of US sanctions against India, it became possible to acquire some components for this project from the US and Israeli companies. Without any delay ISRO successfully launched its first military satellite 'TES' (Technical Experimentation Satellite) into the low-earth-orbit about 450 km above the earth in October 2001. Now data from one meter resolution TES is being used by the Indian security forces. To supplement the 'TES' image, India has approached Israel with a request for 'Ofeq-5' data.[27] The 'TES' is suited for a general identification of Pakistan's gun areas, helipads, logistics areas and even ballistic missile sites.[28]

ISRO launched 'Cartosat-1' into the low-earth-orbit about 400 kilometres above the earth on May 5, 2005. 'Cartosat-1' (1560 kg) is the heaviest Indian remote sensing satellite. It has two panchromatic cameras on board. With a 2.5 metre spatial resolution it is capable of providing clear pictures of all Pakistani missile launch preparations but not their range. Determining their range and trajectory would require a network of tracking and telemetry stations. Cartosat-1 will provide stereo-pair images for the generation of digital terrain models, providing a new capability for mapping the country. ISRO is in the process of launching 'Cartosat-2' by the end of this year.

To end its dependency on American GPS-Navstar, India has expressed interest in taking a $ 345 million stake in European Union's 'Galileo', global navigation satellite system.[29] India is also ready to help complete the Russian 'Glonass', which has been limping along well below strength since the fall of the Soviet Union.

Conclusion and Suggestions

Aerospace remote sensing is a dual use technology. India has made a satisfactory progress in the field of aerospace remote sensing during the past decades and is trying to acquire state-of-the-art electronic systems to make it more effective and meaningful. In view of India's threat perceptions, it is necessary for India to maintain technological edge over her traditional rivals. Indigenous development in this field is necessary because one cannot be fully dependent on other nation for aerospace data and imagery. The reason is that, at present anyone can purchase space imagery, but by the time it is received, it is likely to be several weeks old. While real time information is needed to strengthen C_4ISR capability, modern forces are working on real time intelligence and information. These systems can also be used in managing various types of natural and man-made disasters. The Indian Navy created history on December 29, 2004, by probably being the first to use land-based UAVs (8 Searcher II and 4 Herons) from its naval base in Kochi to find both displaced people as well as dead bodies.[30]

India has maintained the fourth largest army, fifth largest airforce and the seventh largest navy in the world. It is also working hard to develop network centric warfare capability. It will need more development in the field of C4 ISR. Aerospace remote sensing will remain the core element for future development and war. The existing systems must be continuously upgraded to make it more powerful. Greater emphasis should be on UAVs and high-resolution satellites. These can also be enormously used in border management and low-intensity conflicts.

Keeping in view India's growing regional responsibilities and challenges in the first quarter of this century and conceptualizing the security needs the following measures should be adopted to strengthen the notion of national security:

1. Formation of National Surveillance Command (NSC) or National Reconnaissance Command (NRO) with emphasis on including new network of surveillance.
2. Indigenous development of small high resolution satellites, UAVs and electronic payloads should be

initiated on a massive scale to cater the future growing needs.

3. Focussed systematic attempts should be made to acquire a meaningful stake in the European Union's Galileo GPS system so that clear, precise and accurate information can be obtained.
4. Mini AWACs system should be developed within the first decade of this century.
5. The Government should frame a regulatory licensing policy for commercial satellite operators to tap the international market of satellite data and imageries.

NOTES AND REFERENCES

1. Ria Novosti, May 2005.
2. Due to their advanced C4 ISR Capabilities the U.S. forces has won the Gulf war 1991 in 41 days and Gulf war Second 'Operation Iraqi Freedom' in three weeks time.
3. During Iraq War, a total of 1801 Combat aircraft were fielded by the USA, Australia and the UK from March 19 to April 18, 2003. The largest subset of aircraft within this was dedicated to intelligence, surveillance and reconnaissance (ISR) activities. The coalition forces also fielded 80 ISR dedicated platforms in support of their operation. Collectively, these aircrafts are reported to have completed 1000 ISR sorties, and as a result, generated 42,000 battlefield images, 3200 hours of full motion video, 2400 hours signal intelligence (SIGINT) coverage, and 1700 hours of Moving Target Indicator Radar Imagery. Pairs of 'Rivet Joint' aircrafts were used to accurately locate moving targets, such as surface to surface missiles and SAM launchers.

   NCW in the context of 'Operation Iraqi Freedom', Shitanshu Mishra, Strategic Analysis, Oct.-Dec. 2003, Vol. 27, No. 4, p. 555.
4. The US – U_2 (Lockheed Martin fly at altitude 70,000 feet) was the first modern sky plane of which was first flew in 1955. After many modern upgrades, it collected 88 per cent of all battlefield imagery during operation Iraqi Freedom 03. Defence Week, Sept. 22, 2003.
5. Defence News, December 15, 2003. In Afghanistan and Iraq Global Hawk, marks a new era in aerial surveillance, flying hundred of hours over hostile territory, thousands of miles away from its operators without leaving any foot print in theatre of operation from its base in an undisclosed Middle East country. The Iraqi soldiers probably had never heard of Global Hawk. Its high-power cameras of synthetic aperture radar can see targets through the thickest sandstorm. But they were sure something was up in the sky watching them—and that something,

whatever it was, could command their deaths. Defence News, Sept. 22, 2003.

6. Strategic Digest, IDSA, New Delhi, Feb. 04, p. 267.

   In an early 2003 presentation to an international aerospace conference in India, Ovadia Harari, IAI's Chief operating officer noted that UAVs in the near future would be capable of performing attack missions in addition to reconnaissance missions. Typical mission for future UAVs would include all-weather 24 hour reconnaissance and sensor fusion, immediate transfer of information to war fighters weapon system platforms; direct attack on targets and the supply of battle damage assessments. Defence News, May 3, 2004.
7. No. 2, November 3, 2003.
8. *The Hindu*, New Delhi, June 14, 2004.
9. No. 2, May 3, 2004.
10. No. 3, November 2003, p. 1274.
11. *Frontline*, March 11, 2005, p. 133.
12. No. 2, January 12, 2004.
13. Flight International, January 7 – Feb. 2, 2004.
14. 'Application of Unmanned Combat Aerial Vehicles in Future Battles of the Subcontinent', C.N. Ghosh, Strategic Analysis, July 2001, Vol. XXV No. 4, p. 611.
15. No. 2.
16. No. 2, January 24, 2005.
17. *The Hindu*, New Delhi, June 14, 2004.
18. No. 2, February 28, 2005.
19. No. 10, March 22-28, 2005. *Frontline*, March 11, 2005, p. 133.
20. DRDO after spending more than 100 crores had designed radar, high power transmitter antenna, signal and radar data processors and installed the same on a HAL assembled HS748 Avroplane. The defence scientists were in the process of testing the efficiency of the system and in course of one of the testing sorties the aircraft plummeted down to the earth in January 1999, killing all personnel on board and destroying the sophisticated equipments.
21. Aviation Week and Space Technology, April 19, 2004.
22. *Times of India*, LKO, September 15, 2004.
23. No. 10, March 9-15, 2004.
24. Sengupta Prasunk, *Deal for Phalcon Inked Force*, May 2004, p. 38.
25. 'A Display of Air Power' Ravi Sharma, *Frontline*, March 11, 2005, p. 133.
26. *Strategic Digest*, IDSA, New Delhi, August 1997, p. 1285.
27. No. 10, Feb. 17-23, 2004.

Israeli 'Ofeq-5' satellite can cover an area of 500 kilometres and take high resolution panchromatic pictures of an area 12.5 by 12.5 kilometres, at a resolution of 1.8 metres.

Defence News, April 4, 2005.

28. Force, May 2004, p. 18.
29. No. 10, Nov. 11-17, 2003.
30. **No. 18**, p. 55.

ABBREVIATIONS

AWACs	–	Airborne Warning and Control System.
JSTARs	–	Joint Surveillance and Target Attack Radar Systems.
C_4 ISR	–	Command, Control, Communication, Computers—Intelligence, Surveillance and Reconnaissance.
UAVs	–	Unmanned Aerial Vehicles.

12

India's Geopolitical Environment

A.K. Trikha

Introduction

Shorn of academic dressing, geopolitical environment of a country may be viewed as the external environment in which it has to pursue its national interests. Global reach of jet age transportation, high speed space age communication networks, internet, intercontinental range weapon systems and a multitude of other phenomenon of the modern age have so fused man's functional space that national or international boundaries no longer divide or restrict humanity the same way as even a few decades ago. In today's interconnected world, there are any number of sources, players, factors and events, the seamless interplay of which creates the ocean of our environment. Indeed, it is no cliché that any matter of significance anywhere in the world tends to create a global resonance. Power and reach of the media has heightened public awareness of issues, which not too long ago would have been considered remote and inconsequential. Witness how environment, human rights, corruption in high places has come to occupy the centerstage of our perceptions and what a compelling role they have assumed in matters of public policy, shaping national and even international agendas. Societies and nations have thus become conscious of a vast number of issues, each of which has an impact on their perception of the state of their well-being. However notwithstanding the vast and growing spectrum of interests and concerns, which engage all nations, at the core there still remains an irreducible minimum which a nation must pursue at all costs to survive and prosper. India's most vital and fundamental interest may be identified as "Rapid economic growth" to lift its teeming millions out of abject poverty. This is not only a moral imperative but also a critical precondition for continued stability of the nation. All efforts of the Indian state must be directly or indirectly concentrated towards this objective. To be able to pursue this purpose single-mindedly, it needs a favorable international environment, which ensures peace and tranquility on its borders, and facilitates pursuit of vigorous economic activity without any hindrance.

Is India's current geopolitical environment conducive to vigorous pursuit of her vital interests? What road blocks if any, stymied her quest in the past and what the future portends—are some of the questions which this paper would seek to address.

Cold War

To most observers, India's current geopolitical environment appears to be more benign than ever in its history since independence. Indeed objective scrutiny would tend to bear this out to a large extent. Looking back, our troubles started almost as soon as the colonial rulers departed our shores. India's independence created an intractable neighbour on its borders with whom it was at war almost immediately. On a larger canvas, the consensus which the big powers had forged to fight Nazi Germany unraveled very quickly after the War, and the world found itself divided into two opposing ideological camps, each committed to eliminating the other. India believed that it could insulate itself from the debilitating effects of the Cold War by declaring herself non-aligned. It appropriated the right to judge each issue on its own merit without the precoloration of bloc politics. By staying out of power blocs, it felt elevated to a high moral perch from where it could preach ethics of international behavior to all nations constituting the Western alliance, led by the United States were in no mood to being preached at a time when they saw themselves engaged in a mortal struggle against communism. Their attitude was summed up succinctly by John Foster Dulles (US Secretary of State to President Eisenhower) who pronounced non-alignment espoused by India as immoral. As events were to unfold, non-alignment acquired a distinct bad odour. India's credibility as champion of non-alignment didn't earn her any spurs when she failed to criticize Soviet Union's invasions of Czechoslovakia and Afghanistan, and allowed Cuba membership of the 'Non-aligned Club' even though it was firmly in the Soviet embrace. Non-alignment in fact began to appear synonymous with opposition of the United States on virtually every major issue of the day. Thus a perception took root that even if India was formally not part of an alliance, its sympathies certainly lay with the Soviet bloc. Pakistan, on the other hand, always on the lookout to humble India, was soon gathered in an anti-Soviet alliance. This opened the doors to US largesse particularly in military hardware.

The world at this time was going through a period process of rapid decolonization, which resulted in emergence of many more new nations in Africa and Asia. India assumed leadership of this rag tag grouping under the banner of 'Third World.' Its self-assumed championship of the third world propelled it to take many sterile, and unproductive positions in the international fora which helped neither its image nor any of its numerous causes. In 1962, the Chinese whom we had courted as 'Bhai-Bhai' slid down the Himalayan slopes and left us licking our wounds in humiliation. Even the Western powers, which were so keen to enlist any one in their anti-communist crusade refused to extend any meaningful help. We had no friend of any significance anywhere. Our pathetic weakness and isolation emboldened Pakistan in 1965 to go to war in a bid to wrest Kashmir by force. While that attempt failed, India now had two implacable enemies in collusion. In 1971, as the Bangladesh crisis was coming to a head, the situation became so precarious that we were left with no choice but to accept the Soviet embrace. As history was to unfold, Pakistan broke up under the weight of its own contradiction. With a little nudge from India, its Eastern wing became Bangladesh. Usually, liberation from an oppressive regime should have been a cause celebre and India should have been applauded and automatically supported by the free world. But logic of cold war was such that while China was making ominous noises in the North, US served an ultimatum backed by the seventh fleet sailing up the Bay of Bengal. That was a close call and if countervailing Soviet power had not been disposed in

India's favor, history might have been written differently. India had learnt its lesson. In 1974 it surprised the world by exploding a nuclear device, as a result of which its isolation from the western world became even more intense. Sanctions were imposed and all co-operation in the field of nuclear energy was withdrawn. India braved with the sanctions stoically.

In 1979, Soviet Union invaded Afghanistan and started a new chain of events. Sensing a historical opportunity of destroying its mortal foe, US pulled out all stops. Overnight Pakistan became a front line state for the fight against the Soviets and US arms began pouring in. Pakistan invoked *Jehad* and opened scores of training camps to indoctrinate recruits in Islamic fundamentalist ideology and train them in guerilla warfare. Pakistan's ISI became the nodal agency for funneling of arms and funds to the Mujaheedeen forces fighting in Afghanistan. In the prevailing 'any thing goes" environment created to fight the mighty Soviets, ISI was quick to exploit every available opportunity including the rich pickings from the abundant poppy crop of Afghanistan. Flush with narco funds, weapons and a continuous stream of fanatic, die-hard *jehadis* graduating from innumerable Madrassas, ISI grew into a powerful entity—virtually a state within a state—with little accountability to any legitimately constituted political authority. By the late eighties Soviet Union, the mighty super-power was laid low which began the process of its disintegration. Pakistan buoyed by the victory it had engineered and flush with weapons obtained both legitimately as well as stolen, now decided to turn its army of *Jehadis* against India in Kashmir. India had barely got a grip on the Pakistan abetted militancy in Punjab, when insurgency in Kashmir blew up.

By the beginning of the last decade of the 20th century, India was also flat broke. By following a strategy of import substitution led industrial growth; it had isolated itself from the Global trading system. In 1991, its foreign exchange reserves were scraping the bottom of the barrel. With barely a billion dollars in reserve, it had to suffer the ignominy of having to dispatch its gold reserves to London as a hedge against default on debt repayments. Soviet Union, its erstwhile friend and main arms supplier was in its death throes. Insurgency in Kashmir was picking up strength alarmingly. And India had no one to turn to. A bleaker security scenario is difficult to imagine.

Post-Cold War Period—Decade of the Nineties

Subtle changes started occurring with the end of the Cold War. With the meltdown of the Soviet Union, the main bone of contention between India and the West (US) disappeared. While Indian political class as a whole continued to lament the loss of a trusted friend, government of the day was quick to grasp the reality and began to trim its sail with the new winds. At the same time, India took the long leap of faith and shed the socialist baggage of the past four decades, decided to start dismantling state controls and open up the economy to market forces. This initiative had a dramatic impact. On the one hand it shook the Indian industrial enterprise out of its slumber (induced by protected markets) and forced it to compete in the global marketplace, and on the other it showcased to the outside world the enormous potential of the Indian market. Although the processes started nearly 15 years ago have yet to run their full course, yet their impact has been transformational. Liberalization and integration with the world economic system has begun to bear fruit. Exposure to the world markets has improved competitiveness of Indian exports. The liberalized economic regime is attracting foreign investments at a healthy rate. The Balance-of-Payments position, which was so precarious just over a decade ago, looks distinctly healthy and India is sitting on a pot of gold worth about $ 150 billion. With the economy growing at a steady 7% or so, global footprint in the IT and IT-enabled services sectors, there is a distinct sense of optimism permeating the Indian atmosphere. India is being noticed on the world stage.

Impressive as the ongoing economic transformation is, the change in India's geo-strategic environment is even more remarkable. Demise of the Soviet Union deprived India of a veto wielding power in the United Nations Security Council, ended a highly favorable arms transfer relationship which had enabled India to maintain a modern military and virtually insulated it against Chinese blackmail. United States was quick to grasp the emerging possibilities. It was now the sole superpower and undisputed champion of the free world. Soviet Union's passage into history had unhinged a potentially powerful regional player in India. Its sheer size, population, geographical location, and economic possibilities invested it with huge power potential. Coupled to these attributes, it was also a functioning democracy, which could make it a useful ally in maintaining regional stability. The first initiative came soon after the first Gulf War in 1991 in the form of 'Kickleighter Proposals.' The proposals from General Claude Kickleighter, CINCPAC suggested enhanced military cooperation through joint seminars, training and establishment of service steering committees. The two countries engaged in Malabar series of naval exercises. Some rudimentary army and special forces exercises were also undertaken. However, perhaps due to lingering suspicions, each side was reluctant to reveal its hand, and thus the anticipated momentum failed to materialize. Indian Shakti tests in 1998 sent the just budding relationship into a total freeze.

9/11 and its Aftermath

Events of 9/11 were to change the entire chemistry of the relationship. India's swift response in offering unconditional support to the US-led war on terrorism, set the scene for fast paced developments which have been underway since then. United States and India are now engaged in forging a close strategic relationship. The scale of change has been truly remarkable—as aptly summed up by US Under Secretary of State for Political Affairs Nicholas Burns when he wrote "The United States and India are implementing habits of cooperation that characterize US relations with our closest friends and allies." Even a few years ago, such a sentiment would have been unthinkable. In June 2005, the two governments signed a new framework for the US-India defense relationship for the next 10 years. Under the new dispensation, United States has not only indicated its willingness to give India access to the latest in high technology weapon systems but also agreed to consider technology transfers, co-production and joint marketing. Thus if Indian Air Force selects F-16 or F-18 as its fighter of choice, no separate authorizations may be required from the US Government for the related technology transfer. Besides the obvious advantage that such technology transfers would nudge the Indian aviation industry into the next generation, they would also serve as a hedge against arbitrary interruptions such as experienced in the past due to stoppage of essential spares for the Harrier jump jet, Sea King helicopters or contracted services/assemblies for the LCA programme. United States is a generation ahead in cutting edge areas of defense electronics, avionics, satellites and advanced sensors. By allowing access to these technologies, the existing restrictions on dual use technologies would also automatically stand diluted.

In July 2005, Prime Minister Manmohan Singh visited the US, and addressed a joint session of the US Congress (a rare honor reserved for only the closest friends). During this visit, a number of areas of co-operation were identified and mechanisms set in motion towards realizing them. However, by far the most significant outcome of the visit was US commitment to allow India access to advanced nuclear technology for power generation. This would not only benefit our fledgling nuclear energy programme immensely, but also obliquely give us *de facto* recognition as a nuclear weapon state. This reversal of policy of 30 years standing could not have come about without a very serious consideration of costs and benefits. Non-proliferation sentiment in the US Congress particularly in light of the ongoing disagreements with Iran and North Korea over the nuclear issue is still very strong. Therefore, for the President to commit to obtain waiver for India meant risking a considerable amount of political capital, particularly in view of the growing difficulties of the administration's position on Iraq. US will also have to work hard with the 'Nuclear Supplier's Group' both to bring them on board with respect to India as also to plug any openings which this waiver might seem to encourage.

Why did the US do India this favor? It would be naïve to believe that motivation behind the changed attitude of the US towards India is driven by anything but perception of its own interests. While there may be a grain of truth in their being some common ground between the world's largest and the world's most powerful democracy, it cannot constitute sufficient basis to build policy. Instead if one were to focus on what the United States interests in the region are, and what it might expect from India in furthering those interests the answer may stand out in clearer relief. Amongst others, the following factors could have steered the US policy in the new direction:

(a) India's growing power stature, its role as a stabilizing force in the region, and the value of it being disposed favorably towards the United States.

(b) Congruence between US and India's security concerns and US confidence in being able to address them more effectively if in partnership with a strong India.

(c) India's credibility as a responsible power, which can be relied upon to co-operate with the US in strengthening the nuclear non-proliferation regime.

It has also been argued quite convincingly that the real motivation behind America's decision to assist India in building up its strength is to create a counterweight to the growing power of China. However, be it as it may, after five decades of a cold, indifferent (if not outright hostile) relationship, being on the right side of the sole hyper-power at the beginning of the new millennium certainly brightens our geopolitical landscape considerably.

Relations with Neighbours

Relations with our immediate and rancorous neighbours, if not mended, are at least quiet and there is a glimmer of hope that co-existence in harmony may one day become possible. Pakistan, with whom we have the most difficulty, is currently engaged with us in cobbling together a peace process. While potential of a sudden mishap remains high, yet slowly and haltingly the process is moving forward. Terrorism, inspired and abetted from across the border has bedeviled Indo-Pak relations for over decade and a half. So far as we are concerned, it still remains the principal stumbling block. However, there may be some comfort in the fact that the number of incidents and their ferocity appears somewhat reduced. Likewise while cross-border infiltration hasn't ended altogether, the numbers coming across appears much reduced. If one were to take them as straws in the wind, there is reason to be cautiously optimistic of the future. An encouraging aspect of the current peace process (or Composite Dialogue—as the officialdom would put it) is that it is being driven as much by 'people to people' engagement as by governmental processes. Atmospherics or the 'feel good factor' spawned by increasing 'people to people' contact is beginning to acquire a dynamic and momentum of its own and since it is largely based on discovery of common interests, and hard nosed calculation of day-to-day benefits, the process is likely to prove more resilient and difficult to reverse. For example, having opened the long dormant cross-border transport links to facilitate reunion of families, reversing the clock would not be as easy. It may be too early to estimate the degree of impact definitively, but it is likely that as the population of stakeholders in the peace process increases, chances of it getting more and more firmly embedded and getting less accident-prone would also increase. People of Pakistan are India's real constituency. For too long they have lived in a closed system being fed a diet of hate by the ruling class and the Mullahs largely to serve their own ends. India has been the favourite whipping horse to flog for all seasons. Consequently perceptions have hardened and preconceived notions tend to drive the agenda. Government of India, the many organs of the Indian state and even NGOs have not invested sufficient effort and energy in trying to influence the Pakistani population of the merits of a free and open society and the benefits of which can accrue with synergy between two free, open democratic societies. Hitherto India has not demonstrated adequate appreciation of its own 'soft power' and hence this considerable asset of national power has not been invested with any great purpose. Government of India has demonstrated good grasp of this shortcoming and has thus made 'people to people' contact the centerpiece of its strategy of confidence building measures. Relaxation of controls on travel, and the accompanying exposure to reality has come to most people from across the border as a pleasant surprise. If this process is allowed to go its logical way, gradually the many miscued perceptions congealed over the past 60 years, would start melting away. As a matter of abundant caution, it is also being careful to keep the process within the comfort zone of the many influential doubting Thomases on either side of the border. Indian government's actions in his regard when the recent earthquake devastated parts of PoK are illustrative. As would behove a good neighbour, India responded generously with relief material. It was also quick to agree to Gen. Musharraf's proposal to permit people from both sides to traverse the LoC to lend a helping hand to the people in distress. Though largely symbolic, an Indian army border post lent a hand with digging tools, etc. to assist a Pak post opposite destroyed by the trembler. Pakistan's main need was of more helicopters to reach the many remote areas isolated due to collapse of surface communications. Despite its own preoccupation with relief (in which helicopters are always a scarce resource), Indian Government did offer helicopter assistance. Pakistan did not accept it. Perhaps it was too long a leap in one go. Public visibility of Indian armed forces helicopters hovering in PoK skies would have been perhaps too evocative to handle. Not intending to make any political capital out of it, Indian Government played the whole affair very low key—which should have gone down well with people of Pakistan. Both Governments have permitted the local Heads of Governments at Muzaffarabad and Srinagar to publicly announce their desire for a cooperative and coordinated response to the natural disaster, which has overtaken the state. Such actions should help chip away the hard images of each other formed over several decades of mistrust. The scale of disaster in PoK was by far the greater and therefore Pakistan had a much more difficult task at hand. Notwithstanding this difference of scale that the two nations were confronted with, media applauded the swift response of the Indian Government. Indian Army came for special praise both for its efficiency in providing relief and for the deeply sympathetic attitude with which it approached the task. Pakistan army on the other hand was castigated for its flat-footed response. The point here is not of substance, but the perceptions it tends to foster and their impact on how the parties view of each other slowly begins to get transformed.

For some time now (perhaps for the first time since the early nineties) mainstream opinion in Pakistan appears to be veering round to the view that the strategy of terror adopted by the Pakistani state to settle the Kashmir issue has done it more harm than good. That is not to say that there is any erosion of belief in the Kashmir cause which Pakistan has espoused since its creation. But there is a sense that whereas the ongoing *Jehadi* war has not dented the Indian determination any to maintain the status quo, the culture of violence spawned by the Pakistani state has created havoc with its own society and undermined its societal structures. Further after 9/11 the thin, blurred line, which Pakistan attempted to draw between a freedom fighter and a terrorist has disappeared. There is a broad and growing consensus in the civilized world that it would not condone acts of violence against innocent civilians—no matter what the cause or provocation. Therefore, whatever limited legitimacy Pakistani encouragement of terrorism in the garb of 'fight for freedom' might have enjoyed in the past, it has now melted away. As a state, its credibility as votary of a stable international order has also taken a hard knock since the news of promiscuous proliferation of nuclear technology by Dr A.Q. Khan to the various pariah regimes broke. But for the strategic compulsion of co-opting the Pakistan state (through Gen. Musharraf) in its fight against Al Qaeda, US would have put Pakistan on the coals. However even while this marriage of convenience runs its course and Parvez Musharraf frequently applauded as a courageous man, there is no doubt that US has its sights trained both on the extremists as well as Pakistan's nuclear weapons. Having established a large, intrusive and long range presence in the country, US will do all it can to ensure that the enormous threat posed by nuclear terrorism is not allowed to come to pass.

United States has a huge stake in the stability of South Asian region. Any armed conflict between India and Pakistan has the potential of spinning out of control with unpredictable consequences. As of now US is fully committed in its global war against terrorism and would not like any dilution of attention by emergence of another crisis. It is also conscious of the destructive potential of the Kashmir issue, if extremist elements in Pakistan are allowed a free run. Therefore, it will do all it can within its powers to see that Kashmir is not allowed to boil over. Deferring to Indian sensitivities publicly, it has steadfastly refused to assume a mediating role in the dispute. But there is widespread belief that US is behind the scenes to keep the peace process moving. This unseen hand may or may not be responsible, but on the ground there is a definite perception of movement in the right direction. Consequently, it has become possible to put in place a number of 'confidence building measures' and more are on the anvil. In this context while visit of Hurriyat leadership to Pakistan and its talks with the Indian leadership may not amount to too much substance, symbolically they are significant events. Ceasefire on the border has been holding since November 2003 and generally the rhetoric emanating out of Islamabad has also distinctly mellowed.

With the Chinese, while resolution of the contentious border issue doesn't appear any closer, its salience in the context of our developing relationship appears much reduced. It is recognized that the boundary dispute is a legacy of history and thus demarcation of territory to the mutual satisfaction of both sides would take time. Both sides have agreed that confidence building measures in place would be continued and strengthened to keep the borders tension-free until the boundary dispute is finally settled. Going beyond the immediate border issue, an agreement to build a Strategic Co-operative Partnership for Peace and Prosperity was signed during the Chinese Prime Minister Wen Jiabao's visit to India in early 2005. India was invited to the Shanghai Co-operative Organization, driven mainly by China, Russia and other Central Asian States to discuss larger security issues in the region. India was also included in the East Asian Summit in December 2005 to discuss prospects of economic integration of the Asian region. It was a large grouping comprising ASEAN nations, China, South Korea, India, Japan and even New Zealand. If it succeeds in its ambitious agenda, its impact on the region's economies could be enormous. Bilateral trade between India and China is booming. Targets set for 2010 are likely to be met by 2008 and if the present rate of growth is sustained, India's trade with China will exceed trade between India and the US by 2006. It may not be unreasonable to hope that the burgeoning economic ties, coupled with joint/ coordinated approaches on issues of common interest would build a sufficiently strong constituency for peaceful resolution of the border problem even if sometimes in the distant future.

Future Prospects

While survey of India's current geo-strategic environment looks healthy, there is no assurance that the trajectory would remain the same. The international situation is highly fluid and there are several straws in the wind which portend the likelihood of change. United States, which has come to occupy such a salient space in India's geo-strategic landscape is deeply engaged in Iraq—a conflict on whose merits there is no political consensus in India. US had hoped that after removing Saddam Hussein, it would be able to initiate a political process which would culminate in installation of a secular, friendly and democratic regime in Baghdad which would protect its interests in the region. Success in Iraq was to be a harbinger of change in much of the Islamic world which the US perceives as the fountainhead of terrorism because of the absence of democratic political structures. However, for the time being at least, US plans to bring about this transformation seem to be mired in uncertainty. While a national election to form a duly elected Iraqi national government has been conducted successfully, intense insurgency continues to rage in Iraq—taking a terrible toll of Iraqi lives. US casualties are also mounting steadily and clamor to bring the troops home is finding increasing resonance in middle America. The undiminished mayhem on Iraqi streets, despite strong and repeated military actions to flush out militants, suggests that Americans are not succeeding in stabilizing Iraq. Iraqi forces on whose ability to fight insurgency, much hope had been invested, are nowhere near being up to the task. The force is heavily infiltrated by insurgents and even in sheer numbers, accretion of strength is nowhere near expectation. The irreconcilable differences amongst the main claimants to power and absence of any strong legitimate authority to mediate the differences could drag Iraq into a full-fledged civil war. Americans cannot leave Iraq in that state, no matter how vicious the internecine conflict gets. Such a move would seriously erode US credibility and put a question mark on its resolve to stick it out. A disintegrating Iraq would also become a major source of terrorism. Therefore leaving Iraq unless it is stable and friendly and capable of handling its own affairs, is not an option that the US can entertain. US forces are hence committed in Iraq for the long haul. US recognizes this and in fact current spending bill in the Congress includes $ 256 million for creation of permanent bases in Iraq. While insurgency shows no signs of abating, there are signs that US military is already quite stretched and hence as time goes by, its capacity and patience could run even thinner. Therefore it would like to use all its persuasive powers on friends and allies to bring them on board. India fits the bill for this mission admirably. With a million strong army, well-versed in anti-insurgency warfare from decades of experience, there is an asset in being which could be a very useful indeed. However, the fly in the ointment is that there would never be a political consensus in India to commit Indian troops in a war, seen as unjust by majority of the Indian population. So far India has resisted pressure on this account citing domestic security compulsions. However in a worsening situation, US demand could become more insistent, putting the relationship under strain.

Even without US troubles in Iraq spilling over to cast a shadow on Indo-US relations, there are other areas of fundamental disagreement. Many Indians are apprehensive of the designs of the neo-conservative power elite currently inhabiting the corridors of power in Washington. Their aggressive road map of ensuring US global dominance in the 21st century makes many in India very uneasy. US is seen to be engaged in open-ended conflicts which instead of stabilizing the world could be paving the way for even greater instability. While it is acknowledged universally that US military strength is unmatched in range and sophistication, it is still finite and more importantly of little use against the 'hit and run' *fedayeen* or suicide bombers. Terrorism, the major challenge facing the United States (and indeed the world) feeds on humiliation and hopelessness. By its very nature, terrorist groups are fragmented and the perpetrator of indiscriminate violence elusive. Therefore, while use of force is an essential tool in the fight against terrorism, reliance on military alone or even as the major foil to eradicate sources of terror, contains the seeds of aggravating the problem further. In the world as it is today, there are millions of people nursing grievances and identifying United States as a complicit factor in their real or imagined woes. Americans are culturally predisposed to seeking quick, unambiguous solutions—which in real world often don't exist. It is an open question whether the US has the necessary will, patience and political resources to stay the course for the long haul and win the war against global terrorism comprehensively which it has declared itself engaged in. Under the circumstances, how deeply it would get sucked in its unrelenting war on global terrorism and what its consequences would be is hard to predict.

History of our fragile relationship with Pakistan also commends caution. While the current scenario appears hopeful, as so often before, the situation could change quite suddenly and dramatically for the worse. Reasons for this pessimism in outlook are not far to seek because at the fundamental level, there has been no significant change in causes underlying the dissonance in Indo-Pak relations. The impulse of change has to be felt in Pakistan because the root of problems lies within the Pakistani society and its institutions. Unfortunately liberal politics in Pakistan has never had an opportunity to mature adequately, so that it could define Pakistan's nationhood in any terms other than anti-India or to be able to give to the general public a sense where its true interests lay. Whenever a legitimate political process began to take root, military stamped it out under its jackboots. It appropriated (and continues to possess) the exclusive right to define Pakistan's 'National Interests'—which invariably ensured its own pre-eminence in the affairs of the state. Consequently rather than evolving in to a secular, liberal, forward-looking model of its founder's vision, Pakistan has teetered on the brink of being a failed state. A deeply feudal society, out of step with modern social and political trends, infected with extremist ideologies of all hues, failing social indicators and either absence or weak/ineffective civic institutions incapable of imparting a positive impulse for change, is the unfortunate reality of today's Pakistan. It makes for a combustible recipe for radicalization of politics, which may threaten both Pakistan as well as the world around it.

Army is one of the few credible state institutions of Pakistan. It has been in power for much of the time since creation of the state. Even during the brief interludes of civilian governments, it has always sat right on top of the power structure. Therefore, it has always had and continues to have a commanding voice in all matters of war and peace. Given that reality, motivations behind Pakistan army's view of the desired direction of Indo-Pak relations becomes crucial. As it stands, the virus of Jihadi fundamentalism which infected the Pak army during the Zia regime is still alive and kicking amongst the many influential decision-makers. It is their life's mission to see India humbled one way or the other, which compels India never to lower its guard. Besides the historically derived, deep-seated animosity which motivates many in the Pak army, there are a number of other incentives too for the army brass to perpetuate the status quo. Firstly, keeping the Kashmir pot boiling legitimizes the bureaucratic primacy of the military. Also in its perception, it is pursuing a low cost strategy in Kashmir which helps to tie up many hundreds of thousands of Indian troops in counter insurgency grid in Kashmir. While these forces are only a minimal threat in Kashmir, their deployment in Punjab or Rajasthan could be far more menacing. Besides, it still nourishes the hope that by sustaining insurgency at a minimal cost, in the long run it would tire the Indian army out and resolve the Kashmir issue on favorable terms.

International community is becoming increasingly intolerant of terrorism as a tactic, irrespective of the motivations behind it. Pakistan is aware of it and President Musharraf has given repeated assurances in the international fora that he would not to allow terrorism from Pakistani soil. However, the uncomfortable truth is that the infrastructure of terrorism remains by and large intact right under the government's nose. Pakistan Government does not appear to be leaning on the terrorists half as hard as it would, if it were to be serious in its intent. Is the Pakistani state unwilling or unable to stand by its commitments? A charitable view would be that both could be partly true and partly false. Given the restive law and order environment, and the frequent sectarian wars on the one hand, and the intense US pressure to maintain the tempo of operations against Al Qaeda on the Western border areas on the other, Pakistan's ability to seriously curb all militant activity against India could be severely limited. Even more ominously for the Pakistani establishment, another general could be waiting in the wings, if a serious campaign is undertaken to root out anti-India militancy. Be it as it may, so far India is concerned, the threat remains in being, and therefore, every possibility remains that some band of desperados could execute (with or without government support) a large scale strike against a sensitive target—thus nullifying instantaneously years of painstaking efforts at confidence building.

Institutions of the state are weak in Pakistan and there are any number of fault-lines. Therefore, while there is appearance of calm and stability from the outside, the façade could crumble quite quickly as has often happened with dictatorial regimes. Any of these or several other unsavory realities of the Pakistani state, could surface rapidly which could not only send the ongoing peace-process in a tail spin but also plunge the region in a period of uncertainty.

Reversal of course in the relations with China is less likely but cannot be discounted altogether. It is argued that going by geography and power potential China and India are destined to be competitors for the same regional space. Over the past several years of border negotiations, both sides have taken care not to queer the pitch—but significant differences in perception remain. China is wary of the Islamic fundamentalist energy flow from Pakistan—lest the virus might infect its own restive Muslim minorities in the Sinkiang region. Nonetheless, it has continued to maintain close strategic links with that state (including in the crucial missile and nuclear field). The most likely purpose of this alliance is to keep India off-balance. China's scorching rate of economic growth has placed it firmly on the trajectory towards superpower status. Buoyed by self-confidence of achievement, it is bound to pursue aggressively what it perceives as its legitimate national interests. This would inevitably disturb the existing status quo and bring it in conflict with powers whose areas of influence are transgressed. The most likely challenge to the growing Chinese power would emanate from the US because of the global nature of her interests. Both US and China are aware of such a future and adjusting their respective stances in preparation for the forthcoming clash. Vis-à-vis India, China appears to have softened its stand on the border issue and is creating a stake by giving a strong impetus to mutually beneficial economic ties. On the other hand, United States is finally responding to India's aspiration to be a regional power. The remarkable depth which the Indo-US strategic relationship has reached in a short time could be an indication of the American intent to strengthen India as a hedge against Chinese influence in the region.

While China and Pakistan retain the potential to pose a military (including nuclear) threat to India, threat from the other neighbours, i.e. Nepal, Bangladesh, Myanmar and Sri Lanka arises on different counts. Apprehension of being swamped by a powerful neighbour sometimes motivates them to seek countervailing arrangements with other states. Dynamics of their domestic environments also influence much of their behavior. They face a number of problems of different varieties. Often, the powers that be find it convenient to ascribe own failures to difficulties created by India. Demagogy characterizes much of the region's politics, and is frequently used to whip up public frenzy which then has to be factored into formulation of policy. Except for Sri Lanka with which India does not share a land border, with the others the borders are long, sometimes ill defined and often they lie in very difficult terrain. Keeping an effective vigil is extremely difficult. Legacy of history has created populations with close societal and even family linkages on either side of the border. All factors combined create unique problems which tend to vitiate the environment. Mass illegal immigration from Bangladesh illustrates the point. Informed sources suggest that there could be as many 20 million illegal Bangladeshis in India. Most have settled in the North-Eastern states and drastically changed the demographic profiles of the region creating tremendous social tensions. The long, difficult and remote borders also render check on illegal trafficking in arms, narcotics and other contraband goods very difficult. This cocktail of factors has been exploited by hostile agencies to actively support insurgencies in India, thus diminishing its ability to concentrate on its vital task of nation building.

Although the cold war is history now, mutual suspicion between Moscow and Washington has not evaporated altogether. Historical experience of being ravaged by repeated invasions has conditioned Russia to seek security by promoting a number of buffer states on its periphery. This security architecture crumbled at the end of the Cold War. With steady expansion in Eastern Europe, NATO now sits within short striking distance from St. Petersburg. United States has also established large scale military presence abutting Russia's soft underbelly. As the rash of recent political events would suggest, Caucuses and the Central Asian Republics are politically very fragile. The region is generally remote and underdeveloped but has vast hydrocarbon wealth.

This combination of strategic location, underdevelopment and precious resources makes it a potential hotbed of competing interests. Russia is naturally extremely weary. What political coloration develops there would be of significant geo-strategic interest to India.

Besides the needs, aspirations and ambitions of states both within the region and extra regional powers whose power and influence impacts us, some other crucial components also comprise the mosaic of our strategic landscape. For India to occupy her rightful place in the comity of nations or indeed even for survival, brisk rate of economic growth is an absolute necessity. It constitutes our core national interest. Unfortunately India's energy scenario which is one of the prime movers of any modern industrial economy does not present a very rosy picture. Currently it imports 76% of oil and 20% of its gas consumption. Its meager oil production from domestic sources is declining while its demand is increasing annually by at least 6%. Gas production from its existing fields in the Krishna-Godavari basin will also begin to dwindle. In the absence of large scale hydrocarbon resources, it could have filled the gap to a large extent with nuclear power. In Asia, India was a pioneer in the field of nuclear energy. Had we succeeded in harnessing nuclear power more substantially, our dependence on imported crude oil would have reduced. As it stands the nuclear energy component is just 3.7% from 15 nuclear reactors with an installed capacity of 3310 MW. Although it has made several ambitious plans to increase nuclear power generation dramatically, but they haven't delivered on results. Hitherto several constraints have stood in the way of India's nuclear power generation ambitions. To begin with it did not have access to the currently in vogue technology of efficient power generation i.e. Pressurized Water Reactors (PWRs). Currently some 230 PWRs are in use worldwide. Secondly, its uranium reserves are limited and it does not have plants for enrichment from 1% U 235 found in nature to the 4% level required for PWRs. Now with the likely removal of restrictions on access to technology related to civilian nuclear energy, there is reason to hope that the planned target of 20,000 MW of nuclear energy by 2020 may be achieved. However, even if this target is reached, our dependence on import of hydrocarbons is likely to remain a major concern. Therefore, security of hydrocarbon sources and their safe passage to our shores is absolutely crucial to our economic well-being. While India has done a great deal to bolster her energy security, many uncertainties plague the energy scenario. On the one hand global demand for oil is increasing inexorably. On the other, many oil rich states are dogged by instability and their long-term futures remain cloudy. Consequently oil prices have already reached stratospheric levels and much worse is being predicted. Although, the world has absorbed the recent oil price hikes rather well, the long-term impact of unchecked increases is bound to impact growth adversely. Developing economies like India would be the worst sufferers because of diversion of enormous resources towards financing oil imports. Competition for this scarce and strategic resource is bound to create ripples in the geostrategic environment in the coming decades.

9/11 changed the world dramatically. US launched itself in a relentless war against terrorism—a crusade in whose pursuit, it has established a long-term physical presence in an arc stretching from Pakistan, Afghanistan through the Gulf (Iraq, Kuwait, Bahrain, Saudi Arabia, Yemen) into Central Asia. Physical presence of an extra regional power of the footprint such as of the United States is bound to shake triangles which have existed for so long. Political trends towards greater democratization of societies, would sooner or later shake the established power structures. Whether the process would be smooth and orderly or come about violently is an open question.

Of special interest to India is the ongoing turmoil related to Iran. India has deep historical ties with that country and now it is closely tied to its energy security. United States counts Iran amongst 'the axis of evil' and seems to have it in its sights. Consequently, Iran finds itself surrounded from all sides by an arch enemy with unmatchable military capability—an intolerable situation from its perspective. At the moment it appears weak and isolated on the right to its nuclear programme. However, it is too big and important a country and too proud a civilization either to surrender or to live with this humiliation forever. It is also rich in hydrocarbons for which the world is getting more and hungry. How the array of forces would finally align to end this dangerous stalemate would have a significant effect in sculpting the geo-strategic environment of the region.

Conclusion

As one surveys India's geo-strategic landscape halfway down the first decade of the 21st century, the outlook appears promising. The welcome change has come about partly because India chose to rid itself of some long cherished dogmas which had kept her grooved into what was derisively described as the 'Hindu Rate of Growth.' Shedding the burden of socialist baggage, in early nineties she chose to integrate with the global economies and allow market forces to drive her growth. The change has been dramatic. India has emerged on the world stage as one of the fastest growing economies. Simultaneously, it has also begun to look at the world more objectively and weigh issues more on how they impinge on her national interest rather than in ideological terms. In 1997, after years of vacillation, it finally bit the bullet and undertook the Shakti tests. It braved the sanctions which followed but stayed the course. In strategic terms, robust economic performance, and nuclear weapon status (even if unacknowledged) has given her a sense of self assurance which was missing earlier. India is being noticed on the world stage.

The terrorist strikes on the United States on 9th Sept. 2001 and its aftermath has had a global impact. As the United States unfolded its post-9/11 agenda, for the first time since India's independence, there appeared a convergence of interests between the two nations. Consequently today US and India are engaged in building a mutually beneficial partnership. US commitment to help India become a major power promises to open many new vistas of cooperation. Access to sophisticated technologies could help India to accelerate its economic growth and give its people a better life. Waiver of crippling sanctions in the nuclear field would help India expand its nuclear power generation capacity and thus reduce its dependence on imported hydrocarbons. US help in areas of defence can help India build its military strength to protect its vital national interests. Political backing could prove decisive to India's case for a seat in the United Nations Security Council. US also has the capacity to compel Pakistan to end cross-border terrorism which has blighted India for over 15 years. There are thus many benefits which can accrue to India by having a strong cooperative relationship with the only hyper-power of the day.

However, while taking in all the glad tidings, there is a danger of being swept away by overexpectation of benefits without taking stock of the price which one may be called upon to pay. That there is a cold calculation of national interest behind all overtures in International relations is too well-known to bear repetition. While making India a beneficiary of its technical, military and political largesse, United States would certainly have reciprocal expectations of India. India's recent vote against Iran at the IAEA (when Russia and China abstained) is a precursor of the difficult choices, which India may be compelled to make.

There is a commonly held belief that the US is investing in Indian power as a hedge against the Chinese overshadowing the region. India is certainly concerned about how burgeoning Chinese power could clash with its own aspirations of being a regional power. However its sense is that it would rather engage the Chinese in a cooperative mould rather than a confrontational one. Therefore, India would like to avoid being seen as a partner in an alliance to thwart the Chinese power—particularly where her own interests don't appear threatened (conflict over Taiwan, for instance). If Sino-US push comes to a shove, would the US accept a non-committal Indian posture and still continue to contribute to the strength of the Indo-US partnership. The fact is that US is a global power and it has a certain worldview, which in its detail doesn't necessarily coincide with India's. While articulating the kind of world that US would like to see, it is impatient with dissent and would like those whom it considers its friends fall in line. Born out of our respective historical experiences and relative power positions, there are significant dissimilarities in our outlooks. Arrogance of power is writ large in US interactions with the rest of the world. Would India be comfortable in such a relationship, particularly when widely different perceptions have to be reconciled? But all said and done, it may be useful to remember what Shakespeare said:

> There is tide in the affairs of men, which, taken at the flood, leads on to fortune; omitted, all the voyage of their

> life is bound in shallows and in miseries; on such a full sea we are now afloat; and we must take the current the clouds folding and unfolding beyond the horizon. When it serves, or lose our ventures.

Today, there is certainly a tide in the affairs of India and it must be taken at the flood. Given the global footprint of US power, its impact both when in support as well as when opposed cannot be overstated. Strong Indo-US relationship could certainly help in shaping our geopolitical environment favorable to our interests and therefore, we have everything to gain by promoting it vigorously. However, while taking full advantage of this favorable tide in our fortunes, we must also be conscious of the potential pitfalls, even if for no other reason than to avoid disappointment arising out of unrealistic expectations. Caution is also to be commended to ensure that India's strategic space is not crowded by any single power to the exclusion of others. Therefore, even while India and the United States draw closer in response to a perception of commonality of interests, India must continue to widen its options by simultaneously cultivating strong ties with others centers of power.

13

Third Party Mediation (TPM): The Case of India-Pakistan Conflict

Vijay S. Khare

Introduction

The whole world is faced with conflict and violence today. In fact there has been no period in history, which has not witnessed violent conflicts. But at the same time there have been thinker, sages, religious personalities, writer, always-emphasized love, peace, and harmony. Though both trends i.e. of violence and peace and harmony gone together violence and conflict remains predominant in our memory.

The present international system experienced a qualitative transformation following the series of processes sweeping across the world after the collapse of Soviet Union and the communist bloc towards the end of the 1980s. Strategic experts, defence analyst and students of strategic studies, international relation and international politics have been compelled to recast their traditional mode of thinking to make sense out of the turbulence and promise of the emerging world order. A unipolar world order dominated by the United States led alliances of some Western capitalist states has replaced by the bipolarity of the Cold War era. In the process of globalization erosion of state, sovereignty (Evan: 1997, Strange: 1997) extensive economic interdependence, uniform trade and traffic policies enforced by the transnational institutions, technological linkages among states, increased flow of information across the geographical boundaries, international social networking through means of advanced communication and information technologies raise number of issues to developing world. The contemporary regional security environment also exhibits its apparent contradictions. Cold War compulsions exacerbated regional conflict and restricted the ability of the international organization to resolve them. The end of the Cold War was, therefore, seen by many as increasing the ability of the international community to resolve conflicts (Andrew Bennett, Joseph Lepgold: 1993). The advantages of reduced international tension have also reached different regions that were caught in deadly conflicts during the Cold War era. Serious attempts to mend fences between adversarial states in Latin America, Middle East and the Far East have been undertaken. The US brokered a peace agreement after decades of violent conflict in Northern Ireland. Vietnam disengaged from Cambodia and launched initiatives for normalization of relation with China, Vietnam, which had remained isolated from its neighborhood of South-East Asia, has joined the ASEAN. South America's traditional rivals Argentina and Brazil agreed to freeze their nuclear programmes and open their nuclear facilities to inspection by the International Atomic Energy Agency. The Cuban withdrawal from Angola and relation between two Koreas are some other indicators of the propitious effects of the post-Cold War strategic transformation on the regional and sub-regional security environment. However, it can also be argued forcefully that in the era of globalization and new world order, the international community will be less capable of resolving inter-state conflicts in different regions than it was in earlier times (Andrew Hurrell: 1992). Unaffected by the global shift, several areas in the grip of ethnic insurgencies, intra-state clashes, miniaturizations, arms races, terrorism and religious fundamentalism today. The fierce conflicts in the Balkans, civil wars in Somalia, Sudan, Sri Lanka, Chechnya, and the escalation of the India-Pakistan conflict are some illustrations of the destabilizing conditions of the current globalization age. America's wars against Afghanistan and Iraq and the forced regime change brought about in these two states in 2001 and 2003, respectively signify the direction and quality of the international order in the coming years.

Concept of Third Party Mediation

The terms third party and intermediary are both used to refer to a person or team of people who become involved in a conflict to help the disputing parties manage or resolve it. Third parties might act as consultants, helping one side or both sides analyze the conflict and plan an effective response. Alternatively, they might act as facilitators, arranging meetings, setting agendas, and guiding productive discussions. Facilitators will also usually record what was said, and may write up a short report summarizing the discussions and any agreements that were reached. A more active and powerful third party role is that of mediator. Mediators not only facilitate discussions, but they usually impose a structure and process on the discussions that is designed to move the parties toward mutual understanding and win-win agreements. While many different styles of mediation are common, most mediators have the conflicting parties sit down together to explain to each other their views about the nature of the problem and how they think it might best be solved. The mediator often tries to get the disputants to focus on underlying interests (the things they really need or want) more than their initial opening positions (what they initially say they need or want). By clarifying the divergent views and reasons for those views, mediators can usually get the parties to develop a common understanding of the situation, which often yields a solution, which satisfies the interests of all parties. While some mediators take a stronger role in option identification and selection than others, mediators do not have the power to impose a solution. At most, they can suggest a solution, which the disputants may or may not accept. The most powerful third party role is that of an arbitrator. An arbitrator listens to presentations made by both sides, examines written materials and other evidence relating to a case, and then makes a determination of who is right and who is wrong, or how a conflict should be settled. Usually, the arbitrator's decision is binding and cannot be appealed. Thus, the arbitrator is the most powerful type of intermediary. Arbitration works well when the parties simply want a settlement, and do not worry about losing control of the process or the outcome. For parties that want to maintain control, however, the other forms of intervention (mediation or facilitation) are often preferred.

Intermediary Roles and Functions

When impartial third parties intervene in a conflict situation, new relational structures and possibilities for moderating the conflict are created. Introduction of a mediator, for example, changes both the physical and social structure of a conflict. New groups and sets of transactions appear with the third party. The presence of an observer tends to put contenders on better if not their best behavior. Intermediaries facilitate more accurate communication. The issues, interests and needs of the contenders become clearer with the help of such third parties. There may even be someone besides one's adversary to blame, as intermediaries sometimes divert blame toward themselves as a technique for transforming stalemate into resolution. Most importantly, third parties bring additional minds and skills for problem-solving to the conflict. The contenders are no longer on their own.

Multi-Modal Intermediation

Many types of third parties can be introduced in a conflict, simultaneously working together, or at different points in a conflict when their form of assistance is most needed. Lederach (1997) identifies nearly 25 different functions intermediaries perform over the life of a conflict. Intervention could begin with the explorer who assures the contenders that total victory is not the goal of the other side and end with the work of the reconciler who facilitates the healing process. Along the path of resolution, unifier's facilitators legitimate and many other specialist roles are introduced. Such a multi-modal approach is necessary with large-scale conflict such as civil war. An intervention team must use particular skills and relationships with the contenders at the right time, in the right context. Even intra organizational and two-person conflict could benefit from the team approach, though the types of interveners would be smaller. Who is there who could help us out of this conflict? This should be the first question conflict opponents should ask. The more varied their concept of third party the more intermediary potential they will see as they look around. An important function of third parties in a conflict, particularly in its latent stage, is conflict prevention. At the international level, multinational peacekeeping has for almost forty years been a common way of preventing conflict and violence.

International Mediation in the Post-Cold War Era

Third parties mediate based on their desire to make peace, and their own self-interest. Self-interest is the primary motivation for states. States are motivated by defensive and offensive interest. Defensive interests include promoting international stability, and protecting the mediating nation's foreign interests. Often nations will attempt to mediate a conflict in order to prevent rival powers from intervening and expanding their influence. States may also fear being drawn into the escalating conflict. When motivated by defensive interests, mediators often have some stake in achieving particular outcomes. When acting on the offense, states mediate conflicts in order to extend and increase their own influence. For instance, successful mediation may earn the gratitude of other nations. In such cases states usually have less interest in the content of the settlement. As an example of how self-interest motivates third parties, a case of U.S. mediation during and after the Cold War. During the Cold War, the U.S. was quick to mediate international conflicts. By doing so, they extended their influence and blocked expansion of Soviet influence. With the demise of the U.S.S.R., the U.S. has been less eager to intervene. Less powerful nations also act on defensive and offensive self-interests. In addition smaller states may attempt mediation because they lack other foreign policy tools and as a way avoiding is being drawn in to the conflict as participants. Non-state organizations generally emphasize peacekeeping as their main motive. Parties to a conflict accept mediation when they believe it is in their best interests to do so; that is, when they believe that mediation will gain an outcome that is more favorable than the outcome gained by continued conflict. Similarly, parties will accept mediation when rejecting it will result in greater harms. Parties may fear incurring bad relations with the proposed mediating nation or international sanctions if they refuse to negotiate. In addition, mediation may offer parties a way to negotiate compromises without losing face. The mediator may also be seen as guarantor of the final settlement.

Nature of India-Pakistan Conflict

The India-Pakistan conflict is not just a traditional interstate conflict over a peace of land. The causes of this conflict are deeply entrenched in the history, popular psyche, and societies of the two states. Few other international conflicts are as profoundly influenced by historical memories, events and determinants as the India-Pakistan conflict. India-Pakistan conflict bears many features of a conflict between civilizations for survival and expansion. India and Pakistan use cultural and civilization-related parameters to define themselves and their identities. Each state emphasizes the characteristics: tradition, customs, heritage, literature, religion, language, and values, norms that presumably distinguish itself from other. The threat from the other is perceived not just in military or territorial terms but also as a civilization. The popular discourse on India-Pakistan conflict has many similarities to the impending 'clash of civilizations' propounded in a book of the same title by Samuel Huntington. The conflict between India and Pakistan is also rendered untraceable because of the psychological structure of the conflict, and interaction of this structure of the conflict, with the political, historical, and strategic factors.

The Line of Control (LoC) dividing Kashmir is often referred to as the most dangerous place on the earth, the flash point for potential conflict in South Asia (Bill Clinton: 2000). These characterizations took on added meaning after nuclear tests conducted by India and Pakistan in 1998 and the high-altitude war around Kargil in 1999 transformed the strategic environment in the region. The two states have been involved in a relationship of unrelenting hostility ever since their independence from British rule, fighting three full-scale wars in 1947-48, 1965, and 1971, a semi-war in 1999, and coming very close to war in 1955, 1987, 1990, 2001 and 2002. The roller-coaster ride of their relationship short-lived ups but prolonged downs-defies all attempts at conflict management and resolution. The Cold War mindset, as reflected in zero-sum game scenarios, conception of conflict as one the fundamental values, and a nuclear arms race still seems to hold sway over the majority of the people, decision-makers and commentators in the Indian subcontinent. Right since its inception, the Government of India has been paranoid at the thought of international intervention, interference, or even interest, in the Kashmir issue. India opposes third party role in its conflict with Pakistan, it is a fact that India itself has acted as mediator or facilitator in disputes involving other states, and it is not averse to the principle of international mediation general. The directive principle of the Indian Constitution enjoin the Government of India to 'encourage settlement of international disputes by arbitration.' India played a successful mediator role in the UN-sponsored efforts to settle the problem of the repatriation of 1,40,000 Chinese prisoners of war towards the end of the Korean War in the 1950s. The Indian formula was accepted by all the parties—North Korea, South Korea and China. India also acted as a mediator during the 1954 UN conference on Indo-China held at Geneva. Its good offices were used in initiating negotiations between the Government of Sri Lanka and the LTTE in the 1980s. All this makes the Indian stance on mediation in the India-Pakistan conflict seem paradoxical and illogical. However, from the beginning India allowed a role for third party in the Kashmir dispute and in the management of its relations with Pakistan, it has resolutely and consistently opposed any suggestion of formal mediation in India-Pakistan conflicts since the India-Pakistan war of 1971. Simla Agreement of 1972 and Lahore Declaration of 1999 have given more thrust on bilateral negotiations. Several governments have been in power in New Delhi since 1971 war, but the Indian stand on dealing with Pakistan within the bilateral framework. The government, the media, politician, commentators, and the masses in India have been so sensitive to the issue of third party initiative. There was well meaningful proposal of friendly states like Russia, South Africa, Nepal, and Iran to provide assistance in settling India's problems with Pakistan, however, these proposals have been interpreted as threatening to India's sovereignty, integrity and vital national interests. India has favoured a bilateral approach with respect to not only Pakistan but also with other South Asian states. Bilateralism has become one of the core values of India's foreign policy. However, the end of the cold war and era of globalization have changed in the international strategic environment seem to have had little influence on India's stand on bilateralism.

Key Events of Third Party Mediation between India and Pakistan

Water Dispute

The treaty on the sharing of the Indus River water the most significant economic and strategic agreement between India and Pakistan signed in 1960 is an instance of successful mediation in India-Pakistan conflict (Amit Dholakia: 2005). The agreement incorporated most of the proposals of the World Bank. India was also permitted non-consumptive use of the western rivers flowing into Pakistan. It provided for arbitration to settle future disputes and set up the permanent Indus Commission to facilitate regular communication and control over the distribution of water. The treaty created a fund for the development of the Indus basin in which the World Bank and the governments of the US, Canada, UK, West Germany, Australia and New Zealand agreed to contribute about $ 1 billion to finance the construction of large storage dams and other hydrological development work to be undertaken by Pakistan. It seems that Indus Water Treaty would not have been possible without the mediation of the World Bank.

Tashkent Treaty

The Soviet Union mediated between India and Pakistan against the backdrops of the short war between the two countries in Sept. 1965. Soviet Prime Minister Alexei Kosygin offered his good offices to India and Pakistan even as the war was on in early September 1965. After the end of war, the Soviets renewed the offer and attempted to broke a peace agreement. What Kosygin offered was not active mediation, but assistance in bilateral dialogue at a location in the USSR acceptable to both India and Pakistan.

Rann of Kutch

Both India and Pakistan used International arbitration to settle their conflicting claims over the Rann of Kutch. There was a major engagement between both the parties and the British Prime Minister Harold Wilson offered his good offices during the Commonwealth meeting and both parties agreed for a cease-fire. Both countries concluded an agreement in 1965, which stipulated that if there were no resolution of the dispute within two months, it would be submitted for arbitration by an international tribunal. So no arrangement was made in the later two months, the case was transferred to International Tribunal consisting of one judge appointed by India (Alec Bebler of Yugoslavia), one judge appointed by Pakistan (Nasrollah Entezam of Iran), and third judge jointly selected by both the judges (Gunnar Lagergren of Sweden), was constituted by the Secretary General of the UN. In its award made by a majority of two in Feb. 1968, the tribunal awarded 350 square miles of Rann area to Pakistan. Bebler submitted a dissenting note and Indira Gandhi publicly expressed her dissatisfaction, but decided to accept it in the spirit of arbitration.

The Kargil Conflict

During Kargil conflict Clinton's administration took personal interest for the third party mediation and wished to continue playing role in the South Asia. The US is also believed to have influenced the Chinese not to support Pakistan's claim in the Kargil War.

Operation Parakram

After terrorist attack on Indian Parliament both countries mobilized their forces at border level and ready for war. Due to nuclear parity and lack of conventional military capability, Pakistan was not ready for war but tried for third party mediation to resolve Kashmir and other core issues with India. During operation Parakram US had taken keen interest and develop pressure against India and Pakistan.

Kashmir Conflict

India's reference of the Kashmir dispute to the UN in 1948 first began the process of internationalization of the Kashmir issue and mediation by external actors in India-Pakistan conflict. The experience with UN mediation on Kashmir and the attitude of the western powers, particularly the US and the UK in the late 1940s and the 1950s have strengthened India's stand against a third party role. In its view, the UN adopted a pro-Pakistani stand from the beginning because of Pakistan's key role in the emerging strategic interests of the US-led military blocs in South and Central Asia during the early years of the Cold War.

India's Position on Bilateralism

From independence India has argued that as the conflict is between India and Pakistan others cannot be expected to resolve it for them. Third party mediation would encourage needless dependence on outsiders. India feels that the diplomatic strategy of bilateralism also helps avoid internationalization of contentious issue in South Asia and avoid involvement of multiple actors in South Asian region.

Is the Third Party Mediation Possible in Kashmir?

India will never allow any extra regional power for mediation to solve Kashmir issue. Third party mediation could be the beginning of a spiral of similar demands for self-determination and secession from other discontented regions. A major problem in third party mediation is the neutrality of the third party mediation. Indian strategic experts arguing that third party mediation is a conspiracy of the Western states to secure economic and strategic interest in the South Asian region.

Asymmetrical Conflicts and Third Party Mediation

Number of studies have brought out that third party mediation is most effective in disputes involving states with equal power. When the parties possess asymmetrical power, their conflict is not apt for resolution through third-party involvement. There is a marked disparity in the levels of military power between India and Pakistan. Both in conventional and nuclear weaponry, India claims numerical and qualitative superiority. India also enjoys huge economic superiority over Pakistan.

India believes that Kashmir problem is just one of many issues between the two countries. Hence, it prefers a multi-track, composite dialogue covering a wide range of bilateral issues that include, apart from Kashmir problem, Sir Creek, Siachen Glacier, Economic and commercial relation, Nuclear risk reduction measures, confidence building measures, terrorism, drug-trafficking, etc. However India accept Kashmir is 'core issue' whose resolution alone can normalize relation between the two states.

The end of the Cold War has not made third party mediation more effective or successful. Peter Wallensteen and Karin Axell report that of the 43 disputes ending between 1989 and 1993 only 6 ended with mediated agreement (Peter Wallensteen and Karin Axell: 1994). Roland Paris also argues that one of seven UN post-conflict peace building efforts was successful (Roland Paris: 1997). The prime reason for the failure of mediation is also due to lack of understanding of the political, social, and cultural context of the conflict on the part of mediator. The failure of the Lahore and Agra Summits—both organized due to American prodding-demonstrates that an externally-inspired peace process cannot last long, and that the conflicting parties get back to their habitual animosity once the external pressure eases.

The Role of US in India-Pakistan Conflict

US interest and involvement in South Asia have increased in post-Cold War period for two objectives. First, the US attaches the highest importance to the control of nuclear proliferation in other countries, and second America's own strategic interest in Afghanistan and the Middle East in the aftermath of the terrorist attacks on September 11, 2001 have pushed South Asia higher up in its foreign policy priorities. America today enjoys better relations with both India and Pakistan simultaneously than it has at any time in the past. This also makes its involvement than it has at any time in the past.

Conclusion

In the post-Cold War era strategic environment has changing according to technological revolution. Traditional issues of security has no longer survive in the age of globalization. Recent earthquake in Pakistan and financial and managerial support from India shows that there is possibility to resolve core issues between India and Pakistan through peaceful process. However, through confidence building measures and preventive diplomacy also invites third party mediation directly or indirectly. Intervention in the underdeveloped and developing countries in the Asia in the name of human rights, fight against terrorism, elimination of weapons of mass destructions, have challenged to sovereignty of states. To resolve core issues between India and Pakistan there is necessary to proper congenial strategic culture and political institutions. Third party or major great powers may resolve core issues between India and Pakistan through preventive diplomacy and confidence building measures but common will of people is necessary to maintain peace and stability in South Asia.

REFERENCES

Bajpai, Kanti, P.R. Chari, Pervez Iqbal Cheema, Stephen Cohen and Sumit Ganguly (1995) "Brasstacks and Beyond: Perception and Management of Crisis in South Asia," New Delhi, Manohar.

Banerji, Dipankar (2000) (ed.) "Confidence Building Measures in South Asia," Colombo: Regional Centre for Strategic Studies.

Bennett, Andrew and Joseph Lepgold (1993) "Reinventing Collective Security after the Cold War and Gulf Conflict" *Political Science Quarterly*, Vol. 108, no. 2.

Bourton, John and Frank Dukes (1990) "Conflict: Practices in Management, Settlement and Resolution," Macmillan.

Cohen, Stephen (ed.) (1987) "The Security of South Asia: American and Asian Perspectives," Urban and Chicago: University of Illinois Press.

Cohen, Stephen (1997) "The Structural Dimension of Conflict in South Asia," Colombo: Regional Centre for Strategic Studies.

Evan, Peter (1997) "The Eclipse of the State?" World Politics.

Former President Bill Clinton (2000): described it thus just before he embarked on his journey to South Asia in March.

Hurrell, Andrew (1992) "Collective Security and International Security Order Revisited" *International Relations,* vol. 11, no. 1.

Mitchell, C.R. and Webber (ed.) (1988) "New approaches to International Mediation," Greenwood, New York.

Paris, Roland (1997) "Peace-building and the limits of liberal Internationalism," International Security, Fall.

Paul Lederach, John (1997) *Building Peace: Sustainable Reconciliation in Divided Societies*, Washington: United States Institute of Peace.

Rajgopalan, Ragesh (1998) "Neo-Realist Theory and the India-Pakistan Conflict," *Strategic Analysis*, Vol. XXII, no. 9.

Susan, Strange (1997) "The Erosion of State," *Current History*, November.

Wallensteen, Peter and Karin Axell (1994) "Conflict resolution and the End of the Cold War," *Journal of Peace Research*, vol. 31, no. 3.

Zartman, William and Saadia Touval (1985) "International Mediation: Conflict Resolution and Power Politics" *Journal of Social Issues*.

ELECTRONIC REFERENCES

- www.rcss.org
- www.stimson.org
- www.ipcs.org
- www.cisac.standford.edu
- www.idsa-india.org
- www.epw.org.in
- www.satp.org
- www.sipa.columbia.edu/cicr

14

Security Beyond South Asia: The European Experience

Prasad Rane

Introduction

Security as a concept has undergone a tremendous change. This change in the definition of security is spread over the span of around 50 to 60 years since the end of the World War II. The contemporary definition of security has engulfed the conventional definition of security. This has enlarged the security paradigm *per se*. The predominant reasons for this change were the changing nature of the security challenges and threats over the said period.

To understand the contours of the concept of security, it is essential to study the nature of this concept in Europe. As far as the history of International Relations goes, the development of the concept of security was a one of the outcomes of the development of concept of 'nation-state' in the 17th Century Europe. However, pedigree of the concept of security can be traced back in the writings of Hobbes, Locke, and Rousseau.[1] Right since its inception, the concept of security has undergone a lot of change internationally in general and Europe in particular. The World War II left the war-ravaged Europe with a whole lot of problems. When the war ended it had left the West European nations in physical and economical collapse. This left them in no position to address the hegemonic challenge from belligerent Soviet Union. These incidences saw a precursor to the alliance politics in Europe. Then for over a period of 45 years deterrence and balance of power became the *mantras* in defining the security situation.

But the end of the Cold War saw the first paradigm shift. The security did not remain confined to the *mantras* of Cold War. To define and address the security of this new phase some out of box thinking became necessary. 'Interdependency' tried to define the nature of security in this period. What followed was 'institution building' with interdisciplinary approach to address these security threats. The concept of "New Europe" was an outcome of this. The North Atlantic Treaty Organization (NATO) and the European Union (EU) had a major role. But the unfolding post-Cold War period also posed a problem to this combined effort. The problem had its genealogical roots embedded in the history. "Core European" attitude which had now culminated into 'Europeanist' attitude questioned the 'Atlanticist' attitude in the Euro-Atlantic region. With these debates on, the building of a "New Europe" still remains a distant dream.

The present essay envisages seeing the key features in the "Security Thinking" in Europe. The area is vast, but this is a concise and comprehensive effort. The paper also makes an effort to answer a question in the context of what Europe can gain from India in their exercise of building a "New Europe." The post-Cold War phase is very demanding due to growing inter-dependency in the international system. This inter-dependency has ushered a need for the European Union (EU) to have partnerships with various Asian countries. Amongst the Asian countries, China and India are leading on the partnership tables of the EU. As such Europe and India share a lot in common. Their understandings of certain key issues converge at a certain point. The experiences India had over certain issues like multiculturalism, Islam etc. can be of great help for the Europe's endeavour in building a "New Europe."

European "Security Thinking": A "Core European"[2] Dominance

Observations suggest a considerable amount of heterogeneity in the "Security Thinking" in Europe. The reason lies in the diversity of the European history. The European History has been vibrant with wars and conflict breaking out between

European countries. The European continent was never at peace. The perceptions of security in Europe are strongly influenced by the experiences Europe had during the World Wars. However, these experiences are phenomenally divergent as each European country experienced the wars differently. Hence, these different historical experiences shaped different "Security Thinking" in Europe.[3] Hence the entire "Security Thinking" was dominated by the nationalistic feelings for supremacy.

The World War II and the onset of the Cold War was the period mark the first phase of the formation of a new "Security Thinking" in Europe. The entire strategic thinking during this period saw the influence of a "Total War." The emergence of two superpowers, the US and the USSR, saw the international system attaining a bipolar status. This led to contest of two different ideologies, and the battleground was none other than Europe. However, the nature of the East-West rivalry was seen as a continuation of a state-centric behaviour of achieving a regional as well as global hegemony.[4] As stated earlier, conventionally the concept of security was dominated at large by the military security.

The entire continent was confused due to the catastrophic effects of the World War II. With the end of the war Europe was in total shambles. The reconstruction of Europe was the need of the hour. When the war was on, the plans were made for the reconstruction of Europe. The United Nations Relief and Rehabilitation Agency (UNRA) was created in 1943 and remained functional till 1947; a European Central Inland Transport Organization, a European Coal Organization and Emergency Committee for Europe were established and merged in 1947 with the UN's Economic Commission for Europe (ECE).[5] But these efforts were not sufficient for the restructuring of Europe. To suffice the need of reconstruction of this war-ravaged Europe, the US aid via Marshall Plan[6] had to be institutionalised. An aid of around $17 billion was to be offered for the European reconstruction via Marshall Plan. As the Russians turned down the offer for the USSR and its dependent states, a creation of an organization of the European nations for the Plan to become functional, only was restricted to the Western Europe. Eventually, sixteen countries established a Committee for European Economic

Cooperation to assess their requirements. This organization performed its allotted duties from 1948 to 1952 and sequentially was converted to a more permanent structure called Organization for European Economic Cooperation (OEEC).[7] To extend the work of OEEC into the developing areas of the world it was replaced by Organization for Economic Cooperation and Development (OECD) in the 1960. The US and Canada became the full members of the OECD.[8]

All these developments coincided with the procedure Europe was going to start of a political and economic union. With the experience of the World War II, the Soviet threat hovering over the Western Europe, and the onset of the Cold War got the West European leaders convinced that a lasting peace can be secured by getting united. Taking inspiration from a speech delivered by Jean Monnet, the French Foreign Minister proposed an integration of the coal and steel industries in Western Europe. This resulted in the formation of the European Coal and Steel Community (ECSC) by Belgium, West Germany, Luxembourg, France, Italy and the Netherlands in 1951.[9] Jean Monnet became the first President of the sole decision-making independent, supranational body called the 'High Authority.' This marked the beginning of a new era in the history of Europe. Aware of the prerequisites of the era to follow, Europe was on a jumping board to jump and explore the areas in which further cooperation can be achieved.

From 1945 to 1949 the West Europeans were busy in the process of post-war economic reconstruction with the help of the US through the Marshall Plan. Simultaneously, they were keeping a close watch on the Soviet expansionist policies in Eastern Europe. The Brussels Treaty of March 1948 marked the determination of five Western European countries—Belgium, France, Luxembourg, the Netherlands and the United Kingdom—to develop a common defence system and strengthen ties, which would enable them to resist ideological, political and military threats to their security.[10] To strengthen the defence system, negotiations were also held with the US and Canada resulting in the formation of a single North Atlantic Alliance based on security guarantees and mutual commitments between Europe and North America. Denmark, Iceland, Italy, Norway and Portugal were invited by the Brussels treaty powers to become participants in this process. These negotiations led to the signature of the Treaty of Washington in April 1949, which led to a security system based on a partnership among these 12 countries called NATO.[11] Today the membership of NATO has increased to 26.

The international security system underwent a first paradigm shift with the disintegration of Soviet Union. The world is acquiring a 'uni-polar' status underlined this paradigm shift. Since then, the post-Cold War international politics has run into many grooves. The common running thread among all of them has been the paradigm shift from geopolitics to geo-economics instigated by the rigorous spread of globalisation.[12] The spontaneity of the spread of globalisation made people look at the emerging world order through an ever evolving process and made them understand the structural as well as functional dynamism that underlined it. The most important feature of such a dynamic process, which has become the unit of analysis in contemporary international relations, is what many have called 'interdependency.' This has brought the disparate nations of the world closer to one another. But with this, the problems of the nation-states have multiplied.

The end of the cold war on the one hand brought an end to conceptual understanding of security as military security, while on the other it widened the security paradigm. It brought in a set of new security concerns which were more or less non-strategic in nature. With increasing interdependency amongst nation-states, it became a Herculean task for the nation-states to address these security challenges. The problem aggravated with the dawning of these new security concerns on the horizon of security. These security threats were non-strategic in nature,[13] which worsened the things.

How could Europe escape these developments? Rather, these developments marked a beginning of understanding the requirement of a "New Security Thinking" for Europe. With the end of the Cold War Europe underwent lot of structural changes and was waiting for more to happen as the post-Cold War phase was unfolding. The immediate structural changes were due to the disintegration of Soviet Union. As observed, there were two immediate structural changes which posed a serious challenge to

Europe. Firstly, the disintegration of Soviet Union showed the way to a fall of central authority which subsequently created a power-vacuum in the Central and Eastern European Countries (CEEC).[14] This power-vacuum made these countries vulnerable to politico-military-economic challenges. These challenges had the potential to aggravate to instability in these countries. The West Europeans were worried about the challenges due to the spill-over effects in the form of refugees and illegal migration. In addition, the region also confronted some local and internal conflicts over the issues related to border disputes, the status of minorities, domestic power struggles, and rising influence of the ultra-nationalistic groups.[15] This situation made the European security theatre a complex mosaic.

Secondly, as stated above, the set of the non-strategic threats in the evolving international system in the post-Cold War phase also had a brunt over the European security theatre. By then it was understood that instability of any nature throws the window wide open for these new security threats. The inference for the Europeans was very clear that they were seating on a pyre if they allow the power-vacuum to persist. According to analysts like Ronald D. Asmus, Richard L. Kugler and F. Stephen Larrabee:

> ...Europe's new strategic challenges exist almost exclusively along two "arcs of crisis." The first is the eastern arc: the zone of instability running between Germany and Russia from northern Europe down through Turkey, the Caucasus and Middle Asia. The second is the southern arc, running through northern Africa and the Mediterranean into the Middle East and Southwest Asia...[16]

The Europeans understood the demand of this grave situation. The situation had to be dealt with some comprehensive efforts. By then the Europeans also realised that a united effort has to be made to address this challenge. Therefore, this united effort has to come through an arrangement which is equipped to address the challenge of power-vacuum in the CEEC. This arrangement has to be a 'security arrangement' as it is to understand and address the security challenges. Europe had addressed its security needs during the Cold War through institutions like NATO and

ECSC. However, there was a serious problem with these Cold War institutions as they had a state-centric character.[17]

Also, one observes a continued neglect of the CEEC by the Western Europe countries in their respective academic and political discourses. One can analyse this tendency as a Cold War legacy. However, to understand the changing landscape of Europe in the post-Cold War period, Europe has to be treated as a single unit of analysis. There cannot be any 'central' and 'peripheral' issues while addressing the security challenges as the strategic distinction between the two ended in the post-Cold War period.[18] The need of the hour for Europe was to formulate a grand strategy to address these security challenges related to the instability, conflict and restoration of democracy. Europe by now understood that they have to re-organise and harmonise their individual security concerns with the international security concerns which were changing in the post-Cold War period.

However, the European Economic Community (EEC) had proved its incapability while building a consensus on vital issues among its 12 members during the Persian Gulf War and Yugoslav crises.[19] The diversity amongst the 53 members Conference on Security and Cooperation in Europe (CSCE) made it impossible for the organization to take decision in one voice. Obviously, NATO became the final choice to shoulder this responsibility as it had displayed its cohesiveness during the Cold War.

To address these challenges, the Europeans had to take up a project of building a "New Europe" which will be without the 'East-West' dividing lines. 'Cohesiveness' in decision-making and 'Multi-facet' approach were the pre-requisites for the arrangement to address these security threats. The prescribed pillars on which this "New Europe" was to stand were Economics and Security. And, the *mantra* for the success was consensus between all the members on vital issues. Subsequently, a major role for building this Europe was waiting for the two major West European regional organizations—the European Union (EU)[20] and NATO.

Initial the post-Cold War phase saw the Europeans convinced about retaining the US role in Europe for peace and stability. But this conviction did last long. Very soon the Europeans started experiencing certain degree of uneasiness due to the presence of the US troops on the European soil.[21] A worry about the future US role in NATO was the culmination of that uneasiness. West Europeans in general and France in particular even questioned the need for stronger transatlantic relations with the disappearance of the Soviet threat.[22] The French even questioned the US dominance in the NATO which aught to be a multilateral institution.

Given the fact that terrorism is complex; there is, therefore, a need for a multi-dimensional and interdisciplinary approach. However, NATO attempted to expand its strategic horizons realising the need of addressing the present day security challenges to Europe and for staying in the business. The summits in London and Rome, 1990 and 1991 respectively, redefined the new political and military goals for NATO in the 'Strategic Concept.'[23] NATO adopted the policy of transformation and change through expansion. In brief, a new US-European Union (EU) consensus to find new meaning and goals for NATO was crafted through 1990s onward. This further added to the worries of the West Europeans. With the proposal of an eastward enlargement of NATO,[24] the Europeans foresaw a shift in the US strategic priorities. This led to the St. Mâlo Summit on December 4, 1998, between the French and the British to affirm on the EU's determination to establish ESDI. During the Summit British Prime Minister Tony Blair and French President Jacques Chirac issued a joint statement on European Security and Defence Initiative (ESDI) which intended to provide capacity to conduct autonomous actions. The St. Mâlo declaration stated that,

> ...the Union must have the capacity for autonomous action, backed up by credible military forces, the means to decide to use them and a readiness to do so, in order to respond to international crises.[25]

The EU's determination to establish ESDI and gain autonomy worried the US. This also brought the EU and NATO at loggerheads. The US feared a duplication of NATO with the formation of ESDI. These concerns were voiced at the semi-annual NATO Foreign Ministers' meeting in Brussels on December 8, 1998, by none other than the then US Secretary of the State Madeleine Albright. The concerns were raised with the mention of the US demand of a stronger European Pillar in the Atlantic Alliance.[26] In the same context she mentioned about the US supporting an ESDI "within the Alliance," and referred to the subsequent support the US may extend for any effort which will enhance the European capability. Her famous judgment on the three standards on which the ESDI should stand soon became famous as the 'three Ds." The judgment says,

> The key to a successful initiative is to focus on practical military capabilities. Any initiative must avoid pre-empting Alliance decision-making by de-linking ESDI from NATO, avoid duplicating existing efforts, and avoid discriminating against non-EU members.[27]

Since then, in spite of several efforts, there is no cohesion between these two, NATO and EU, which were supposed to play a key role in building a "New Europe."

The terrorist attacks on the World Trade Centre on September 11, 2001, confirmed the capability of 'terrorism' to pose a threat. These events exposed the vulnerability of a traditional institution of 'nation-state' against a non-state entity called 'terrorist.' In the wake of these attacks on the United States, the members of NATO invoked the treaty's mutual defence guarantee, i.e. Article 5,[28] for the first time in the alliance's 52 years. The most interesting thing happening with this invocation was something no body had imagined when the Article 5 of the Treaty was being finalised in the year 1949. This first invocation saw the Europeans coming to aid of the Americans and not the other way round.[29] Subsequently NATO undertook two operations, Afghanistan and Iraq as a tactical change in its process of adapting a multi-focal approach.

Subsequently, serious contentions stirred up in the Atlantic Alliance. The "Core Europe" has shown serious reservations over the 'out-of-area operations.' These reservations were due to difference in strategic priorities which the "Core Europe" dominated EU and the US dominated NATO had since the end of the Cold War or before that also.[30] Since the end of the Cold War the major differences were over the approach towards the 'the states of concern.' The Europeans preferred 'negotiations' to the US belief of the policy of 'containment.'[31] These different approaches literally brought a rift in the EU-NATO relationship during the US operations in Iraq.

Nevertheless, the events of September 11 and the subsequent war in Iraq compelled the Europeans to consider an exercise in the strategic thinking. This also led to intense debates in strategic thinking throughout Europe. This endeavour marked an attempt by the Europeans to translate their policy practice into strategy.[32] The comprehensiveness brought in strategic thinking of Europe culminated in forming the European Security Strategy (ESS).[33]

Conclusion

Going through the developments above, one sees a clear cut influence of a "Core European" egocentric behaviour on the "Security Thinking" in Europe. This influence is at two levels:

- Firstly, the "Core European" attitude towards the US unilateral approach.
- Secondly, the "Core European" attitude amongst themselves.

When the "Core European" countries were worrying about the influence of the US in Europe, they were also worried about the change in the US strategic priorities. However, in spite of a lot of pessimism about the US unilateral approach towards security issues, the West Europeans are always haunted by a fear of the entire West Europe returning to what French analyst Francois Heisbourg called *"la geopolitique de grand'papa"* (old-style geopolitics) if the US leaves Europe. These worry buds out of the realisation of a fact that due to the US leadership of NATO, the entire West Europe stayed as a one unit. Under the NATO, the West Europeans learnt the benefits of multilateralism due to cooperation. Now if the US leaves Europe, they may soon return back to the historical positions, and the security and defence related areas would retrogress from multilateralism to nationalism.[34]

The West Europeans are also aware about the inefficiency the military structure will acquire if the EU hypothetically gets a complete autonomy in dealing with the security related matters. They have even realised that for building up of a "New Europe," the economic stability is not sufficient. It has to be supported by a military strength which can consolidate security. To serve this purpose, the EU and NATO have to complement each other. Perhaps these realisations have restrained the Europeans from agitating the demand of complete autonomy.

With this the "Core Europe" has worries amongst themselves also. With the unification of Germany, this worry has increased a lot. They want the US to be there to constrain the strength and power of the newly unified Germany. The main worry was that a unified Germany may dominate the political and economic centrestage of Europe. So, to prevent Germany from 'Germanising Europe' and instead 'Europeanise Germany' there was a need for Europe to stand as a cohesive unite.[35] Secondly, France is worried about the changing nature of Europe from *Franceophone* Europe to an *Anglophone* Europe.

Way Ahead

With this situation, one gets the feeling that to bring homogeneity to the 'Security Thinking" in Europe, Europe first has to stop lingering in history, its warring past. Otherwise, "New Europe" on a new Security Premises will remain a distant dream. Secondly, Europeans should start looking outwards in their approaches towards security. The lack of outward thinking on security issues has prevented EU of becoming a strong political unit at the international theatre.

Reviewing its relations with the South Asian countries, Europe can benefit a lot from these countries. The EU already has three major "Strategic Partnerships" in South Asia: EU-China, EU-India and EU-Japan. It can be a learning experience for the Europeans while consolidating their partnerships with these countries. In particularly, EU can learn a lot from the experiences of India.

EU-India relations go back to the early 1960s; India was amongst the first countries to set up diplomatic relations with European Economic Community (EEC). The bilateral agreements between the two were signed in 1973 and 1981.[36] EU-India relations are structured up on the 1994 Cooperation Agreement,[37] the 1993 Joint Political Statement and the 2000 Lisbon Summit. Since then six EU-India Summits were held. Still one can say that this partnership is in a phase of infancy. Yet, EU can learn a lot from India as their understanding on certain key strategic and security related issues converge. Indian experience in multiculturalism can be of great help in addressing the problems Europe has within its continent. India has been facing the bane of terrorism since long. However, Indian system has prevented a spill-over of this problem in the adjacent region. The cognitive approach India had adopted in addressing the issue can be a worthwhile experience for the Europeans.

As stated in the discussion throughout this essay, Security as a concept has undergone tremendous change. In addressing the security-related issues today, a holistic approach is pertinent. To have a secured place for humanity, solutions to the security problems should be built upon the experiences of all countries. Europe is not an exception to this. To build a "New Europe" in particular and a stable and secured system in general, convergence of understanding of security becomes a precursor.

NOTES AND REFERENCES

1. Sujit Lahiry, "Concept of Security: A Theoretical Analysis", *Journal of Peace Studies*, 11 (4), October-December, 2004, p. 58.
2. The notion of "Core Europe" was invoked by Jürgen Habermas-Jacques Derrida manifesto. The notion manifested by them was different from both the British and the 'new' European candidates for EU membership. They sought to build a Common European Identity upon the social-democratic traditions and enlightenment. The notion of "Core Europe" raised a great amount of passionate reactions from the scholars across the Atlantic. For the sake of information, the term *'Kerneuropa'* was originally coined in a highly influential policy paper published during 1994. This policy paper was written by Karl Lamers, then Foreign Policy Spokesman for Germany's Center-Right Christian Democratic Union (CDU), together with Wolfgang Schäuble, the then CDU Chairman. The paper argued about a "Core Europe"—Germany, France and the Benelux Countries—as a driving force in the then ongoing project of the economic and political integration of the European Union (EU). The title of the paper was; Karl Lamers (1994), "Strengthening the Hard Core", in Peter Gowan and Perry Anderson (ed.), *The Question of Europe* (Verso, London, 2000), pp. 104-16. But one can find a some enlightening discussions by various scholars on the notion of "Core Europe" in Daniel Levy, Max Pensky, and John Torpey (ed.), *Old Europe, New Europe, Core Europe: Transatlantic Relations After the Iraq War* (Verso, London, 2005). The present paper makes use of the term "Core Europe" to identify the fissures in the "Security Thinking" in Europe. The present paper also argues that the "Core European" identity of the

"Security Thinking" in Europe has several limitations to serve the dream of a "New Europe."

3. For a detailed record on the different "Strategic Cultures" in Europe refer Adrian Hyde-Price, "European Security, Strategic Culture, and The Use of Force," *European Security*, 13 (4), 2004.
4. Edward A. Kolodziej, "What is Security and Security Studies?: Lessons from the Cold War," *Arms Control*, 13 (1), April 1992, p. 1.
5. Peter Calvocoressi, *World Politics 1945-2000* (Pearson Education Limited, England, 2001), p. 215.
6. In June of 1947, the then US Secretary of State, General Marshall advocated a plan at Harvard. The plan was for the entire Europe (including the USSR) an economic aid for the recovery up to 1951 on the basis that the European governments would accept the responsibility for administering the programme and would themselves contribute to European recovery by some degree of united efforts. As it was advocated by General Marshall, the plan bears his name.

   For the details regarding the recovery of Western Europe and the Marshall Plan refer, Peter Calvocoressi, *ibid.*, pp. 215-28; Michael J. Hogan, *The Marshall Plan* (Cambridge University Press, Cambridge, 1987).
7. Organization for European Economic Cooperation (OEEC) came into being on April 16, 1948. It originally had 18 participants: Austria, Belgium, Denmark, France, Greece, Iceland, Ireland, Italy, Luxembourg, Netherlands, Norway, Portugal, Sweden, Switzerland, Turkey, United Kingdom, and Western Germany [originally represented by both the combined American and British occupation zones (The Bizone) and the French occupation zone]. The Anglo-American zone of the Free Territory of Trieste was also a participant in the OEEC until it returned to Italian sovereignty.

   See http://www.oecd.org/document/48/0,2340, en_2649_201185_1876912_1_1_1_1,00.html
8. Twenty countries originally signed the Convention on the Organization for Economic Co-operation and Development (OECD) on December 14, 1960. Since then a further ten countries have become members of the Organization. For the list of the member countries of OECD, see http://www.oecd.org/document/58/0,2340,en_2649_201185_1889402_1_1_1_1,00.html
9. The Treaty establishing the European Coal and Steel Community (ECSC) was signed on April 18, 1951 in Paris. The Treaty entered into force on July 23, 1952 and expired on July 23, 2002.
10. The Brussels Treaty was signed on March 17, 1948, at Brussels. Text of the Treaty is available at http://www.nato.int/docu/basictxt/b480317a.htm
11. For history of NATO and the basic treaty, see NATO-OTAN, NATO Handbook, 2001, pp. 29-30.

12. Lynn E. Davis brings out the influence of Globalisation on security:

"Globalisation is a multidimensional phenomenon: Information technologies, along with a variety of other technologies, are developing rapidly and spreading widely. Trade is expanding globally, as is the flow of private capital and investment. Interdependencies are growing in all aspects of our lives. These developments create real possibilities to achieve economic prosperity, spread political freedom, and promote peace. Yet they are also producing powerful forces of social fragmentation, creating critical vulnerabilities, and sowing the seeds of violence and conflict. Economic crisis extend across state borders and are producing global hardships. All these are aspects of what is commonly referred to as 'globalisation,' and all have important security implications."

See the Issue Paper of RAND by Lynn E. Davis, *Globalisation's Security Implications*, RAND, 2003, p. 1.

13. The spectrum of these non-strategic security threats ranges from terrorism to environmental problems on one side, and, energy security to rights of the unborn on the other. 'Economic' in particular can be called as a strategic parameter of security. However, the September 11 attacks by *Al-Qaida* on the US brought 'terrorism' at the forefront of this set of non-strategic parameters.

14. The "Central and Eastern European Countries" (CEEC) are those European successor states of the former Soviet Union and other formerly Communist states in Europe.

15. See Arthur R. Rachwald and Gale A. Mattox, "Introduction: European Security and the Enlargement of NATO" in Arthur R. Rachwald and Gale A. Mattox (ed.), *Enlarging NATO: The National Debates* (Lynne Rienner Publisher, London, 2001), p. 10.

16. Ronald D. Asmus, Richard L. Kugler, and F. Stephen Larrabee, "Building a New NATO," *Foreign Affairs*, 72 (4), September/October 1993, p. 29.

17. The understanding of security still lingered in the Cold War as the emergence of Security Studies as an identifiable sub-field of International Relations was closely related to the Cold War. Even the scholars like Bull (1968), Martin (1980), Nye and Lynn-Jones (1988) in their works, identified Security Studies as a study of threat, use and control of military force and a conflict between states and societies. During the Cold War Military threat was treated as the only threat to Security. To study the debates on these issues in detail, refer: (i) David A. Baldwin, The Concept of Security, *Review of International Studies*, Vol. 23, (1997), pp. 5-26; (ii) David A. Baldwin, Security Studies and the End of the Cold War, *World Politics*, Vol. 48 (1995), pp. 117-41; (iii) Stephen M. Walt, The Renaissance of Security Studies, *International Studies Quarterly*, Vol. 35 (1991), pp. 211-39.

18. During the Cold War the security concerns of Western Europe were considered as the central issue, whereas those related to Central and

Eastern Europe were considered as the peripheral issues. Asmus, Kugler and Larrabee bring out this distinction. According to them, *"the potential locus of conflict in Europe during the Cold War was located along the old inner-German border."* They further elaborate, *"Many Western policymakers cling to the Cold War distinctions between Western Europe, which is implicitly defined as vital interest, and Eastern Europe, which is seen as a secondary or peripheral concern."*

Ronald D. Asmus, Richard L. Kugler, and F. Stephen Larrabee, "Building a New NATO," *Foreign Affairs*, 72 (4), September / October 1993, pp. 29-30.

19. The original members of the European Economic Community (EEC) were Belgium, France, Federal Republic of Germany (FRG), Italy, Luxembourg, and The Netherlands. Denmark, Ireland, and the United Kingdom joined in 1973, Greece in 1981, and Portugal and Spain in 1986; the former East Germany was admitted as part of reunified Germany in 1990.

    This is summarised from the information available on the European Union (EU) available at http://www.itcilo.it/english/actrav/telearn/global/ilo/blokit/eu.htm#History.

20. The Treaty of European Union was signed in Maastricht on February 7, 1992. This Treaty introduced new forms of cooperation in the areas like defence and justice and home affairs between the member state governments. This additional intra-governmental cooperation other than the existing 'Community' system paved way to the creation of the European Union (EU). The adoption of the Maastricht Treaty also envisaged the inter-governmental Common Foreign and Security Policy (CFSP).

    The details regarding the Treaty of European Union including the entire Treaty is available at http://europa.eu.int/eur-lex/en/treaties/dat/EU_treaty.html

    About CFSP, see Treaty of European Union, especially, "Title 1: Common Provisions, Article B regarding CFSP." This is also there in Article J.4. Cited in Robert E. Hunter, *The European Security and Defence Policy: NATO Companion—or Competitor?* (RAND, 2002), pp. 2-3.

    For more information on Common Foreign and Security Policy (CFSP) visit http: //www.europa.eu.int/comm./external_relations/cfsp/intro/index.htm; http://www.europa.eu.int/comm/external_relations/esdp/

21. Dr. Willem F. van Eekelen, *The Changing Environment of Transatlantic Relations* (A report from the European Strategy Group, IFRI, 1991), p. 71.

22. Jiri Sedivy and Marcin Zaborowski, "Old Europe, New Europe and Transatlantic Relations," *European Security*, 13 (3), 2004, p. 188.

23. The Alliance Strategic Concept agreed by the Heads of States and Government participating in the meeting of North Atlantic Council in

Rome on November 8, 1991 is available at http://www.nato.int/docu/basictxt/b911108a.htm

24. Invitations were issued to three new members from Central Europe—Hungary, Poland and Czech Republic during the NATO's Madrid Summit held during July 8-9, 1997. Eventually, these three countries formally acceded to the North Atlantic Treaty and joined the Alliance in March 1999 and participated in the NATO Washington Summit held during April 23-24, 1999 as members. This was the first expansion of NATO since the end of the Cold War increasing the membership of NATO to 19. On the invitations issued to Hungary, Poland and Czech Republic see the Madrid Declaration on Euro-Atlantic Security and Cooperation issued by the Heads of State and Government on July 8, 1997 [Press Release M-1(97)81] available at http://www.nato.int/docu/pr/1997/p97-081e.htm

25. See *Text of a Joint Statement by the British and French Governments*, Franco-British Summit, St. Mâlo, France, December 4, 1998, paragraph 2.

    The text is also available in the chapter 6 of the Document on European Security and Defense Identity (ESDI) of the BASIC RESEARCH REPORT on "A Risk Reduction Strategy for NATO" which can be accessed at http://www.basicint.org/pubs/Research/1999riskreduction 7.htm

    Also, cited in Jolyon Howorth, "Britain, France and the European Defence Initiative," *Survival*, Vol. 42, No. 2, Summer, 2000, p. 43.

26. ESDP / ESDI were the initiatives based on the goals set by the EU Treaties of Maastricht (1992) and Amsterdam (1997). The US and NATO had strongly supported it. See NATO Ministerial meeting of the North Atlantic Council, Final Communiqué, M-NAC-2 (93)70, Brussels, December 2, 1993, paragraph 2 for its support to the emerging ESDI. This is available at http://www.nato.int/docu/comm/49-95/c931202a.htm

27. Refer to the text of the US Secretary of the State Madeleine Albright's remarks to the North Atlantic Council Ministerial meeting at Brussels on December 8, 1998. For a detailed discussion on the "three Ds" refer Robert E. Hunter, *The European Security and Defence Policy: NATO's Companion—or Competitor?* (RAND, 2002), pp. 34-44.

28. The Article 5 of the NATO Treaty reads:

    "The Parties agree that an armed attack against one or more of them in Europe or North America shall be considered an attack against them all, and consequently they agree that, if such an armed attack occurs, each of them, in exercise of the right of individual or collective self-defence recognised by Article 51 of the Charter of the United Nations, will assist the Party or Parties so attacked by taking forthwith, individually, and in concert with the other Parties, such action as it deems necessary, including the use of armed force, to restore and maintain the security of the North Atlantic area.

Any such armed attack and all measures taken as a result thereof shall immediately be reported to the Security Council. Such measures shall be terminated when the Security Council has taken the measures necessary to restore and maintain international peace and security."

The entire document of the treaty is available at http://www.nato.int (i.e. NATO Homepage).

29. Philip H. Gordon, "NATO After 11 September", *Survival*, Vol. 43, No. 4 (Winter 2001-02), p. 89.
30. Philip H. Gordon and Jeremy Shapiro, "A European Front", *San Jose Mercury News*, June 20, 2004, p. 2.
31. See the Report of an Independent Task Force sponsored by the Council on Foreign Relations, *Renewing the Atlantic Partnership* (2004).
32. For a comprehensive analysis of the European Security Strategy (ESS) refer Sven Biscop, *The European Security Strategy: Global Agenda for Positive Power* (Ashgate Publishing Limited, England, 2005).
33. The European Security Strategy was adopted in Brussels on December 12, 2003, by the European Council. The document can be accessed from the European Union Website.
34. Robert J. Art, "Why the Western Europe Needs United States and NATO," *Political Science Quarterly*, Vol. 111, No. 1, Spring 1996, pp. 4-5.
35. Germany after unification played a central role in the European Economic Integration. The French and the British were aware of the German power. So, they were worried about the integration process which may possess a German character. For good amount of analytical reasoning on this issue please refer Robert J. Art, "Why Western Europe Needs the United States and NATO," *Political Science Quarterly*, 111: 1, Spring 1996.
36. See, http://europa.eu.int/comm/external_relations/india/intro/index.htm
37. The Cooperation Agreement was signed between the European Community and the Republic of India on partnership and development on December 20, 1993. The Council of the European Union was represented by Wily Claes, Minister for External Relations of the Kingdom of Belgium, President-in-Office of the Council of the European Union and Manuel Marin, Member of the Commission of the European Communities. The Government of India was represented by Sri Pranab Mukherjee, Minister for Trade. See the Cooperation Agreement on http://europa.eu.int/comm/external_relations/india/intro/agree08_94.pdf

15

The Nuclear Dimension of India's Security

Shankar Roychowdhury

In Indian mythology, divinely created weapons like the Brahmastra were endowed with catastrophic powers of destruction, and specifically forbidden to be used by protagonists except in the most dire emergencies because of the horrendous disasters likely from their fallout. Nevertheless, our sagas record that ultimately these weapons had to be employed at various critical junctures when all else had failed to stop the onslaught of demons and demi-gods. The parallels between these mythological weapons and nuclear weapons in real life are irresistible, even as we progress into the twenty-first century. Crisis estimation and its management are all relative to human perceptions, which ultimately decide the magnitude of any contingency, and also the appropriate weapons to be employed in each case. Concepts of active warfighting in a nuclear conflict developed for the Cold War are no longer considered relevant in the present geopolitical context and nuclear weapons are now regarded as purely political instruments of proactive coercion or protective deterrence, notwithstanding their radically different characteristics and capabilities. But nevertheless, like the mythological *Brahmastra*, in the ultimate analysis nuclear weapons, though capable of mass destruction, are essentially weapon systems, to be used only in extremis, as final fallbacks when no other options are perceived to be available. They are not mythological—they exist in real life and cannot be wished away. Their presence serves both deterrence as well as coercion, and it would be irresponsibly escapist to philosophise that they are entirely political assets, never to be used in war, because, if in spite of all efforts, crises do escalate beyond an acceptable threshold of criticality and the existence of the nation itself is at stake, nuclear weapons, if available, are likely to come into play. The near-death experience of the Cuban missile crisis between the USA and the Soviet Union that almost ignited in 1962 is a classic example of deterrence that nearly failed.

Hence, while assessing its security environment in the initial decades of the new millennium within the regional environment of South Asia, India has to take cognizance of past history and present developments particularly in respect of the Islamic Republic of Pakistan and the People's Republic of China where the potential nuclear dimension is always a reckonable background factor. In this context, one of the most significant geo-strategic elements in the case of Pakistan, is its territorial contiguity with northern and western India, exactly similar to that between East and West Germany during the Cold War. Consequently, missile flight times both ways would be extremely short, allowing almost no early warning or reaction time prior to impact. It will generally not be feasible to differentiate between the nature—conventional or nuclear—of incoming missiles, and there will naturally be a strong tendency on both sides to treat every incoming missile as a potential nuclear carrier, increasing manifold the chances of a nuclear war by accident. Most of Pakistan's heartland, including its major population centers lie within coverage of even short-range missiles from India, as also do many important Indian towns and cities from Pakistan. In such a setting, even tactical battlefield missiles like the Indian Prithvi or the Pakistani Hatf I and M 11 assume a quasi-strategic significance for attacking value targets on homeland territory of both countries. Proximate contamination from drifting nuclear fallout will be the greatest threat, not only to India and Pakistan, but also to third countries in the vicinity like Afghanistan, Nepal, Bhutan, Sri Lanka, or Bangladesh as well large areas of the adjacent oceans. There will truly be nowhere to run and no place to hide in the event of a nuclear war in South Asia. The situation is almost totally reversed in respect of China, where the heartland is a great distance away from mainland India, while most of the latter lies within medium range coverage from the border regions of China. Nuclear missile carrying warships or submarines in the oceans around peninsular India will add to the complexity of the overall equations, which can be further compounded if the Islamic Republic of Iran comes on stream too. In view of these, India has adopted the concept of "protective deterrence by second-strike" as its core nuclear doctrine, derived from Prime Minister Atal Bihari Vajpayee's statement in Parliament calling for strategic capabilities based on the principles of "a minimum credible deterrent, no first use, and never to be used against countries which did not possess nuclear capabilities, either their own, or under protective treaty with a nuclear weapon state." It is an eminently suitable nuclear doctrine for the complex geo-strategic realities of the South Asian subcontinent.

A high "nuclear threshold" for conflict resolution at the sub-conventional and conventional levels, and forestall use of nuclear weapons, is therefore, one of the basic requirements of national security. This has a special relevance in an environment where internal stability itself may become a flashpoint through terrorism and insurgencies externally engineered by hostile or potentially hostile nuclear weapon states, like the prolonged low intensity proxy war sponsored by Pakistan in Kashmir and Punjab since 1984, and its sudden high intensity spike at Kargil in 1999. The hostilities of the Indo-Pak situation in the West have percolated eastwards to Bangladesh as well, which seems to be reverting to its earlier status as the eastern wing of an undivided Pakistan, encouraging anti-Indian sentiments and feeding separatist aggravations in India's North East. For India, the "nuclear threshold" has therefore to be a composite process relevant to external as well as internal threats, synergising effective diplomacy and strong conventional military forces, with political sagacity, good governance, adequate police and paramilitary forces, and efficient and responsive civil administration, to establish a system of layered fire-breaks at different levels to defuse outbreaks before they escalate into an irretrievable trajectory. But in the ultimate event of that threshold finally being crossed, then awaiting across it must be the ultimate deterrent of nuclear strike forces. This is the outline pattern India has chosen to follow.

The nuclear dimension of the India's military security in the twenty-first century comes within the continuum of a process ongoing in the country since the 1960s, its most recent update being the meeting between Prime Minister Dr Manmohan Singh and President George W. Bush in Washington on 18th July 2005. Jawaharlal Nehru, free India's pre-eminent founding father and first Prime Minister, initiated the Indian nuclear programme for purely civilian usage. Subsequently however, the adverse security environment after the Sino-Indian border war of 1962, the Sino-Pak Treaty of Friendship in 1963, followed by the first Chinese nuclear test in October 1964 at Lop Nor, caused the then Prime Minister Lal Bahadur Shastri to authorize commencement of SNEPP (Subterranean Nuclear Explosion for Peaceful Purposes), a nuclear programme with military linkages, which ultimately resulted in the so-called "peaceful nuclear explosion" (PNE) of a non-weaponised device ten years later at Pokhran in 1974 ("the Buddha has smiled"). The period after Pokhran I witnessed considerable political turmoil in the country including the imposition of Emergency by Mrs Gandhi, her electoral defeat and subsequent re-election, Operation Blue Star and the assassination of the Prime Minister in 1984. Their cumulative effects diverted attention away from the nuclear programme, and created a prolonged hiatus almost upto 1989 during which there was no perceptible progress. This delay of nearly fourteen years in development of nuclear weapons after the initial success of Pokhran I was an irrecoverable strategic setback whose long term fallout would return to haunt the national policy-makers perhaps for all time to come. It was a lost victory of critical dimensions, more so because during this period Pakistan acquired the working design of an already tested nuclear weapon from China in 1983, placing India in a situation of nuclear asymmetry with its hostile neighbour. The Indian nuclear weapons programme was resuscitated by Prime Minister Rajiv Gandhi on assumption of office, but the damage had already been done. Nevertheless, the programme remained an article of faith with successive Indian prime ministers, irrespective of political affiliations or personal opinions, and was assiduously nurtured notwithstanding intense pressures to "cap, roll back and eliminate" it by the United States and other western nations. If media accounts are to be believed, India came close to nuclear testing on several occasions during this time but backed away under American pressure. However, in accordance with his undertaking during his election campaign, Prime Minister Atal Bihari Vajpayee ordered the second series of Indian nuclear tests to be carried out soon after he assumed office, which were carried out at Pokhran on 11th May 1998. The tests, designated "Operation Shakti," involved one 12 kiloton (KT) fission, one 45 KT fusion, and three sub-kiloton underground explosions conducted almost surreptitiously, under the shadow of severe displeasure by the United States, which in the end was miffed that its super-sophisticated systems of strategic surveillance as also other sources of intelligence could not detect the preparations. But their credibility and dramatic impact was trivialised by incredibly irresponsible statements of some politicians in the immediate aftermath and above all by an abjectly exculpatory letter to the President of the United States of America by no less than the Prime Minister of India himself, besides an abruptly declared unilateral moratorium on further nuclear testing. It was officially stated this single Shakti series of five underground tests had in fact generated enough data adequate for further nuclear weapon design refinement and upgradation through computer simulations only, without recourse to further "hot testing." The government's contention did not find too many takers in the country. India's efforts to appease the United States, akin to that of an errant schoolboy caught stealing forbidden fruit, were seen by many to have restricted Indian options, apparently for all times to come. Nevertheless, Operation Shakti was the watershed that propelled India into nuclear weapon status. Not unexpectedly, Indian claims after Pokhran II have been questioned and disparaged elsewhere too, especially by several Western commentators (plus of course Pakistan) on the basis of seismic data recordings, to which the Indian nuclear establishment has replied. While adverse comments by Western and Pakistani sources need not be taken seriously, domestic public opinion too must exercise caution in uncritically accepting the government statements, particularly with regards to its claims of total adequacy for the future developments. Indian scientists, notably those in Government establishments, are notoriously prone to over optimistic public statements, as experience of the Defence Research and Development Organization (DRDO) in other fields has repeatedly demonstrated. So, at the end of the day, how is Operation Shakti to be ultimately assessed? A one-shot experiment, apparently never to be repeated, has it really generated the ability to upgrade our nuclear weapons and graduate from fission technology to thermonuclear weapons of proven reliability through laboratory testing alone? Or, has the government made a deliberate decision to base India's future capabilities on fission weapons only and not progress thermonuclear weaponisation further? Warhead yields would be a critical factor within the subcontinent in an Indo-Pak contingency, because of likely proximate contamination of neighbouring countries from nuclear fallout. Thermonuclear weapons could perhaps be counter productive in this setting, and fission weapons could produce the desired effect. But matters could be different in the Sino-Indian context, where the balance of capabilities is of an entirely separate order thermonuclear weapons would be necessary to achieve true deterrence. No satisfying answers to all these conundrums are available in the public domain, though their outcome is of critical relevance to the country's future deterrence capabilities. At this stage, all that can be devoutly hoped that Prime Minister Atal Behari Vajpayee's decision to announce a unilateral moratorium on nuclear testing after Pokhran II in 1998 was not yet another major strategic blunder of the same magnitude as Prime Minister Indira Gandhi's decision not to expeditiously push for weaponisation immediately after Pokhran I in 1974.

"Second Strike" is essentially a concept of retaliatory retribution—"delayed but assured" based on a counter value strategy, which primarily targets population centers rather than military assets. Depending on the situation, second-strike retaliation may be immediate or delayed. Strategic resources will require high survivability against a first strike, and thereafter retain the capability to deliver assured retaliation to create the strongest punitive effect with counter value strikes, primarily targeting population centers. For India, the ultimate responsibility for planning and execution of nuclear second strike after its political approval devolves on the newly constituted Strategic

Forces Command, which is still in process of evolution. For the present, the new Command is constituted around a fairly rudimentary triad of nuclear-weapon, capable fighter-bombers with the Air Force and land based ballistic missiles with the Army but the ultimate aim would undoubtedly be to develop the classic triad of land, air and naval launch systems, with increased range and capabilities, capable of reaching critical strategic objectives in great depth, but these are unlikely to materialize unless accorded special priorities. Fighter bombers and toss bombing with gravity bombs are perhaps the most basic and primitive system of nuclear delivery having the least assurance of penetration, but there are not many alternatives available at present. Present resources are the short range missile Prithvi (150/250 km range, 1000/500 kg warhead) and medium range ballistic missile Agni I (2000-2500 km range, 1000 kg warhead) together with Jaguar, Mig 27, Mirage 2000, and Sukhoi 30 aircraft, with possibly a Brahmos cruise missile element to follow. The Prithvi is essentially a short range tactical missile for supporting the land battle upto the operational depth of the battle area. While it has absolutely no relevance for deterrence in a Sino-Indian context, it does acquire a degree of pseudo-strategic capability in an Indo-Pak situation, because even with its limited range it can still reach major value targets across the border with a nuclear warhead. It is obviously a weapon of the very last resort, but such as it is, it does exist. Agni I is a true ballistic missile which can cover all of Pakistan, but not major value targets in the mainland China. Development and deployment of a follow-on series of intermediate range and intercontinental ballistic missiles are essential. It is understood that Agni II is in the pipeline, while Agni III and even Surya are appearing in the media as part of sensational reportage. Amongst aircraft, the Mig 27, like the Prithvi missile, is a fairly outdated Warsaw Pact aircraft originally designed for close support of land operations (a sore point with the Air Force!). Though nuclear capable in theory, they should be discounted as viable assets for nuclear delivery. The Jaguar is somewhat more viable in this role, but only the Mirage 2000 and Sukhoi 30 can be reckoned as true frontline strategic assets, though it is not known how many have been modified for carriage of nuclear weapons. The

Indian Navy is not known to possess any nuclear assets as at the time of writing, but would obviously plan to acquire an adequate fleet of nuclear propelled submarines in the future with submarine launched ballistic or cruise missiles. Not too much is known about nuclear warheads (and rightly so), but these are sometimes surmised as based on the original 1974 Smiling Buddha fission device, weaponised and fielded during Operation Shakti in 1998. On a conservative estimate, this would place them in the 12 to 15 KT range, which, if anywhere near correct, might lead to the further conclusion that the yield is too small for assured effectiveness against hardened military targets like missile silos or deep underground headquarters. The Brahmos, a supersonic cruise missile with land, sea, sub-sea and air configuration, a stated range of 270 km, and a 200-300 kg warhead, is scheduled for introduction into service around 2007. A nuclear payload for Brahmos would have to be in an extra-light configuration, possibly at the sub-kiloton level, making it at best a flyweight nuclear weapon with limited deterrent effect, but nonetheless one more option available. It is also thought that nuclear warheads and the trigger mechanism will be demated from the missile systems during peacetime storage and held at dispersed safe locations in custody of separate non-military agencies, to be reassembled at selected areas before launch by aircraft or ballistic missiles. The mode of storage and modalities of re-assembly are definite pointers towards strategic acceptability of delayed second strike as an option. In the meanwhile, procedures for reassembly in a viable time frame under multiple scenarios will require to be developed and operationalised.

The requirement of nuclear warheads to achieve a perceived level of minimum credible deterrence has been frequently assessed, analysed and speculated upon by many commentators, whose estimates have varied from sixty to six hundred, with an acceptable median assessment of one hundred and fifty to two hundred warheads (less reserves). Official figures for this will never be known, but an important factor here will be the availability of fissile material from which warheads are to be fabricated. Enriched plutonium (Pu 239) is the basic fissile material for the strategic nuclear programme, primarily derived in residue from natural uranium used as fuel rods in nuclear reactors. Uranium is a strategic natural resource (like oil) of which there are only limited deposits in India, and even here, politicized agitation is holding up exploration and industrial exploitation. However, there are fairly abundant resources of thorium, but the crossover stage from uranium to thorium-based technology still has to go an appreciable distance. This is an area of concern in the weapons programme which will have to be resolved.

The decision to use nuclear weapons would of course be vested at the highest level in the person of the Prime Minister, who will do so in consultation with the Cabinet Committee on Security, supported where necessary by other national mechanisms like the National Security Council. Thereafter, operational control should devolve through the Defence Minister to the Chiefs of Staff Committee (including the Chief of Defence Staff as and when positioned) who will be supported by the Integrated Defence Staff, and exercised through the Strategic Forces Command, employing strategic assets held by the two (or later all three) Services. With the establishment of Strategic Forces Command as an inter-Services entity the task of putting the military framework for strategic command and control in place has commenced but will require extensive training and work ups especially with the interlocking political and civil systems, particularly the multiple agencies involved with reassembly of nuclear devices in storage, as well as establishment of hardened national command posts and EMP-proofed communication links. All these have presumably been taken in hand. Strategic Forces Command was to have been directly responsible to the Chief of Defence Staff (CDS), but this has not happened so far, because of obvious reasons. As things stand, the Strategic Forces Command (like its other inter-Services counterpart the Andamans and Nicobar Command) is controlled directly by the Chiefs of Staff Committee through the Headquarters Integrated Defence Staff. This unscheduled delay has perhaps been fortuitous, because the proposed command channels would have been unsatisfactory, without any particular advantage in respect of oversight or responsive command and control. The present system regarded as ad hoc is in fact much more logical, and should continue as a permanent measure whether the long awaited headpiece of the Chief of Defence Staff finally arrives or not.

A connected aspect of India's nuclear weapons programme is the total exclusion of the Indian military from every aspect of its development and progress, a phenomenon seen nowhere else in the world. It is a strangely disturbing conundrum to which there can be only conjectures, and no clear answers. The question in one word is—Why? Why has there never been any formal or even informal interaction, consultation or participation on the weapons programme by the armed forces? Does it stem from a mistrust of the armed forces by the political leadership? Are there subterranean misgivings that given an occasion, India's armed forces could turn rogue? If so, does this extend to other aspects as well? Perhaps its origins lie in the personality and perceptions of the nation's first Prime Minister, Pandit Jawaharlal Nehru himself, which he brought to his office during an unbroken and almost unchallenged tenure of almost twenty years from 15th August 1947 until his demise in harness on 27th May 1964. It can be speculated that it may be rooted in Pandit Nehru's strong aversion to militarism, developed in his formative early years as a Fabian socialist, continued after he assumed office and unfortunately found a focus in his own armed forces. As Prime Minister, Jawaharlal Nehru was impatient with professional military advice if it ran counter to his political visualizations, and downplayed the role of the armed forces in the consultative process of government even on matters of national security, an inexplicable and illogical bias, but an unstated but very obvious vote of no confidence. Professional military opinion was at a discount, and the nation lost on the council table the advantages wrested on the battlefield, or suffered traumatic humiliation, ignominy and grievous loss of life in avoidable military disasters. The premature referral of Kashmir to the United Nations in 1947, before establishment of a favourable situation on the ground, as well as piecemeal establishment of isolated outposts strung out along the Sino-Indian border in 1962, leading to the humiliating defeat and loss of life in the border war with China, both came about primarily because military advice to the contrary was ignored. Leaving these issues aside, he also totally rejected nuclear weapons on ethical and moral grounds. Pandit Nehru set the guiding principles of India's nuclear policy, and proclaimed that India would never make nuclear weapons. The decision to unilaterally foreclose the country's nuclear options was momentous in its implications, but here too, taken without any reference to the defence forces. Later, in the interregnum after Pokhran I (1974), the political pronouncements of so-called "nuclear ambiguity," were again made without consultations with the armed forces. The Nehruvian mindset continued to keep the armed forces in darkness about domestic nuclear developments, even though by now there was reliable intelligence that Pakistan had already become a covert nuclear weapons power with clandestine support from China and North Korea. The armed forces were only too aware of the *de facto* adverse nuclear asymmetry with Pakistan, but totally unaware of any Indian attempts to redress the balance and progress towards indigenous nuclear-weapon capability. Nevertheless, though dismayed and irritated by what appeared as a charade to create a smokescreen over the lack of progress after Pokhran II, they blindly soldiered on, stoically shouldering the ultimate responsibility for defence of the country with or without the necessary resources. But amongst themselves the Defence Services could have done better. In the absence of government directives, which was nothing unusual, inter-service rivalries stymied coordinated attempts at the level of either the Chiefs of Staff Committee (COSC) or the moribund Director General Defence Planning Staff (DGDPS) to develop provisional Joint Services nuclear doctrines on which operational contingency planning could be structured. Some Services took their own individual initiatives in this respect, others preferred to await official intimation in this regard. But these were perforce single-Service formulations, not disseminated or accepted outside each service. In the end, each went his own way, and nothing of note emerged. It is to be hoped that with frequent articulations of the concept of inter-Services synergy, matters will improve in future.

But notwithstanding all the foregoing, a full scale nuclear conflict between states is an extremely unlikely possibility, except under extraordinary circumstances totally unforeseen as yet. However, nuclear terrorism by non-state extremists is a different matter altogether and presents a very credible "future shock" contingency. One to ten-kiloton miniaturised man-portable nuclear munitions—the "nuclear suitcase"—are said to have produced in the Soviet Union during the Cold War for "special operations" by their covert agencies, and there are disquieting reports that some of these are now untraceable in the chaotic aftermath of the disintegration of the country. There are also reports that organizations of international jehad like Al Qaida and its associated agencies in Pakistan like the Lashkar-e-Toiba, or Jaish-e-Muhammad are attempting to covertly acquire or make such weapons. If these attempts are successful, one of the possible contingencies for India could be a nuclearised re-run of the Bombay blasts of 1993, or the recent Delhi blasts in 2005. As for all types of terrorism, defensive measures against nuclear terrorism too, will primarily have to be police and intelligence oriented, based on intensely active intelligence capabilities together with smart pro-active police forces, who have to be lucky every time. If such a catastrophe does occur, and shows up the familiar pattern of jehadi sponsorship from across the border (which is the case with most such terrorist attacks as of now) it would undoubtedly constitute a major escalation of the ongoing proxy war—a sort of "nuclear Kargil" as it were—which would demand an appropriate response. India's current nuclear doctrine of second strike would then require to be re-evaluated in the context of receiving a "covert first strike" from a neighbouring country, by an act of nuclear terrorism which can be "plausibly denied" by the latter. Under these circumstances, will (or can) India retaliate according to its established doctrine? These and many others similar to it, are some of the dilemmas of the "New Deal in Terrorism" in the nuclear age, which the India's security agencies and strategic community will have to face up to urgently if they are not to be overtaken by events.

In conclusion, conceptualisation of security in the twenty-first century will depend very much on the tide of world affairs during the millennium, which, as of now is shrouded in uncertainty thick obscurity. Indeed it cannot be otherwise, but judging by trends at this stage, the outlook for peace, at least in the early decades (say upto 2015 or even 2020), does not appear too promising. Rivalries brought forward from the recent century have not subsided, but merely reconstructed into other shapes and forms, from geopolitical to ethno-religious, Cold War into War on Terror, manifested in the spread of fundamentalist terrorism and ethnic conflicts, intra-society, sub-national, as well as non-state. In a fast globalising world, many contingencies with potential for conflict may arise. The reasons remain undefined as yet, but diminishing natural resources, water in particular, could possibly be amongst the most frequent causes. But in all this, the nuclear dimension, civilian as well as military, will remain an important component of future security equations.

16

Military and Security Perspectives

V.P. Malik

Introduction

Each civilization gives rise to its own way of waging war. The Prussian military thinker Clausewitz noted, "Each age has had its own peculiar forms of war.... Each, therefore, would also keep its own theory of war." The industrial revolution ushered in a new dimension of mass-produced weaponry. The strike capability of combat forces focused on reach, mobility and destruction power. The length of the sword, the range of the aircraft or missile, the number of combat forces, how fast they can be committed, how deep they can be sustained, what total damage can they achieve on the adversary: all these became key combat capabilities affecting the outcome in a conflict. Such capabilities reached their near total extreme in the past half-century. This also brought about the likelihood of the mad level of mutual assured destruction, if any nuclear military powers ever decide to go for an all out war.

Changing Paradigms of Security and Spectrum of Conflict

Over the last few decades, particularly after the end of the Cold War, a distinctive feature of the strategic and security related environment has been the unprecedented and sheer dynamics of change in the concepts, paradigms and complexities of national, regional and global security. There are three main reasons for these changes. Firstly, the rapid advances made in science and technology, particularly in the field of information technology. Secondly, globalization, multilateralism, and regionalism are replacing bilateral international relations and a straitjacketed concept of sovereignty. And thirdly, a more liberal approach to security; there is now a greater focus on peace, development and cooperative security; most people would like to see stability at national, regional and global levels to continue. There is thus a new salience and awareness of the comprehensive nature of security. This includes in its ambit the traditional defence-related threats, but no less importantly, challenges in societal, political, economic, technological and environmental dimensions as well.

It is also evident that these changes are being understood better and more easily by liberal and stable democratic nations than nations ruled or dominated by the military, or quasi-democratic countries. Although the situation in this respect is much better in India than what prevails in Pakistan, the full impact of these changes is yet to be felt adequately in our security planning and management.

Trends and statistics of the last 50 years have shown that the armed conflicts around the world have been gradually moving down the paradigm scale of intensity as well as inclusivity. Potential nuclear war has given way to restrained nuclear deterrence. Total war, even a conventional war, has yielded to 'limited war,' 'restricted war,' and several types of 'low intensity conflicts.' The empirical evidence points towards a significantly lowered probability of a regular high intensity war leave alone a regional protracted war. There are several reasons for this trend:

- The attention of international relations and national attention has shifted markedly towards developmental economics, commerce and trade issues. Global and regional trade and economics of international finance have made more and more nations interdependent in a free market and export-oriented world. High-speed long-range communications have shrunk the world. Even the insular and inward looking nations have no options but to join 'internationalization' and 'engagement' thus reducing the chances of open or intense conflicts. The trend is to focus on peace and development and most people would like to see this stability to continue.

- The challenges of human development, including international efforts to enlarge peacekeeping and peace enforcement. It includes issues like human rights, international laws of war, protocols on nuclear, biological and chemical weapons and efforts to prevent collateral damage. There is close monitoring of conflicts and conflict situation by the media and it ensures greater public accountability of governments.
- High cost of maintaining standing Armed Forces and costly new weapon systems and equipment. There is likelihood of heavy civil and military casualties on account of greater lethality and reach of sophisticated conventional and non-conventional weapons.
- Destruction of enemy's military potential and occupation of large foreign territories: these are not easily attainable military objectives even when an armed conflict is between unequal enemies, as we have seen in Palestine and Iraq.

However, this does not mean that any nation is prepared to compromise on its security, or give up its efforts to become powerful. With the paradigm shift in the nature of security (military and non-military), the military has a tougher job today to be prepared for this elongated spectrum of conflict ranging from Aid to Civil Authority, counter terrorism, different levels of conventional war, to a war involving Weapons of Mass Destruction.

Revolution in Military Affairs

Due to Revolution in Military Affairs (RMA), the industrial character of armed conflict capabilities is shifting to a new form; based on knowledge and information. The RMA has three basic constituents:

- **Technology.** Integration of new technology into existing weapons systems and integrated C4ISR (command, control, communications, computers, intelligence, surveillance, reconnaissance);
- **Doctrine and Operations.** Experimenting with technology to create new types of warfare; and

- **Organization.** There can be no RMA without far reaching institutional changes like jointness, better defense management, integration and other means of achieving synergy.

It is the synergy among these three constituents that will bring about RMA. It enables continuous surveillance and precise surgical strikes on command and control nodes, strategic facilities, combat reserves, and combat support facilities in depth. It also enables getting at the adversary's nerve centers; with precision attacks or through electronic warfare and cyber attacks, as happened in the Gulf War, Iraq War, and in Afghanistan.

New developments in weapons, equipment and other capabilities give rise to new tactics and strategies. Due to faster technological progress, military doctrinal revisions are now needed more frequently; every 5-7 years, instead of 25-30 years as was the case earlier. There is much greater emphasis on the versatility of the combat forces. The military has to be more innovative, receptive to new ideas, and changes.

Nature of Wars that India may Fight

It is necessary to identify in broad terms the nature of conflicts or wars that India may be involved in, the limits and opportunities that influence the political and military objectives, and the circumstances that might present themselves in the conduct of such wars, especially to the different components of military power.

Nuclear War

I believe that nuclear weapons are political weapons and not military weapons. Also, no one wants a nuclear war. But then as long as there are nuclear weapons around, they could be used.

What are the chances of a nuclear war in India-China-Pakistan scenario? Given the fact that all three states possess nuclear weapons, proximity of India to Pakistan and China, have unresolved territorial/boundary disputes, the authoritarian structure of Pak and Chinese politics, a nuclear war between India and Pakistan/China, although extremely unlikely, cannot be altogether ruled out. Going further with such an unlikely but not an improbable assumption, in the foreseeable future, an

India-Pakistan nuclear war could be considered more likely than an India-China one. The fundamental reason for that is that currently China in relation to India is a status quo power while Pakistan is a revisionist power. Unless India threatens to use force to recover lost territories, which appears unlikely, India and China are not likely to go to war. While Pakistan, as a revisionist state, can be expected to continue to look for opportunities to wrest Kashmir or any other part of territory from India and/or continue with proxy war. What are the pathways to a nuclear war between India and Pakistan? These are given in succeeding paragraphs.

- **A Surprise First Strike.** Pakistan may calculate that its massive first strike will wipe out all our nuclear assets and also deals such a psychological blow that Indian leadership submits itself to Pak demands. This is highly improbable. Firstly, Pakistan does not have adequate military capability to wipe out Indian assets, which are more and widely dispersed. Secondly, it will have to contend with a very serious global reaction for breaking the 50 years old nuclear taboo. India and other nations will not let Pak survive, at least not in its present form.
- **Escalation to Nuclear War.** This is probable only if India launches a conventional war in retaliation to Pakistan's proxy war and crosses its nuclear threshold. These thresholds are not as low as Pak wants us and other nations to believe. It is likely to happen only when there is a clear spectre of a very major loss of Pak territory or a military defeat. Although very unlikely, this scenario cannot be altogether ruled out.
- **Accidental Nuclear War.** Accidents, misperceptions, and unauthorised actions by military in Pakistan without adequate nuclear CBMs between India and Pakistan could cause this. If both sides maintain their assets in demated posture, political and military confidence building measures and hotlines continue to be active, there is hardly any chance for this.

It is clear that due to horrendous destructive power of nuclear weapons, the probability of their use on the sub-continent would remain extremely low. Do remember that even a miniscule probability inhibits political leaders, particularly the democratically elected leaders, from taking a chance with nuclear weapons. For that reason, in a likely conflict situation, the political leadership in a democratic set-up tends to be more sensitive and exercise greater control on such weapons.

A Conventional War

With nuclear weapons here to stay, it is hard to see a large-scale 1962, 1965 or 1971 type conventional war between India and Pakistan, or even with China. In future, therefore, the probability of an all out high intensity regular war between these nations will remain fairly low. Even when a conventional war does break out, the war is likely to be limited in time, scope and space: some people call that a sub-conventional war, or a limited conventional war. The Chinese call these "local border wars." Such a conflict could also spread out in time, in what could possibly be termed as a war in 'slow motion.' It will have to be conducted within the framework of carefully calibrated political goals and military moves that permit adequate control over escalation and disengagement. This, however, does not rule out a larger scale conventional war where there is greater asymmetry of power.

A Limited War[1]

A limited war implies limited political and military objectives, not to hurt the adversary excessively at any one time; limited in duration, in geography, and in the actual use of forces level. It could also be limited in the quantum and pace of application of firepower. According to Ariel Levite, "The employment of the military in Limited Wars is far removed from the classical "no holds barred" attitude. It is typically characterized by severe limitations and constraints imposed by the political leadership on the employment of the military. Limitations are widely understood to mean in this context capping of the objectives for the military campaign, while constraints refer to restrictions imposed on the military conduct of that campaign by its political authorities."[2]

The military implications on the ground are integrated capabilities, shallow objectives, rapid concentration and launch, multiple choices/thrust lines, short, sharp intense action, surprise, continuous surveillance, multiple choices/thrusts and shallow objectives, maximum use of forces (including Special Forces) and force multiplier, and a pro-active deployment stance.

The likely duration of the war and time available to the Armed Forces to execute their missions and achieve politico-military goals would be crucial for their planning and conduct of operations. In a 'reactive' situation (like the Kargil war), this duration can be prolonged. However, the duration available will be much less if we deciding to take the initiative.

There is a linkage between deterrence and escalation. Capability to wage a successful conventional and nuclear war is a necessary deterrent. A war may well remain limited because of a credible deterrence or Escalation Dominance. Escalation dominance means that one adversary has overwhelming military superiority at every level of violence. The other will then be deterred from using sub-conventional, conventional or nuclear war due to the ability of the first to wage a war with much greater chances of success. It means that more room is available for manoeuvre in diplomacy and in conflict. Limited war does not mean limited capabilities. It refers to the use of those capabilities.

In a limited war, politico-diplomatic factors will play an important role. Careful and calibrated orchestration of military operations, diplomacy and domestic environment is essential for its successful outcome. Continuous control of the 'escalatory ladder' requires much closer politico-civil-military interaction. It is essential to keep the military leadership within the security and strategic decision-making loop and having a direct politico military interface. During a conflict situation, all participants must remain in constant touch with political leadership as was done during the Kargil war. Ariel Levite writes, "Furthermore, the military employment in Limited Wars is typically also subjected to constant senior military and often also political monitoring, oversight, intervention, and at times, even micro-management. This level of scrutiny and intervention has been made possible by the dramatic evolution of modern secure communications system, and has become politically or militarily attractive if not necessary by the growing transparency of developments on the battlefield in which Limited Conflicts are fought not only to the highest military echelons and civilian consumers in the chain of command (through real-time broad band secure communications between sensors) but also increasingly to the media as well."[3]

The fundamental point in a limited war is that it is a political process conducted for bargaining. The aim is not to win but rather not to lose and to fight in such a way that the enemy is forced to settle for peace and concede politico strategic advantage. When a war starts to move down the intensity spectrum, victory and defeat shift more into the political, economic and psychological dimensions. And perceptions are as important as reality. The political goals may be limited but are synergised in a way that optimizes them in our favour by maximizing the strengths and minimizing the effect of our weaknesses.

Counter Terrorist/Insurgency Operations[4]

India has a population of over 1 billion spread over 3.1 billion sq kilometres. We have people speaking 16 major languages and 200 dialects. There are a dozen ethnic groups, seven major religious communities with several sects and sub-sects, and 68 socio-cultural sub-regions: all part of a developing, semi-literate society. There are rapidly rising social, political and economic aspirations of groups in our multi-ethnic, lingual, cultural and communal social structure. The ancient, multi-ethnic and multi-cultural diversity has ethno-binding as well as ethno-competitive affects that make our national security quite complex. It is for this reason that developing India and its multi-ethnic society has been facing insurgencies and terrorism ever since independence.

We have been one of the longest victims of terrorism. But we have also handled terrorism successfully in Mizoram, Punjab and several other parts of our country. More importantly, we have not allowed terrorism to politically or economically destabilise our nation. Over the last five decades, we have developed a wealth of experience and capability in dealing with terrorism and insurgencies.

India adopts a comprehensive approach to counter terrorism and insurgencies. We believe that such operations would be effective only if there is a multi-pronged approach based on a national consensus. Our approach treats terrorism and insurgencies phenomenon with political, economic, social, perceptual, psychological, operational and diplomatic aspects, all of which need equal and simultaneous attention. It seeks a holistic approach to all these dimensions. Therefore, we have the system of unified command in terrorist affected areas under a Governor or the Chief Minister, with committees made up of all the earlier mentioned functionaries.

We also believe in a healthy, well-functioning democracy, good governance, and a secular and liberal mind-set, which makes no distinction between the majority and the minority, and treats everyone equal in the eyes of the law. Firmness and determination in action, tampered by a civilized, democratic and patient behavior by the State, have been the hallmark of India's counter-terrorism policy.

The aim of the security operations is only to isolate and arrest or eliminate the hardcore secessionist elements and to deter their supporters. The security forces use a stick and carrot approach and employ the principle of 'use of minimum force' during such operations—not the overkill required in a war. The security forces not only fight militants and anti-social elements, but also reassure innocent people feeling insecure or neglected due to inadequate civil administration. Tough measures lead to increasing alienation. Conversely, attempts to appeasement carry the risk of being read as a sign of weakening resolve. We have to find the right balance.

With experience, we have realized that we need specially organized, equipped and trained, areas-oriented security forces to deal with insurgencies and terrorism. Special Forces, Rashtriya Rifles, Assam Rifles, Rapid Reaction Force etc. are some examples. These forces, and those who work alongside, need training for local terrain people, their language, customs, and traditions. Special training schools have to be established for this purpose.

During sustained operations, the security forces involve senior and respected citizens, and professionals, as a link between them and the locals. They also form citizens' committees to learn about their difficulties, and hold meetings with them as frequently as possible. Along with sustained operations, small and large-scale civic action programmes are undertaken. In some areas, the Indian Army formed the Army Development Group and launched Operation Sadbhavana (Goodwill) for this purpose. The overall aim is to win the hearts and minds of the populace.

Emerging Techno Military Trends

At the operational level, there are emerging techno military trends that I feel are of particular significance to India. They influence defence planning, structure of the Armed Forces, their deployment pattern, conduct of war, and most importantly, the decision-making apparatus. Military technology, and some as a result of dynamic strategy considerations, is driving these. These trends are given below.

Network Centric Warfare

Wars are fought in three domains: Physical, Information, and Cognitive. The Physical domain is the existing situation that the military seeks to change. It includes the reality parameters of strength, weapons, disposition and so on; all very clearly measurable in terms of overall combat power. The Information domain is where information is created, collated, manipulated and shared, and ultimately utilized by commanders and subordinates. The Cognitive domain is the mind of the participants and relates to the perceptions, awareness, understanding, beliefs and values, which give a final shape to their decisions. This is the domain of intangibles, leadership, morale, unit cohesion, level of training and experience, situational awareness and public opinion. Battles are actually won and lost in this domain. With the help of information technology, the realities of the physical domain are converted into selected data, information, and knowledge by the systems in the information domain. And these further assist the leaders in the making judgments and taking decisions in their cognitive domains. A right kind of synchronization in time and space, resulting from conscious coordination and collaboration of the three domains would lead to a winning act.

Network Centric Warfare (NCW) recognizes the centrality of information and its potential as a source of power. It is described as "...the linking of platforms into one shared awareness network in order to obtain information superiority, get inside the opponent's cycle, and end conflict quickly." NCW networks all three domains individually, and collectively, to achieve synchronized effects. It enables a force to generate increased combat power in the battle space, achieve greater speed of command, and increase lethality, survivability and responsiveness. The NCW rests on the premise that the power of force grows proportionate to the extent of networking among the weapons, sensors and the command and control elements. NCW not only enhances awareness, it reduces the time for decision-making at higher levels of command.

Blurring Separation between Tactical, Operational and Strategic Levels of War

The separation between tactical, operational and strategic levels of warfare is blurring. While there was always some degree of overlap between these levels, due to the increasingly pervasive influence of Information Technology (IT) on warfare this overlap is increasing. As stated earlier, over the years, the range and lethality of weapons has increased and the time to target has reduced. The battle space has expanded in all the three dimensions. In a digitised battlefield, timely access to intelligence can be matched with operational mobility with great effect. Enhanced mobility, long reaches in targeting and effective command and control have obscured tactical and strategic boundaries. A small military action along the Line of Control, or a terrorists' act in the hinterland of the types that we have seen in the recent past, tend to become issues for consideration and decision-making at the strategic level. It is a situation wherein a junior military officer is expected to understand political considerations, and the political leader to know the tactical and operational considerations.

Faster OODA Loop

On account of IT enabled networking centric capabilities, and the blurring distinction between the levels of warfare, the Observe, Orient, Decide, and Act (OODA) cycle has to be traversed much faster. In effect, we have to break into enemy's

OODA cycle, and ensure quicker action while the enemy is still/kept disoriented. We need more effective integrated Command, Control, Communications, Intelligence (C3I) systems and faster decision-making at tactical, operational as well as strategic levels of command. Not only OODA, but also the cycle of collection, collation, synthesis and dissemination of information has to be speeded up and made real time. It means all three services becoming network centric.

Integration, Jointness and Interoperability

There is the aspect of integration, jointness and interoperability, as explained below:

- Defense policy and planning has to be based on collective defense forces' influence and potential and not of any individual Service. We have to think in terms of integrated capabilities and synergy among the forces for optimum utilisation of military power. Synergy can be ensured only when our war fighting aims, goals, resources and techniques are harmonised by a single doctrine. We need a joint services doctrine at the earliest.
- Our experience since the 1980s has been that the external and internal security is meshed more than ever before.
- Greater liaison, coordination and interoperability for operations is needed by the Army with agencies responsible for internal security than hitherto. It also requires compatibility of equipment, as much as possible, particularly the communication equipment.
- There is an increasing trend towards interoperability of defence forces. The backbone of such interoperability is sets of common interoperable standards and operating procedures. This trend is becoming increasingly significant, especially in the context of UN Peacekeeping Operations.

Extensive Use of Space Technology and Satellites for Surveillance, Communications and Location

Rapid and responsive military operations require timely and accurate reconnaissance reports, weather monitoring, precise navigation and long haul fail-safe communications. In Iraq, Global Positioning System (GPS), Global Information System (GIS) and satellite communications systems were used for detecting, identifying, monitoring, tracking, and ultimately destroying enemy resources. A soldier on the ground would use a laser range-finder linked to a GPS receiver to get a target's coordinates, send them to command site hundreds of miles away, which would then send them to a bomber for loading into GPS-enabled bombs that could be dropped accurately from a height over 30,000 feet. Indian aspirations for RMA would remain unfulfilled till we are ready for the NCW. The first and foremost requirement for which is a communication network that allows interoperability of the highest order among all the constituents of war fight machinery.

Use of Force-Multipliers

The concept of calculating conventional force levels to achieve an objective has been radically altered on account of force-multipliers. A small well equipped and better trained force can cause much more devastation and accomplish more than what was possible earlier.

Rapid Mobilization

The sooner an intervening force can arrive to influence the course of a military event, the smaller the chance that the conflict will devolve into firepower intensive, wasteful slugging match. Rapid mobilization out paces enemy and has the same asset as surprise. We need to review our mobilization plans, particularly in the limited war environment. It may be necessary to carry out strategic re-locations of some our combat formations, particularly those that take a long time to move and deploy. Also, we need not wait for full mobilization of the entire theatre or border (Op Cactus in Maldives and Op Prakaram).

Surveillance and Intelligence

Without adequate intelligence and continuous surveillance, even the best of plans cannot succeed. We require a very clear strategic, operational and tactical picture and assessment with the help of all possible technology and human intelligence. We have to obtain real time intelligence, and ensure that it reaches those who need it in time.

Surprise

In a limited war, due to short duration, surprise as a factor becomes more important than ever before. Strike the enemy at a time or place or in a manner for which he is least prepared. A pro-active strategy and a pre-emptive plan have a distinct advantage in a limited war.

Fire Power

The basic engine of attrition will be the synergised and integrated applications of firepower; artillery, missiles and all other firepower. Massive and surgically applied firepower will cause disruption, destruction and dislocation, and provide a decisive edge in a war. Firepower must break the enemy's will to resist before close combat begins. While operating in a firepower intensive environment, air delivered firepower, and the extended killing zone permitted by precision-guided missiles and artillery, will not only affect enemy's morale, it also offer the greatest freedom of movement to the maneuver element. In difficult terrain conditions like Siachin, Kargil and areas of North-East, we must have a clear perception of what firepower and technology can or cannot do. However, in counter insurgency and anti-terrorist operations, it may not be as effective as some of us tend to believe.

Precision-Guided Munitions

Lethal munitions and precision targeting, unavailable till very recently, promise to provide an unprecedented edge against enemy, however, well-equipped and steadfast, if he can be found and fixed. In Kosovo, about half the ordnance dropped was precision-guided; it was about two-thirds in Afghanistan and in Iraq it was more than 70%. Eighty per cent of the smart bombs struck within a few metres of the aim points. These bombs are much cheaper today.

Airpower

Let us not underestimate the airpower. Control of air is the single greatest firepower advantage. Airpower is also decisive because it can cause heavy and precise destruction, provides mobility, aerial observation, and close air support. Make close air support most responsive to your needs.

Helicopter Support

You cannot fight a battle without the aid of helicopters, for they provide all types of support, including fire support. The more this (helicopter) support is integrated with the fighting formation the better. Armed helicopters and long-range rocket artillery will lessen the problem of integrating aerial close support by taking over several difficult close air support fighter-bomber tasks.

Small-Scale Operations

In a limited, or small-scale war, tempo and speed dictate that light; highly mobile infantry and commando forces make up the majority of the force. We need more Special Forces.

Electronic Warfare

A conflict in future could well be decided on the basis of better exploitation of the electro-magnetic (EM) spectrum. Its impact is all pervasive: to aid anti-terrorist operations, prevent attacks against civilian or military targets. The e-bombs would have the advantage of no collateral damage and lesser likelihood of loss of life. Concerted R&D and user innovations into the varied uses of the EM spectrum are an urgent requirement. We also require systems and trained manpower for Information Warfare.

Information War

The Iraq conflict was the first fully IT-enabled war. Instant firepower was matched by instant communications and instant interpretation. The conflict showed how the very character of information is changing. The new form of war reporting catches events at their source, when they are still history's raw material. The earlier robust reporting gave way to brittle reporting. The result was wide; unpredictable swings in public sentiment, compounding the government's challenge of building support for the war.

These days, it is not possible to resist the pressure to be opened. The lesson, therefore, don't try. People—whether analysts, journalists, investors, employees, or members of the public—have high standards and increasingly consider the ability to know everything, as quickly as possible, to be their right, an entitlement rather than a luxury. The Pentagon used daily briefings, broadcast live, to put the scattered pieces of embedded-journalist reporting into context. Even though that context could be disputed, it was still the earliest, most robust, and best-integrated message available. Also, the U.S. government managed its communications effort from the very top. It appointed a Brigadier (Vincent Brooks) one of its brightest officers, to deal with daily briefings at Central Command headquarters in Qatar. In Washington, the secretary of defense and chairman of the Joint Chiefs of Staff held almost daily meetings with the press. The most important lesson from the Iraq war is that managing real-time communications is as important as managing real-time processes.

Military Vision

Conservative institutions like Armies tend to focus on past successes rather than failures when seeking a vision for the future. The Bangladesh and Kargil successes must be treated with great caution. The circumstances that so favored maneuver in Bangladesh, or did not favor in Kargil due to limited deployment, are not likely to be repeated. In Kargil, although we gained a victory and succeeded in achieving our political and military aims, let us not forget our intelligence and surveillance failure. We must be more innovative and adaptable to new techno-combat environment. Let us not be afraid of making changes.

Conclusion

War, as Clausewitz has aptly noted, has always been a continuation of politics by other means. Recent wars have involved a much greater level of integration of politics and military planning and execution. Even when diplomacy has run its course and a decision to employ the military is made, the political leadership seldom allows autonomous conduct of the war to the military and tends to reassert its authority when military operations reach their logical conclusion on the battlefield. In practice, we are seeing a continuing erosion of the dividing lines between war and politics.

The question that arises, 'are we, therefore, adequately equipped and trained for the more likely form of warfare or the less likely form?' Are we prepared for yesterday or tomorrow's war? Have we taken into account the nuclear thresholds with two of our more likely national security challengers; however grey those lines maybe? How relevant are our large, heavy and cumbersome combat organizations like the strike corps? Is there a need to review some of our combat organizations and operational concepts that go along with them? These are important questions. The Armed Forces must review these aspects while working on their Defense Plans. I believe that some of our combat organizations can be reduced in size; made speedier, more versatile and more flexible. It is time that we started thinking about greater combat effectiveness of our Special Forces, Combat Groups, Commands and Battle Groups and other equivalent formations. Having several large, unwieldy and expensive strike corps for conventional deterrence that tend to sit out of the war when it actually happens is not a cost effective military strategy. We could consider splitting one of them into Battle Groups initially.

We need much better integration of surveillance and operational resources (satellite imagery, air reconnaissance, radars, armed helicopters and so on) to reduce mobilization and force generation time. 'Anticipation' of a war, or in the battlefield, can be substantially improved when we deploy force multipliers effectively.

Currently, our operational planning caters more for reactive all out conventional war settings and much less for 'pro-active' limited war scenario. A reactive strategic culture tends to erode our deterrence capability. Our mobilisation, particularly of the Army, is time consuming and prone to losing strategic and tactical surprise. Besides, the Army cannot be expected to sit through the 'air dominance' period required by the Air Force. In the current strategic environment, there is a need for the Armed Forces to prepare different level joint plans, which can be implemented at a very short notice/during the course of mobilization. Such contingency plans and their full implications would need prior politico military discussions and 'in principle' approval of the Cabinet Committee of Security.

Lastly, with the conflict becoming multi-dimensional, the Armed Forces require geo-strategically aware and somewhat specialised political guidance, and networking. We also need to re-organize the networking system of the Armed Forces within, and with other agencies that have an important part to play in future wars. The Armed Forces, Intelligence Organizations, the DRDO, Atomic Energy Commission and the ministries of Defence, External Affairs, Home, Finance, Communications, Surface, Sea and Air transportation and so on; all have to work with speed, in a true spirit of cooperation, understanding and mutual confidence. Only then it would be possible to win any kind of wars.

NOTES AND REFERENCES

1. This is based on a talk given by the author in IDSA seminar on *Limited War* in January 2000.
2. Ariel Levite (of Israel), who I believe is the only other strategist outside India to have written on the subject of Limited Wars in Recent Years, in his Paper *Force and Statecraft: The Challenge of Limited Wars for Defence Planning* presented in the IDSA on January 26-29, 2001.
3. *Ibid.*
4. Based on talks given by the author on *Global Terrorism* to an annual conference of the American Jewish Committee in Washington DC in May 2003 and to the National Institute of Defence Studies, Tokyo in November 2003.

17

Military Perspectives of Security

H.M. Khanna

GENERAL

The Nation-State has been and continues to remain the essential unit of identification of the peoples on the globe. The concept of the nation-state is unlikely to disappear into oblivion in the foreseeable future. As long as the nation-state exists, its accompanying concepts of territorial and military security shall remain the dominant elements in the continuum encompassing the various aspects of the security of a nation-state. The rapid pace of globalization of national economics has, however, made several inroads into a related concept of the absolute sovereignty of Nation-States.

The search for security is a continuous and evolving process in the lives of individuals, groups and nations. The need for security ranges from ensuring survival, achieving freedom from want and fear, to attaining and maintaining a hard-won feeling of peace and prosperity. It is proverbial, however, that one man's security breeds another man's insecurity. This realist aspect of life further reinforces centrality of military and territorial security to ensure survival, growth and development. The total package addressing the nature and type of security needs of a nation derives itself from the state of social, political and economic development as well as the geopolitical compulsions confronting its region and neighborhood.

Challenges to security in the twentieth century were met by the traditional methods of defence and deterrence; development and use, if necessary, of preponderant military power in the areas of conflict. It resulted in two devastating world wars; development, proliferation and stockpiling of weapons of mass destruction (WMD), with adequate mega-tonnage to destroy the world many times over, and an emerging possibility of militarisation of space.

Many a security analysts and practitioners rue the certainty and stability associated with the period of the Cold War. The inability of the Soviet Union to keep pace with the military-technological challenges and competition resulting in its disintegration; put an end to the Cold War and its attendant relative stability. The end of the Cold War, however, opened up many of the otherwise dormant fault lines, making the world considerably less stable, and permitting series of regional conflicts to blow up. The Cold War, *de facto*, turned out to be a 'virtual war,' providing a loose rein to the theorists and analysts. They progressively came up with theories and concepts of massive retaliation, flexible response, and mutual assured destruction (MAD) depending upon the state and sophistication of nuclear arsenal at the disposal of either side, knowing fully well in their hearts that a nuclear war is neither fightable nor winnable.

The dissolution of the Soviet Empire and the emergence of the USA as a military hyper-power and the sole superpower, with no challengers on the horizon for at least a quarter of century, has given a new dimension to the security landscape around the globe. Other major developments affecting the security landscape in the foreseeable future are: the information, communication and technological revolutions underway, the increasing globalization of economies and their dependence on assured transfer of resources and expansion of markets; oil shock and energy crises; a perceived threat to the ecological balance around the globe; and last but not the least, the emergence of terrorism as the dominant form of conflict. These developments have provided the security analysts, theorists and practitioners a much wider canvas to paint the various non-military aspects of security into prominence. The dominant theme in each of these perspectives is how to save the world from itself, and to control the human greed and lust for power. The contours of the security debate now stands considerably expanded. Besides security analysts, theorists and practitioners; experts and specialists from many other disciplines to include the scientific community, economists, behavioral scientists, corporate and industrial world, and academicians have a contribution to make in the developing concept of an all encompassing security. The military perspective, while continuing to hold the high ground in the security domain, needs to be tampered with inputs from other disciplines.

'Human security' is the new fashionable mantra amongst the security analysts. It is, however, essentially a philosophical concept, or at best a strategy, which is difficult to practicalize. In essence, it approximates the ancient Indian percepts of *'Loka Samastaha Sukhino Bhavantu'*[1] *and 'Vasudev Kutumbhkam.'*[2] Thousands of years later, these percepts still remain the ideals; yet to be practicalized.

This paper aims at analyzing the contemporary and the unfolding global and regional geo-strategic environment with a view to crystallize the nature and scope of the roles that are likely to be assigned to the military predominant aspect of security to ensure the stability and balance required for growth and development.

The Global Geo-Strategic Environment

Major developments of the last quarter of a century or so, which have been the determinants of the contours of the contemporary geo-strategic environment, are:

(a) The unflattering exit of the Soviet Union from Afghanistan; providing a boost, in the process, to the political ambitions of the Islamic fundamentalists.

(b) The dissolution of Soviet empire due to its inability to keep pace with military-technological competition; and a resultant crumbling economy.

(c) The emergence of the USA as the world sole super-power and a military hyper-power with no challengers in sight for at least another quarter of a century.

(d) Oil and energy crises.

(e) The info-tech revolution and the globalization of the world's major economies.

(f) Spread of Islamic fundamentalism and its emergence as a potent force in the geopolitical arena.

(g) Emergence of terrorism as the dominant form of warfare in seeking to enforce socio-political change.

(h) Over-exploitation of the world's natural resources posing a perceived threat to the earth's ecological balance; leading to phenomenon like the puncturing of the earth's protective ozone layer and global warming.

(i) A perceived threat of the proliferation of the WMD, and more dangerously the increasing possibility of the WMD and falling into unscrupulous hands for use as weapons for mass-terror.

The compelling pace of change is the defining aspect of the twenty-first century. The stability and certainty of the Cold War period has been replaced by instabilities around the globe and a comparatively uncertain security calculus. With globalization, geo-economics have overtaken geopolitics as the primary determinant of the policies of nation-states and their groupings. The political and social institutions around the globe have, however, been unable to adapt to the punishing pace of change; and continue to grope around to find a way forward; to face the challenges posed by the post-Cold War realities. They shall have to display much greater dynamism to retain their relevance.

Europe is the only part of the world that has reaped a cognizable peace dividend at the end of the cold war. Its constituent nations were not only able to effect a considerable drawing down of their armed forces; the conventional or nuclear threat to their security has receded into the margins of their security calculus. EEC and NATO have expanded themselves eastwards to incorporate into their fold; a large number of countries comprising the erstwhile Warsaw Pact. In fact, the primary focus of Russia and her erstwhile allies in the Warsaw Pact has shifted towards acceleration of the rate of their economic development. The focus of the security concern of Western Europe revolves around retaining and maintaining its stature as the most prosperous region of the globe as well as to protect and advance the quality of life of its peoples. In this regard, their chief concerns are the threats emerging from the growing inequalities in the globalized and increasingly inter-dependent world; and a possible interruption of the flow of resources and expansion of their markets. The doomsday scenarios for them are: a massive migration of population consequent to a possible man made or natural disaster, and materialization of the self-fulfilling prophecy of the of civilizations.

Except for the now controlled and possibly capped convulsions in the Baltic region; Europe, in conjunction with North America, enjoys a perceptively greater permanence of political, social and economic stability than any other part of the globe. This has enabled them to bring into the frontline of their security concerns the non-military threats to their security encapsulated in the theme of human security. Economic compulsion have forced the nation states of Europe to grudgingly cede a part of their national sovereignty to the supra national institutions of the region. This has also diluted the significancc of territorial boundaries converting them into soft borders. Security of the region is considered to be a co-operative effort. Consensus and not coercion is the dominant currency of the inter-state transactions. "Soft power" involving persuasion and diplomacy are the preferred method of conflict resolution. However, soft power can only make an impact when duly backed up by the existence of a credible military strength and capabilities constituting the "Hard Power." This is to be co-operatively generated especially for conflict resolution tasks outside the region.

The USA's role in the defense of NATO powers in Europe now stands considerably diluted. USA, however, remains the senior partner for military defense of the security interests of the developed world around the globe. Retention of its status as the world role superpower, and military a hyper-power remains at the core of its security concerns. There is a perceived arrogance of power associated with this extraordinary power wielded by USA around the world. Most countries have persistent 'Love-Hate' relationship with the USA; and USA is also not hesitant in dishing out prescriptions for what is most suitable for growth and development of individual countries or regions.

While the US shall not willingly give up its exalted power status, the world is already being seen as becoming multi-polar, especially in terms of economic power; which is considered to be the defining element of power in the twenty-first century. China with her continuing double-digit growth rates is expected to pose a serious challenge to the US supremacy in the foreseeable future; especially in the economic arena. Europe and Pacific Asia are already reckonable and growing centers of economic power. Unlike the earlier defensive strategy of 'confrontation and containment' to meet the ideological challenge posed by communism, a more dynamic strategy of 'Engagement' has been evolved to meet the challenges to USA's economic supremacy. The economies of individual countries of Europe and Pacific Asia and more recently even China have got so enmeshed into the US economy that individual countries or grouping would have unpalatable effects on themselves while posing an economic challenge to the US. A multi-polar world is more likely to have multiple but co-operative centers of power. This provides the footprints of the emerging balance of power equations in a multi-polar world.

The USA triumphed in the Cold War, but USA itself did not reap any peace dividend. In fact, peace did not really break out at the end of the Cold War; it only opened up cultural and ethnic fissures; breeding instability around the globe. The US defense spending has only soared with time reaching anything between 400-500 billion dollars, which no other country or grouping has the ability to match. The USA has an unbridgeable lead in military technology especially in the new disciplines comprising the heart of the ongoing Revolution in Military Affairs (RMA); the expanding frontiers of missile defense as well as the military use of space. There are no challengers on the horizon to compete with the US in the area of military technology, and the US intends to keep it that way. Maintaining and widening this lead is her 'mantra' for retaining her pre-eminent status; as well as an insurance against any breakdown of the balance of power equations, or emergence of a world order contrary to her liking. The struggle for a place at the top table in the emerging New World Order is an evolutionary process and may take a better part of the first quarter of this century to crystallize. The developed worldviews stability as the perpetuation of the status quo. This paradigm is sought to be challenged by new players seeking a place of prominence in the power structure at national or international level, generating social and political turbulence in the process. Only North America and Europe are considered to be stable and enjoying what has been termed as 'stable peace.' The remainder of the globe is considered as being in turmoil. The other regions and countries have been variously described as being in state of ugly stability, unstable peace or dynamic instability depending upon the turbulence and turmoil being perceived as capped or boiling below the surface, or having surfaced to threaten the existing stability. The world is, therefore, destined to face regional instabilities till a new stable world order emerges, duly backed by vibrant, invigorated and effective social and political institutions.

The erstwhile colonial powers of Europe have a culture of effective use of a combination of hard and soft power to prevent conflict, and if necessary, resolve the conflict situation in their favor. The US record in this dimension is less than flattering. Although the US may have salvaged some pride; yet Korea and Vietnam were not exactly success stories. The more recent "Gung Ho" interventions in Somalia, Iraq and even Kosovo have exposed the limit of the use of military power in a sub-conventional warfare environment. Hopefully, some lessons may have been learnt from this unabashed use of military power. The isolationist USA of the pre-World War II era had assumed the role of a moderator against the colonial powers' unabashed use of its military power. Perhaps, it is now the turn of Europe to act as moderator in the exercise of use of military power by USA due to the preponderance of its power. The outline of the division of responsibility for conduct of stability operations around the globe appears to have crystallized. The US will be the lead player and do what it does best; use its enormous logistic capability and worldwide reach to the deploy and use its overwhelming military capability in the area of operation, duly supported by its allies or the coalition of the willing. The US operations will be in the nature of quickly in and as quickly out. The European allies will be the lead players for the conflict resolution phase. The allies unable to participate due to national policies or sensitivities will bear the appropriate burden of the cost. The developments in Afghanistan and the increasing emphasis on out of area and stability operations in NATO are pointers in this direction. Be that as it may, there exists a distinct perception of European powers distancing themselves from the US due to its unilateralist and overbearing approach. The possibility of the European powers mounting an economic challenge to the US in foreseeable future, in furtherance of their economic interests cannot be ruled out.

Germany and Japan are established economic powerhouses and they would have to be given a place at the top table in the emerging power structure. They would have to supplement their conventional warfare capabilities in tune with their economic power for defense of their interests. Equally, they would, in time, have to shed their inhibitions about out of area operations. For the foreseeable future, they will continue to rely on their strategy security alliance with the US and its nuclear umbrella.

The rise of China as an economic power, with its continuing high growth rates, has brought a new element into the global power equations; as well as a dominant influence in the regional security calculations. China is seen not only as a rival and a competitor in the economic arena but also as the only country capable of mounting a challenge to the US supremacy in any foreseeable future. The Asian region as well as the world will have to adopt to accommodate this emerging phenomenon; especially Japan, Korea and Russia in its vicinity with a history antagonistic relationship with China.

The Regional Geostrategic Environment

The recent devastating earthquake with its epicenter in Pakistan-occupied Kashmir (PoK) has displayed the geographic frailty of South Asia. Equally frail is the geostrategic environment and the security stability of this region. This region encompasses the bulk of the elements known to be the causes of conflict. It has experienced, in the last half a century or so; a geographical partition of India involving the turbulence and miseries of mass migration of population, three mid-intensity conventional wars between India and Pakistan, and a plethora of semi-dormant and active insurgencies fuelled by local, regional and extra regional powers in pursuit of their interests.

It is in South Asia that three of the world's great civilizations; the Hindu, the Buddhist and Islamic civilizations converge. If Samuel Huntington's perspective of the clash of civilizations becomes a self-fulfilling prophecy, then; South Asia lying on the fault-lines of three great civilizations is sitting on a powder keg.

Endemic and persistent poverty is the essential identity of this region with majority of its countries lying at the lower end of Human Development Index (HDI). Ethic and religious antagonisms and discrimination based on caste, color, creed and religion continue to permeate the socio-cultural milieu. Socio-political turbulence is a continuing theme of this region.

The great power interests in this region revolve around the emerging markets of the thickly populated and fast growing countries of the region; the vital need to keep the shipping lanes of the Indian ocean open for transportation of goods and raw material; and perhaps more immediately to retain and maintain a bridge head for access to the huge reservoir of oil in central Asia. The USA has long-term interest in building a counter-weight to the growing Chinese power.

Within the region there are no nations enjoying any cognizable measure of lasting security stability. Despite the existence of convulsions in many of its parts, the wonder is the contemporary prevalence of a perceived stability in the region. Perhaps the explanation lies in religion pervading the lives of the people; and tolerance and fatalism being part of their culture. A survey of the region may elucidate this.

Separatist Tamil Insurgency has bedeviled Sri Lanka for many decades. The existing but tenuous ceasefire and the ongoing negotiations brokered through the Norwegians have not made any significant headway towards a solution. The turbulence generated by the Sinhala-Tamil rivalry and confrontation appears to be a long-lasting phenomenon of the Sri Lanka's socio-political milieu. Burma has for long remained isolationist under the persistent military rule with essential links only with China. Its political institutions and democratic aspirations remain suppressed under the weight of the military rule. Considerable turbulence can be expected when the military is forced to give up its assumed role of governance.

Endemic poverty in Bangladesh, the regularity of its devastation by floods and cyclones, sensitivity of its ecological balance to global warming, and continuing migration of its population towards India, constitute the essential elements of the threat to security in its region. After over three decades of its liberation from the dominance of the erstwhile West Pakistan, Bangladesh has yet to evolve a balance between its Islamic identity and predominance of its essentially Bengali culture. The fragility of its political institutions is evident from its political history; assassination of its creator soon after independence followed by long period of military rule, and thereafter alternating transfer of power between the daughter of its founding father and the widow of its military ruler. Of equal concern is the growing influence of the Islamic fundamentalist and the safe sanctuaries available to them.

The seven sisters[3] comprising the north-eastern region of India have been experiencing varying degree insurgency over a long period. The insurgent organizations find succor, shelter and assistance from their camps and organizational structure resident across the border in Bangladesh and Burma. In some of these areas, however, the writ of the local Burmese or Bangladesh government also does not run.

Nepal is in the throes of socio-political turmoil engineered by the ultra left Maoist insurgency which now controls a large chunk of the countryside as we move westwards from the capital city of Kathmandu. Political consensus appears to have broken down. The monarchy has assumed control. The authority of the monarchy, considered to be a revered institution only a few years ago, is now being openly challenged. The Nepalese Army, the mainstay of the king's power, is fully stretched to keep the insurgency under control. Nepal's internal stability stands seriously threatened with attendant consequences for the neighboring states across the Terrai region. Externally Nepal's attempts at flirtations with Pakistan and China at the cost of its traditional and kinship relations with India has done her more harm than good.

The fulcrum of the security-stability equilibrium lies in the India-Pakistan equation. India is not only the most populous and largest country of the region, but also its largest, and of late the fastest growing economy. India, by virtue of its size and location is destined to play pivotal role in the growth and development of this region. Establishment of SAARC is an essential but hesitant first step in this direction, whose potential is yet to be realized. Pakistan, however, is not prepared to concede the centrality or primacy of India's role. Pakistan, since its very birth has assumed for itself the role of a competitor and a challenger, sworn to fight what it terms as India's hegemonistic designs. It has been prepared to pay any cost for attaining, retaining and maintaining a position of parity with India. Zulfiquar Ali Bhutto swore to acquire a nuclear capability even if it meant eating grass. Nawaz Sharif carried out competitive testing of nuclear weapons to display this achievement of parity in the nuclear arena. Anti-India orientations have formed the basis all her external pacts and alliances as well internal propaganda. At the foundational level, Pakistan's Islamic identity remains at odds with India's secularism; and with a confrontationist attitude based on inherent insecurities. The persistence of the imbroglio in Jammu & Kashmir is only symptomatic of the inability to find practical ways of co-existence of these basic foundational ideologies. Besides her determination for keeping pace with numerical and military technological superiority enjoyed by India, Pakistan has a pro-active and offensive-defense strategy to neutralize India perceptible conventional superiority. Jammu & Kashmir's Muslim majority status and the existence large pockets of Muslim majority areas; which in sum contain Muslim population equivalent to, if not larger than Pakistan's own population, offer Pakistan the opportunity to engineer and sustain active insurgency in Jammu & Kashmir, as well as carry out sabotage and subversion in the rest of India.

It is only recently that Pakistan appears to have realized the enormous cost to herself of carrying the burden of incessant competition in military power and capabilities vis-à-vis India; as well as the backlash on her own stability of fuelling fundamentalism in support of her designs in Jammu & Kashmir and her ambitions in Afghanistan. There is an off-quoted saying that Pakistan is run by 'Allah, Army and America.' The Pakistan army has assigned to itself the role of not only defending the territorial frontiers but also the ideological frontiers of Pakistan. Pakistan has been under direct Army rule for a major portion of its existence, and the Army has been the final arbiter of the political orientation of its rulers during the remaining period. Pakistan's political institutions stand stymied by the overbearing power of its armed forces. Allah's mystical hand must have been behind the creation of situations in Afghanistan meriting America's active intervention in the region. Each time Pakistan was approaching economic bankruptcy or near failed status. First, in the form of Soviet intervention in Afghanistan, raising the status of Pakistan to the front line state. Again, after 9/11 Afghanistan became the first target of the American wrath seeking vengeance against the Al Qaida based in Afghanistan. On both occasions Pakistan was the recipient of a substantial American largesse both in terms of economic aid for stabilization of her economic health and military equipment for boosting her military capabilities.

The historical background of the Indo-Pak relations does not inspire much confidence for the present bonhomie in Indo-Pak relations to last over of a long period. If it does last and enlarges its domain, it should be considered as Allah's grace for prosperity of this region. It cannot, however, be a planning criterion for considerations of security.

Afghanistan fits the criteria of a failed state. It has a turbulent history. Seldom has the writ of its rulers' run to include the control of the countryside. Its innumerable tribes are fiercely independent and have yet to be tamed. Even the British only launched punitive expeditions; but never attempted to retain full control over it and tribes inhabiting the countryside. Powers intervening into Afghanistan have invariably had their hands scorched. The present US incursion into Afghanistan may have destroyed the Al Qaida infrastructure existing there; but the odds are stacked against taming of Afghanistan into a functional democracy.

India has traditional good relations and strategic interest in Afghanistan as well as the oil rich central Asian countries. Pakistan, however, considers Afghanistan to be its backyard; providing it the much needed strategic depth. It is this perception of treating Afghanistan as its backyard, which may have been the motivation for Pakistan being drafted willingly for the US escapades into Afghanistan. Afghanistan remains the unstablest of the countries in the South Asian Region. Pakistan may have yet to experience the full extent of the backlash emerging out of her policy of promoting Islamic fundamentalism in pursuit of her ambitions in Jammu & Kashmir and Afghanistan.

India thus has, perhaps, one of the most threatening external security environments. It is flanked by nuclear armed China and Pakistan with thousands of miles of disputed and fully manned borders with both countries, and large tracts of her territory being either under adverse occupation or claimed by other parties. Pakistan swears by her all weather friendship with China substantiating the perception of the existence of a Pak-China nexus against India. When compared to 2.5 million strong modernized Chinese PLA, and technologically competitive 650,000 strong all volunteer Pakistan army; even the 1.2 millions strong duly modernized Armed forces of India look comparatively miniscule. A war on two fronts involving both Pakistan and China, even though an unlikely and unrelishable possibility, it must figure into reckoning of security parameters of India. The big power rivalry over the control and domination of the oil rich central Asian Region and the existence of an unstable Afghanistan in our vicinity has definitive security implications for India in the foreseeable future. The gravity of this scenario pales into insignificance the security implications of the inherent instabilities in Burma, Bangladesh and Sri Lanka. India's large heartedness towards its neighbors permits even the Bangladesh rifles to unhesitatingly activate their border without fears of substantive repercussions or reprisals.

Internal threats to India's security are even more concrete and real when compared to the perceived short-term and long-term external threats. A multilingual, multi-religious and multi-ethic India faces division based on caste, color, creed, religion or region. Despite the much touted poverty alleviation programmes, encapsulated in the political slogan of *Roti, Kapda, aur Makan* with *Rozi* also figuring into it of late; or the more recent emphasis on caring for the *am admi* poverty remains endemic with regularity of visitations by drought, cyclones, floods and earthquake. The revolutionary expansion of the communication network through Radio, TV and telephone has further raised the awareness and expectations of people. The state, however, just cannot generate the resources to match these expectations. Maintenance of internal stability is, perhaps, the most challenging of India's problems concerned with security.

India has a creditable record in facing the internal challenges to her integrity and security. It stands out as the exception amongst the post-colonial countries to have successively carried out peaceful transfers of power amongst the various contending political institutions; as opposed to repeated coups with long periods of military rule in other newly independent countries. The off-quoted saying in the form of wall graffiti in Karachi in respect of Pakistan is "We are sorry for this temporary democratic interruption, Military rule will be resumed shortly." The comparatively mature socio-political institutions in India have enabled her to successfully battle a spate of insurgencies. The separatist insurgencies in the North-East have been successfully checkmated and gradually losing their steam. The Sikh insurgency in Punjab has been decisively beaten, with remnants licking their wounds in their havens in Pakistan and some Western countries. Even in the Jammu & Kashmir, the fight against Pakistan inspired and backed militancy and terrorism, prosecuted by Islamic fundamentalist based across the border is over the hump with the security forces having regained the control of the high ground in the military space. The message is loud and clear that there is no military solution to the Jammu & Kashmir problem. The bulk of the credit for this must go to the tenacity displayed by the security forces. There is strong lobby in the country which believes that the country is being held together by the professionalism displayed by the armed forces and internalization by the armed forces of the principal of civilian supremacy.

Socio-economic turbulence is a continuing process, which provided the themes for political agenda of the various political parties. The threats posed by the Ultra left PWG terrorism in many of the Indian states; the growing threat of Islamic fundamentalism from within India; the interstate wrangling over resources like water and electricity; a relative absence of job opportunities, and internal fallout of the effects of globalization, WTO accords are amongst the many issues capable of rocking the countries internal stability and security. The country could be engulfed by a political Tsunami if the political leaders are unable to display the sagacity and the political wisdom required for meeting the challenges posed by the non-military aspects of security.

Military Perspective and Non-Military Aspect of Security

Security is an all-pervading issue, which provides the background for the action carried out by individuals, social groups, states, nations, and the international organizations. There has never been nor can there be a purely military perspective of security. In the developing and actual conflict situations, where violence and coercion become the dominant currencies of transactions the military perspective of security assumes over arching dominance to restore order and stability. The all-inclusive perspective of human security is the strategy for conflict resolution phase.

During periods of peace, the non-military aspects of the security of individual and groups; like the security of food and shelter, security of income and job opportunities, security of health and environment lie in the routine functions and normal domain of politicians, social workers, administrators, scientists, engineers as well as the corporate world. Their contribution towards the achievement long-term stability and security has now been highlighted by the increasing globalization. In fact, the developed world having pushed the military threats to their security to the margins and arrived at the stage of stable peace, now seeks long-term stability and peace. The answer lies in the developing ideological formulation of Human Security.

Human security is now a global ideological formulation of security which is an all inclusive concept to include fight against terrorism, drug trafficking, AIDS, environment degradation and illegal immigration; preservation of ecological balance; ensuring water and energy security as well as programmes for banishing of extreme poverty.

Non-Military aspects of security and the ideological formulation of Human Security are add-ons to the Military dominant perspectives of security, which shall continue to form the foundational basis of all the security-related formulations.

On ground, it shall imply an expansion of the traditional roles of military to include areas, which lend themselves to exploitation of the inherent strengths of the military organizations, their power and extensive logistical capabilities. Besides the capability of playing a lead role in the fight against terrorism and drug trafficking, the military's inherent strengths have considerable scope for exploitation in Green field development projects in underdeveloped terrain; dealing with restoration of normalcy in the event of ecological or natural disaster; alleviation of human tragedy in war torn areas.

The Evolving Nature of Warfare

Unacceptable destructive and devastating power of the WMD especially the nuclear weapons, has limited their role to deterrence which essentially lies in the psychological domain. Countries with ambitions to develop or procure WMD face definitive prospect of inviting the general displeasure of the comity of nations, but more importantly of the wrath and punishment by members of the exclusive nuclear club. However, the distinct possibility of procurement of WMD by the unscrupulous non-state actors or terrorists, represents a doomsday security scenario. Prevention and pre-emption is the strategy against such a development. While nuclear warfare shall remain at the apex of the continuum of the type of operations to be conducted by the military; it remains not only a remote possibility but also an impracticable enterprise.

Historically, the advent of new technologies has brought about revolutionary changes in the conduct of warfare; the Soviets termed them as military-technological revolutions. The accelerating pace of the advance in science and technology has also generated the ongoing revolution in military affairs (RMA). Although the principles of war have remained constant and shall continue to do so; their inter-se importance and the methods of their application are bound to undergo a change with the incorporation RMA into the military systems. The advances in technology are only enablers; revolutionary changes emerge out of their practicalisation and incorporation into the existing systems. The revolutionary aspect of the RMA relates not only to the additional power and capacity generated by the new weapons and related technologies but also accompanying revolutionary changes required in the organizational and non military aspects of military systems for the application of the capability. "A revolution in Military affairs is a major change in the nature of warfare brought about by innovative application of new technologies which, combined with dramatic changes in military doctrine and operational and organizational concepts, fundamentally alters the character and conduct of military operations."[4]

The ongoing RMA is qualitatively different. It does not relate to changes brought about by singular development of the earlier times like the advent of gunpowder, creation of mass armies, development of fighter aircraft or submarine, or nuclear weapons. It is based on the expanding horizons of a wide spectrum of new technologies, which individually and collectively affect the entire range of military systems. The rate of change is so fast that even the developed industrialized countries have been unable to keep pace with it. The US army while still in the process of practicalising the vision 2010 has already been pushed to crystallize the contours of what it calls the Army after next (AAN).

The RMA promises much. Space based surveillance systems and weapons may generate new power and capabilities for offense and defense. The incorporation of fully developed Kinetic energy weapons; directed energy weapons; and Ballistic Missiles Defense Systems will completely alter the nature of conventional warfare. In less than two decades the Army after next may be configured around individuals acting as weapons systems; self-contained for long duration and wielding the power and capability exceeding those of the present-day sub-units; duly assisted by bio-genetics technologies and bionic men. Maneuver by fire may become the dominant and decisive form of maneuver. Special forces may be the basic unit of the infantry. The tactical concepts may evolve around 'disengaged combat' with emphasis on Special Forces and effects based operations. The conduct of close quarter battle may fade away. The concept of network centric warfare having been practicalised, the operational level of war may be eliminated. The disabling technologies are likely steal a march over technologies for destruction. Clausewitzian thought centered on destruction and annihilation may be less relevant than Sun Tzu's formulation of winning the war without fighting a battle as the guiding principle for conduct of warfare. Psychological aspect of war may be the defining theme of warfare; involving use of technology to incapacitate organizations and military systems; coupled with the use of psycho-technology to alter the perceptions and political beliefs of the decision-maker amongst both the allies and adversaries. The information and psychological warfare may not remains support systems but may graduate towards becoming lead players.

On the ground, the contemporary and fielded in service aspects of the RMA are so far essentially based on the advances in technology related to computers and electronics. The two areas that have undergone revolutionary changes are Information Warfare and Precision Targeting. The circular error of Probability (CEP) of even the long-range weapons has already been reduced to less than ten metres and continues to shrink further. Although rather one-sided; and *de facto*, assuming the form of a firepower demonstration on the ranges, the Iraq war amply brought out the rapid expansion of military power generated by application of RMA technologies. The doctrinal and organizational changes, however, have yet to catch up.

Both time and space appear to have shrunk in the last half a century or so, and this is reflected in the pace of change. RMA may, in fact, may turn out to be an evolutionary phenomenon. Witness the successive development of weapons and their effect on evolution of new tactical and strategic concepts in conventional warfare in Europe. The development of assault breaker missiles to cope with threat posted by massed armor, development of the concept of follow on forces attack (FOFA) as ranges and capability of weapons got enhanced, the doctrine of Air Land Battle, and fielding of ATACMS, JSTARS and Precision interdiction strikes. The developments of the RMA shall gradually find their way into the armories of other big powers, middle ranking powers and even poorer countries depending upon the gravity of assessed conventional threat and state of their economic health. The matured military system integrating the developments of RMA shall generate power and capability to cause destruction equivalent to or even exceeding the use of WMD. Conventional warfare may be itself become a prohibitive exercise. The response to the above developments has been the evolving concept of Asymmetric Warfare, which displays the potential of becoming the dominant form of warfare in the twenty-first century.

Asymmetric Warfare

Post-Second World War, none of the conventional wars resulted in bringing about any territorial or Socio-Political changes; status quo continued to persist after the war in each case. All political or territorial changes in this period were effected through unconventional warfare variously termed as revolutionary wars, national or liberation movements. The objectives were political; and they invariably resulted in partial or complete achievement of their objectives in bringing about political change. Unconventional wars have become the favored medium of bringing about political change. The armed forces professionals brought up in the culture of destructions and annihilation, attrition and maneuver, fight to the finishes and unconditional surrender have been slow to adjust to the realities of unconventional warfare being the persistent form of warfare. A variety of terms like counter Guerilla Warfare, Counter-Insurgency, Low Intensity Conflict (LIC), Stability operations, Support operations and more recently military operations other than warfare (MOOTW) have been used to distinguish military participation in unconventional warfare from their primary role in conventional or nuclear wars. The ground reality, however, is that the destructive power associated with nuclear weapons and more recently even conventional wars have made them unacceptable options; and unconventional war is likely to remain the persistent form of warfare in the 21st century.

Sophisticated counter-insurgency techniques, revolutionary advances in mobility of forces, modern capabilities of surveillance, info and spy-war have made it impossible for any new socio-political or religion inspired movement to mount a conventional military challenge; like the early revolutionary movements in China or Vietnam or the Sadinista and the like. The twenty-first century terrorism is the mutated form of the twentieth century revolutionary warfare, which aims to achieve similar political objectives without having to fight pitched battles of the conventional military arena. The objectives continue to be political change and alteration of the power equations in a nation, region or the international arena. The new incarnate unconventional warfare adopted by the Islamic Fundamentalists has already acquired transnational dimension and status, with displayed potential to grow into what has been termed as hyper-terrorism with ambitions to acquire a clandestine nuclear capability.

The term Asymmetric Warfare recognizes the dominant role to be assigned to the military; but with the liberty to use its power and capability severely curtailed by environmental, cultural, ethical and other considerations of Human Rights. For the terrorists, however, it is uninhibited total war only limited by the resources at their disposal, giving the terrorists a tactical advantage.

The terrorists generate their strength from political mobilization, use of coercion and protracted violence as the dominant currency of their transactions with governments, national and international organizations, as well the general population and their supporters. Pitched battles of the conventional battle space are to be avoided, but hit and run raids into this space are launched with regularity by innovative use of modern technology; by improvised but powerful weapons and missiles to cause awesome death and destruction. The aims of the operations in the military arena are psychological attrition of the security forces and their supporters; ensuring the terrorists' own survival through offensive defense; and to retain and maintain a stalemate for continuance of future operations. The entire exercise is a stamina game to provide a base and a platform; as well to gain time for attaining ascendancy in the political arena.

The disaster that struck the USA on 11th September 2001 and its aftermath represents the opening rounds of the war against terrorism. It broke the myth of invulnerability of the US homeland, and posited a symbolic challenge to the USA's economic and military supremacy. The US retribution in Afghanistan and Iraq was instinctive and spontaneous. USA has won the first battle with ease based on its overwhelming conventional superiority. Whether she can display the resilience to win the peace and thwart the long-term designs of the Islamic fundamentalists is an open-ended question. As it stands today, the terrorists appear to have psychological ascendancy in both Iraq and Afghanistan. Despite physical destruction of the bulk of its infrastructures in Afghanistan, the Al-Qaida retains its worldwide spread of networks and strike capabilities. It is evident that the world is in for a long and protracted struggle in view of the vital political and economic stakes involved. The Al-Qaida ambitions are assessed as gaining control of the Islamic World through spread of Islamic fundamentalism, with a view to establish the equivalent of the erstwhile caliphate. The overall aim being to alter the balance of power in the International arena.

India's Security—Military Perspectives

The seeming stability structured around a manipulated consensus; an accelerated rate of growth of the Indian economy rivaling that of China; the emergence of a burgeoning and increasingly prosperous middle class, lifting India to the status of a favored emerging market must not be permitted to lull us into a sense of complacency or wish away the enormity and gravity of the nature of external and internal threats to India's security and integrity.

The recent Indo-Pak bonhomie or the ongoing India-China negotiations aimed at a border settlement, have yet to show any significant forward movement or concretized results. The ground reality remains a near permanent eye ball to eye confrontation both along the line of control (LoC) with Pakistan; and the line of actual control (LAC) with China. Hyper active militancy in Jammu & Kashmir, persistent insurgency and militancy in the North-East and expanding reach of the Maoists and PWG in the heartland, and communal riots occurring in repeated succession have to form the basis of our security calculus.

China has a domineering attitude. Pakistan displays an attitude of arrogance based on her perception of an ability to negotiate from a position of strength; derived out of her displayed nuclear weapons status and her assessment of a capability to indefinitely continue with terrorism in Jammu & Kashmir duly controlled, generated and inspired by her. The debilitating effect on the military and the psychological impact on the administration is to be treated as a pressure point to obtain concessions. Her repeatedly testing of the threshold of India's tolerance is indicative of this perception and a newfound confidence. Pakistan, however, has her own internal instabilities. Her present seeming politico-social stability is imposed from above by a near dictatorial military dominated regime; however benevolent be the projection of its dictator. The perceived dominance in Pakistan by Punjab and the Punjabis of the power structure, suppressed Baluch and Sindhi nationalism, the historically untamed independent nature of its tribes inhabiting the border regions of Baluchistan and NWFP have the potential blow up into conflict. Of graver concern for India is the increasing political role and power being assumed by Islamic fundamentalist organizations and political parties. A Pakistan imploding from within, or a Pakistan dominated and governed by Islamic fundamentalist is a much graver threat to India's security than the present day confrontationist military ruled Pakistan. Post-1971, a wide range of Indian commentators predicted a gradual marginalisation of Pakistan. This type of wishful thinking is inappropriate security planning criteria. Pakistan has repeatedly demonstrated her resilience; we must plan to keep under check a vibrant but antagonistic Pakistan. The strategy to be adopted in this regards is the strategy of 'compellance;' to be achieved by developing the appropriate diplomatic and economic strength; and coercive conventional military capability and superiority. Despite the nuclear stand off, there remains ample scope for conventional military response to Pakistan repeatedly crossing India threshold of tolerance, especially in Jammu & Kashmir; with a view to deliver hurting military blows and in the process test and stretch Pakistan's threshold of conventional tolerance, while still remaining within the assessed nuclear threshold.

India and China are competitors in the global economic arena. Both China and Pakistan would try to limit India's regional power status. China will thus remain India's long-term security threat. This does not by itself imply a lasting adversarial relationship between India and China. Cooperation between India and China can enhance the global status and reckoning of both the countries and provide stability in the region. China has global power ambitious with focus towards USA, Japan and Russia, who pose the greater threat to her security and ambitions. Tibet and Sinkiang represent China soft underbelly. China has over a period, considerably enhanced her logistic capability in Tibet, which needs to be reckoned with by the Indian security planners. The military strategy against China has to be based on nuclear deterrence and conventional 'dissuasion.' The rugged and prohibitive nature of the terrain comprising of high altitude and glacial mountain favoring the defender as well as the possibility of generating superior air capability based on airbases located in the plains are favorable factors on the Indian side. There is a necessity to improve the logistic and communication infrastructure on our side of the border to ensure that the humiliating experience of 1962 is never repeated.

The nature and quantum of external threats to India's security are predictable; and remain well within the capabilities of duly modernized professional Indian Armed Forces to cope with and neutralize. It is the internal threats that pose a greater danger to India's security and integrity.

India lives in three distinct echelons. A prosperous top echelon composed of the rich and upper middle class enjoying standards of living comparable to those of developed world. A burgeoning and ambitious middle and lower middle class concentrated in bigger towns and metropolitan cities seeking upward mobility and a secure future for their children. A large un-empowered chunk of the India's population lives in abject poverty eking out a survival existence; frequently uprooted by natural or man made disasters. In addiction to this there are horizontal and vertical division in terms of North-South divide, division based on caste, color, religion or regions. Social turbulence is endemic and lends itself to exploitation by the power seekers to cause conflict and confrontation between communities. The 1984 Anti-Sikh riots in Delhi and the more recent communal carnage in Gujarat represent only the tip of the iceberg. India's socio-political systems have tremendous resilience and have been constantly bringing into the power structure the un-empowered communities and classes to develop a stake in the existing institutions and structures. Reservations for the scheduled castes and tribes as well as the OBC represent positive action in this direction. Rampant corruption and lust for power can break down so far manipulated political consensus and let loose the political equivalent of a Tsunami. Center-state relations and inter-state rivalry and disputes over sharing of waters and electricity are persisting areas of discord. The essential elements of human security can no longer be treated as routine administrative functions. They have to become a part of the overall package of national security; a necessary add on to military security; and to be executed with the same degree of seriousness.

The focus on human security is the South Asian Region in general and India in particular implies a role expansion for the armed forces. The armed forces must not now treat their role in meeting and neutralizing the internal threats to security as their subsidiary role. They must plan for and be capable and ready to undertake operations along the entire spectrum of military and military-assisted operations. Extending from disaster relief and aid to civil authorities, to stability and confidence building operations, counter-terrorism as well as the broad and better tasks of conventional and nuclear warfare. It needs to be emphasized that in our regional context; Human security does not constitute an alternate approach but is an essential supplement the basis concept of national and territorial security. It is my view that the core issue between India and Pakistan is security. The problem in Jammu & Kashmir is only a symptom of this security-insecurity complex. Shifting the focus of the security concerns in Jammu & Kashmir from territorial security to 'Human Security' can provide the outlines of the resolution of the Jammu & Kashmir imbroglio.

Conclusion

The basic unit of identity around the globe is the Nation state; and its accompanying concept of territorial security remains the foundational basis of the security calculus among nations. Human endeavours and actions of groups, communities and the comity of nations revolve around the search for security, peace and stability, growth and development. The overall security calculus must, therefore, reach down to the individual and extend upwards to include regional and global security.

The certainty and stability associated with the cold war has given way to the existing comparative uncertainties and instabilities. The entire gamut of the security calculus is in a state of flux. The world is now divided into areas of peace and stability comprising bulk of Europe and North America and the areas of 'turmoil' comprising the rest of the regions on the globe. The primary threat to the security of the developed world comes from the hot spots of instabilities spread around the globe; and attempts to alter the existing balance of power presently titled in their favor, as well as the threats emerging from over exploitation of the earth's resources and the resultant ecological imbalance.

The destructive power associated with WMD makes their use impracticable and abhorrent. The info-tech revolution has engineered the RMA, which has enabled revolutionary advances in precision targeting and destructive power of conventional munitions and promises much greater generation of power and destructive potential of conventional forces and weapons. In effect, this may make the likelihood of a war between symmetrically equipped conventional forces also a remote possibility. Asymmetric warfare promises to be the dominant form of warfare in the twenty-first century.

Trans-national terrorism with networks spread across the globe; employing innovative use of technology for operations is the new mutated form of insurgency adopted by the Islamic fundamentalists to post a challenge to USA and her allies. Terrorism is to be used as the vehicle to first gain control of the Islamic World and eventually to effect a change in the existing world order. Asymmetric warfare is likely to be the dominant form of warfare in the twenty-first century; it enables exploitation of the weakness of the security forces and full exploitation of terrorists' strengths and resources.

The concept of 'Human Security' aims at moderating the existing turbulence and turmoil with a view to prevent its development into violent conflict. It is a preventive concept with equally useful application for post conflict resolution. Controlled and judiciously applied military force is the only way to maintain and restore order in the developing, active and persistent conflict situations.

In the South Asian environment, internal security threats are many and varied. It implies an expansion of the military's role across the entire spectrum of military dominated and military assisted operations. Incorporation of Non Military and Human Security aspects into the National security calculus alone can minimize the chances of sub-surface turbulence transforming itself into violent conflicts.

NOTES AND REFERENCES

1. Meaning; may the entire human race live in peace and happiness.
2. Meaning; all the living beings on this planet are one family.
3. These the states of Assam, Nagaland, Meghlaya, Manipur, Mizoram, Tripura, and Arunachal Pradesh.
4. Andrew Marshal, Director of office of net assessment, office of the secretary of Defense, USA.

18

Military Industrial Base: Is India Inching Towards It?

M.R. Joshi

Introduction

The production of military hardware and weapons in India could be traced back to the early nineteenth century, when the British Empire was trying to consolidate its base in India. Although the earlier periods saw some fierce battles, the weaponry required by the princely states was not produced through any organised industry. Therefore, the British model of the Ordnance factories came into existence through the network of the Ordnance factories, which still forms the major component of the Indian Defence production. These Ordnance factories were primarily meant for fulfilling the British Army's requirements and thus were oriented to meet the war shortages. No real Research and Development activity was undertaken by these factories. If one looks for the first indigenous weapon development effort in the country, he will find Tipu Sultan's experimental development of the Rocket as the most significant achievement. Although the concept was exceptionally good, it was produced without appropriate engineering. The shortfalls noticed from the concept to production were made up by the British, who took a sample to the U.K. and perfected it through proper Development and Engineering methods. Thus came the revolutionary Congreve Rocket in the Britishers' arsenal. The things have changed a lot in the past two centuries; but the major weakness of the Indian industry does not appear to be corrected over these 200 years. This paper attempts to take a stock of the industrial base available within the country and to examine if it has the capacity to convert itself into a military industrial base.

India's Defence Expenditure

India's military spending is always on the rise although the hike in spending varies from year to year. Currently, the budget is pegged down to Rupees 830 billion. The experts feel that this is not enough to fund the badly needed modernisation programme. Therefore, the budget is bound to cross a trillion rupees threshold in the next couple of years.

The modernisation and military acquisition programme that India has set for itself needs appropriate and sustained increases in the capital component of the budget. The fact that there has been a marginal drop in the rate of increase this year is worrying the operational planners.

India, one of the world's biggest arms buyers with one million-plus troops, is looking for 126 new jet fighters to replace an accident-prone fleet of Russian-built MiGs, an anti-missile system from the United States and rocket launchers from Russia. In the recent past, India has bought the Phalcon radar system from Israel for 1.1 billion dollars, a used aircraft carrier from Russia for 1.5 billion dollars, 66 Hawk jet trainer planes from Britain for 1.45 billion dollars and recently six Scorpene submarines from France for 3 billion dollars. The last deal with France is for import and building of the submarines at the Naval Dockyard. This single deal amounts to approximately 20 per cent of the annual defence budget.

India's Congress-led government came to power in May 2004 on a pro-poor ticket and with outside support from the leftists. So it is under pressure to funnel money into the health, education and social sectors to keep its political coalition intact. The Finance Minister managed to use its budget allocation for the current financial year of 770 billion rupees in full by allocating additional rupees 250 billion for social programmes like health care, education and poverty alleviation. This is seen by some as an effective way of reducing the Defence budget share in the Government spending. Secretary (Defence Finance) in her brief to the Finance Ministry has stated that the country needs to hike its defence budget by more than 35 per cent to Rupees 1.12 trillion, compared to the current year's Rs. 83 billion. This means that the defence budget would be pegged at four per cent of the GDP.

When one looks at the entire economic scene from a statistical perspective, lie finds that the total budgetary outlay of Rs. 213,000 crores is spent on a population of 1.05 billion or Rs. 2,028 per citizen. Let's call this figure DevX. Similarly, the Rs. 83,000 crores spent on defence translates to Rs. 790 per citizen. Let us call this expenditure the Defence Expenditure Index (DefX). With these two figures now available, we can look at the Development-to-Defence Ratio (DDR), which tells us how much is being spent on defence vis-à-vis on development. The current DDR is about 2.57. That is, we spend 2.57 times as much on development as we do on defence.

Is that good? Since the great majority of the Indian people live in difficult conditions, it follows that this ratio of development-to-defence spending is too low. To understand this further, let us look at development measures for nations that are comparable to India. We could benchmark our DDR to the Human Development Indices (HDI) of these nations—Argentina, Mexico, Brazil, and Sri Lanka—and use that as a target that can be realised over a period of time. HDI figures are shown below:

Country	*HDI*	*Rank*
Argentina	0.844	34
Mexico	0.796	54
Brazil	0.757	73
Sri Lanka	0.741	89
India	0.574	124

The objective of this paper is not to examine the statistical data related to defence spending as a percentage of GDP or as a percentage of the Government spending. The Defence spending ultimately will depend on our security perspectives and the role India should play in the region. There should also be no compromise on the objective of attaining a sustainable development. The defence budget can be seen as a drag on our development if 'we' are spending on defence by funding 'their' Research and Development. On the contrary, we could also see the defence spending as a catalyst to our development and as a vehicle to create a strong Science and Technology Base within the country. This approach can finally enable us to realize competitive advantage in the highly hostile commercial world. This paper intends to examine the Science and Technology base, Industrial Infrastructure and the effect of globalisation on our National Security policies.

Could India's Military strength and defence spending help the nation to achieve higher levels of technological competence? Could that lead us to self-reliance? Will this help us gain a crucial advantage in the industrial world where our commercial products will be world class and globally competitive? If the answers to these questions are in the positive, we can achieve higher growth rates, which in turn can sustain higher levels of Government and defence spending. Only then, there is a strong case for creation of a Military Industrial Base.

In the recent years, the Indian economy is growing very rapidly. The corporate India has made tremendous advances into the world markets. Our Information Technology (IT) industry has became a role model for many other countries. It is not the IT sector alone, our pharmaceutical industry, design capabilities and some of the manufacturing sectors are making their mark on the global scene. There are acquisitions, joint sectors and foreign direct investments coming into news. It is no more a one-way traffic; but even Indian business houses are acquiring companies abroad. Most of these developments are taking place in the private sector. The Government and Public sectors, on the other hand, are performing by exception. There is a huge infrastructure built up over a long period, the good portion of it could still be used profitably.

The globalisation in the non-strategic and the commercial sectors has brought about major changes—especially change in the mindsets. Similarly, new equations in international relationship are getting established. We can still live in peace with collaborations with Russia, the United States, France, Israel and Italy. However, without having a strong Science and

Technology base in the country itself, these collaborations will have no meaning. Let us, therefore, take an overview of the existing industrial infrastructure available within the country and assess as to what extent it can be used to meet the challenges of the twenty-first century war machines.

Science & Technology in India

The Science and Technology activities in the country are so far limited primarily to the Government sector. The following are the four major S&T organizations within the country.

(a) Council of Scientific and Industrial Research (CSIR)
(b) Department of the Atomic Energy
(c) Indian Space Research Organization (ISRO)
(d) Defence Research & Development Organization (DRDO)

Out of the above, DRDO is the youngest and yet the largest organization. Although each organization is created for its own specific objectives, there is a air amount of interaction between them. Together, they employ around 20,000 scientists and engineers and share the annual budgets of approximately rupees 10,000 crores. There is always a debate in the media and strong criticism, especially of the DRDO programmes. Yet there are quite a few significant achievements to their credit. Today, India has achieved a status of a nuclear power, having its own delivery system, capable of designing and launching its own satellites. All this would not have been possible if the four S&T organizations would not have created the infrastructure and the competence in strategically sensitive areas. Without resorting to any clandestine means, India has exploded the myth of the Missile Technology Control Regime (MTCR). The question is "Could we have not done better if we had harnessed the full potential of the country including the private sector and the academics?"

Before we proceed further to the issue of privatisation, let us have a brief overview of some of the facilities that are available within the country for design, development and manufacture the military hardware. Appendix 'A' lists the four major S&T organizations that are within the domain of Government sector while appendix 'B', 'C' and 'D' lists the PSUs that are directly relevant to the production of weapons and the systems for military applications.

Even today, many weapon system development programmes are undertaken with the active participation of the private sector. But, the number of companies having adequate skill sets, infrastructure facilities and will to work in this high risk area are only a few. Appendix 'E' lists a typical world-class company which has come forward to participate in the weapon system development programmes and has made a significant contribution to our national efforts.

The Evolution of the Defence Industrial Base

The concept of the defence industrial base is, in many respects, an artefact of that unusual period in the world history. It came as a natural sequel to the industrial revolution triggered by James Watt's steam engine in the year 1762. Each new invention thereafter was being looked upon as a potential military weapon. This process was accelerated during the World War II, culminating in the development and use of an atomic bomb. The British, German and other European countries were strong proponents of using the industry for military purpose. This continued till the World War I, wherein the United States did not play a major role. Soon thereafter, the erstwhile leaders were pushed in the background by the American inventions in the early twentieth century. Yet, till the beginning of the Cold War, the United States did not have a distinct industrial sector that was dedicated to design and manufacture of the weapons. Instead, the U.S. government pursued a peacetime strategy of maintaining arsenals for critical, defence-unique capabilities like munitions and warships while contracting out most supply and service requirements. In times of crisis or war, the government would turn to the larger national industrial base as the foundation on which to build the necessary productive capacity. The differentiation between commercial companies and those supplying defence products to the government was a function of the inherent differences in the goods themselves. After the World War II, the U.S. and its allies had to build and deploy in peacetime the weapons and forces they would need to fight a possible war with the Soviet Union and its allies. A permanent state of war required a "permanent" defence industrial base. For the first several decades of the Cold War, government R&D, primarily for military purposes, was the major force driving technological innovation in the U.S. government procurements. This created a pull for private sector R&D. In a number of cases government funding and private sector R&D acted in a mutually reinforcing manner to accelerate the development and commercialisation of new technologies. As a result, defence-oriented companies were required to develop structures and practices to enable them to adhere to federal contracting practices, standards and specifications, and regulations. The costs associated with conforming to acquisition regulations and contracting requirements were factored into the price of the firms' products.

After the end of the Cold War, DoD not only purchased fewer new weapons but reduced its research and development into follow-on weapons systems. Since 1990, overall defence spending has fallen by nearly 28 per cent.

The new technologies that have now to be adopted alter the value-added chain in production. Whereas thirty years ago "metal-bending" was the most lucrative stage in manufacturing, today the most value is added in the "systems integration" stage, that is, the stage in which manufacturers integrate micro circuitry, sensors, and weapons systems into a complete platform. For instance, in today's combat aircraft nearly 50 per cent of the final costs come from the avionics, sensors, fire control and weapons systems, components that three decades ago comprised barely 20 per cent of the total costs. Defence industries have reorganized and consolidated in a manner that reflects an attempt to capture a greater share of this systems-integration business. By becoming vertically integrated, they can capture the value-added work at the systems and subsystems stages of production. These trends are pinching defence industries from both sides: while federal outlays for defence have fallen, technological complexity of weapons have increased the costs associated with developing and producing new generations of weapons. The American Military Industry is, therefore, looking for Foreign Military Sales (FMS) with the government support. The American model of a Military Industrial Base, therefore, has no relevance to the ground realities that exist in the Indian subcontinent.

One of the strong points about the U.S. industry so far was the close interaction between the industry and the academics. This produced some spectacular results in the past including the breakthroughs achieved in atomic science, aerospace and communications. The Internet developed in 1969 under the DARPA programme was initiated to link various universities and industries. When the American industry was losing an edge over the Japanese in the 1980's, DARPA's concurrent Engineering Research Center developed the tools and practices to maintain the competitive advantage. Apart from this, Lockheed's Skunk Works concept made a significant contribution to the revolutionary developments of Space vehicles to stealth bomber within very short time frames, with small teams and small budgets. Appendix 'F' gives a glimpse of some of the programmes completed as Skunk works while Appendix 'G' shows the latest anti-ballistic missile—THAAD, developed using concurrent Engineering as the core technology.

Let us examine the Israeli model. Israel has focused on the technologies and weapon systems that are most relevant to their national security. Although, there was a tacit U.S. support to Israel's Defence efforts, she never underestimated the importance of self-reliance. Thus over the past fifty years, she has designed, developed and produced a number of world class systems that satisfy their national security objectives. Today, they are the world leaders in the field of unmanned vehicles. In the field of ammunition, they have total capability to get their requirement of guns, vehicles optoelectronics and even radars. In the field of missile technology, development of Arrow missile is a striking example. A joint venture with the U.S., Arrow is mostly funded by the U.S. while the entire development is carried out by the Israelis. Today, after a development and evaluation period of 12 years, Arrow has proved its capabilities as ABM beyond any doubt. Israel considers it as its own solution to the National Missile Defence (NMD); while the Americans have signed an agreement for the technology transfer of the missile for production by their giant multi-national-Boeing.

How has Israel achieved this? Israel's military industry is a conglomeration of a few large size companies supported by a host of small scale industries having a strong technology base and knowledge content. Seemingly complex components, devices and sub-systems are designed and produced by these small companies while the major players simply integrate them. They have thus an advantage of both a small scale, knowledge based industry and a large industrial house. This must not be confused with the Indian scenario where a number of small sector industries (SSIs) support the primary manufacturer as an ancillary having low cost and flexibility. But these SSI units have no competence in the design field.

Appendix 'H' shows some of the Israeli weapons produced by their own in-house R&D in association with the small and large sized private sector.

The Indian Scenario

The weapons and ammunitions are being produced in India for the past 200 years. During the pre-independence years, the production centers and facilities were established purely to meet the interests of the British Empire. Initially, these were to fight against the princely states and the natives and later to meet the shortfalls caused by the two world wars. Thus came into being most of the Ordnance Factories, whose number has now grown up to 39. These factories, especially during the post-independence periods, could not keep pace with the changing technologies and therefore were relegated to produce the traditional weapons and clothing. Occasionally, they could attempt trying with new technologies with mixed results. The Government was in a real dilemma. On the one hand these factories could not be closed since they employed a large work force and any reduction in it would pose a major social and political problem. On the other hand, these factories could not migrate to the new advanced technologies due to 'ageing'. To meet the newer technological challenges, the Government created a new infrastructure in the form of public sector. Some of the PSUs came under the exclusive domain of the Defence Ministry, while the others catered for different ministries.

Over the years, the Defence PSUs have created a huge infrastructure and have acquired certain level of competence in the high technology fields. Many of the PSUs are dedicated to the long-term programmes like shipbuilding or license production of military aircraft. However, some of them have a good R&D competence. Hindustan Aeronautics and Bharat Electronics can be seen as good examples of this. However, these units act in isolation and therefore, it is very difficult to find synergy between other institutions and these PSUs in the common field of technological specialisation. Some exceptions could be found like the Missile Development Programme or the LCA project. But, even in these examples, the ego factor is more dominant than the collaborative team effort. One of the PSUs, although part of the Ministry of Defence, contributes only 20 per cent of its efforts to Defence. The customer for them is someone other than Defence services.

The Science and Technology programmes were initiated under the newly created Research & Development organizations which were constituted in the first decade after the independence. Thus came into being the Department of Atomic Energy, Indian Space Research Organization (ISRO), the Council of Scientific and Industrial Research and lastly the Defence Research and Development Organization. However, there is not much interaction amongst them. DRDO's Missile development programme and the LCA project however could bring about a welcome change in the attitudes. The five decades that have elapsed after the formation of these S&T organizations, some maturity has been achieved. However, much more is yet to be accomplished. Focusing only on the DRDO, one can see a sea change in the competence building within the organization resulting in some major breakthroughs in the development of strategic weapons. Achieving the status of a nuclear power is no mean task. This speaks volumes for the S&T organizations in the country.

From the services viewpoint, however, DRDO has fallen too much short of their expectations. The services want operational readiness through filling up of their inventories with the state-of-the-art weapons and systems, which should be in a condition of operational readiness all the time. They have no patience to wait for the development process to be completed and deliveries made thereafter. They really want a solution from Concept to Disposal with the Integrated Logistics Support. The services note the following shortfalls in the existing systems:

(a) Lack of pro-active initiatives and long-term planning.
(b) Development period is too long, some times threatening technological obsolescence.
(c) Frequent performance shortfalls and cost overruns.
(d) Too many departments involved in the procurement process, invariably leading to blame-game for non-performance.

The natural choice for the user then is to follow the import route to ensure operational readiness. This is at the expense of self-reliance. The newly introduced structure of the CDSS and Defence Procurement Agency is trying to co-ordinate the entire process; but the same is particularly directed to inter-services coordination and does not address the inter-organizational issues.

The Impact of Globalisation

The globalisation process that was triggered by the split of the Soviet Union in 1991 can be a double-edged weapon. One way to look at it is the conquest of the domestic markets by the erstwhile rulers. The other side of globalisation is the opening up of new avenues for utilizing your own skilled manpower. India's advent in many new technological fields, such as Information Technology, Pharmaceutical industry and even in Design and Manufacturing technologies have brought rich dividends. The foreign exchange reserves have grown to a record high of $ 145 billion with Sensex crossing 8,000 mark. There are academic studies carried out in the U.S. indicating that they are losing a vital advantage to India and China. The quality and the number of engineers graduating every year from India far surpass the American figures. There are mergers and joint ventures and the traffic is two-way. Although India is far away from achieving the status of a developed nation, it does not stop her to realize its full potential to utilize the unique skill sets that are relevant to the IT revolution.

We have already seen Israel's achievements as the Technology Donor in the exclusive field of strategic weapons. Can India aspire to do something like that? The answer, at least for the present, is emphatic 'No'. We have not learnt many lessons from the history books where Tipu Sultan's revolutionary concept of a Rocket failed in the battlefield simply because it was not technologically mature weapon. It took Congreve to do the remaining work to perfect the technology and use it with striking effect on the battlefield. Even today, technology transfer is our major problem. What we achieve in the laboratory cannot be achieved in the field. The reason being that the entire history of development such as process details, are not captured on-line. Here again the compartmentalized structure used in the weapon system development is our major problem. The need of the hour is to form multi-disciplined, multi-organizational cross-functional teams, the members of which always carry out conflict resolution by concensus. The IGMDP tried to achieve this with a limited success. Whatever has been achieved is not sustainable. Just like Team-India, can Team-Industry concept work? Has the private sector some good experience in this field—since their ultimate success is measured in the profitability of the organization.

Understanding all the major issues involved, the Government of India has a vision to create India a defence industrial base capable of producing world-class products, at highly competitive prices. This vision is in line with the liberalized economic policies, which are routed in ever-expanding globalisation of the economy. The performance of our existing R&D base, when considered with the large sized industrial infrastructure, both in the private and public sector makes us take a major decision about associating the private sector in our defence R&D and production process. We are no more simple technology recipients through TOT agreements; but deserve to be treated as equal partners in the process of new Defence products including weapons. The Indo-Russian joint venture 'BRAHMOS' is a striking example to support this statement. Appendix I shows the cruise missile developed jointly in record time. This is more significant when one considers that the technologies used are really the-state-of-the-art.

Although this vision and policy statement is quite impressive, could we achieve such a revolutionary change in the near future? After all, more than the technology, the mindsets are more difficult to handle. And if we consider the traditionally old organizational structures with the bureaucratic and political roadblocks, it looks next to impossible. We could be satisfied if we make a progress in the right direction even at the snail pace.

Looking from purely a technological angle, it must be admitted that the Government sponsored R&D organizations have been successful to lay a strong foundation to the technology base that is required to design and develop state-of-the-art weapons and systems. Although some times it looks like a mirage! Many advanced weapons and systems are now within our reach, thanks to the excellent infrastructure and highly skilled manpower that has been created by these organizations. That is the key behind initiating joint ventures with the technological giants worldwide. Yet, these organizations do not appear to have reached a critical mass. The private sector, with a few exceptions, lacks such a strong R&D base. It has certain advantages though, like the flexibility, cost consciousness, scheduling and quality systems. If a properly enabled business enterprise wants to enter the field of Defence production, it is now possible. The striking example is Larsen & Toubro Ltd. who has invested in the technologies over a fairly long period. Today they can talk in terms of independently leading a weapon system development programme (collaborative efforts are not precluded), which can make them competitive in the world markets. The first beneficiary will, of course, be Indian Defence. L & T will however maintain its position as a leader in the industrial world and can soon expect to get a technological advantage for their core sector activities.

For deriving the benefits of synergy between the Private and Public sectors, the Government needs to take some proactive steps for the purpose of confidence building. They should assure certain share in production as a return of investment made against R&D efforts. Already, thirteen private sector firms have been short-listed for such a collaborative effort. The exclusive facilities that may be needed to be established at high costs should be funded by the Government and set up within the premises of the Private Sector for operation, maintenance and exploitation. Also the false sense of secrecy need not hold up certain information that may be vital for developing new weapons and systems. All the artificial barriers that have been created should be slowly removed in order to facilitate team building. Similarly, exports of defence products can be best handled by the private sector, which has marketing skills and presence in the foreign markets for their own commercial products. And finally, the Government should not differentiate between the Private Sector which will form a part of the military industrial base and the other organizations under the Ministry of Defence.

Conclusion

Indian Government has good intentions behind creating a Military Industrial Base. This will bring all the players from the government sector, public sector and the select private sector under one umbrella. Considering the trend of continuously increasing defence budgets, India has no other option than to make best use of every rupee spent on procurement. The existing mindsets, false concepts about secrecy, improper planning, programming and budgeting, political roadblocks and other social issues are the major obstacles that have to cross before we get some tangible results from this marriage. Considering these aspects, the following actions on the part of the government will prove to be confidence-building steps:

(a) Identify select private sector industry houses and establish an intense dialogue with them.

(b) Identify pilot projects that have a high probability of success.

(c) Assure making up of the shortfalls in infrastructure if the industry is willing to invest in Research and Development.

(d) Encourage cross-organizational co-operation and team building.

Creation of the Military Industrial Base could be the next sequel to the successful completion of the first stage covering the above issues. Till this is done, the Military Industrial Base will only prove to be a mirage.

APPENDIX 'A'

Major Science & Technology Organizations of India

DEPARTMENTWISE R&D FUNDING (Rupees in Crores)	
ISRO	3,100
DRDO	2,800
ATOMIC ENERGY	2,000
CSIR	1,600
DST etc.	350
TOTAL	9,850

DRDO Mission

Develop infrastructure and quality manpower and build strong indigenous technology base.

APPENDIX 'B'

The Indian Ordnance Factories

OFB

The power of PEACE and the power to preserve peace—that's OFB. For two centuries OFB has lent strength to India's voice in the world, deterred aggression in the 19th century battles, two World Wars and skirmishes in the 20th century. With its vast inventory, OFB is the prime supplier to the Armed Forces of India, its Police and Para-military forces and also caters to global requirement.

That's OFB—the force behind Armed Forces for global peace.

Jurricans are still being produced by the ordnance factories.

APPENDIX 'C'

The Bharat Earth Movers Ltd.

- PSU under MOD
- Catering mostly for Ministry of Coal and Mines

BEML is a major player in manufacturing earth moving equipment, dozers, excavators and railway coaches. It also produces military vehicles like Tatra. The technologies have been mostly imported from the east European countries, Japan and Korea. BEML is also a major manufacturer of Railway coaches.

BEML has started catering for the Indian Army's obstacle crossing equipment such as the Czechoslovakian PMS Bridge and the indigenously developed Sarvatra multi-span bridging system. Yet over 80 per cent of the sales of this Defence public sector comes from the Coals and Mines sector. It also depends heavily on the foreign principal for the subsystems and components of military vehicles like Tatra.

Tatra mounted Indian Bridge. Sarvatra – A world class multi span Bridging system, developed by DRDO. The famous PMP/PMS bridge designed by the Soviet Union and license produced by BEML.

APPENDIX 'D'

Hindustan Aeronautics Limited

The history of the Indian Aircraft Industry can be traced to the founding of Hindustan Aircraft Limited at Bangalore in December 1940 in association with the erstwhile princely State of Mysore and Late Shri Seth Walchand Hirachand, an industrialist of extra-ordinary vision. Government of India became one of its shareholders in March 1941 and took over the management in 1942. Hindustan Aircraft Limited was merged with Aeronautics India Limited and Aircraft Manufacturing Depot, Kanpur to form Hindustan Aeronautics Limited (HAL) on 1st October 1964.

Today HAL has got 16 production units and 9 research and design centres spread out in seven different locations in India. Its product track record consists of 12 types of aircraft from in house R&D and 13 types by license production. HAL has so far produced about 3352 aircraft (which include 11 types of indigenous design). In addition, HAL has successfully completed many systems updates and integration tasks. HAL has 9 Research & Design Centres engaged in the design and development of combat aircraft, helicopters, aeroengines, gas turbines, engine test beds, aircraft communication and navigation systems and mechanical system accessories. Equipped with the latest facilities, the company is backed by high profile, highly skilled manpower with an impressive track record of more than five decades of rich experience in all disciplines of aeronautics.

APPENDIX 'E'

Defence

L&T has issued letters of intent (LOIs) for industrial license for a wide range of products, after the Government of India's decision to open up Defence production to the private sector. The LOIs issued to L&T cover design, development and construction/manufacture of warships, submarines, weapon platforms and launchers, field and air defence guns, anti tank weapon systems, missiles, rockets, torpedoes, land/naval mines including associated systems and subsystems, Radar, Sonar, sensors, armoured and combat vehicles, airborne assemblies, systems and equipment for aircraft, helicopters and UAV, etc.

Systems

Naval Engineering Systems

- Controllable Pitch Propeller Systems
- Steering Gears and Fin Stabilizers for warships
- Helo Landing Grid & Traversing System
- Winch and Handling Systems for Active/Passive Towed Array Sonar with customized handling systems and wet end integration and installation
- Specialized hull fabrication

Missile Systems

L&T offers missile systems and sub-systems, refurbishment/ upgrade, ground support systems and testing of missiles.

- Metallic systems and sub-systems: L&T manufactures various missile systems and sub-systems hardware such as combustion casings, in exotic metals including titanium, aluminium alloys, aluminium magnesium alloys, 15CdV6, AB2, maraging steel, etc.

Composite systems and sub-systems: L&T has in-house facilities for design and development of advanced composites, backed up by computer-aided simulation of multi-layered composite structures, characterisation of reinforcements and matrices, coupon testing, design and development of toolings, prototype manufacture, advanced non-destructive testing.

APPENDIX 'F'

Lockheed's Skunk Works Concept

Flying has always claimed a special grip on the imagination. The faster planes fly, the more fascinating they become. This is especially true of military aircraft because of their speed and maneuverability superiority over other types of aircraft. In addition, many are the products of highly classified programmes, which makes for very little public insight into their secrets. Only one company in the history of the aerospace industry has produced so many secretive and inspiring aircraft that it is considered a legend. This is the Lockheed Martin Skunk Works, America's most secret and successful aerospace operation.

Chief Engineer of Lockheed Martin, Clarence "Kelly" Johnson started the Skunk Works in 1943, after designing two of the most famous commercial airliners in the world, the Lockheed Electra and Constellation. The Skunk Works' official name is "Lockheed Martin Advanced Development Program." Skunk Works is listed in the Random House Dictionary: "Often a secret experimental division, laboratory or project for producing innovative design or products in the computer or aerospace field."

The idea of the Skunk Works was to stay away from bureaucratic management, enabling the engineers to work quickly and efficiently with a minimum of corporate oversight. It requires a great deal of faith in its leader by corporation executives, who generally have no idea what is going on in there. The Skunk Works has since been emulated by Ford Motor Co., McDonnell Douglas, and many others as a means for developing products quickly cheaply, and effectively.

1. **The spy plane U-2:** America's most vital tool during the pre-satellite period, that began over flights of the Soviet Union.

2. **Blackbird:** A successor to the A-12 airframe, the SR-71 Blackbird has held the title of fastest airplane in the world since it was built over 30 years ago.

3. The F-117: Stealth Fighter was the first operational airplane in the world with a radar cross section the size of a marble.

4. F-22 RAPTOR: As America's air-dominance fighter for the 21st century, the F-22 Raptor will replace the F-15.

APPENDIX 'G'

THAAD—National Missile Defence System

Theater High Altitude Air Defense System Elements Thaad Radar

The THAAD weapon system consists of Launchers, Missiles, Battle Management Command, Control, Communications, Computers and Intelligence (BMC4I) units and THAAD Radars. These elements work in concert to detect, identify, assign, and destroy incoming theater ballistic missiles.

Missile: The Missile comprises a single-stage solid propellant booster and a kill vehicle with a gimbal-mounted infrared seeker. The booster incorporates thrust vector control, and the kill vehicle has a high performance divert and attitude control capability.

Launcher: The THAAD Launcher is based on the U.S. Army Palletized Load System, or PLS. Dormant missiles are launched on command and the launcher has a rapid reload capability.

BMC4I: Battle Management/Command, Control, Communications, Computers and Intelligence units are mounted on High Mobility Multi-Wheeled Vehicles (HMMWV's). These are hardened shelters for the management of all Force and Engagement operations.

THAAD Radar: The x-band radar will perform multiple functions in the typical battle scenario. It is used for surveillance and tracking and is the communications link with the missile during flight.

APPENDIX 'H'

The Arrow, an anti-ballistic missile system, is displayed for the first time at The Palmachim Air base in Israel, November 7, 2002. The missile, untested in combat, will be Israel's last line of defense if the enemy launches Scud missiles attack. The Arrow 2 approaches the target at a speed of Mach 9.

The Arrow 2 theatre ballistic missile defence system has been developed by the MLM Division of Israel Aircraft Industries and is in operation with the Israeli Defence Forces. The system, carrying the codename Homa or Fence, is to be deployed in three batteries including one battery near Tel Aviv and one to the south of Haifa. The first battery became operational in 2000.

The demonstrator phase of the programme began in 1988 when the US Department of Defense Strategic Defence Initiative placed a contract on the Electronics Division of Israel Aircraft Industries to build and test the Chetz. The demonstrator phase of the programme began in 1988 when the US Department of Defense Strategic Defence Initiative placed a contract on the Electronics Division of Israel Aircraft Industries to build and test the Chetz.

In February 2003, IAI signed an agreement with Boeing to establish the production infrastructure to manufacture components of the Arrow missile in the US. Boeing will be responsible for the production of approximately 50 per cent of the missile components in the US. Boeing will produce various missile components and co-ordinate the production of existing Arrow missile components already being manufactured by more than 150 American companies. IAI will be responsible for integration and final assembly of the missile in Israel.

APPENDIX 'I'

Brahmos—Indo-Soviet Joint Venture

Brahmos is a Supersonic Cruise Missile that can be launched from submarine ship, aircraft and Mobile Autonomous Launchers. The missile is launched from a Transport-Launch Canister (TLC), which also acts as storage and transportation container.

Primarily Brahmos is an anti-ship missile. It has the capability to engage land based targets also. The missile can be launched either in vertical or inclined position and will cover 360 degrees.

19

Patent and Security Issues

Vishal Katariya

Introduction

The protection and commercial exploitation of intellectual property rights such as patents, trade marks, designs and copyright are seldom confined to one country and the introduction of a foreign element inevitably raises potential problems of security ranging from private international law, establishing which court has jurisdiction and which is the applicable law to securing the recognition and enforcement of foreign judgments. For example, will a foreign defendant be subject to the jurisdiction of the English courts if he includes his English distributor to infringe a patent in England? What law will apply to a trade mark licensing agreement for the UK market made between a German and a French company where the parties have not expressly chosen which law governs their contract? And are an author's rights determined by the same law as that governing the issue of the transferability of copyright?

"Information is a weapon in the modern day and age," says Shannen Coffin, a lawyer at Steptoe and Johnson and a former U.S. deputy assistant attorney general from 2002 to 2004. "And that is a serious concern for national security."

Internet users hoping to protect their privacy by using anti-virus software, *Web anonymizers*, false identities and disabled cookies on their computer's Web browser have something new to worry about a patent filed by the *National Security Agency* (NSA) for technology that will identify the physical location of any Web surfer.

Patent 6,947,978, granted this week, describes a process based on latency, or time lag between computers exchanging data, of "numerous" known locations on the Internet to build a "network latency topology map" for all users. Identifying the physical location of an individual user, reports CNET News.com, could then be accomplished by measuring how long it takes to connect to an unknown computer from numerous known machines, and using the latency response to display location on a map.

While most users are unaware of it, their computers are able to "ping" website addresses to trace the route their connection took and how much time was required to complete the operation. Likewise other computer users—hackers, for example—can ping their computer as well when connected to the Internet. It is this feature that the NSA's patent seeks to exploit.

The NSA patent does not describe the intended use of the technology by the agency, noting only general uses like measuring the "effectiveness of advertising across geographic regions" or flagging a password that "could be noted or disabled if not used from or near the appropriate location," according to CNET News. But given NSA's status as the nation's premier cryptologic organization, it is unlikely that the technology will be used to improve advertising.

NSA is so secret that its acronym has been said to stand for "No Such Agency." According to its website, "the National Security Agency/Central Security Service...coordinates, directs, and performs highly specialized activities to protect U.S. government information systems and produce foreign signals intelligence information. A high technology organization, NSA is on the frontiers of communications and data processing. It is also one of the most important centers of foreign language analysis and research within the government." *Post-9-11, if bin Laden goes online, NSA may actually know where he is.*

Security Concerns due to Government Control over Certain Inventions

One of the prime duties of the government is to provide secure environment to its citizens which would *inter alia* take care of the well-being of the nation. In order to secure the citizens, governments need to safeguard themselves from real and potential threats, from known and unknown enemy. Some countries take excessively cautious approach to tackle such threats which takes the shape of intrusion at times. Such intrusions are in the form of monitoring the national patent office for inventions which may enhance or jeopardise national security. On monitoring the inventions coming to the patent office, government may be able to acquire such invention for national use with little or no monetary benefits to the inventors.

Monitoring the inventive activities of their own citizens provides the government with a two edged sword. Firstly, they can monitor and determine inventions going to the patent office which might be potentially beneficial to the government and secondly, acquiring such inventions minus the R&D expenditure is far more economically lucrative than running monsterous, secretive and hence expensive R&D facilities on public money.

When New England inventor Philip French had his epiphany 15 years ago, he didn't dream it would lead to an invention that would be pressed into service in a top-secret government project, or spawn an epic court battle over the limits of executive power. He was just admiring a tennis ball.

The ball's seam, with its two symmetrical halves embracing each other in a graceful curve, intrigued him. "I thought, my god, I bet you can do something with that kind of shape," he recalls. He was right. French and two colleagues went on to design and patent a device now called the *Crater Coupler*, a simple, foolproof connector for linking one pipe or cable to another without nut threads or bolted flanges.

Lucent wanted to evaluate the Crater Coupler for use as a fiber-optic "wetmate" an airtight connector for two fiber-optic cables designed to operate underwater. It was part of a contract with a U.S. government agency that, the company said, would have to remain unnamed. "It was a secret black job, they couldn't divulge what it was for," says French. "Who it was for, the Navy or the CIA, or who knows, they never said."

The inventors agreed to help Lucent try to adapt the Crater Coupler to the company's needs, with the expectation that Lucent would license the group's patent if it all worked out. The inventors sent over plans, sketches and a model, and French began consulting and advising a Lucent engineer in monthly phone calls.

After about a year of development and testing, Lucent had good news for the inventors: The device passed all the tests, shaming a competing, clunky design that French says resembled an old thermos. But when the inventors got on the phone with Lucent's lawyers to discuss license terms, the company dropped a bomb. "Almost the first thing they said was, 'Well, we don't have to do anything, because this is under some sort of provision for military secret stuff where we don't have to pay anything,'" says French.

Never passed by Congress, the privilege has its roots in English common law and was cemented into American jurisprudence by a landmark 1953 Supreme Court case titled *U.S.* v. *Reynolds. In Reynolds,* the widows of three men who died in a mysterious Air Force crash sued the government, and U.S. officials tried to quash the lawsuit by claiming that they couldn't release any information about the accident without endangering national security. The Supreme Court upheld the claim, establishing a legal precedent that today allows the executive branch to block the release of information in any civil suit—even if the government is not the one being sued.

Under *Reynolds*, the head of a federal agency must personally intervene to invoke the privilege. In *Crater* v. *Lucent*, it was Richard J. Danzig, then-secretary of the Navy, who did the honors. In a March 1999 declaration, Danzig claimed that permitting Crater to pursue a legal inquiry into the government's alleged use of their coupler would tip off U.S. adversaries to certain highly classified government operations and "could be expected to cause extremely grave damage to national security."

Judge E. Richard Webber granted the government's request immediately, and blocked the Crater inventors from obtaining any information from Lucent or the feds about the government's alleged use of the Crater Coupler or any other coupling device.

Steven Aftergood, Director of the Federation of American Scientists' Project on Government Secrecy says, "The privilege has worked very effectively for the government. In almost every case where they've invoked it, it leads to the termination of litigation."

The device is interesting on its own, but the broader legal legacy of the invention may be more important. In a little-noticed opinion this month, a federal appeals court ruled against the Crater Coupler patent holders and upheld a sweeping interpretation of the controversial state secrets privilege, "*an executive power handed down from the English throne under common law that lets the government effectively kill civil lawsuits deemed a threat to national security, even if the state is not a party to the suit.*"

The ruling is notable as a rare appellate interpretation of the state secrets privilege as it applies to patent holders. As such, it is a potentially worrying development for inventors particularly those developing weapons, surveillance and anti-terror technologies for government contractors who may find infringement claims dismissed without a hearing under the auspices of national security. It also offers a fascinating, if limited, view into the machinery of official secrecy at a time when the privilege is being exercised as never before.

"It's the most powerful privilege the government has," says William Weaver, senior adviser to the National Security Whistleblowers Coalition. "It's the nuclear option. It never fails."

Security Concerns due to Individual Control over Inventions Important for the National Security

Instances where an individual invention in a particular area is a matter of national security and concern is not new. However, to be able to monitor such inventions, albeit, at the patent filing stage, gives the government a primary control over and potential ownership of an invention which would be beneficial to national security if controlled by the government and hazardous to national security if reaches the hands of an adversary. Most nations of the world have enacted their patent laws to augment their control over such inventions which would primarily fall under the premise of this topic.

Some of the provisions in the National Patent Acts to safeguard National Security:

A. Indian Patent Provisions

The Indian Patent Act, 1970 Section 102 provides for acquisition of inventions and patents by the Central Government.

According to the Section 102 of The Indian Patent Act, 1970, the Central Government may, if satisfied that it is necessary that an invention which is the subject of an application for a patent or a patent should be acquired from the applicant or the patentee for a public purpose, publish a notification to that effect in the Official Gazette, and thereupon the invention or patent and all rights in respect of the invention or patent shall, by force of this section, stand transferred to and be vested in the Central Government.

B. United Kingdom Patent Provisions

Attention is drawn to the provisions of section 23 of the United Kingdom Patents Act, 1977 (as amended by the Patents Act, 2004 with effect from January 1, 2005).

Under these provisions, certain patent applications may not be filed abroad by a person resident in the United Kingdom, unless permission is obtained from the comptroller. These are patent applications which contain information relating to military technology or information the publication of which might be prejudicial to national security or public safety. For such patent applications, permission to file abroad should be sought from the comptroller, unless an application for a patent for the same invention has first been made in the United Kingdom, and six weeks have elapsed from the date of such application and no directions prohibiting publication or communication have been given or all such directions have been cancelled. Requests for permission from the comptroller to make an application abroad should be made even if, for example, such an application is required by contract with a foreign firm.

C. United States Patent Provisions

The United States Code title 35 section 5.1 provides details for applications and correspondence involving national security. This section requires that the applicant in a national security classified patent application must obtain a secrecy order pursuant to § 5.2(a). If a national security classified patent application is filed without a notification pursuant to §, the Office will set a time period within which either the application must be declassified, or the application must be placed under a secrecy order pursuant to §, or the applicant must submit evidence of a good faith effort to obtain a secrecy order pursuant to § from the relevant department or agency in order to prevent abandonment of the application.

If evidence of a good faith effort to obtain a secrecy order pursuant to § from the relevant department or agency is submitted by the applicant within the time period set by the Office, but the application has not been declassified or placed under a secrecy order pursuant to §, the Office will again set a time period within which either the application must be declassified, or the application must be placed under a secrecy order pursuant to §, or the applicant must submit evidence of a good faith effort to again obtain a secrecy order pursuant to § from the relevant department or agency in order to prevent abandonment of the application.

Furthermore, all the applications on inventions made outside the United States and on inventions in which a U.S. Government defense agency has a property interest will not be made available to defense agencies.

Security Concerns due to Jurisdictional Issues

Interestingly, not all the inventors would necessarily file a patent in their home country. Some inventors, may, forgo their national patent rights and file a foreign application on a potentially dynamic invention which would be beneficial to their country. For example, if an Indian scientist, without informing the Indian patent office, files an application in the US, the USPTO may process the application and issue a patent, which, if commercialized, create a threat to the Indian national security. Such a scenario is not very uncommon. The problem further arises, if the US government monitors and acquires such patent filed by an Indian scientist. The problem would be to find ethical owner of such patent. Would the United States Government be able to defend their ownership of such patent which was filed by an Indian national without the express permission from the Indian Patent Office? The answer is complex. However hypothetical it may appear, such cases would not remain rare in near future. Illustrated here are few such concerns:

A. Problems due to territorial nature of IPR

The first set of security problems arises out of the territorial and exclusive nature of intellectual property rights and their close link with competition law. The country that grants the intellectual property right typically also deals with its validity. However, there might be occasions where a foreign court, for example in infringement proceedings, has determined the validity of a foreign intellectual property right. Will an Indian court recognize the foreign judgment and authorize its enforcement in such a situation? And is it only the validity point that creates these problems? Arguably, a territorial right applies only in the country that granted it and maybe its infringement should exclusively be dealt with by the courts of the granting country. Would that mean that a foreign judgment would not be recognized and enforced even if it deals only with the infringement issue? Would any other solution offend against public policy?

A second set of problems surrounds the recognition and enforcement of foreign interim orders. Should an Indian court recognize and enforce such an order which was, for example, granted by a Dutch court in a case of alleged infringement of Dutch, English and French parallel patents? The Dutch court may have taken jurisdiction to grant an extra-territorial interim order on a basis which is not readily accepted by the Indian courts. Does that influence the decision at the recognition and enforcement stage?

B. Problems Arising due to Counterfeits

One of the major security concerns in dealing with intellectual property is the international dimensions of trade in counterfeit and pirated goods from the late 1970s. The best method of preventing this practice was to stop production of such goods at the source itself. But the practical reality made it difficult to achieve. The strengthening of customs controls was advocated as a means of preventing counterfeit and pirated goods from reaching their target markets.

In modern warfare, counterfeits are employed to destabilize the economy of the enemy state. Counterfeits could be in the form of currency or trade items. It is trade items that this paper is expressly going to limit itself to. Border security measures were thought of as the instrument to combat international commercial counterfeiting and piracy from the earlier years. But the concept underwent many developments in the recent years. A requirement to resort to border security measures is now firmly incorporated in the TRIPs Agreement. In addition, the World Customs Organization has sought to facilitate the implementation of this part of the TRIPs Agreement by issuing a model law to give national customs authority's powers to prevent cross-border traffic in counterfeit and pirated goods.

The TRIPs Agreement obliges the member countries to adopt procedures to enable an intellectual property right holder to make application in writing to competent authorities. This can be made on valid grounds of suspicion that the importation of counterfeit trademark or pirated copyright goods may take place. The application may request the customs authorities to suspend the release of such goods into free circulation. However, what are the provisions to counter security concerns when member countries adopt procedures to enable an intellectual property right holder and his rights which in turn might be a security breach? Such questions have not yet gather momentum in the TRIPs and WTO negotiations but are, nevertheless, on the minds of the negotiators. Law is the sovereign pinnacle of a country and most countries would appreciate minimum foreign intervention in such sovereign matters. However, with globalization, such concerns do take a back seat and thus give rise to potential security concern.

In addition, it is essential to reiterate that such foreign treaties and trade related understanding sometimes come to rescue in a situation which would turn into a security breach. The TRIPs mandate on border security measures had been incorporated under Section 53 of the Copyright Act, 1957 that deals with the importation of infringing copies. Accordingly, the owner of the copyright in any work or his duly authorized agent can make an application to the Registrar of Copyrights on the payment of the prescribed fee. After inquiry, the Registrar may order that copies made out of India of the work, which if made in India would infringe copyright, shall not be imported. The registrar of

Copyrights or any person authorized by him in this behalf may enter any ship, dock or premises where any such copies are kept and may examine such copies. The copies to which any order is made by the Registrar shall be deemed to be goods of which the import has been prohibited or restricted under Section 11 of the Customs Act, 1962. Section 11 of the Customs Act, 1962 deals with the prohibition on importation or exportation of goods. Section 11(2) (n) of the Act specifically refers to the prohibition on importation or exportation of goods to protect patents, copyrights and trademarks. However, all copies confiscated under Act shall not vest in the government but shall be delivered to the owner of the copyright in the work.

In *Gramophone Co. of India Ltd.* v. *Birendra Bahadur Pandey,* it was held that the word import in Sections 51 and 53 of the Copyright Act means bringing into India from outside India and this is not limited to importation for commerce only, but includes importation for transit across the country. This interpretation is in accordance with international conventions and treaties between India and Nepal. An order under Section 53 of the Act may be made even in respect of infringing copies of artistic works that have been brought to India for transit across India to Nepal. On the order being made, the offending copies are deemed to be goods whose import has been prohibited or restricted under Section 11 of the Customs Act. Then the relevant provisions of the Customs Act are to apply, with the difference that confiscated copies shall not vest in the government, but shall be delivered to the copyright owner.

C. Article 16 (4) Of the Brussels and Lugano Conventions

This provides that the following courts shall have exclusive jurisdiction, regardless of domicile:

In proceedings concerned with the registration or validity of patents, trade marks, designs, or other similar rights required to be deposited or registered, the courts of the Contracting State in which the deposit or registration has been applied for, has taken place or is under the terms of an international convention deemed to have taken place.

Scope of Article 16(4)

(i) Regardless of Domicile

So strong is the desire to allocate jurisdiction under Article 16 that it applies regardless of domicile. It is an exception to the normal rule under the Brussels and Lugano Conventions that the defendant must be domiciled in an EC/EFTA Contracting State.

Conclusion

The protection and commercial exploitation of intellectual property rights in the international playing field would inevitably give rise to security concerns. Moreover, the concept of security could be rather complex from different viewpoints. A person may not be aware of grave security concerns if he is all but interested in patenting his invention. Similarly, governments may not accord personal sentiments when it may encroach on personal property of an individual in the garb of security concerns.

The advent of internet has made things even more cumbersome for the national security when a click of the mouse would send substantial vital information from one corner of the room as effortlessly as we pass a cup of tea from one corner of the room to other. It would be pertinent to end the paper with the remark which was mentioned earlier in this paper, "Information is a weapon in the modern day and age and that is a serious concern for national security."

REFERENCES

Backman, Michael and Charlotte Butler (2002) *Big in Asia: 25 Strategies for Business Success*, Palgrave Macmillan.

Baxter, J.W. (1968) *World Patent Law and Practice*, London: Sweet & Maxwell.

Commission on Intellectual Property Rights (2002) *Integrating Intellectual Property Rights and Development Policy*, Report of the Commission on Intellectual Property Rights, C/o DFID, London: September/November [www.iprcommission.org]

Duran, Luis-Alfonso (2002) "Whither goes the International Patent System?" *AIPPI Newsletter*, No. 5, June, pp. 11-15.

George, J. (1999) "Issues of Public Administration: Towards a New Managerialism" in K.S. Ramachandran (Ed.) *Economic Agenda for the Next Millennium*, Institute of Management Technology (IMT) Research Series-03, Excel Books, New Delhi.

George, J. (2003) "Patently Absurd: Bartering Away Innovative Intellectual Capabilities," *Mainstream*, Vol. XLI, No. 20, 3 May, pp. 26-28.

Krasser, Rudolf (1995) "Developments in Utility Model Law," *International Review of Industrial Property and Copyright Law (IIC)*, Vol. 26, No. 6, pp. 950-63.

Pellegrino, Giovanni (1999) "Harmonization of the Existing Utility Model Protection Systems (including EU)." AIPPI Report Q117A to Council of Presidents Meeting, Oslo-September. www.wippi.com/.

Wendland, Wend B. (2002) "Intellectual Property, Traditional Knowledge and Folklore: WIPO's Exploratory Program," *International Review of Industrial Property and Copyright Law (IIC)*, Vol. 33, No. 4, pp. 485-504.

WIPO (2001) *Intellectual Property Handbook: Policy Law and Use*, WIPO Publication No. 489 (E), Geneva: pp. 40-41.

WIPO (2002) "Conference on the International Patent System March 25-27," *WIPO Patent Agenda*, http://patentagenda.wipo.int/index.html.

20

Biting Bytes and National Security

Aniruddha G. Joshi & Ankush R. Kulkarni

Introduction

In the past few years Information Technology has changed the ways of business transactions, government operations and national defense. All these activities now rely on an interdependent network of information technology infrastructures called cyberspace. Cyberspace is gaining more importance day by day. While its penetration in the society is getting deeper, threats in cyberspace have also risen dramatically in the past few years. As networks are removing the barriers and crossing the boundaries between the countries, national security issues need to be given special attention. A national strategy is required to secure the cyberspace. That should provide a framework for protecting the information technology infrastructure thereby protecting financial and economical health of the nation.

Knowledge and information are two of the most important components of today's world. With the emerging trends in technology, information is being gathered, analysed and delivered more quickly and effectively. The advancements in information and communication technology in past two decades have transformed the way organizations and communities create, manage or distribute the information. All the data required in policy and decision-making can be made available accurately and selectively at a click of a button thereby the process of decision-making can be executed efficiently. In today's business arena, IT has become the premier productivity driver. The potential of IT is such that one can hardly find a field which cannot remain untouched with it. IT has the potential to bring in smart changes in biotechnology and health care services, scientific research and education, production and automation, defence and warfare, banking and governance, media and entertainment and other walks of life too. An individual's personal health record can be stored at some location and made available to the doctor attaining that patient in case of any emergency. This can save his life. Todays syndromic surveillance systems in integration with automated decision support tools help clinicians in tackling the disease outbreaks or bioterrorist events this leads to provide better public health security. The results of any scientific experiment can be made available to the researcher at the other end of the world. The web-providers facilitate the participants to interact actively with the speaker sitting at a far end of the world. The knowledge involving the production and other business processes can be shared remotely. E-banking helps the customer with hassel free instant money transfer. Since knowledge and information are the basic ingredients of food security and are essential for facilitating rural development and bringing about social and economic changes, United Nations Food and Agriculture Organization hosts some workshops discussing the role of IT in rural development. With e-mails and internet chatting a layman can also make his presence feel everywhere in the world.

When we think of above things which are getting internetted at fast pace, it is nacessary to think about security over the network and its changing dimensions in todays futuristic world. Previously people were developing new technologies and were training others to use that technology. The paradigm is shifting today and technologies being developed are too simple for the layman to use. People have started using new technology without knowing the basics working at its root. This makes the scene more dangerous. Now we must understand the difference between 'doing things right' and 'doing the right things.'

Indian Scenario

India has already started taking initiatives in handling the use and misuse of digital resources and cyberspace. Establishment of Computer Emergency Response Team (CERT) is one of the right steps taken to assure users safety. Apart from that few other organizations are also coming up. IT Act, 2000 is also in place. After the recognition of use of digital resource, India also started taking steps towards security of the communication infrastructure, but it was not on the high priority (Cyber Security Information Dissemination, Dr. K.K. Bajaj, Cyber Security Seminar, 21-22 April 2005). CERT India have mission to enhance the security of India's communications and information infrastructure through proactive action and effective collaboration. As all other countries India also has reactive services like providing single point of contact for reporting problems, sharing information and lessons learnt, preventing the damage which may occur by known or unknown threats. We also have to think about protecting the people, economy and national security as cyberspace and the digital resources are getting used for many things. We still need to go a long way. We still lag behind the other nations in user awareness. Common user should be given rigorous training to transform him to a smart user who can handle and respond to the security incidences happened to an individual or organization. Project India Cracked was one project that had been monitoring Indian websites. The main objective of the project was to bring to notice the large number of Indian themed website defaced by the hacker community. Unfortunately this project is no more updated now and it has been closed. But the previous statistics are available online. www.zone-h.org is another website that keeps the records of latest defacements all over the world. CERT publishes website defacement statistics at regular intervals. Let us have a look at these statistics.

Statistics of defaced Indian Websites

(Defacement statistics from 1 Jan. 2005 to 30 Sept. 2005)

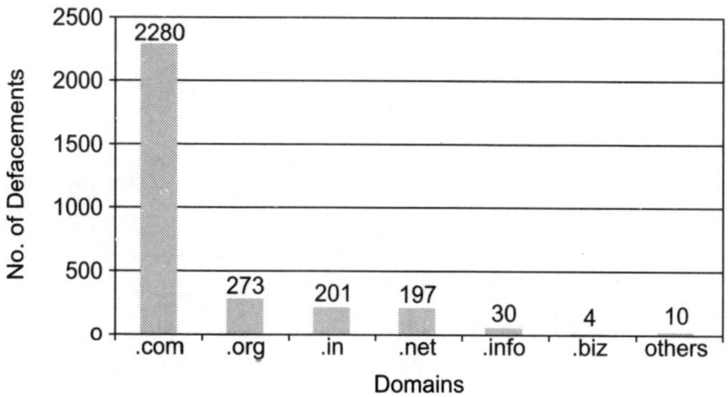

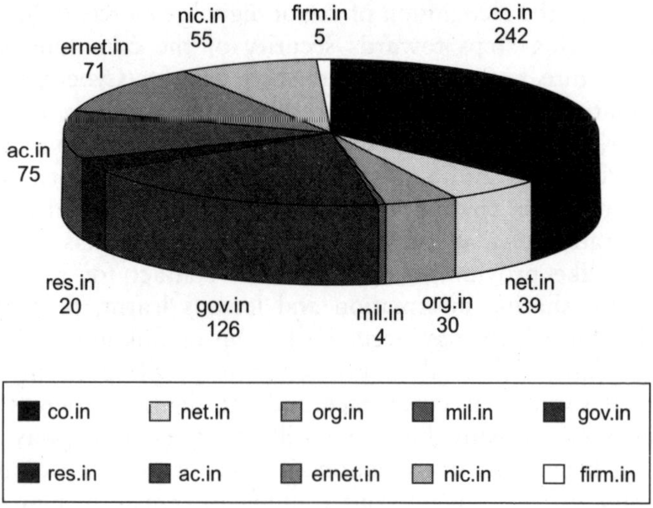

More than 150 hacker/hacker groups have been responsible for defacing Indian websites. The hackers/hacker groups responsible for the highest number of defacements in country code top level domain — ccTLD defacements are shown in Table 1.

Table 1: .in defacements hacker-wise

Defacer	*Number of defacements*	*Percentage of total .in ccTLD defacements*
AIC	97	14.54
Silver Lords	57	8.55
GForce Pakistan	41	6.15
FBH	37	5.55
powHACK	31	4.65
TimeOut	18	2.70
WFD	17	2.55
TheBuGz	14	2.10
m0r0n and nightman	13	1.95
TechTeam	13	1.95

The group AIC (Anti India Crew) has defaced the most number of .in ccTLD sites. They were responsible for around 15% of the total .in ccTLD sites defaced. The other top defacers are Silver Lords, G-Force Pakistan and FBH (Federal Bureau of Hackers). In fact, the top 4 defacers together were responsible for more than 35 per cent of the total defacements. Interestingly, the members of the top four hacker groups are said to be predominantly from Pakistan.

The break up of the .in ccTLD sites defaced by the top five hacker groups is shown in Table 2.

Table 2: .in defacements hacker by second level domain

	.co.in	*.gov.in*	*.org.in*	*.net.in*	*.nic.in*	*.ac.in*	*.ernet.in*	*.res.in*
AIC	26	10	7	7	14	13	15	5
Silver Lords	30	1		3	6	3	12	1
Gforce Pakistan	6	2		4	12	4	9	4
FBH	16	13	1	2		4		1
powHACK	13	16	1			1		

The group powHACK has the highest number of defacements for the .gov.in domain, as shown in the Table 3.

Table 3: gov.in defacements hacker-wise http://www.cert-in.org.in/knowledgebase/whitepapers/analysis_defacewebsites.htm

Defacer	*Number of defacements*	*Percentage of total gov.in defacements*
powHACK	16	12.60
FBH	13	10.24
Fatal Error	12	9.45
AIC	10	7.87
DarkBicho	4	3.15
GhostIRC	4	3.15
TheBuGz	4	3.15
Abunasar	3	2.36
Gantep	2	1.57
Gforce	2	1.57

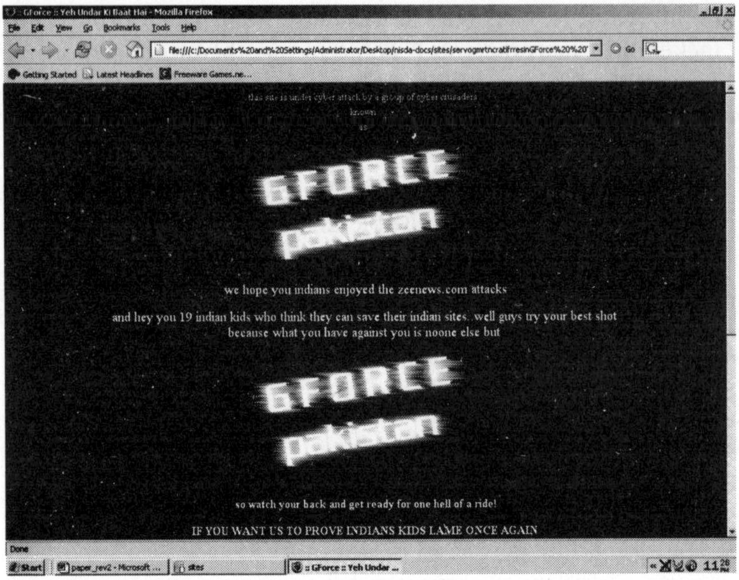

Defaced Website: An Example

We can learn many lessons from the statistics mentioned above. As we all know that cyberspace is an unavoidable place for everybody to be present everyday. Cyberspace is also working as a powerful medium of the communication and presentation. As it is not fully controlled by anybody and everybody has rights to be present in the cyberspace, acts like defacements are playing vital role in common people. Defacements can be used for propaganda, advertisements etc. Some hackers deface the website to spreadout anti-national messages. Some intend to show the vulnerabilities only. They do it for fun or to prove their expertise. But when it comes to defacement of Indian websites the propaganda of Pakistan supported *jehad* in Kashmir takes the centrestage. The first cyber-war between India and Pakistan started after India carried out its nuclear tests in May 1998. A group of hackers called milwOrm, immediately broke into the Bhabha Atomic Research Centre's website and posted anti-India and anti-nuclear messages. Since then, hackers from both sides have been using the Internet as a medium to popularize their political agendas and this demonstration is gradually leading to cyber-terrorism. In response to Pakistani hackers' activities Indian hackers take 'cyber revenge' by attacking Pakistani network, spreading worms and viruses, defacing their sites. Indian snakes, desi hackers, white snake and True Indian are some of the Indian names active in this field.

India in International Scene

As mentioned earlier internet does not know the national borders. Acts like IT Act, 2000 can be implemented in one nation. Such acts becomes powerless outside the nation. So global efforts are necessary to tackle the problem of cyber war. India is trying to be an active element on the international scene so far as cyberspace and cyber security is concerned. We have also taken initiatives like U.S.-India Cyber Security Forum. Here we are convening both government and industry collaboration to identify areas for collaboration in combating cyber-crime, cyber security research and development, information assurance and defense cooperation, standards and software assurance, and cyber incident management and response.

Under Secretary of State for Political Affairs Marc Grossman, in prepared remarks, stated that the U.S.-India Cyber Security Forum "holds great promise for future cooperation." Indian Head of Delegation, National Security Council Secretariat Joint Secretary Arvind Gupta, delivering a statement to the Forum on behalf of J.N. Dixit, India's National Security Advisor stated that "Securing cyberspace will remain one of the biggest challenges facing the international community for years to come and this Cyber Security Forum has emerged as an important bilateral mechanism to address such issues".

The first meeting of the U.S.-India Cyber Security Forum was held in New Delhi in April 2002 in recognition of the increasing interdependency between India and the United States in the information technology arena. Cooperation between the United States and India is of growing importance as U.S. government and corporations utilize information technology companies in India at a rate of about $9 billion annually. "As this trend increases, it is crucial that our governments and private industry work together to ensure an environment for secure transactions, networks, and software development," said U.S.

State Department Assistant Secretary for Political-Military Affairs Lincoln P. Bloomfield, Jr., the U.S. Head of Delegation.

During the conference United States and India reaffirmed their commitment to cooperation on securing cyberspace by establishing five joint working groups and identifying action plans for each. Future efforts will include workshops in New Delhi and Washington and scientific exchanges. Representatives of private industry similarly identified areas to strengthen cooperation.

Internationally, as we know, United States has already spoken about the National Strategy for securing the cyberspace. All over the world most of the developed and developing countries have started taking measures for securing information infrastructure. There is a move to protect the debilitating disruption of the operation of information systems for critical infrastructures and, thereby, help to protect the people, economy, and national security.

We are learning: Miles to go before we sleep

We must act to reduce our vulnerabilities to cyber threats before they can be exploited to damage the cyber systems supporting our Nation's digital infrastructures and ensure that such disruptions of cyberspace are infrequent, of minimal duration, manageable, and cause the least damage possible.

Securing cyberspace is an extraordinarily difficult strategic challenge that requires coordinated and well focused efforts from entire society—government, state and local government, the private sector, and the people. One of the important things is public-private partnership as this partnership can give India the cutting edge technologies and the skilled manpower. Establishment of public-private architecture for responding to national-level cyber incidents has become essential now. There should be organized and prioritized efforts in this regard. It requires initiatives from governments, private companies, organizations and individuals. The speed and anonymity of cyber attacks make it difficult to distinguish among the actions of terrorists, criminals and nation states, a task which often occurs only after the fact, if at all.

Strategy should include prevention of cyber attacks, reduce the vulnerability to cyber attacks, and minimize damage and recovery time from cyber attacks. To achieve many things technical sophistication is required. We also require to think about encouraging the developments and expanding cyber warning and information network support.

It needs to be stressed that India's national security and defense is not solely the duty of the Indian Armed Forces. India's national security and defense is equally the responsibility of all its citizens. They must not only study military matters, but also be alive to dangers to India's security, both from external and internal threats. Cyberspace is becoming a nervous system in many areas like banking and finance, transportation, information and telecommunications, energy, postal and shipping industrial base, government, industrial base, health, agriculture etc. Healthy functioning of cyberspace is essential to our economy and national security. Securing cyberspace is a difficult strategic challenge that requires coordinated and focused effort from our society.

REFERENCES

- www.zone-h.org
- http://attrition.org
- www.cert-in.org.in
- http://journalism.uts.edu.au

21

Revolution in Military Affairs and Changing Patterns of Wars

D.B. Shekatkar

There have been profound scientific, technological changes in 20th century which have altered our perceptions of the nature of future wars or conflicts and the mechanics of its resolution. There has also been a sea-change in the way nation perceive themselves and each other in the international system. While the military will continue to be an important and critical element of national power, economical and technological strength will influence the armed power. Indian governing mechanism, defence forces and defence research and development establishments require creative adaptation, determination and fundamental changes to be able to respond effectively to the nations need in future.

Revolution in Military (defence) affairs occurs when the application of new technologies in to military systems combines with innovative operational concepts and organizational adoption in a way that significantly increases combat effectiveness (both offensive and defensive mechanism) and fundamentally alters the character and conduct of military campaigns as we have been witnessing in various conflicts all over the world. The railroad, rifle and telegraph revolution of the mid-19th century displaced the Mughal and Nepoleonic era of warfare. The aviation, mechanisation and radio revolution of the early 20th century produced the blitzkrieg form of land warfare and strategic aerial bombardment while displacing the battle line at sea. The nuclear weapons, ballistic missiles made tremendous impact on the strategic aspects of warfare, the use of space and satellites then further revolutionised the warfare as we witnessed recently during Afghanistan and US-Iraq conflicts.

Innovations in technology and doctrine are the harbingers of change not only in the conduct of warfare but also in strategic parameters and calculations. Controlled changes lead to evolutions and evolution out of control leads to revolution. They render obsolete or downgrade existing means and methods for planning, execution and conclusion of war. Military revolution tend to bring about new forms of military operations. For example, the interwar period of the 1920 and 30's brought about mechanised air land warfare, strategic bombardment and integrated strategic air defences. It is worth considering if prior to World War I, the world had ever experienced a strategic submarine blocked.

New revolutionary dimensions in waging warfare have always slumped the adversary since the advent of civilisation and is not a contemporary phenomenon as has been hyped by many. Technological changes and upgradations have always been there, what is new is the term Revolution in Military Affairs (RMA). RMA is nothing but an improvement in the combination of national and military vision, philosophy, doctrine, organisation, technology, strategy and ever changing tactics. Another very important aspect is the National Will to usher in RMA !!

Historical events and experience of human kind offers some interesting insights as to the character of military revolutions themselves, the impact on the military perspectives of security, use of total combat power and military forces keeping in view the prevailing geo-strategic environment and also insights that in some cases clash with conventional wisdom over the conduct and outcome of military campaign and future military changes and competitions. The recently terminated conventional US-Iraq and Afghanistan has brought to focus some important issues and realities which need serious consideration:

(a) The present emerging military revolution is driven by rapid advances in information and information related technologies. Fabrication of "false intelligence" based on non-existent facts. Use of information technology, space, combined with propaganda skills to mislead the world and own nation regarding justification of conflict or war.

(b) While technology has proved and will continue to be a key element in a military revolution, it is not the only element from which competitive advantage is derived. Technically speaking US-Iraq war was over on 19th April 2003 with the well publicised fall of the Statue of Saddam Hussein, has the outcome of the war been on expected lines? Technically the conventional war was over but in reality the new and more dangerous campaign commenced and it continues even today!

(c) Having an early lead in developing the new form of warfare that defines the revolution is no guarantee of long-term success (Indian Air Force and Indian Navy need to seriously ponder over the outcome of US-Iraq war). The casualty figures of US Army, British Army and other contingent after 20th April 2003 and the death of thousands of innocent Iraqi civilians also needs serious and honest consideration.

(d) The emergence of insurgency and civil warlike situation in Iraq has proved that transformation paths may be diverse—relatively small and unorganised competitors (non-state actors and unidentifiable actors) are likely to emerge and compete quite effectively and dangerously; as many as symmetric competitors.

(e) While the entire process of transforming to a new warfare regime tends to take a generation or may be even longer but where the shift comes it comes and manifested quite rapidly, offering little time for the adversary and lagging military competitors to adopt.

(f) The shape, size and competitive dominance of so-called superior organization or superpower to exploit the military revolution and over all gains is typically short lived.

(g) Manageable, combat effective, well organised, equipped, trained and motivated combat oriented defence mechanism will have the advantage of competitive dominance and be able to exploit military revolution. In India there is a serious and urgent need to re-assess, re-evaluate and reorganise India's defence mechanism and philosophy. We continue to carry the historical load of 2nd World War experience and combat philosophy while we claim that we are preparing to face the challenges of 21st century. While this may be true in the air-conditioned operational, planning and conference rooms of various power centres, the ground realities need serious scanning and reconsideration! This is a issue for separate and serious consideration and debate.

RMA pose challenge to national security, leaders charged with national vision, philosophy and strategic planning. The world environment is full of uncertainties, shocks and awe. Recent events in Middle East, South Asia, Afghanistan, Central Asia should be an eye opener to the entire world. There is a new emphasis on regime shift, shift in the governing mechanism and philosophy to the liking and convenience of just few (unfortunately not from the region or nation where the "shift" is being advocated or encouraged). Economic and Military diplomacy is predominantly impacting the foreign policy and diplomacy. For example, the timing of regime shift is often unclear. While new forms of military operations may emerge, the scale at which they can be conducted may be critical in determining military advantage. Yet it may be difficult to assess accurately the "Scale Factor." While certain military systems or capabilities may be identified as element of the coming military thought process (military regime; not to be confused with military dictatorship for national governance); it is not often clear what specific attributes they should possess. Much talked about "anti-missile defence system" is an example. While it may be true in case of just few countries in the world, is it really applicable in Indian context? From where can we expect a missile threat? Of course the answer is obvious. But should we not take into consideration the geographical distances, time required to identify and assess the threat, response time, passage of information, decision-making process and authority, communication of directive to meet the threat and "respond." Are we serious? Thus the priorities (e.g. size, range, speed, armament command and control linkages) that should be given greatest weight in designing, developing and fielding new systems and capabilities are often unclear.

Compounding the problem, important assumptions must often be made under conditions of relatively high uncertainties with respect to the basic characteristics of emerging military environment and threats. Will they be offensive or defensive dominant? To what extent does the scale of effort determine such dominance? Will the military dominance remain stable or dynamic? Despite the fact that the nuclear weapons have been developed and demonstrated in India's neighbourhood, there will always be a possibility of Kargil like episodes. Strategy and defence planners must always remember the fact that during Kargil conflict Pakistan's foreign minister during an interview on BBC channel very clearly emphatically and repeatedly stated that "there will be ten more Kargils in future." He knew what he was talking about. We must always remember that Kargil may not happen again in Kargil Sector, but Kargil like situation may develop or may be created anywhere else in India. The place, timing, mechanism and methodology will be decided by those who want to create "ten more Kargils." We must always remember the philosophy of Chanakya and Kalhana-Rajtarangani (though it is not written in "English" with which India's governing and defence mechanism is more familiar than the Indian languages) that "for a Saint it is right to see the same in every person—but for a ruler (monarch) and soldier it is a great fault and can be source of disgrace." There is a need to analyse the possibility of threat of ten more Kargils in the light of philosophy of Chanakya.

The strategy and defence planners' challenge with respect to coping with RMA is further compounded with the geopolitical, geo-economical and geostrategic flux. The emergence of power centres and distribution of power in the world and particularly in the region today is significantly different from that which existed during Cold War. The future promises even greater change, with the rise of regional powers such as China, Japan (though self limited) and a recovering power in Russia. The information revolution will induce major shifts in wealth and power to those states best able to exploit. How will these changes, combined with emerging RMA, influence the long-term relationships and the balance of military power among these powers? This important question will continue to tax even the most talented strategic planners.

The requirement for a conceptual approach is clear when the changing features of our regional and national security environment are considered in terms of constants, trends and shifts. Constants are those features that endure over time. Trends describe those aspects that are changing permanently in the long term. Shifts describe those elements that can change temporarily in short-term. The higher the degree of change greater the need for innovation to manage it. The most enduring feature of India's strategic environment should be the Indian Ocean Region, Central Asian Republics, Middle East, Asia Pacific Region and SAARC Region. India must have a global vision, to promote and protect India's long-term interests but our prime focus must remain the immediate neighbourhood and region.

Strategic Mega Trends

While analysing the Military Perspectives of Security and RMA there is a need to discuss strategic mega trends, which will influence the security environment and perspectives.

(a) Space power and control of space has assumed greater importance. The dominance of space will also result in dominance of global environment and human behaviour.

(b) The centre of gravity of geo-strategic scenario is shifting to Asia, Asia Pacific and Central Asia.

(c) Geopolitical uncertainties and unpredictabilities are likely to persist.

(d) There is a shift from geo-political to geo-economics. This shift to geo-economics will dictate geo-strategy, foreign policy and politico-military dependency and partnerships.

(e) Revolution of rising expectations will continue in coming decades with ethno-religious, ideological overtones to social and political interactions.

(f) Transformation of conflict is well under way, with substantively reduced threat of nuclear and general war and regular prolonged conventional war significantly giving way to non-standard conflicts and wars (like Kargil episode).

(g) Possibility of availability of nuclear technology in the hands of non-state actors (with no specific recognition and accountability) can act as trigger for Afghanistan and Iraq like war. A use of nuclear device by non-state actor as well as chemical-biological weapons may trigger use of conventional nuclear weapon by the powerful nations whose national interest and security may perceived to be under threat. Risk and dangers of nuclear proliferations have increased.

(h) The so-called war against terrorism can trigger conventional war as the world has witnessed in Afghanistan and Iraq. Iraq war has proved that it is easier to start a war, but it is difficult to terminate the war at a point of gain, which is convenient to the attacker. "Consequence Management" after the war is a serious business and cannot be ignored.

(i) Public opinion restraints both national and international on conventional conflict would remain a major factor. If ignored it can create a major crises. Yet in some cases decision to go to war may be influenced by the interests of some influential powers and international players.

(j) Political diplomacy is being supplemented by politico-economic and politico-military diplomacy.

(k) NATO's area of influence and area of operations is advancing Eastward. NATO's presence in Afghanistan should not be seen in isolation but strategically NATO has covered Southern Flank of Russia and Western Flank of China. India too cannot remain unaffected.

Both the presence of NATO in proximity to India is bound to influence strategic calculation sooner than later.

(l) Presence of American forces in Pakistan should be a cause of concern to Russia-China and of course to India. The American presence in Pakistan should not be seen only in the context of the so-called war against terrorism but in long-term strategic context and implications.

(m) The decline of American supremacy in the world has commenced and no one but only Americans can arrest the decline. A weak America will influence world geo-politics. We need a strong but accommodative and sober America.

With American support and encouragement power equations in our neighbourhood have radically changed. The presence of NATO and America in Afghanistan and Pakistan respectively should be seen in context of move to counter Chinese advancement towards Middle East by using shorter land route via Pakistan and at a later stage through Iran. While Pakistan has been accorded the special status, usefulness of Pakistan and Americas views on Pakistan may change and special status may be reviewed if the terrorists and jehadi elements now hiding in Pakistan began to trickle back into Afghanistan to fight against NATO and USA, and also when they gain strength in Iraq and Saudi Arabia. It should, therefore, be obvious that the security perspectives of any nation is a dynamic phenomenon which like the shifting course of river, form new patterns and demand ongoing examination and response. America's long-term interests in starting strategic partnership with India needs to be considered carefully.

We are located in the close proximity of regions of considerable instability, making the security environment complex. World's strategic waterways pass through Indian Ocean. We have uneasy and disturbed neighbourhood. There is a history of conflict and mistrust, we have live borders, LoC, LAC. Our neighbours on Eastern and Western flank are promoting, propagating, exporting and sustaining fundamentalists tendencies. Our Eastern and North-Eastern region has been subjected to demographic changes which is most likely to be part of well thought-off and executed plan of some of our neighbours. Though the nuclearisation of the subcontinent may have altered the situation, but space still exists for limited conventional war.

Changing Nature of War

In the past five decades, warfare has moved down the paradigm scale of intensity and inclusiveness. Potential nuclear warfare has given way to nuclear deterrence, with more and more small nations trying to possess nuclear technology and capabilities to deter possible adversaries. The total war has yielded to limited, irregular or unconventional war. Use of military power for coercive diplomacy has increased but without actually resorting to war. The events world over points towards significantly lower probability of prolonged regular high intensity war, leave alone a regional protracted war.

It would be difficult to identify political objectives that would justify a protracted total war between nations. Also war may no longer be taken to the logical conclusion of military victories as was the case in the past. War would be conducted with the objective of achieving political success, rather than a total military victory! Even the US multinational forces could not achieve a total victory in the Gulf war, Afghan war and Iraq war.

Due to RMA, space domination and progress in information technology, the armed conflicts in future will be based on full knowledge and detailed information about each other. It would be difficult to ensure and achieve total "strategic deception" against adversary. A war in future will be influenced by strong limiting factors, the most important of which will be the need to avoid a nuclear exchange. The increasing costs of weapon systems and problems of replenishment and prolonged sustenance of forces in battle area will impose their own dynamics in limiting the scope and direction of future war. (It would be interesting to analyse as to why Pakistan made an offer of ceasefire along the LoC in J&K. It was not the desire to progress towards peace with India but the logistics and sustenance on two fronts. Along Afghanistan border the operations against the so-called Taliban or Al-Qaida terrorists and sustenance of terrorism in J&K and keep the LoC activated !!) Even if a conventional war breaks out it is likely to be limited in time, scope and space. A nation which can clearly define achievable political goals would have an inherent advantage.

Operational environment in future conflicts conventional or even non-conventional would be characterised by leathal, near continuous, high tempo operations (as witnessed in Afghanistan and Iraq), in extended geographical areas, with accent on simultaneity. Therefore, there is a need to evolve systems that can generate greater speed and fluidity of information flow and promote a responsive and effective decision-making process. Manoeuvre war in all types of terrain will hold the key and not attrition war. There should be no doubt whatsoever that it will require total synergy of joint services and entire defence and security mechanism, duly supported by internal and external diplomacy. Therefore, there will also be a need for more frequent military doctrinal and strategic revisions. The doctrine for next thirty years at least should be based on 21st century technology, based on accurate and actionable intelligence and information, which should enable flexible engagements ensuring land, air, space and sea dominance with improved lethality as well as readiness (we cannot have the luxury of time and space of 1971 war) while ensuring shared situational awareness.

Technological race will force us to achieve next higher range, accuracy, lethality, mobility and distant sustenance. Therefore, the criteria for military doctrine for achieving combat capability, combat effectiveness duly supported by quality human resource should be "ruggedness, reliability and redundancy."

In 21st century military might alone may not now constitute the predominant element of national power, though it would remain a major ingredient. Economic, technological, industrial and information strength will dominate the military power as the most important determinant of national status in the emerging world order. Economic security of a nation will be the first form of security because every thing else will flow out of that. Therefore, armed power supported by adequate industrial and economic power will constitute the main safeguard against a threat to a nation's security and well-being. Once again the philosophy of Chanakya needs emphasis:

> If you know your adversary
> And if you can deter them
> You will live in peace
> For hundred years...

Conclusion

As we are progressing through the first decade of 21st century we must recognise and accept the fact that our national security apparatus requires reorientation and radical restructuring to meet the challenges of global and regional security environment. Our armed forces have high reputation for living upto the nations expectations but we cannot afford to rest on our laurels. The world marches on. We have not only to stay in step but even a step ahead. Today, there is a recognition that national security encompasses much more than mere territorial integrity and preventing external military aggression.

Technology is the key to the future. Warfare in future will wear a new face which we must learn to recognise, accept and be prepared to confront. This calls for a paradigm shift in attitude. Only then we would be able to evolve new strategies, doctrines and concepts that are appropriate for the challenges of the future.

Further, we should not lose sight of the fact that, though technology offers much RMA is revolutionising the warfare, it is the rank and file (our young leaders and soldiers) that will use it. Thus the soldiers, sailors and airmen, young junior leaders (our cutting edge) of the future should not only possess essential traditional combat skills but also have the capabilities to assimilate these technological advancements to analyse and act appropriately in the rapidly changing operational environment.

There is a sudden awakening and realisation in the western world and USA "that India is emerging as a formidable economic power, regional power of 21st century. What have been the sources and incentives of this sudden awareness? What are the ground realities? Is it that Delhi, Mumbai, Bangalore, Chennai, Kolkata, Noida and Gurgaon represent India? There is a need to be practical about the ground realities in different parts of India and in our neighbouring countries. Let us be careful that we do not get led to a garden path and get trapped in the economic "*Chakraviuwh.*" USSR was projected as superpower. Overnight it got dismembered under its own weight! Who pressed the remote? It is questionable if USSR was really a superpower or it was forced to be a military power without adequately backed by strong economy and strong political base.

It would be pertinent to mention here that during my command of 8 Mountain Division among all the foreign terrorists (mostly from Afghanistan and Pakistan) who were killed in Kashmir during 1995-96 and over 1200 terrorists who surrendered with their weapons and equipment all of them had a part of Urdu poem in their personal diaries stating that:

Kal Roos ko bikharte dekha tha,

Ab India tootta dekhenge.

Ham barq-e-jehad ken sholon mein

Amrika ko jalta dekhenge.

Meaning that "we saw the disintegration of USSR, we will now see the dismemberment of India, we will see America burning in the fire of *jehad*!!" This philosophy and ideology was in 1995-96. It manifested in America on 9/11! The world has been changing thereafter rapidly. It will continue to change rapidly. Prudence demands that we remain in tune with ground realities otherwise we may be caught again and face another Kargil-like situation! Would we like to be caught again.

Finally once again it would be appropriate to learn from the philosophy of Chanakya:

The weak have one weapon,

The errors of those,

Who think—they are strong!

22

Secure Access to Space

Pramod Kale

On the 21st November 1963, a Nike-Apache rocket was launched from the Thumba Equatorial Rocket Launching Station-TERLS near Thiruvananthapuram. The payload released Sodium vapor in the upper atmosphere and the trail was photographed from four different locations. This effort was started as international cooperative effort in space research. A large number of scientists were interested in carrying out rocket experiments very close to the geomagnetic equator. We can certainly say that our efforts for the development of Space Technology seriously started then. In the last twenty years or so our national life, our economy has been impacted by the Space Technology Applications. The development of Space Technology and applications of the space technology for the social and economic development of our country was not just a dream or a vision of Dr. Vikram Sarabhai. In fact it was a vision that he shared with us and gave a direction for the development of the technology. He showed us the purpose for which the work was required to be carried out.

Today we are operating a large number of communication and remote sensing satellites of our own and there will be many more to come. The utilization of these satellites has now to be described as "Operational Space Services." While we consider the progress made so far, the plans for the future, we must consider the question, "How Secure is our access to Space?" We take it for granted that our access to space, our ability to develop, fabricate, integrate, test and launch our own satellites using our own launch vehicles will continue unhindered. Even now as we are using our own communication satellites, some of the operational space communication services are dependent upon the use of international and foreign owned satellites. A large number of transponders on our satellites are being used by international organizations. This is as it should be. This type of interdependence results in equitability, business growth and mutual security. A large number of countries are now availing remote sensing services through the use of our remote sensing satellites.

The satellites that we make, the launch vehicles that we make, are not entirely made in government laboratories. A large number of large and small industries are involved in various activities for making them. By and large the industries contribute as subcontractors. We need now the industry to take up the work, not as subcontractors but as prime contractors, capable of providing a total satellite or a launch vehicle.

During the years when there was an "Embargo" on sale of certain goods, including test equipment from USA and some other countries, certain of our own Indian industries were not ready to work with the Indian Space Research Organization, Department of Space (DOS), Department of Atomic Energy (DAE) and Defense Research and Development Organization (DRDO). We have gone through that period and developed the necessary resources and technologies. The geopolitical situation has undergone a sea change now.

We need to capitalize on the gains of those years. We need to have a strong commitment about "Self-Reliance." We need to get to the position of not allowing the situations to develop where the recurrence of the embargo could happen and if it happens we must have alternate strategies. We have the resilience but what we must have is the will and determination. During the time when embargo was present we did not give in. Some of our programmes were delayed but we persisted in developing alternate sources. A large number of these sources were indigenous. As students of Dr. Vikram Sarabhai we learnt from him, "When options are closed, resources arise." Even when the easy options of import were available, we knew that we had to develop the necessary technologies for the launch vehicles. There was job satisfaction for the working scientists, engineers and all the staff, there was pride in our work.

When we consider secure access to space, it does not mean only the physical security of space installations. We can achieve secure access to space through constant vigilance about the international and national situations. We have to keep on using the space technology for national development. This does not mean that we should develop systems only for our use. We need to take initiatives to promote our operational services and make them available to other countries in cooperative as well as commercial manner.

Today following are operational space services:

- Telecommunications
- Data communications
- Networking
- Mobile communications
- Television broadcasting
- Radio broadcasting
- Navigation and position determination
- Meteorological earth observations
- Meteorological data collection and dissemination
- Disaster warning systems
- Remote sensing of earth resources
- Earth imaging for surveillance
- Telemedicine

Only when we consider the scope and economic impact of these services on our national day-to-day life, we can understand the meaning of secure access to space. Try to imagine what would happen if our services like Television broadcasting or the VSAT services which are the mainstay for our stocks and shares trading business are disrupted. Our entire IT industry or IT enabled service industry is today dependent upon the availability of reliable space communication services. Denial of any such service to us will need to be considered to be threat to our national security.

Some of these services are well regulated in terms of international regulations and applicable space law. We need to be vigilant about the developments going on in these fields. We need to be constantly looking out for the opportunities as well as the threats. There is a major scope for Universities and Educational institutions for carrying out studies and analysis in the field of international relations, international treaties, international trade scenarios and space law.

Secure access to space means that we should be able to use our operational space services as required by us and in the manner determined suitable by us. We have to develop our capability to launch eight to ten satellites per year for own needs. Once we develop that capability, we need to expand our space industry to cater to needs of other countries in a commercially viable and competitive manner. The development of the aerospace industry should not be considered as projection of power, it should be considered to be projection of industrial capability. We must have a real long-term perspective of our industrial capability.

During the nineteen sixties and seventies the European Space efforts were driven by their needs to have cooperative approach for the development of a European launch vehicle. The initial efforts had resulted in failures. At that time France had finally taken a different approach. France had decided that as a country they must have their own launch vehicle. The initial denial of the launch and later use of the Symphonie satellite developed by France and Germany had resulted in their taking the decision to embark on the independent development of European aerospace capability. France had taken the lead in the development of the Ariane satellite launch vehicle. France and Germany had decided on two major projects—Airbus Industries and Arianespace. Outcome of that policy decision are all too visible for us to see and learn from. We need to learn from history of these projects to appreciate the meaning of industrial security.

There was a time, twenty years ago when we were trying to expand our own space communication networks. The industrial capability was there and therefore we could do it. We could not seize the initiative and use that capability of delivering the ground equipment for export. Again now as the space communication requirements are growing we need to make a concerted effort to design, develop, manufacture and deliver end to end systems.

The new technologies are all science-based. We adopt many of these new technologies without consideration to the scientific aspects. Thus the technical know-how obtained remains in use for a limited period of time. Further product development, product improvement and continuous manufacturing requires specific attention to the scientific details. It is important to "know why" if we want to proceed and keep up the pace of the technological developments.

Services and manufacturing should go together. Our IT and IT enabled services are generating a large amount of money. Our main advantage is considered to be our ability to transact business in English. This type of boom is not going to last more than a few decades. This is not generating industrial infrastructure. China, Korea and Japan are fast catching up with their IT industry and their determination to learn the English language. We have the basic industry, the basic knowledge but large mass production is missing. We need to modernize our manufacturing processes. Our economic development, independence and security is going to come from our agriculture, biotechnology, textiles, trade, commerce and our manufacturing industry.

At one time we were not able to meet our demands for food material. The Green Revolution and the White Revolution coupled with a spell of more than fifteen years of normal to good monsoon has brought the stability to our food production. At one time countries like Nigeria and Indonesia were net exporters of energy. We have to study the history of these countries to understand why they have now become net importers of energy.

We are dependent upon import of natural gas and hydrocarbon oil for energy requirements. Our requirements of the energy are going to constantly increase. Our projections indicate that we will have to necessarily depend upon the import of hydrocarbons to meet our growing demands. Our imports in that sector alone are touching 70 per cent. In such a scenario we must have strong base for export of products and services for maintaining healthy balance of payments. Some of our traditional exports are facing heavy competition and we must find more and more avenues for export.

We could target Operational Space Services for that. Such services will not be only for products but could also be for end to end systems. This will require adoption of a long-term policy to work towards such a goal in a self-reliant manner. Such a policy will also ensure our secure access to space, since we would have then established a strong collaboration of the industrial manufacturing capabilities and the research and development capabilities of the national scientific establishments.

23

Human Rights and the Implementation of Programmes Related to Human Rights Studies in Indian Universities

K.B. Powar

Human Rights, simply stated, are the rights that accrue to an individual for the reason that he or she is a human being. The most basic rights are the ones that relate to life, liberty and security. To these may be added the right to live with dignity. These rights are equal and inalienable, and universally available to the human family. On December 10, 1948 the United Nations General Assembly adopted the Universal Declaration of Human Rights (United Nations, 1948). Article 1 of the Declaration states that "all human beings are born free and equal in dignity and rights." Article 3 emphasizes that "Everyone has the right to life, liberty and security of person." Article 12 states that "No one shall be subject to arbitrary interference with his privacy." Article 18 provides for freedom of thought, conscience and religion and Article 19 for freedom of opinion and expression. Article 26 gives everybody the right to education. Significantly, the Universal Declaration on Human Rights, in its preamble, calls upon every individual and every organ of the society to promote respect for these rights through teaching and education.

Violation of human rights is unfortunately common. Human rights are violated on a large scale during wars, and armed conflicts. This happens in spite of the fact that the basic rules of international humanitarian law have been laid down in the Geneva Conventions and their Additional Protocols, (International Committee of the Red Cross, 1983). In times of peace human rights violations are common in countries under dictatorship but are also known to take place in the most open democracies. Unfortunately, as pointed out by Mani (2001), the seminal problem of all laws, including humanitarian law, is the yawning gap between precepts and practices. Possibly, the best way to control the violation of human rights is to educate people about their rights and raise an outcry against violation.

On account of the alarming rise in armed conflicts and other forms of violence in different parts of the world—most of which are internal in character—countless innocent people have to face hardships and suffering. Political or social actions aimed at alleviating the hardships can be successful only if there is a foundation of humanitarian laws that protect the rights and dignity of individuals and groups. International humanitarian law is a very important branch of international law, which regulates situations of international and internal armed conflicts basically by making it obligatory for parties in a conflict to spare persons not participating in hostilities, and by restricting excessively dangerous or indiscriminate means and methods of warfare. Another humanitarian problem that has to be dealt with is that of refugees. Those who leave their country on account of a well-founded fear of persecution for reasons of race, religion, nationality, membership of a particular social group or political opinion and take refuge in another country ought to be protected on humanitarian grounds. A number of legal developments in this respect at the national and international level have taken place. These can be covered under the sub-category of 'refugee law.'

During last few years, much attention has been focused on human rights issues in our country. However, until recently subjects like humanitarian law and refugee law were largely neglected. There is a need to rectify the situation. While doing so it must be remembered that humanitarian law, refugee law and human rights are related to each other. Although their fields of application and the ways of achieving their objectives may be different, they all essentially deal with the broader aspect of 'human security.' In the ultimate analysis, they are concerned with protecting human life and safeguarding human dignity.

The fundamental rules of humanitarian law are applicable in times of international and non-international armed conflicts. Strictly speaking, they may not be directly applicable in times of internal disturbances, violence and tensions. However, the basic principles of humanity on which they are founded are extremely relevant in situations falling outside the purview of armed conflicts and must apply even in situations of internal violence and disturbances. This finds support in the Constitution of India, in national laws, and in human rights instruments to which India is a party. From this point of view the efforts being taken at the international level to enlist and adopt, at all times, fundamental standards of humanity, or minimum humanitarian standards, are based on basic elements enshrined in the concept of human rights, humanitarian law and refugee law. This also makes the study of humanitarian law and refugee law important for students of law, political science, defence studies, journalism and other subjects.

The Universal Declaration of Human Rights says that education should promote understanding, tolerance and friendship among all nations. In the context of humanitarian law, this is very important because knowledge of this law will undoubtedly help in promoting these ideals. In 1977, the Diplomatic Conference on the Reaffirmation and Development of International Humanitarian Law made a number of suggestions in this respect. These included:

1. Encouraging the authorities concerned to plan and give effect to arrangements to teach international humanitarian law in a manner suited to international circumstances;
2. Undertaking the training of suitable persons for the teaching of humanitarian and related laws;
3. Recommending that the appropriate authorities intensify the teaching of international humanitarian law in universities (faculties of law, political science, medicine etc.); and

4. Recommending to educational authorities the introduction of courses on the principles of international humanitarian law in secondary and similar schools.

Realising the importance of dissemination of international humanitarian law, the Geneva Conventions of 1949—which constitute the core of international humanitarian law—provide that it is the responsibility of all states parties to the conventions 'to disseminate the text (of the conventions) as widely as possible in their respective countries, and in particular, to include the study thereof in their programme of military and if possible, civilian instruction, so that the principles thereof may become known to the entire population.' This provision is reiterated in the first Additional Protocol of 1977 of the Geneva Conventions.

Clearly, the international community considers the promotion and dissemination of the knowledge of humanitarian law as a means of ensuring respect for the rules of this law. India, with its huge educational infrastructure and network must take a lead in this respect. It may be mentioned that Sassoli and Bouvier (1999) have given considerable attention to teaching of humanitarian law in universities. They have also provided possible teaching outlines for general and special courses in international law, national and international criminal law, refugee law, journalism, etc. Evidently, the universities can contribute substantially to the cause of promoting respect for human rights. Study and the field of application of international humanitarian law, by virtue of its very nature, is related to various academic disciplines. First and foremost, it is a branch of international law and, hence, its study in the Faculty of Law assumes considerable significance. Since wars and armed conflicts are invariably and essentially linked to political factors, an understanding of laws governing armed conflicts by students of political science is equally important. At the same time, if students of defence and strategic studies who specifically deal with issues concerning wars, armed conflicts, military strategies, defence, etc., will be better equipped to understand these issues if they are familiar with laws applicable to the phenomena of wars and armed conflicts. As noted earlier, application of international humanitarian law has the effect of promoting certain human rights in times of armed conflicts and safeguarding human dignity to the maximum extent possible, those who undertake the study of human rights ought to know the basic principles, fundamental norms and rules of international humanitarian law.

It is against this background that, in early 1998, the Indian universities were approached by the International Committee of the Red Cross and the United Nations High Commissioner for refugees, through the Association of Indian Universities, to promote the study of human rights and international humanitarian law. This marked the beginning of systematic efforts to promote humanitarian law, including refugee law, in Indian universities.

It is heartening that the process of national consultation, drafting of syllabi, preparation of reports of consultative meetings and recommending them to concerned academic establishments has been taken up seriously. Five syllabi have been drafted through consultative meetings involving experts. While drafting the syllabi some models developed at the international level were taken into consideration. During the period 1998 to 2002 consultative meetings of experts were organized (Kadam and Bhalla, 2004), and curricula developed, for the following courses:

1. Human Rights and International Law on 23rd and 24th May 1998.
2. Defence Studies and International Law on 30th Jan. 1999.
3. International Humanitarian Law and Refugee Law for Human Rights on 6th November 2000.
4. International Humanitarian Law and Refugee Law for Political Science Course on 26th April 2002.
5. International Humanitarian Law for Journalism and Mass Communication Courses on 10th September, 2002.

The course modules finalised at these consultative meetings have been circulated to the universities for possible adoption, either in full or in part. Presumably, these modules have been placed before the Boards of Studies in different universities that finalise their own curricula. The modules are available at the office of the Regional Delegation, International Committee of the Red Cross, Sundernagar, New Delhi.

The position regarding the status of the teaching of humanitarian law was reviewed at a Consultative meeting of Vice Chancellors and legal experts held at Pune on 17th August 2005, and a strategy for follow-up action has been drawn up. This includes developing curricula for other subjects in social sciences, organizing refresher courses for teachers, creating an electronic network for university teachers working in the area of human rights and humanitarian law and introducing short-term diploma and certificate courses.

Once humanitarian law and refugee law become a part of syllabi of Indian universities, it will be necessary to ensure that those who are required to teach these modules are adequately trained and provided with sufficient literature. The universities and affiliated colleges must, therefore, encourage their teachers to participate in training programmes, refresher courses, workshops and seminars on these subjects. Teachers of Law will find the on-line web-based distance education Diploma in International Humanitarian Law offered by the National Academy of Legal Studies and Research University of Law, Hyderabad to be useful because of its innovativeness and convenience.

It should be possible to include some basic information on these aspects in secondary school education. A study of the basic principles of humanity and ideals of the Red Cross movement at a younger age in schools will have a positive impact. It will also provide a basis for understanding humanitarian law concepts at a later stage during the course of higher education. For this purpose, it will be appropriate to convince the national secondary school syllabi prescribing bodies like the Central Board of Secondary Education, the Indian Council of Secondary Education and the National Council for Educational Research and Training, as also the Ministries of Education in various States, to include some lessons at appropriate level in secondary school education, in the Social Studies stream.

By way of conclusion, it may be said that the present initiative taken by the ICRC to promote the study of humanitarian law and refugee law must be responded to by educational bodies as well as institutions involved in higher education. It is hoped that all the Indian universities find these modules useful and incorporate them in appropriate courses of study conducted by them. Further, it is hoped that the present effort to promote study of humanitarian law and refugee law at the university level will also encourage other developing countries to undertake similar action.

Acknowledgements

The author gratefully acknowledges the inputs provided by Dr. Umesh Kadam of the Regional Delegation of the International Committee of the Red Cross, New Delhi; and Dr. Veena Bhalla of the Association of Indian Universities, New Delhi. The lead taken by the International Committee of the Red Cross, New Delhi, the Office of the United Nations High Commission for Refugees, New Delhi, and the Association of Indian Universities, New Delhi in organizing meetings aimed at developing and implementing human rights education programme is unique. The development of curricula was possible because of the critical inputs provided by various experts.

REFERENCES

DCIHL (1977), Final Act of the Diplomatic Conference on the Reaffirmation and Development of International Humanitarian Law Applicable in Armed Conflict, UK misc. 19 Cmnd. 6927.

International Committee of the Red Cross (1983), Understanding Humanitarian Law: Basic Rules of Geneva Convention and their Additional Protocols, ICRC, Geneva.

Kadam, Umesh and Bhalla, Veena (2004), Development of Curricula for Study of Human Rights, Humanitarian Law and Refugee Law, *Higher Education Policy and Practices*, 2(1): 31-33.

Mani, V. S. (2001), International Humanitarian Law: An Indo-Asian Perspective, International Review of the Red Cross, 83(841): 59-75.

Sassoli, Marco and Bouvier, Antoine (1999), *How Does Law Protect in War*, ICRC, Geneva (Chapter 9), p. 1493.

United Nations (1948), *Universal Declaration of Human Rights*, http://www.un.org/overview/rights.html.

24

Need for Military Sociology in Asian Universities

Leena Parmar

The problem of the influence of military organization on society on the whole has failed to attract the attention of social scientists. To be sure, much has been written about war, its alleged evil or beneficial affects, its causes and the possibilities of its abolition. But only a few writers/scholars appreciated the importance of military factors in shaping societies.

Sociology formed no tradition based on the study of military institutions and war and their effects on society until after the Second World War. The early history of the discipline suggests that it might have been otherwise. The experience of the French Revolution and its aftermath is sometimes considered an important reason for the efforts of August Comte and others to establish Sociology as a disciplined science of society. As is well-known, Herbert Spencer documented the connection between military development and social change. If his formulation of the transition from militant to industrial society now seems too simple, current studies by Anthony Giddens, Michael Mann, Charles Tilly and others show that the line of inquiry Spencer opened was no dead end. Yet , sociologists of Spencer's time and over the next half century failed to pursue these ideas; certainly the greatest minds in sociology did not. Even Max Weber, who was keenly aware of the importance of war and military organization in social life, wrote only a few pages on the subject. We can point to some exceptional cases in the United States: Lyford Edwards's *The Natural History of Revolution*, Pitirim

Sorokin's *Fluctuations of Social Relationships, War and Revolution*, and the multi-volume collaborative work, *The American Soldier*, edited by Samuel Stouffer. But as exceptions, with limited resonance in Sociology, these confirm rather than challenge the judgment that sociologists paid little attention to questions about the armed forces and society. At the middle of the last century, there was no strong history of research on the topic, as there was about the community, the family, inequality, or ethnic groups. Nor was institutional support in place to lead one to expect any change in the situation. Why, then, did this change occur? The important factors include a general widening of the scope of empirical research to encompass studies of national (not only local) communities and institutions, rapid expansion of and funding for the social sciences after the war that provided an impetus for increased specialization with each discipline, increased support by foundations especially by the Russell Sage and Ford Foundations, for university programmes concerned with matters of the professions and national security, and the increased presence and might of American (and other) armed forces mobilized during peacetime to contend with the tensions of the Cold War. But these general factors, however important, fail to explain the particular course that led to the establishment and institutionalization of a sociological tradition of military studies. For this purpose, we must focus on the contributions made by Morris Janowitz, who is commonly believed, with good reason, to have founded 'Military Sociology." In the 1950s, while still a young man and with a growing reputation as a careful student with an insight of political sociology, Janowitz undertook an institutional analysis of the professional armed forces, which led to the publication in 1960 of his famous book, *The Professional Soldier*. In it, he applied available sociological concepts in a new way to formulate a number of innovative and interrelated, but not easily exhausted, hypotheses about military organization in modern democratic societies. These hypotheses gave coherence to a sociological approach to the study of military institutions and provided directions for future research on the subject.[1]

Military sociology, in some ways, is a peculiar discipline. Yet, as this paper is intended to show, it is a multi-faceted, rich discipline. Military sociology is not a mere hyphen-sociology implying that it is a sub-discipline of sociology. This is indicated by one of the most renowned and prestigious journals in which the findings of military sociological research are published. This journal, *Armed Forces and Society*, established in 1974 by the initiative of one of the disciple's most respected founding fathers, Morris Janowitz, is sub-titled *An Interdisciplinary Journal.* Indeed, Military Sociology moves beyond traditional disciplinary boundaries. It takes resort, e.g. to history, political science, international relations, ethnology, and psychology and also to economics and philosophy. This makes working in the field thoroughly attractive and intellectually stimulating.

At the same time, we think that modern societies are in need of Military Sociology. In democratic political systems, in particular, Military Sociology is crucial in ensuring the democratic, civilian control of the armed forces and in helping to establish democratic civil-military relations (see Kummel/Bredow, 2000). Thus, Military Sociology is a social scientific undertaking for both politics and the military. This puts Military Sociology in some kind of a hinge function and makes Military Sociology a double-edged sword. In most cases, then, the ambivalence in attitudes towards Military Sociology stems from the perspective one takes. For the military, Military Sociology was largely seen as one of a multitude of instruments to ensure the smooth functioning of the armed forces. In their view, military sociological research (often funded by the armed forces or by the ministries of defense themselves) was an overwhelmingly practical endeavor and socio-technological in character. For large parts of Western societies, Military Sociology was terra incognito. Those who knew about it were mostly distrustful of military sociologists who were thought of as more or less accomplices in a thoroughly militaristic project, i.e. helping to militarize societies. This perception was corroborated in the wake of the strengthening of the peace movements in various Western countries following the Vietnam War gaining dramatically in strength in the late 1970s and early 1980s. For academia, Military Sociology was hardly a scientific undertaking at all. Military sociologists were accused of mere empiricism and socio-technology. Their work was regarded as theory-free, status quo oriented and thus inherently uncritical. This is reflected to date in the face that there are only handfuls of people allover the world who are holding chairs of Military Sociology and who are teaching genuine Military Sociology.[2]

In the present paper, the term military sociological research denotes scientific analyses of the military institution, both in its professional and organizational dimensions, its roles and missions, as well as its relations with the state and the parent society, though the conceptual and methodological tools of the social sciences, mainly sociology, political science, economics and law. Situated at the crossroad of social sciences, from which it draws its resources, it has, therefore, a multidisciplinary outlook.[3]

Military sociology is branch of sociology refers to that branch of intellectual understanding by which causalities associated with society, state and defense forces interface are produced in objective manner.

Military Sociology in this way is an analysis of how dynamics in the relationship amongst state, society and defense forces occur.

Civil-military relations constitute a major aspect of national and international security policy and most importantly civil-military relations has to be seen in the societal side of civilian control, which is particularly relevant in open and democratic societies. This dimension refers to the legitimacy of the military in relation to society and the societal acceptance of the military regarding its roles, abilities, and its goals and procedures. In today's research agenda on civil-military relations, there is a new postmodern view of the role of the militaries after the Cold War period. Charles C. Moscos, John Allen Williams and David R. Segal have described this new approach in "*The Postmodern Military—Armed Forces after the Cold War*" (2000). They argue that there is an organizational change in postmodern military development taking place which involves: Civilian-military interpenetrating both structurally and culturally, smaller differences within armed services in regard to rank, branch, etc., evolution from classical war-fighting to homeland defense and other nontraditional missions such as humanitarian interventions and Peace Support Operation (PSO), the use of military forces in internationally sanctioned missions, participation in international military forces, and combating sub-national threats like terrorism, ethnic violence, etc.[4]

The emergence, acceptance and institutionalized recognition of Military Sociology is intimately related to academic sub-structure as well as wider societal-structure. The military, as a sub-system of society, is characterized by distancing from people, relative isolationist aloofness and a distinct non-civilian sub-culture and sub-structure. The need for such distinctiveness is related to the tasks, functions, and responsibilities, which are assigned to military. Essentially, military personnel are trained and motivated to protect the country from external invasion. The emergence of nation-state gave primary to boundaries of a country and the notion of sovereignty necessitated its total protection. Historically, India has existed as a cultural entity with different political sovereignties. The supremacy of culture over polity was the basic character of India which was recognized and accepted through classical texts, social institutions, cultural ethos, myths, rituals, religions, castes, family and village communities. The contextual diversities discerned at empirical level revealed the compositeness of Indian social structure and culture which was obtained through the essence of catholicity and pluralism ingrained in transcendental-cognitive and emotive aspect of India and Indianness. The military, historically, was contextually organized, reorganized with multiple and ever changing alliances.[5]

The sociological understanding of military system has not yet come of age in India. The system, by its nature and character, necessitates certain legitimate degree of non-accessibility, secrecy and disciplined silence. The sociologists presumed that if it is a closed system, any intellectual intrusion might lead to consequences, which may not be in national interest. Presumed ethical, moral and national interests and closed structure of military have led to self-denial of Military Sociology in India.

The sources of understanding sociological dimensions of military in India are largely autobiographical, biographical, memoirs, records, reports and newspaper reporting. Such sources are certainly useful but have meaningful biases, revealing self-glorification or national patriotic overtones. The objective and facts-oriented analytical aspects of military system cannot be achieved unless the social scientists have access to the reality of military system through appropriate techniques and methods of inquiry coupled with theoretical and conceptual framework.

In recent times Stouffers work on *American Soldier* is considered one of the very few pioneering studies on the sociology of army social structures, personnel and social psychology which is based on scientific method presented in a systematic form. The first two volumes (Volume-1: Adjustment during Army Life, Volume-2: Combat and Its Aftermath) describe the substantive results relating to these two subjects collected in the course of the research programme. The volume-3, experiments on Mass Communication describes the effectiveness of films and other mass communication devices, whereas Volume-4, deals with the methodological report. The research effort reported in these volumes is very impressive. *The American Soldier* was an official programme of the Information and Education Division of the army. This very fact demonstrated how rapidly the social sciences were becoming respectable in the United States. The fact that it did start and on the whole was a great success—an administrative success and also a scientific success—has undoubtedly, set the pace for later development. Robert S. Lynd reviewed, the first two volumes of *The American Soldier* in the New Republic under the heading "The Science of Inhuman Relations." An extract, quoted in Continuities, reads: ("These volumes depict science being used with great skill to sort out and to control men for purposes not of their own willing. It is a significant measure of the importance of liberal democracy that it must increasingly use its social sciences not directly on democracy's own problems, but tangentially and indirectly...in the present case, in army research on how to turn frightened draftees into tough soldiers who will fight a war whose purposes, they do not understand. With such socially extraneous purposes controlling the use of social science, each advance in its use tends to make it an instrument of mass control, and thereby a further threat of democracy.[6]

Sociological studies of military necessitate democratic framework of society, if they have to be fact based and valid. The U.S. and some other countries of the West have undertaken several studies in the area of Military Sociology. The US defense department sponsors and finances sociological studies in areas, which can be of help for them from strategic point of view. In India there have been biographical, autobiographical and accounts of memoirs wherein military has been discussed as a part of perceived experience. However, there is hardly any work in Military Sociology in India.

The Social Science perspective in Military studies has yet not come of age. The reasons for this neglect lie in the dominant paradigm in Military, which is mechanistic and technologically oriented. The need of security by every nation is legitimate concern of a state. However, no nation can afford to permit use of technologically equipped weaponry which would lead to its own destruction, in the wake of large scale war, obviously there are equally powerful reasons for preparedness and yet restraint. Reconciliation between the contradictions of Military preparedness and maintenance of peace is part of holistic perspective of Military Sociology. Wars are not won or lost by weaponry. There are dimensions of domination, power, morale, commitment, traditions and worldview, which need to be studied and analyzed in the cultural and social context of every society.

The military sociology nevertheless provides several important and relevant dimensions of study and enquiry.

- Military organization-hierarchy.
- Rules and regulations.
- Division of labor.
- Discipline.
- Recruitment.
- Training.
- Socialization.
- Reward.
- Punishment.
- Promotion.
- Job-satisfaction.
- Morale.
- Commitment.
- Interpersonal relationship.
- Civilian-military relationship.

- Military in peace and war.
- The sub-culture; the sub-structure.
- The tensions and anxieties.
- Alienation, the psychosis.
- Fear.
- The war and peace.
- The generality of social structure and specificity of military structure.
- The role of family members.
- The traditions of military.
- The level of aspirations.
- Motivation.
- Heroism.
- Honor.
- Recognition.
- Frustration.
- Factions, feuds.
- The health and sickness.
- Recreation and leisure.

These are some of the significant dimensions for sociological studies, which need to be analyzed keeping carefully in view of the national interests.

Lt General A.M. Vohra (former Vice Chief of the Army Staff and a well-known defense analyst on national security issues) writes "Service in the Armed Forces takes us to all parts of our large and diverse country from Kashmir to Kanyakumari and from Jaisalmer to Jorhat and makes us feel one with all castes and creeds. The base for this feeling is provided to us in our units and formations. Many units have a mixed class composition and units of Arms and Services in the formation give us exposure to our countrymen from all parts of the country. Thus the Armed Force serve the cause of integration and are recognized as an important factor in keeping India together. There is a direct connection between the image and the ethos of the Armed Forces. The parchment of Commission that an officer receives from the President reads, "I, reposing special trust and confidence in your fidelity, courage and good conduct appoint you...." It goes on to charge the officer to "carefully and diligently discharge your duty.... And to obey such directions... that you shall receive...and observe such rules, regulations, orders...." The core values that emerge from the "Parchment" are courage, fidelity, which is faithful performance of duty, good conduct and discipline. Other values follow from tradition and the ways of life or the style of functioning in Armed Forces; loyalty, which works both ways to subordinates and superiors, initiative, cooperation and a sense of urgency, of getting on with the job, of not letting the grass grow under one's feet. "No doubt that we, in the Armed Forces, and our countrymen are proud of our achievements in the wars that independent India has fought, and our people are appreciative of the hazards and the hardships faced by those guarding our borders or tackling insurgencies. Recent opinion polls tell us that they are conscious of our professionalism, and dedication and devotion to duty. Our countrymen give us high marks for upholding the desired value system. Please compare this with the conclusion reached through another opinion poll which indicated that 84 per cent people think that politicians are responsible for communal tension and violence, almost 46 per cent believe that politicians are dishonest and as much as 81 per cent believe that corruption is eroding all organizations to a greater or a lesser degree.

At a panel discussion on 'The Image of the Armed Forces' held at the USI under the chairmanship of Lt. Gen. A.M. Vohra a number of relevant issues were raised:

(1) If the image of the Armed Forces is high, why is there is shortage of officers? Why does the profession not attract the right type of youth, which would ensure a higher percentage of selection by the Boards.

(2) The image is high but it seems that this is not matched by the respect for the Services. The politicians take the military for granted. The bureaucrats look down upon them and jealously guard all decision-making as their prerogative.

(3) The youth does not seem to attach much importance to the image. Apart from the hard life in the Services,

the poor prospects (only 0.6 per cent become General Officers as against 39 per cent reaching the level of Joint Secretary and above in the IAS).

(4) Within Services, there is a general feeling that a person is not getting his due. A Colonel or a Brigadier now does what a Major or a Lt Colonel did in the old days. The attempts to increase higher ranks by cadre reviews have not been a success. It has lowered the prestige of rank and has not solved the problems of poor prospects, poor emoluments and early retirement.

(5) The politicians are guided purely by the bureaucrats as they lack understanding and do not find the time from their political preoccupation with their constituencies to get to know the fundamental issues.

(6) The military need to build influence and harness a lobby of ex-servicemen who have a 'voice' in the rural areas.

(7) There is no future in the Armed Forces. Their role is not understood and the senior brass is unable to do anything as they have no clout in an environment of bureaucrat guided and controlled politicians.[7]

In the Indian context, since the nation has continued to face some or the other form of national crisis or threat to its security since independence, the military continues to be looked upon as the pillar of national stability and integrity. There are basically two reasons why a soldier has continued to be traditionally accorded social acceptance. First, from ancient times, soldiers have enjoyed a higher status in society and, secondly till India got her independence in 1947, military profession was the main employment. It provided the youth an outlet to earn a livelihood.

It is sociologically important to note that the Indian Army fought World War I and II and many campaigns in Asia and Africa over the last two centuries, but not from any sense of loyalty to the throne of England or to the Viceroy of India. As a sense of nationalism was lacking, there was no notion of ensuring Indian security and enhancing national interests. The motivation was primarily allegiance to the regiment. It was the desire not to "let the side down," a sentiment not easy to describe, that really encompassed the contours of professionalism. This was the basis of the army's corporate identity and remains so largely today.[8]

Armed force organizations have two major foci of significance in any society. One is the role of such organizations as far as external use, either for defense or aggression, is concerned. The other is the use of such forces for the internal maintenance of order. To understand any organization we have to study the culture of that particular society. Nevertheless, it will be worth while to consider some definitions briefly. Tylor says that 'culture or civilization is that complex whole which includes knowledge, belief, art, morals, law, customs, and any other capabilities and habits acquired by man as a member of society.' Linton equates culture with "social heredity." Lowie calls it 'the whole of social tradition." All three statements use the term 'social' or 'society,' but in an attributive or qualifying sense. We can accept this: society and culture, social and cultural, are closely related concepts. Roughly, then, we can approximate what culture is by saying it is that which the human species has, this would include speech, knowledge, beliefs, customs, arts and technologies, ideals and rules.

Each country has a separate national character, identity and culture. It is worthwhile to study the cross cultural identities to understand the pattern of army socialization and the social organization. For an example, studies of organizations, especially military organizations has great potentialities in South-East Asia regions. India, Pakistan, Bangladesh and Sri Lanka are neighbors and each has a separate military organization, history and culture. It would be worthwhile to study the military issues, which are raised in this paper. What type of social organizations these countries have? What are the cultural and national identities of these countries? What is the role of military socialization on the army as such? Does socialization in the army in other countries work as the same direction as it does in India? Can we do a comparative study between underdeveloped and developed countries? We may highlight a few issues, which may be studies by sociologists and psychologists both.

The Indian Army has grown and evolved through experiences and shared ethos of its tradition and glory. The shared tradition of the Army is characterized by its apolitical nature, which has revealed remarkable continuity, despite changes in the type of government at the center. The country has witnessed several political crises but all political analysts in the country have always ruled out the possibility of Army dictatorship. This is not only due to the democratic institutions of the country, but largely because of the political nature of Indian Army and its officials who have scrupulously avoided any alignment with individuals or political parties of the country. Such a character of the Army has led to mutuality of confidence and support between two major institutions related to governance and protection of the country. The parliamentary system of government and military organization for defense have developed interpersonal confidence in their specified areas of functioning. The Indian soldier has heterogeneous social and cultural background which, in fact is a replica of Indian society and culture. The recruits come from different regions, linguistic background, castes, religions, classes, and family background and differ in their process of pre-army socialization.

It is significant to note that despite the heterogeneity of background, the military system has superimposed upon them the uniformity and homogeneity of military culture of routine work, duty and styles of life. This synthesizing of micro-level distinctive background and macro-level military super imposition has created national integration. Increasingly more and more people from such castes entered the military organization, which earlier were though to be related to their performance of sacred rituals or trading.

The conventional notion of security has been and remains State-centric with military as its major instrument, entrusted with the duty to defend the territorial integrity of the nation-state. No doubt, safeguarding territorial integrity from external aggression is most vital for the honorable existence of any nation-state.

However, there are equally, if not more vital concerns and facets of security, that are often, ignored in the specialized security discourse of military strategists, where the concerned area is ravaged by militancy, hatred and innocent killings. Military security through armed and ammunitions with latest equipments often neglects the social structures, people's movements, and non-state actors, thus making the entire process elitist, parochial and often insensitive.

The changing nature of Civil-Military Relations in Asia has been focus for any serious scholar of peace and security. Military professionalism is an influential but controversial concept in the study of civil-military relations. The Indian military has been unique among the armies in the developing world in several ways since the historical background and political context is different in each country. Yet, the framework enables us to study some of the trends of institutional development in Indian military organization. Since the relationship between the military and society in each social system also reflects national and cultural considerations, the need of the hour is to understand developmental trends over time through imperial research findings.

India is the world's largest and most populous democracy and largest developing country with a democratic system. Surrounded by military-dominated and non-democratic states, it represents one of the most interesting cases of firm, stable, and authoritative civilian control of the military. It is remarkable that the appalling problems of low economic development, sharp differences in income, mass poverty, over-population, illiteracy, ethnic antagonism, absence of any linguistic unity, cultural fragmentation, social diversities, and a complex class system do not seem to hinder civilian control of the Indian military. The two neighbors of India—Pakistan and Bangladesh—are comparable or closely matched to her in a number of ways yet display divergent patterns of civil-military relations.[9]

In contrast to the Western world, where we find by the end of the Cold War, changes in the security concerns, which led to formal re-definition of their major missions. Indian Army still focuses on what Moskos calls "defense of their homeland," but at the same time participates in international peacekeeping operations, and other humanitarian operations. But if we try to look into the military functions today, we definitely find some minor shift from primarily war fighting or war deterrence to military deployments for peace and humanitarian purposes. This may be due to the change in the threat perception from Pakistan and China. The shift is towards peace missions, humanitarian activities of the armed forces, and simultaneously we find some changes in public attitude and opinion. These are the areas, which are of utmost interest to the Military Sociologist.

To conclude one can say that a system, which is responsible for the maintenance of territorial sovereignty of a country, and which supports the internal security system obviously has paramount significance for sociological inquiry. Cross-national researches should be undertaken so that social, psychological, cultural aspects could be examined on a continuous basis. Sociologists should be able to assess the deeper aspects of resentment, frustration and aspirations to understand different societies in a broad framework.

A syllabus can be formulated to study military sociology as follows:

1. Meaning of military sociology, nature, scope, conceptual construction of military sociology.
2. Structure and organization of defense forces—in different phases of Indian history.
3. Defense bureaucracy and civilian bureaucracy.
4. Roles of defense forces in national calamities, social and cultural calamities.
5. Roles of defense during war.
6. Defense forces as total institutional complexes (life style).
7. The relationship between state and defense forces—the civil military relationship.
8. The relationship between society and defense forces:
    (A) societal perception.
    (B) perception by defense forces.
9. Defense forces and international/global organization.
10. Can society survive without defense forces? The necessity of military sociology.

NOTES AND REFERENCES

1. James Burk. "Morris Janowitz and the Origins of Sociological Research on Armed Forces and Society." *Armed Forces and Society: An Interdisciplinary Journal*, Volume 19, Winter, 1993.
2. Gerhard Kummel & Andreas D. Prufert, Military Sociology, *The Richness of Military Sociology: An introduction—Nomos Veriagsgeseiischarft*, Baden-Baden, 2000, pp. 7-8.
3. Michel Louis Martin, *French Military Sociological Research: A Still Promising Field*. Military Sociology, The Richness of Military Sociology: An introduction—Nomos Veriagsgeseiischarft, Baden-Baden, 2000, p. 22.
4. Jordan Baev & Edwin R. Micewski, *Civil Military Relations*, Nation Defense Academy, Vienna, 2005, p. 5.
5. Leena Parmar, *Society, Culture and Military System*, Rawat Publications, Jaipur, p. 21.
6. Robert K. Merton and Paul F. Lazarsfeld, *Continuities in Social Research: Studies in the Scope and Method of The American Soldier*, The Free Press of Glencoe, New York, 1955, p. 157.
7. Lt. Gen. A.M. Vohra, PVSM (Retd.), The Image of the Armed Forces, *U.S.I. Journal*, January-March 1998, p. 27.
8. Muthiah Alagappa, *Military Professionalism in Asia*, East-West Center, 2001, p. 22.
9. Stephen P. Cohen, 'Civilian Control of the Military in India,' Claude E. Jr. Welch (ed.), *Civilian Control of the Military: Theory and Cases From Developing Countries* (Albany: State University of New York Press, 1976), pp. 43-64.

25

Rational and Problems of Strategic Studies in Indian Universities

P.A. Ghosh

Introduction

Till recently, scholars from strategic studies perceived threats to national security mainly from the military angle and accordingly threats posed by adversary states were evaluated in military terms. Hence, counter measures that were suggested revolved around the policy of acquiring adequate military capability. This model of perpetual adversary relationship and politico-military responses, with the primary thrust on arms build up, though valid for the developed states, is not an appropriate model for the developing countries like India. Unlike developed states, which enjoy a degree of political, economic and social stability, the developing states are facing problems of national integration that pose the primary challenge to their national security.[1] Thus, it would not be wrong to state that while the developed states face challenges to their national security from military angle which are posed by their adversaries, developing states face primary challenge to their security from forces that impede national integration from within. A domestic threat often combines with external threats to compound the challenge to its national integration. This multi-faceted dimension of national security is promoting scholars from the developing countries to take a new look at conceptualizing "security" in the 21st century and to develop methodology of academic approaches to security studies. A crucial issue is related to their concept of national security need to be evaluated from the larger perspectives and to the context of challenges arising not only from international, regional environment but also within for a country like India.

Over the last two decades, particularly after the end of Cold War, debate on national security has significantly brought definitional changes. One can observe that there has been a paradigm shift in these vital areas of investigation involving from state security to like human security and sustainable development. That security has an extended meaning beyond its obvious military connotations is increasingly being understood by the scholars in India; there is better appreciation now of its non-military and human dimensions. Hence, the state needs to cater for its own security and simultaneously, the security of its individuals, which has acquired equal, if not greater significance with the passing years. Hence, the imperative necessity arises to provide for good governance to achieve the ends of both state and individual security. Non-conventional security challenges mainly arises from lack of economic, cultural, religion and political stability, natural disaster, health-hygiene, ecological and environmental degradation. Thus, threats to national security could emulate from many directions, which are not necessarily merely military in nature. In order to deal with such complexity nation-state need to develop comprehensive capabilities rather than mere military build. With the end of the Cold War the vision of a new world order has not been spelt out clearly. In this transitional phase the traditional concept of national security as understood exclusively in military terms and its association with the narrow state structure can no longer be considered adequate. The conventional understanding of security is no longer found to be a politically relevant because national security is dependent on and inseparable from the human security. The notion of security has spanned from territorial integrity through national interest and the political, economic and social well-being to the government policy aimed at the creation of favorable national and international conditions for the protection or extension of national interests against existing or potential enemy threats.

Issues and Changing Concept of National Security

The existing state centric approach to national security confined to the defence of the country against territorial aggression has been widened to the idea of security that is inclusive of larger sets of threats to the people of the state. In this context, arrival of the nuclear weapons on the Indian subcontinent, have added urgency to the need for fresh look at national security beyond its military dimension. Hence, a wider range of issues that includes economic, environmental, societal, education and governance in addition to the political and military factors deserve a comprehensive attention to the national security. Moreover, 9/11 incident and post-development in global politics has further accelerated the security discourse to new angles; a crucial issue is related to the concept of security.

The traditional perception of national security in terms of military preparedness has not been adequate to fulfil the requirements of all the people. Because, in the case of common men, women, children, and workers and other vulnerable groups and people living within the precincts of what is called a state territorial sovereignty. Hence, there is an urgent need to redefine security and broaden its framework. Even while a state has been equipped with all kinds of sophisticated military weapons and with a world destroying capability, it appears to be defenseless against the kinds of threats that are not coming from similar military sources. These threats originate from other sources, which have not received adequate attention. In this context, a traditional disregard of the earth's environment, a multifactor system has led to its degradation and caused progressively increased threat to security. Due to environmental degradation, it has devastating consequences on state's economy, food production and above all the very survival of the people. In an eco-geographical region inhabited by different nations, economic activities on the part of a state can result in environmental scarcity of resources and as a consequence, affect the people and the economy of another neighboring state. Further, in a situation of deepening economic crisis, declining agricultural productivity as social effects of the environmental degradation, there will be displacement of people as environmental refugees not only from one region to another region within a state but also from one state to another state, causing groups identity conflict among the various social, ethnic, cultural and religious groups of the receiving state. Group vs. group conflict ultimately transform into a state vs. state conflict creating a separate security threats to both the states. Environment, therefore, has now become the major security issue transcending any other single issue dealing with the culture, health, spirituality, wealth and leading to a dramatic paradigm shift from the security of the land mass and its resources as an exclusive possession to the environment security and mastery of the environment as an ultimate assurance of sovereignty.

Besides, environmental degradation due to the pressure of population growth and as a part of fulfilment of a development process, results deep financial crisis and fails to cater to the basic needs of the people. Consequently, people faith on the capability of the state and its associated institutions will decline giving rise to a disruption in its political and social institution. Existing social divides will be further widened generating a kind of relative deprivation conflict among various social groups and individuals. Environmental, health, ecological, social and economic security—it becomes readily evident that is an all embracing phrase that need to be anchored in the security of states as well as in condition of human security, because all are inseparable among the elements of all and cannot be achieved in isolation unless all are fully attained. It is pertinent to state that in truth security is far too interdependent an issue to be defined in purely military terms. It can no longer be my security against yours, but my security and your security in a single planet where all are equal stakeholders. Full realization of this and a clearer definition will perhaps take some more time yet, but the concept and relevance of human security vis-à-vis state security is growing and entering the international debate.

National security affairs partially overlap traditional fields of "international politics," "foreign affairs," and "diplomacy" but also differ from them to some extent. Specialist does not completely agree on just where the dividing lines should be drawn. In general, national security focuses more than these fields on the role of force in relations among nations, and the implications of advancing military technology. It focuses more than "international politics" and similar academic subjects on policy: what should a country do about an existing or foreseeable threat, and how should it go about deciding? Also strategic studies revolved around the relationship between military power and political purpose. In a more broad sense, it is the rational assessment and determination of a nation interest and priorities and of the ways in which those objectives may be achieved.[2]

Technological uncertainty and rapidly changing international circumstantial environment including nuclear, cross-border terrorism, energy crisis, etc. gives national security affairs somewhat different flavors from many other fields involving the analysis of contemporary socio-cultural, psychological, economic and political issues. So far, national security as an academic field dominated by policy analysis and relatively is lacking in general theories. Most of the national security literature does not concern itself with drawing general conclusions or developing theory. Rather, it explicitly or implicitly assumes a technical and situational context similar to the one actually existing at the time of writing, and goes on to examine policy problems and associated intellectual problems that exist within that context and derive their meaning and force from it. Beyond this there is an additional domain that not all national security specialists would regard as part of their field: basic research in conflict resolution and security may be reduced or increased, or the full menu of means for reducing, managing, mitigating, and resolving human conflict. Providing more understanding into these subjects is among the most important contributions the security field, broadly defined, could make.

In this context, no national security definition as a field of academic discipline has been generally accepted; none may be possible. In general, it is the study of the security problems faced by the nations, of the policies and programmes by which these problems are addressed, and also of the governmental processes through which the policies and programmes are decided upon and carried out. As practiced in American research institutes, governmental agencies and universities, it naturally focuses on the problems, policies, and processes of the United States government.

Broadly, concept of national security is to be seen for a country like India not only states security but also to people security. In this context, it may be stated that national security is the ability of a nation to protect its internal values from external threats—such as individual rights, personal freedom, the pursuit of happiness, peace, prosperity, economic well-being and protecting whole socio-political entity, which means overall development of a nation and ability to lead better lives of its people. Thus, national security policy is an integral part of government policy intends to create favorable socio-economic and political conditions for the protections or extension of these vital national values against existing and potential adversaries.

Rational

The main objective of national security studies is to create national consensus around some common values and establish coherent and united society. Hence, the analysis of national security issues are vital in terms of national values presupposes an integrated and stable society in absence of conflicts. But, in reality most of the nation states are confronted with serious internal problems, which impinge on their behaviors and position. In this context, the linkage between internal and external setting is the *sine qua non* of national security in a system dominated by nation states. Specifically, in the case of third world state, the cooperation on internal level holds the key to their security and stability, as the domestic cohesion is the inevitable basis for consensus for nation-building process and national integration.

National security or strategic studies encompass a complex variety of issues and sought to answer was how peace is maintained in a society of sovereign states. Such studies required multi-dimensional approaches for the formulation of a unified theoretical orientation. The problem of national security for a country like ours, which has experienced a series of catastrophes from without, has to be formulated in terms of larger goals and aspiration. Briefly, we may think of three such objectives: (a) National stability and integrity, (b) Social, political and economic progress, (c) Peace and stability in our relations with other states.[3] However, India's security policy basically a policy aimed at to defend territory, sovereignty and freedom. These seem to be inadequate for a variety of reasons, prominently, because it fails to make a distinction between external and internal threats to its national security and its magnitude and linkages between both. Addressing the threats to the core values emanating from within the state often makes a nation susceptible to the external threats. In this context, incorporating diverse social, ethnic and religious group, India's core values that stand out would naturally include social, political and economic democracy, these core values must be reflected to the nation-building process. The erosion of any one of these is bound to erode the legitimacy of the state and hence constitutes a threat to its security. Although external and internal security issues are substantially different in nature, they often are interrelated.

In recent years insurgency, cross-border terrorism in the form of secessionist movements have been cropping up in the entire north-eastern region and in many parts of India. Its social and economic scenario always in turmoil has become more tumultuous with the waves of globalization and in the information revolution. The latter has brought in the environment of high expectation for better living and a desire for equality. Security concept should be conceived for the society that has a large gap between poor and rich for centuries, where information flow is now causing high expectation for better life to catch up with the rest but lack of opportunities find frustration leading to social tension, agitation and violent expression. Conflicts have also been emanating from social and economic injustice, ethnic consciousness and sub-nationalism. Diverse conflicts—political, social, economic and psychological, borne out of self-consciousness, aspirations and self-identity in the backdrop of globalization of values, freedom and democracy are dotting India. National security is at stake if this freedom is not channelised, constructively.

Cultural Nationalism and Ethnic Consciousness

The dissolution of former Soviet Union seem to have eroded the very sanctity and legitimacy of pluralistic societies as well as the multi-ethnic, multi-lingual and multi-religious states. India has enough of these fissiparous tendencies. Emergence of sub-regional ethno linguistic centrifugal trends in India's politics is causing severe strain on India's resources. Caste-based, religion-based and ethnic and linguistic parties are challenging the consolidation of the Indian republic in political as well as territorial terms. Center-state relations are under stress because of the growing demand for restructuring relation between the central and the state government with a view to delegating more power and jurisdiction to the state. Criminalisation of electoral politics and politicization of criminals, increasing level of corruption, communal violence in certain parts of the country and many other issues have become major source of security threat. These threats manifest themselves mainly in the form of ethnocentric nationalism, religious fundamentalism or militant demands for redistribution of the economic and political power within the state. It may be noted that in coming decades internal threats are going loom larger than ever before due to variety of reasons. The most extreme danger would be possible break-up of multilingual federal republic of India, if the attitudes of affected people were not changed towards governance. The factors that could work towards the breakup are: the erosion of spiritual, moral and ethical values; disregard for human rights; religious intolerance; in economic growth, standard of living and quality of life or any combination of these. Besides, political parties exploit these for short-term gains. Hence, it creates a doubt about India's prospect and its ability to retain its unity amid its diversity. The complexities of these threats and their transnational character demands in-depth analysis of issues involved with each set of threats, with a view to generate well informed debate and also to redress people grievances and thereby winning the hearts and minds of people involved directly or indirectly enabling them to join in the mainstream. These internal dimensions to India's security threats have not been given adequate attention by the policy-makers.

Against such background, analysis of socio-cultural, economic, political and demographic relationship of the society is important for proper understanding of national security parameters of the Third World countries. It can be rightly said that the Third World countries suffer from scarcity of literature from correct perspectives to formulate national security policies. Because national security of a state is interwoven with its internal structure as it largely determine its external environment. Therefore, Third World country is still dependent on Western literature to understand the security problems of their countries and formulate security policies. The Western analysis is mainly on military strategic dimensions of the particular group of people have less relevance for the Third World countries.[4]

After 59 years as an independent nation, India is now poised to emerge as a major player in world affairs. But to perform well, we need to remove the debilitating factors from our foreign and defence policy decision-making process. Moreover, nowadays security threats posed are very sophisticated in nature and they range over the whole spectrum of conflicts, from direct military threats to indirect threats. The problem of national security is now far more complex and needs to be handled with great caution, which demands greater involvement of population intellectually for the formulation of a unified theoretical orientation. It may be stated that it is the business of every citizen to be defence conscious. The bureaucratic process model, due to the compulsions and complexities of nuclear age, must give into a larger political process model where inputs from the intellectuals at large must become an essential and meaningful necessity. Such exercises concerning our national security can hardly be carried out under governmental control institution. Hence, we must conceptualize security differently for 21st century because the forces we have to fight are changeable and unpredictable. It is no longer Himalayan border we are fighting for, we are fighting forces external and within that are dynamic, to secure people in the new age of knowledge economy.

It may be correct to state that often our foreign policy decision has been ad hoc, responding to given circumstances, rather than pursuing well laid down objectives. A former Foreign Minister (1967-1970) Dinesh Singh stated that foreign policy-making has been "one of carrying on, merely responding to situation."[5] The experience of Ministers of External Affairs since then is not different. The best illustration of such example is Rajiv Gandhi period of ad hoc decision-making. Because, the then government in its own wisdom deployed military force to safeguard her national interests beyond territorial limits. It has firmly indicated India's national interests in South Asian Region and that she has the political will to pay the price for the same. Indian Peace Keeping Force (IPKF) was sent to Sri Lanka without any national debate. IPKF mission in Sri Lanka became a national disaster where more than one thousand Indian soldiers lost their lives without achieving the objectives, either of disarming the LTTE or of protecting the Sri Lankan Tamils. Tamils, who were then looking at India as their only saviors, began to call IPKF as innocent people killing force! India lost her leverage both with Sri Lankan as well as Indian Tamils.[6] That the decision was an ad hoc one is clear, because, while the Indian soldiers were fighting against the LTTE in jungle, Indian intelligent agents were arming the Guerrillas, even treating the injured LTTE men in the hospitals of Tamil Nadu! The same hospitals were also treating the IPKF![7] It was due to over-centralization of foreign policy-making by the prime minister.

The Indian military intervention in Sri Lankan internal crisis was under great public and press criticism within and outside our country. In the wake of all these developments, the Government of India had to absurdly terminate the IPKF action in the mid of its fight against Tamil guerrillas, as a corollary the IPKF also had no popular support or sympathy for the cause of their actions. It will remain as a virgin record for future historians, strategic analyst and commentators, etc. for productive assessment of IPKF achievement in Sri Lankan domestic conflict in totality.

Against this background, strategic analysis in its first step always have to be made 'policy relevant' and hence the need for inputs from the intellectuals at large, intellectual activity by definition has to be confined to individual outlooks uninfluenced by institutional or political rational. It may be stated that basic research conducted in India in the field of pure science has always been 'policy relevant' with the ultimate aim of application. Intellectual analysis must be free from Governmental standpoints, which need not be part of government organizations. Policy relevant study in pure sciences resulted several options that are available for technology and not *vice versa*. The phenomenal progress of Indian science is because of the Indian science policy focusing on 'relevancy of research to provide innumerable alternatives.' Basic research in strategic studies has never been fully geared up to make them applicable for Policy alternatives like in pure science. With nuclear proliferation in South Asia, the complex interests of many extra regional power in Indian Ocean and West Asia, it is absolutely essential for India to ensure that the finest minds in every branch of social science are encouraged to apply themselves to understand the needs of our national security and help the Government with a variety of policy alternatives which are "policy relevant."

Universities, Research units and individual researchers in India, which constitute the cream of thinking manpower, thus must be the focus of attention of the Ministry of Human Resources and the University Grants Commission. Every nation of the Western World utilizes this tremendous talent. The US is certainly the envy of all because they have been able to use this vast "think tank" manpower even commercially. In the nuclear age, it will be an irretrievable folly to be merely reactive to aggression. One has to develop the concepts of preempting to deter the occurrence of aggression. It is the liberal education system of the Universities, which opens the vision of intellectuals to formulate strategic doctrines in which the institution of the Armed forces and its supporting elements of bureaucracy can be made to interact with a view to preempt a possible aggression. At a functional level only when intellectual inputs give 'policy alternatives' for "Policy orientation" can the political decision-maker implement the true fruits of strategic analysis?[8]

Strategic Studies as an academic subject is neither too old nor too recent. It was only after 1945 that the United States and former Soviet Union along with the conglomerate of nations of Western Europe began thinking in peacetime about strategy, i.e. the relationship between military power and political purpose. Concepts of strategy encompassed a new dimension due to the introduction of nuclear weapons. Strategy, thus not only got mixed up with the evolution of new strategic doctrines to safeguard national security, but also generated a new breed of experts from amongst the intellectuals, civilian bureaucrats and practicing soldiers, who could be held accountable. Since then a group of people have made an identical profession as strategic analyst in many research institutes and universities, who provides policy alternatives to the government for policy orientation.

Third World countries or less developed countries, which emerged after the end of Second World War generally, faced a situation of insecurity from their immediate neighbors and from the crushing influence of either of the superpowers. The developed countries influenced each new nation of the Third World politically, economically, socially and militarily. The struggle to exist as viable political units, autonomous in them with the goals of developments for total transformation, became the prime target. Devoid of military powers in comparison to the superpowers, the first task of the Third World countries was to develop a national security programme, to deter secessionist and disruptive movements and protect against external threats from immediate neighbors. This led to the evolution of contemporary national security strategy at the conventional level.[9] Nowadays, security threats posed are very sophisticated in nature and they range over the whole spectrum of conflict, from direct military threat to indirect threats. Therefore, national security analysis is now far more complex and has to be handled with great caution mixed with clear vision and perseverance. Such exercises demand greater involvement of population in matters of security, both intellectually and physically.

Therefore, for a country like India, national security and national integration is to be preserved by all the people by involving themselves in the affairs of national security, not superficially but intimately. Hence, the study of strategic studies should continue and more to be undertaken in the universities under liberal education system and research institutes with open mindedness in view to develop proper thinking and mate correct assessment in the context of India's national security. And this would result more realistic and relevant appreciation of our overall defence and security problems in relation to India's role in the management of world affairs for today and tomorrow.

Problem

"Defence and Strategic Studies" has acquired a distinct academic place through undergraduate, postgraduate and research studies in a large number of Indian Universities and colleges. The origin of the National Security studies in India can be traced back in the different historical formulations of the concept of vital national interests. In India, till the sixties and seventies, although certain elements of the conceptual evolution on national security could be found in the writings of some Indian writers like K. Subrahmanium and Raju Thomas, who are the key figures of security studies. Also many American and West Europeans had written acceptable thesis on India's security problems than Indians themselves. Amongst all notable important works are: "India's Quest for Security" by L. Kavic; "Krishna Menon's View of the World" by Michael Breacher; "The Indian Army" by Stephen P. Cohen—all North American University Professors. Before introduction of this subject, the subject matter were studied partially in terms of National Defence or Military Security and varied emphasis on military expenditure as a part of political science, diplomacy, history and geography. This subject came to exist in Indian universities when she faced a situation of insecurity from her immediate neighbors and from the crushing influence of one of the superpower, she had to struggle to exist, as viable political units became the prime target. Since introduction of this academic subject in Indian Universities, three expert committees, so far, were asked to submit status report on the subject appointed by University Grants Commission. All the three expert committees reviewed the case and submitted their findings. Following were the main findings of the committee (Please refer report of the UGC Committee on Defence/Strategic Studies, 1987, pp. 8-9):

1. Defence and Strategic studies being an academic discipline have vast potential in national life and suggested to include the subject in the academic curriculum of Universities at undergraduate, postgraduate and research level, as it would give more viable policy options to deal with complex issues of national importance and to generate a national security consciousness.
2. Defence and Strategic studies being an academic discipline, it should in no way be connected with either the National Cadet Corps or practical aspects of military training.
3. The present infrastructure in the universities for teaching and research in this subject is inadequate. Therefore, an earnest endeavor should be made to develop Defence and Strategic studies departments in Indian universities. To

achieve this end the commission may give from time to time ad hoc grants to build up infrastructure and departmental library.

4. The development of Defence and Strategic studies in the universities should be monitored closely by the UGC by a standing committee of experts in this discipline.
5. In view of the present security environment of the country an intensive effort may be made to promote a general awareness for national security in the country. The committee would, therefore, recommend that the other faculties of the universities might be asked to assign an academic paper on 'National Security' in order to motivate the young generation to study the issues connected with national security of the country. In order to strengthen the existing departments it is absolutely necessary that there should be a close interaction between senior academics and senior defence service officers.
6. In recent years national security studies has attained great importance in view of the strategic environment of the country. It is, therefore, in the national interest that one or more advance research centers be established in this subject.

Findings

I have had opportunity to visit many Universities, where this intellectual academic discipline has been introduced at undergraduate, postgraduate and research level. Based on my own study, following are the main findings:

1. In India, the average national security awareness on the part of our citizen is less than poor, intellectual input less than satisfactory for the academic and theoretical growth of this vital discipline.
2. In many universities and affiliated colleges the existing infrastructure for teaching and research in this subject is inadequate. Moreover, amongst all, many faculties are appointed as subject teacher who do not have background of security studies and hence less trained to contribute

for theoretical growth of this academic discipline. They have been appointed to teach this subject due to their commission rank as NCC officer.

3. Although UGC expert committee clearly stated that Defence Studies in no way be connected with NCC or military training programme, many universities till date follow syllabus of NCC.

Recommendations

Due to India's present complex security environment and issues involved in it an intensive and extensive study be made to conceptualize security parameter and promote security awareness amongst people and for theoretical growth of this subject. For the purpose of fulfilment of above condition following recommendations may be accepted, to improve quality of research and teaching in this subject:

1. UGC and Ministry of Human Resources need to provide all required financial and logistic support to all the universities and their affiliated colleges for theoretical growth and academic excellence of this subject. It is imperative to promote more serious thinking on national security studies in the existing University Departments in our country.
2. UGC need to make it compulsory to follow unified syllabus throughout the country, although few optional papers may be included on the basis of regional demand.
3. It is pertinent to state that job opportunities in this subject is very less, as this subject has not been introduced at school level. Therefore, it has attracted only few bright students, who contributed to the academic excellence of this subject. Therefore, it is essential to attract more numbers of students to undertake such study of national importance. Hence, there is an urgent need for inclusion of this subject, as early as possible, as one of the optional paper in Union Public Service Commission and State Public Service Commission.

NOTES AND REFERENCES

1. K.R. Singh, Occasional paper circulated in School of International Studies, Jawaharlal Nehru University, New Delhi.
2. Hedley Bull, "Strategic Studies and Its Critics," *World Politics*, July 1968, pp. 593-94.
3. Prof. Gautam Sen, presently Director, NISDA, Pune, circulated occasional paper when he held position as head of the Department of Defence and Strategic Studies, Pune University.
4. Dr. P.A. Ghosh, "Ethnic Conflict in Sri Lanka and Role of IPKF," (APH Publishing Corporation, New Delhi, 2000), p. 5.
5. Quoted from the article of Prof. P.M. Kamath, "India's National Security Policies," in Madhya Pradesh *Journal of Social Sciences* (Vol. 3, No. 2, 1998), p. 33.
6. *Ibid.*, pp. 33-34.
7. Quoted from Oral History of many senior officers, who were directly involved in IPKF operation in Sri Lanka.
8. Prof. Gautam Sen, *op. cit.*
9. Prof. Gautam Sen, *op. cit.*

26

Position and Polemics in National Security Studies in Indian Universities

Rajendra Prasad

Introduction

- 'Security' is everybody's business and concern—individuals, groups, nations, comity of nations, etc.
- In literal sense, it means "freedom from insecurity."
- In practical sense security is interpreted in both the terms: Ends and Means.
- The terms 'National Security' has long been used by policy decision-makers and military leaders to articulate a 'policy objective' with reference to 'Vital National Interests.'
- Social scientists reference: An analytical concept and a field of study.
- SP is: Conceptualising 'National Security' as an integral component of the multi-disciplinary subject of "Defence and Strategic Studies," encompassing: History, International Relations, Sociology, Economics, Psychology, Geopolitics, Strategic Thought and Theorisation, Conflict Resolution, Management and Transformation, Science and Technology and Peace and anything else as field of inquiry to serve the multi-faceted cause of 'Ends and Means' of National Security of India.

Development of the Concept of 'National Security' and Its Study in India

- Perception/misperception of India's strategic culture could be highly debatable, ranging from denial to acceptance.
- The Development of 'National Security' as a distinct academic field of interest and as a 'golden point' of study in the broader framework of "Defence and Strategic Studies" in many Indian universities and colleges owes much to the following defining factors:
  - Historical Legacy;
  - Geopolitical and geo-strategic manifestations;
  - The first Pak attack on J&K and our response;
  - The Chinese occupation of Tibet and our response;
  - The Chinese occupation of Indian territory in the Himalayas and the NEFA debacle of 1962;
  - 1965 War with Pak;
  - 1971 War with Pak and the emergence of Bangladesh;
  - Kargil War 1999 and fresh look for border management;
  - Challenges of secessionism and insurgencies in the North-East, Punjab and J&K;
  - The IPKF misadventure in neighbouring Sri Lanka;
  - Cross-border terrorism in the J&K in 90s and beyond;
  - Rise of ethno-religious fanaticism, violence, organised crime and narco-terrorism through Golden Crescent and Golden Triangle as a menacing monster against India in the post-Cold War era;
  - Rise of India as a Nuclear Weapon State (NWS) against the wishes of opposing 'Nuclear Haves';
  - Illegal migration across the borders;
  - Realistically speaking, in the long journey of over five decades by India as a nation-state, the aforesaid factors have set forth the contours of her ends and means of 'National Defence' or 'Military Security' as

an integral part of the overall theory and practice of National Security in the changing political, strategic and military scenario.

- The conception of National Security is narrowed down by cosidering it merely in terms of 'National Defence or Military Security' and varied emphasis on military expenditure, security arrangements, alliances, force structures, military doctrines, future power projections, border management, and so on. These are, at least in India's case, manifestations of historical legacy, burdens of history, and geopolitical and geo-strategic developments in the South Asia region. At the same time, India has also experienced a complex inter-play of internal posture and international political pressures. Thus, for any articulation of security, we must bear in mind that the 'price of security' as the burden of historical fears, tensions and conflicts are indispensably paid by the nation-states and India is no exception in this regard (Prasad, 2002).
- Thus, the origins of the concept of National Security, at least in India, can be traced back in the different historical formulations of the concept of vital National Interests. Although certain elements of the conceptual evolution could be found in the writings of some Indian writers like K. Subrahmanyam, who is known as father of Indo-centric National Security Studies, the contemporary realities call for the Indian strategists and scholars to go through our ancient literature of diplomacy and strategy. For stance, Bhisma's advice in the *Shanti Parva* of *Mahabharata;* the wisdom of *Hitopadesha* and the common sense of *Panchtantra*. We also have Kautilya's *Arthashastra* to fall back in terms of strategic soul-searching.
- The wisdom inherent in them is not blocked by any ideological vagaries or hang-ups. To my mind, the ultimate wisdom lies in the fact that any change that

undermines National Security is unacceptable. Former Defence Minister of India, Mr. Jaswant Singh aptly defines that "National Security, above all, is the preservation of the core values of our Nation; the political, economic and social well-being and preservation of our state, the inviolability of our territorial boundaries and the maintenance of national interests within the strategic frontiers of India" (Singh, 1996, p. 19).

Promoting National Security Studies in Indian Universities through Teaching and Research

At present, India has the second largest educational infrastructure with more than 300 Universities, 12,000 Colleges, 3.5 lakh teachers and nearly 5.5 million students (Peerzade, 2005). National Security as a strong component of "Defence and Strategic Studies" with its broad integrals has acquired an identifiable place through undergraduate and postgraduate teaching and research in a large number of Indian Universities and Colleges situated in the states of UP, MP, Maharashtra, Haryana, Punjab, Delhi, Tamil Nadu, Chandigarh (UT), Tripura, West Bengal and Uttarakhand.

At present in India, National Security studies as the core subject matter of strategic discipline are being promoted through teaching and research in the residential campuses of 14 universities, and UG and/or PG teaching, as the case be, in more than 118 colleges affiliated to many other universities in the above-mentioned states. We have, thus more than 469 teachers, 44,850 UG students, 1081 PG students and 110 Diploma students. These data have been collected and computed by me through various sources and field work. Tables 1 and 2 are self-explanatory and substantiate the objectives of presentation.

Teaching and research are two prime complementary pursuits. Without research, the existing stock of knowledge would never thrive in the universities. In the present strategic environment, it is imperative to promote more serious thinking and works on National Security and Strategic studies in the existing University Departments in our country, giving more thoughtful attention to the problems of national and international life. The UGC Committee on Defence Strategic Studies (1987) has gone a few steps further to emphasize that "...Universities may be asked to assign an academic paper on 'National Security' in order to motivate the young generation to study the issues connected with the national security of the country" (UGC Report, 1987, p. 9).

Table 1: State/UT-wise Representation of National Security Studies in Indian Universities (Residential Campuses)

	Faculty	*UG*	*PG*	*DIPLOMA*
UTTAR PRADESH				
DDU Gorakhpur University	14	650	100	50
Allahabad University	8	500	30	
Lucknow University	5	200	10	
BHU University	3		30	
Kashi Vidyapeeth, Varanasi	2	150		
CSS University, Meerut	3		15	
UTTARAKHAND				
HNB Garhwal University, Srinagar, Garhwal		350	40	
HNB Garhwal University, New Tehri		250	10	
HARYANA				
MD University, Rohtak	2		40	
PUNJAB				
Punjabi University, Patiala	5		35	
CHANDIGARH (UT)				
Panjab University, Chandigarh	5		30	
MAHARASHTRA				
University of Pune	5		50	
TAMIL NADU				
University of Madras	4		40	
DELHI				
Jamia Milia University, New Delhi	3		30	

Table 2: State-wise Colleges Teaching National Security in Affiliating Universities

State/Affiliating University	*Colleges*	*Faculty Strength*	*Student Intake in UG*	*Student Intake in PG*
Uttar Pradesh	Ishwar Saran College, Allahabad	3	400	—
Allahabad University, UP	Allahabad Degree College	3	250	—
	S.P. Mukherjee Govt. College, Phaphamau, Allahabad	2	70	—
D.D.U. Gorakhpur University, UP	D.N. College, Gorakhpur	3	360	—
	Degree College, Bhatawali Bazar, Gorakhpur	2	245	—
	Pt. Jawahar Lal Nehru College, Maharajgunj	3	450	—
	A.P.N. PG College, Basti	5	435	15
	S.H.K. PG College, Basti	4	500	—
	Pt. Mahadev Prasad Shukla College, Gaur, Basti	1	80	—
	St. Ramkrishana Paramhans College, Basahiya, Sant Kabir Nagar	1	205	—
	Degree College, Lakshmipur, Sidharth Nagar	1	50	—
	MMM Degree College, Bhatpar Ran, Deoria	2	450	—
	Degree College Bishokhor, Maharajgunj	1	50	
Purvanchal University, Jaunpur, UP	UP College, Varanasi	4	40	—
	Degree College Sakaldiha, Varanasi	2	300	—
	Swami Sahajanand Degree College, Ghazipur	2	300	—
	PG College, Ghazipur	3	450	—

Table 2 *contd...*

State/Affiliating University	*Colleges*	*Faculty Strength*	*Student Intake in UG*	*Student Intake in PG*
Purvanchal University, Jaunpur, UP	Samata Degree College, Sadat, Ghazipur	2	300	—
	DAV College, Azamgarh	4	450	—
	Shibl National College, Azamgarh	3	500	—
	Ramdev Krishak Degree College, Surai, Azamgarh	2	350	—
	MM Town College, Ballia	9	2500	—
	SC College, Ballia	4	1150	—
	Kunwar Singh College, Ballia	5	950	—
	Degree College, Dubey Chhapra, Ballia	2	200	—
	Degree College, Bansdih, Ballia	1	150	—
	Maryada Purushottam Degree College, Ratanpura, Mau	3	200	—
	TD College, Jaunpur	7	450	40
	SGR College, Dobhi, Jaunpur	8	550	50
	Mohd. Hasan PG College, Jaunpur	2	550	50
	Rashtriya PG College, Jamuhai, Jaunpur	4	400	10
	G.B. Pant College, Pratapganj	2	300	—
	Govt. Degree College, Naini, Allahabad	2	500	—
	Ram Shankar Balgopal College, Ghazipur	2	450	—
	K.B. College, Mirzapur	4	800	—

Table 2 *contd...*

State/Affiliating University	*Colleges*	*Faculty Strength*	*Student Intake in UG*	*Student Intake in PG*
CSS University, Meerut, UP	Meerut College, Meerut	5	300	100
	SSB College Hapur, Meerut	6	400	10
	RSS College, Pilkhuwa, Meerut	2	450	—
Dr. RML Avadh University, Faizabad	KS Saket College, Faizabad	10	1000	25
	LBS College, Gonda	6	800	35
	Kishan Degree College, Babhnan, Gonda	3	1200	—
	PB College, Pratapgarh	2	1000	—
	RR PG College, Amethi, Sultanpur	2	1000	—
	MD PG College, Pratapgarh	3	1000	—
	Ganpat Sahay College, Sultanpur	3	800	—
	Sant Tulsidas Degree College, Kadipur, Sultanpur	1	300	—
	BBD College, Paruiya Asharam, Ambedkar Nagar	4	60	—
	Degree College, Lalganj	2	500	—
Kanpur University, UP	VSSD College, Kanpur	7	450	30
	DAV College, Kanpur	14	500	25
	PPN College, Kanpur	3	250	15
	Feroze Gandhi College, Rai Bareli	4	400	—
	Baiswara Degree College, Lalganj, Rai Bareli	3	450	—
	Public Degree College, Bidhuna, Kanpur Dehat	1	150	—

Table 2 *contd...*

State/Affiliating University	*Colleges*	*Faculty Strength*	*Student Intake in UG*	*Student Intake in PG*
MJP Rohilkhand University, Bareilly, UP	Bareilly College, Bareilly	10	700	50
	R.P. PG College, Meerganj,Bareilly	5	450	35
	SM College,Chandausi	5	600	—
	Hindu College, Moradabad	10	850	—
	KGK College, Moradabad	5	850	—
	JSH PG College, Amroha	3	200	—
Bundelkhand University, Jhansi, UP	Atarra College, Atarra, Banda	2	200	—
	Pt. Jawahar Lal Nehru College, Banda	3	250	—
	DAV College, Orai	4	300	—
	Gandhi College Orai	3	200	—
Madhya Pradesh				
Devi Ahilya University, Indore	Govt. Science College, Mhow	4	180	20
Vikram University, Ujjain	Govt. KP College, Dewas	1	350	—
Baraktullah University, Bhopal	MVM, Bhopal	6	480	20
Rani Durgavati University, Jabalpur	Govt. Science College, Jabalpur	1	200	—
Awadhesh Pratap University, Rewa	Govt. Science College, Rewa	1	200	—
Jiwaji University, Gwalior	Govt. Science College, Gwalior	6	400	30
	MLV Arts & Commerce College, Gwalior	4	500	30

Table 2 *contd...*

State/Affiliating University	*Colleges*	*Faculty Strength*	*Student Intake in UG*	*Student Intake in PG*
	Govt. MJS College, Bhind	4	900	35
	Mansingh College, Gwalior	3	300	10
	Jain College, Bhind	2	100	—
	Kamal Singh Degree College, Moh, Bhind	1	200	—
	Govt. College, Alampur	1	100	—
Chhattisgarh				
Pt. Ravi Shankar University, Raipur	Govt. Science College, Raipur	3	200	30
Tamil Nadu				
University of Madras	Guru Nanak College, Chennai	5	350	—
	Govt. Arts College, Ooty	2	200	—
	Voorhese College, Vellore	2	200	—
Haryana				
MD University, Rohtak	University College, Rohtak	2	225	—
	Govt. College, Ateli, Mahendragarh	2	300	—
MD University, Rohtak	Govt. Women's College, Narnaul, Mahendragarh	3	225	—
	Govt. Boys College, Narnaul, Mahendragarh	4	250	—
	Govt. College, Nangal Chaudhary, Mahendragarh	2	250	—

Table 2 *contd...*

State/Affiliating University	*Colleges*	*Faculty Strength*	*Student Intake in UG*	*Student Intake in PG*
	Govt. College, Bahadurgarh, Jhajjar	3	200	—
	Govt. College, Jhajjar	2	200	—
	Govt. College, Jhajjar, Baudhkala, Bhawani	2	200	—
	Govt. College, Meham, Rohtak	3	300	
Kurukshetra University	Govt. Science College, Karnal	3	300	—
	Govt. College, Hissar	5	300	—
	Jat College, Hissar	5	300	—
	Govt. College, Adampur, Hissar	3	300	—
	Govt. College, Bhattukala, Hissar	2	300	—
Punjab				
Punjabi University, Patiala	Mahendra College, Patiala	5	400	—
	Modi College, Patiala	1	250	—
	Khalsa College, Anandpur Saheb, Ropar	2	100	—
Chandigarh (UT)				
Panjab University, Chandigarh	Govt. College, Sector 46, Chandigarh	1	50	—
	Govt. College, Sector 11, Chandigarh	2	80	—
Tripura	Govt. Arts College, Tripura	3	30	—
Uttarakhand				
HNB Garhwal University, Sri Nagar, Garhwal	Govt. Degree College, Joshimath, Chamoli	1	40	—
	Govt. College, Gopeshwar, Chamoli	1	100	—
	Govt. PG College, New Tehri	1	120	6

Table 2 *contd...*

State/Affiliating University	*Colleges*	*Faculty Strength*	*Student Intake in UG*	*Student Intake in PG*
	Govt. Degree College, Vedikhal	1	50	—
	DVS College, Dehradun	1	150	—
	SGRR College, Dehradun	1	50	—
	Rath Mahavidyala, Pattani, Pauri Garhwal	1	60	—
West Bengal				
Calcutta University, Kolkata	Bangbhashi College, Kolkata	NA	NA	—
Maharashtra				
Unversity of Pune	Bhonsala Military College, Nashik	3	50	10
	Someshwar College, Someshwar Nagar, Barmati	2	20	—
	PC College, Baramati	2	25	—
	Wadia College, Pune	1	20	—
	Art, Science & Commerce College, Ahmad Nagar	1	20	—
	Degree College Sinnar, Nashik	1	20	—
North Maharashtra University, Jalgaon	10 Colleges	20	400	—
Baba Saheb Ambedkar Marathwara University, Aurangabad	3 Colleges	6	60	—
Swami Ramanand Tirth University, Nanded	10 Colleges	20	400	—

Changing Nature of National Security Under the Shadow of Globalisation

We are now faced with marked shifts, adjustments, re-adjustments and transformations in the domain, range and scope of security, both traditional as well non-traditional. Thomas Friedman argues that, "the traditional boundaries between politics, culture, technology, finance, national security and ecology are disappearing (Friedman, 2000, p. 9). All of these are aspects of what is commonly referred to as "globalization," and all have important security implications.

Security is no longer confined to the traditional approaches of preserving and protecting territorial integrity and national sovereignty against external dangers and, more importantly, attempting for relative freedom from harmful threats and challenges emanating either from external or internal sources, or a combination of the two. In the age of globalization, while interdependence has become norm, armed conflicts, economic imbalances and social dislocation outpass the progress. The events of gross violations of human rights and disrespect for humanitarian principles continue to affect the globe.

It requires to adopt a people-centric approach to security. The new face of security is increasingly being revitalised as—

"security of the people, not just territory; security through development, not arms; security of all people everywhere—in their communities and in their environments."

And, with the gradual progression of 21st century, South Asians are bound to realise all these in big way. With ongoing developments, dynamics of India's national security in 21st century can be analysed on the basis of a model suggested by this author elsewhere (Prasad, 2000).

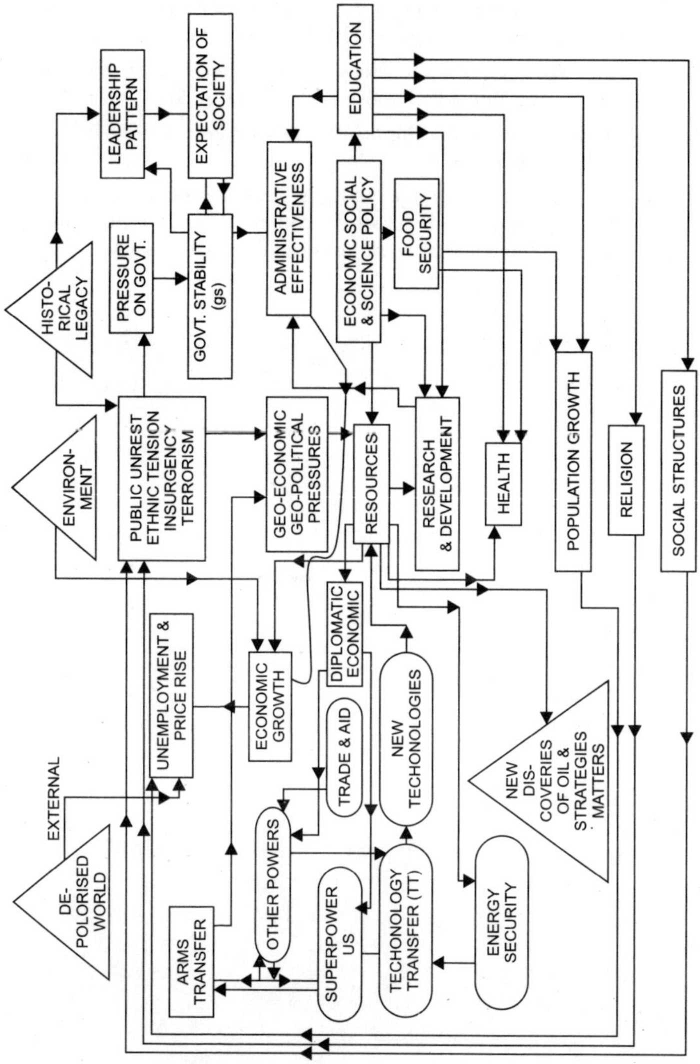

National Security Dynamics in 21st century

REFERENCES

Friedman, T.L., *The Lexus and the Olive Tree—Understanding Globalization*, Ankar Books, New York, 2000, p. 9.

Prasad, R. (ed.), *India's Security in 21st Century. Challenges and Responses*, Dominent Publishers, New Delhi, 2002, Chapter I on Introduction.

Peerzage, S.A., "Some Economics Issues in Financing Higher Education," *University News*, Vol. 43, October 10-16, 2005, p. 9.

Singh, J., *National Security—An Outline of Our Concerns*, Lancer Publishers, New Delhi, 1996, p. 19.

Tables 1 and 2 are based on the author's data collection from various universities and individuals across the country as part of the study thus undertaken Computational work has been done accordingly.